TEXTS BY
MARCO CATTANEO
JASMINA TRIFONI

GRAPHIC DESIGN
PATRIZIA BALOCCO LOVISETTI

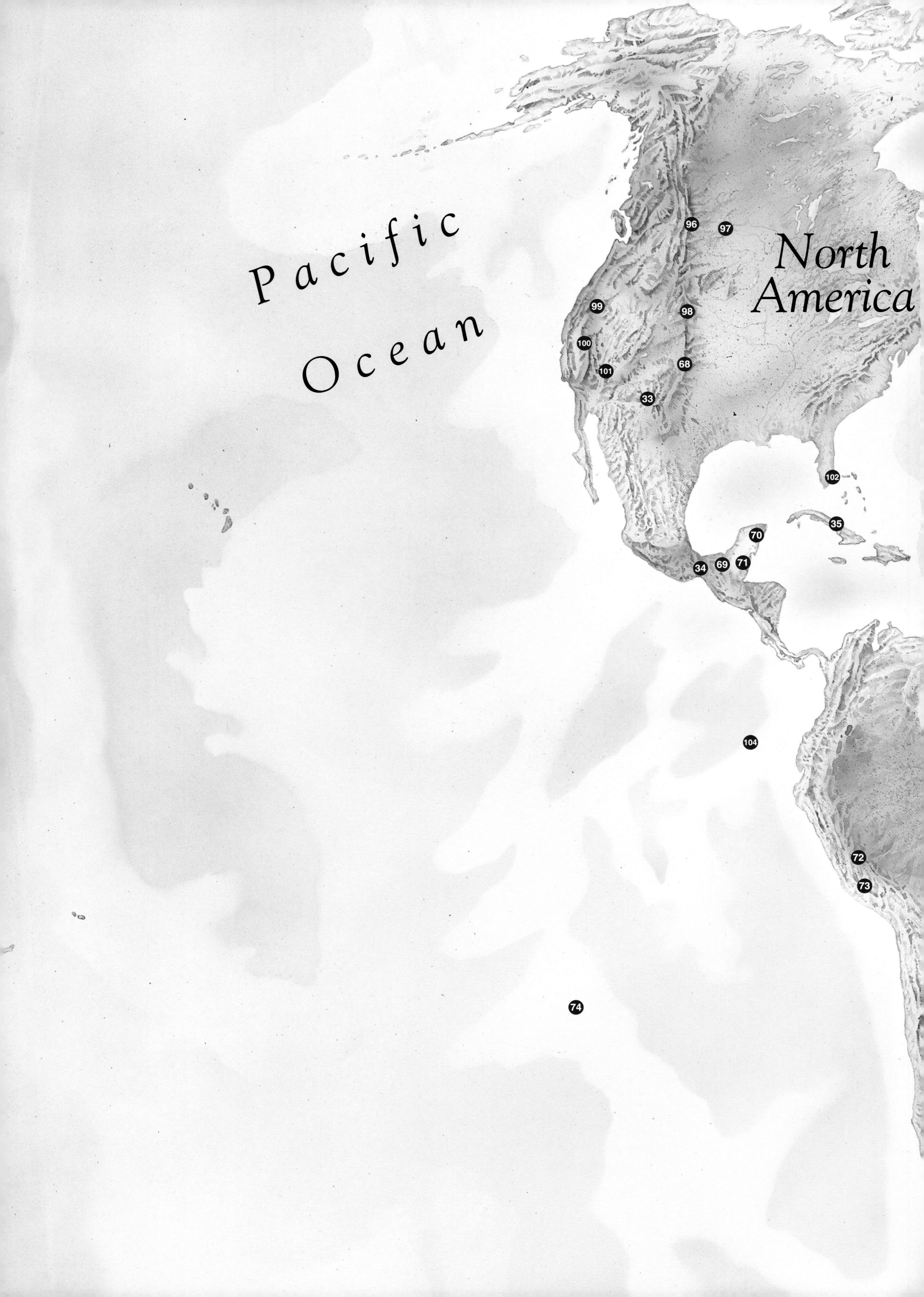

Pacific

Ocean

North
America

96   97

99

98

100

101   68

33

102

35

70

34 69 71

104

72

73

74

Europe

Africa

Atlantic Ocean

South
America

200 GREATEST DESTINATIONS

ART, HISTORY, NATURE

vmb
PUBLISHERS

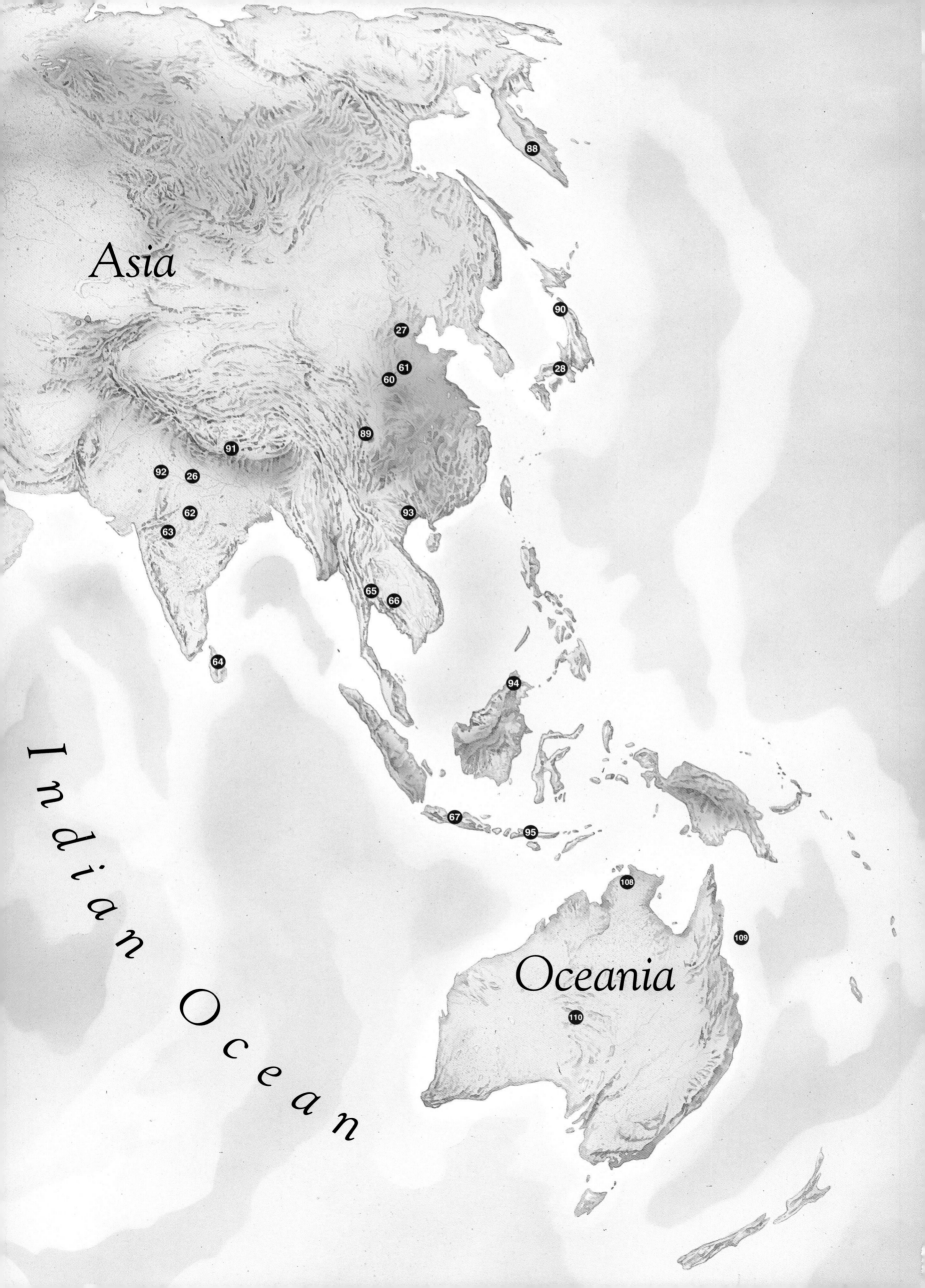

Contents

The Treasures of Art

Ancient Civilizations

Nature Sanctuaries

Contents

2 *The star, the emblem of the Sun King, shows Apollo, the god of peace, the arts, medicine and light. All the decorations that Louis XIV wanted in Versailles palace mixed images of the god and the king in a form of identification that came to symbolise the French monarchy.*

vmb
VMB Publishers®
An imprint of White Star S.p.A., Italy

THE GREAT BOOK OF
WORLD HERITAGE SITES
© 2005 White Star S.p.A.
Via Candido Sassone, 22/24
13100 Vercelli, Italy www.whitestar.it

ISBN: 978-88-540-0683-6

Reprints:
2 3 4 5 6 7 12 11 10 09 08

Printed in China

Taken from:
World Heritage Sites
I volume - The Treasures of Art
© 2002 White Star S.p.A. - ISBN 88-8095-970-0
TRANSLATION: TIMOTHY STROUD, C.T.M. MILAN

World Heritage Sites
II volume - Nature Sanctuaries
© 2003 White Star S.p.A. - ISBN 88-8095-989-1
TRANSLATION: TIMOTHY STROUD

World Heritage Sites
III volume - Ancient Civilizations
© 2004 White Star S.p.A. - ISBN 88-540-0228-3
TRANSLATION: TIMOTHY STROUD

Preface

The UNESCO Convention Concerning the Protection of the World Cultural and Natural Heritage is an international agreement with a dual value: it sanctions an inextinguishable link with the past, but is also something that we experience today and will bequeath to future generations. The Convention, signed in 1972, has made great progress. Since then, 167 nations have ratified it, thus offering their own contribution to the recognition of the unique value of the selected sites.

The world's cultural and natural heritage represents a priceless resource for life and inspiration. The exceptional nature of its recognition by UNESCO resides in its very significance. The World Heritage sites belong to the whole of mankind, regardless of geographical boundaries. Recognition of the unique value of these sites must be a commitment for humankind in its entirety, especially for young people, assuming a universal significance.

This handsome new White Star publication represents a well-designed yet enjoyable contribution to the idea of recognition of and respect for the World Heritage sites as a fundamental element of thoughtfully considered and appropriately made choices for present and future development. A forceful project is required to deliver this invaluable heritage to future generations, so that young people may in turn be stimulated to conserve it with respect and sensitivity, but also with imagination and attention to the means of production of wealth, an inestimable treasure. And the knowledge of this World Heritage it, formed by projects such as this, is an irreplaceable instrument.

This volume's high-quality text and the splendid pictures chosen from previous volumes make it first and foremost a compendium, a special selection of the finest sites inscribed in the World Heritage list. However, it should be clearly stated that the book also acts as a means of shaping consciences, a tool for the acquisition of awareness of sites that belong to the entire world's population, becoming a sort of "intellectual and visual certification" of the work that UNESCO and its member states have achieved over the past thirty-three years.

UNESCO, a great international coalition, under the banners of peace and culture, has taken up the mission of protecting and safeguarding those sites or properties that, due to their natural characteristics, historical importance or spiritual significance, surpass all frontiers or boundaries, becoming the common heritage of all mankind.

Today we find ourselves onlookers – sometimes bewildered and often disinterested – of a world that is silencing cultural diversities through rapid globalization. The World Heritage sites are, however, the clearest sign of diversity and thus oppose standardization. This is precisely where UNESCO comes in, to protect and safeguard the equal dignity of all cultures and "their vocation to enrich themselves and permeate each other." In 2005 UNESCO is also the lead agency for the UN Decade of Education for Sustainable Development.

Prof. Giovanni Puglisi
President of the National
Italian Commission for UNESCO

8 An immense gorge gouged out by the Colorado River, Arizona's Grand Canyon is 278 miles long and just over 1 mile wide. It was first placed under protection in 1893, became a national park in 1919 and has been a World Heritage site since 1979.

Introduction

UNESCO's World Heritage mission is a long success story. The idea of creating an international movement to protect the heritage of humankind had already started to gain ground following World War I. However, the need to protect the world's most important works from decay was not felt until the end of the 1950s, in 1959 to be precise, when the waters of the Nile started to fill the reservoir of the Aswan Dam. The experts warned that unless steps were taken, the water would submerge the Temples of Ramesses II at Abu Simbel, considered among the greatest architectural masterpieces of ancient Egypt. UNESCO thus launched a campaign to save the temples, raising $80 million, which was sufficient to dismantle the monuments and move them to a safe site, in a spectacular operation that lasted until 1966.

During the same period other campaigns were launched to protect such masterpieces of art as Venice and the Borobodur complex in Indonesia. UNESCO started to draft a convention designed to protect the world's cultural heritage, while the International Union for Conservation of Nature drew up a document for protection of the planet's natural wonders. The two proposals were presented to the United Nations Conference on the Human Environment, held in Stockholm in 1972, and were combined in the founding convention of the World Heritage List, which was approved in Paris by the General Conference of UNESCO on 16 November 1972 and came into force on 17 December 1975.

The ambitious aim of UNESCO (the United Nations Educational, Scientific and Cultural Organization) is to identify, study and safeguard monuments, complexes and sites – both manmade and natural – of outstanding historical, artistic, scientific, naturalistic, archaeological or anthropological value.

Today, 30 years after its adoption, ratified by 180 nations, the World Heritage List is an extraordinary inventory of places and works that includes about 800 sites in 135 countries and simultaneously encompasses both the history of humankind and that of the Earth, offering a precious means for "reading" nature, culture and the deep bond that unites them. It is, in short, the historical memory of the planet.

The purpose of this work is to provide a cross-section of the incalculable heritage protected under the auspices of UNESCO. In order to orient ourselves and our readers to such an extensive and varied survey, we have chosen to divide this book into three sections, dedicated to the treasures of art and architecture, natural havens, and ancient civilizations, respectively. Whereas the distinction between cultural and natural sites is already explicitly defined within the scope of the Convention, it proved more complex to draw a dividing line between architectural monuments and sites of archaeological interest. A purely temporal criterion would probably have distorted the historical reading. Consequently, we have considered it appropriate to include all the continuously inhabited properties in the section dedicated to art and architecture, even though some of these could have been included in the archaeological heritage list for chronological reasons.

We have had to limit ourselves to choosing a relatively small number of World Heritage properties owing to reasons of space, and this selection was very difficult, and in many cases painful. We have nonetheless tried to offer a view or general picture that – however partial – does not discriminate against any country or culture and is as complete as possible. We have also tried to encapsulate in the texts not only the intrinsic value of the heritage of each property, but also the accompanying historical and geographical background. This is because the World Heritage is not a list of sites, but the legacy that we have been left by those who came before us and that, with the contribution of everyone, we will leave to those who will follow us.

10 The eighth-century Stele H was created as one of a pair erected in the Great Plaza at Copán. At that time the Maya kingdoms were prosperous but fragmented. However, within two hundred years they all disappeared for reasons unknown: a devastating people's revolt, an epidemic, over-exploitation of the soil, famine ...

The Treasures of Art
introduction

The convention establishing the UNESCO World Heritage List was approved just 30 years ago. Today the List features over 400 properties deemed to be irreplaceable parts of the architectural and artistic heritage of humankind. This overview of cultural sites covers a time span of almost 2,000 years, illustrating the recent development of human civilization and recounting the progress of art, knowledge and religion throughout history.

In such a framework, it is not surprising that over half of this extraordinary architectural and cultural heritage is located in the Old World. During the Christian era, Europe has witnessed a flourishing of civilizations unparalleled in the other continents that have given rise to extremely far-reaching artistic and architectural movements – from Gothic and Renaissance to Baroque and Neoclassicism, right up to the modern currents – but also to local, and sometimes even individual, artistic scenes, which have produced a legacy of inestimable value.

The driving forces of this unrivaled process were undoubtedly the economic and technological development that has always given Europe a privileged status, but also the cultural boosts produced by Christianity and its diffusion and subsequently by the organization of nations, from large empires to the small duchies of Renaissance Italy. Consequently this overview of the most important artistic and architectural monuments includes entire historical centers of cities that have left their mark on long periods of European history, such as Venice, Prague and Paris, along with the palaces of the great dynasties that ruled the continent, from Versailles and Westminster to Schönbrunn, Potsdam, and St. Petersburg. It also features the Vatican City, a symbol of Christianity and incredible distillation of Italian art, and the visionary works of two genial figures of modern architecture, namely the Belgian Victor Horta and the Catalan Antoni Gaudí. Although not included in the selection featured in this book, European culture is also represented by the emblems of the Industrial Revolution, such as the Völklingen Ironworks in Germany, the Verla Groundwood and Board Mill in Finland, and works of engineering such as the Mill Network at Kinderdijk-Elshout in the Netherlands and the hydraulic boatlifts on the Canal du Centre, in Belgium.

However, while Europe accounts for the lion's share, we should not forget the other continents. Asia, in particular, whose huge dimensions enabled it to witness the flourishing of the most diverse civilizations, cultures and religions, is represented here by the marvelous legacy of Islamic architecture contained in cities such as Damascus and Esfahan, and Istanbul that was for many centuries – and still is – the gateway between East and West, as well as the art of two empires, Chinese and Japanese, whose traditions and histories are no less complex and articulate than those of Europe. The heritage of Africa and the Americas, on the other hand, prevalently consists of architecture that reflects the influence of Islam in the Mediterranean area and the European conquest in the New World. However, there are plenty of exceptions, such as the Pueblo de Taos, an old Native-American settlement in New Mexico, the Cliff of Bandiagara, in the Land of the Dogons in Mali, or the royal complex of Fasil Ghebbi in the Gondar region of Ethiopia.

The artistic and architectural heritage united under the aegis of UNESCO cannot be considered merely an inventory of sites and monuments. It is instead a precious tool for tracing the step-by-step development of the stages that have marked the development of human civilization through history, which allows us to observe the progress of all the cultures at a single glance.

13 A view of the historic center of Cairo, showing the minarets of the fourteenth-century mosque of Sultan Hassan and the Rifai mosque, which was completed in 1911.

Bergen

NORWAY

BERGEN
REGISTRATION: 1979
CRITERIA: C (III)

It is in Bergen that, in a certain sense, the story of haddock is written. Here the fish arrived from the ports of northern Norway to be smoked – there were 23 different types with just as many prices and customers – and stored in large warehouses before being loaded onto ships headed throughout Europe. Stockfish was for at least four centuries almost the only Norwegian export.

The roots of Bergen – the ancient wharf of Bergen built on the east shore of the Vågen (bay) – are closely connected to the medieval origins of the town founded by King Olav Kyrre around 1070. By the thirteenth century, the wharf was the crowded commercial and economic center of the town, where 30 or so warehouses stood to hold the goods that arrived from the British Far Øer (Faroe Islands) and the Baltic coast.

In 1360, the economic life of Bergen's port reached a turning point when it was chosen to be a *Kontor*, or a trading office of the Hanseatic League, along with Novgorod, Brugge (or Bruges), and London. From that moment and for the next four centuries, German traders held a monopoly over the port, the name of which is in fact a contraction of a Norwegian word, *tyskerbryggen* (wharf of

the Germans). In exchange for the stockfish, for which there was great demand, particularly in Catholic countries, the Norwegians received cereals, as very little grew in those latitudes, and precious goods like fabrics, pottery, glass, and wine from the Rhine valley.

Bergen *Kontor* was an exclusively male community whose members were strictly forbidden the company of the local women. Wives, fiancées, and female company of various types were only allowed on the site between spring and autumn each year and had to return home for the remaining months.

The community eventually reached

14 Many of Bergen's wooden buildings have been destroyed by fires over the centuries. Those that remain were built at the start of the twentieth century yet faithful to the original style.

15 top Now crowded with pleasure boats, Bergen Wharf (the name is a contraction of Tyskerbryggen, meaning "wharf of the Germans") was one of the main centers of the Hanseatic League, the powerful trading network that for nearly 400 years linked northern Europe's major ports in an economic alliance.

15 center A view of the top of Vågen fjord. Bergen Port formed the nucleus of the city of Bergen and is still located on the eastern shore.

15 bottom Painted bright colors, Bergen's port warehouses now accommodate artists' studios, restaurants, and the Hanseatic League Museum.

1000 resident Germans and was governed by its own rules, among which the most important was the ban on lighting fires. The houses in Bergen, often containing shops, were two- or three-story buildings called *lofts* made entirely from wood, with residential rooms on the upper floors and plank roofs covered with tiles. Even the narrow passageways between buildings were paved with planks. At the rear of each *loft* were the *schøtstuer*, communal rooms where the traders met at the end of the working day. Despite the severity of the regulations, Bergen was repeatedly ravaged by fire, but on each occasion the buildings were rebuilt according to the same criteria. The need to restart trading quickly prevented any evolution in the constructions' design, thus the layout of the port area remained unaltered over time.

At the start of the seventeenth century, the trading network of the Hanseatic League began to weaken as many European nations took back control of the trade of their own goods. In 1630 Norwegian merchants began to buy the first warehouses, and a century later the Germans owned only nine. On October 17, 1754, the *Kontor* of Bergen passed permanently into the hands of the Norwegians, but they maintained the

existing regulations and even kept German as the common trading language.

After 1850, however, the Industrial Revolution made its effects felt on the coasts of Scandinavia, and the traditional stockfish industry suffered at the hands of other types of business. The port area soon proved to be inadequate, and on December 31, 1899 the *Kontor* was shut down.

Since then, Bergen has suffered a series of misfortunes. In 1910 the buildings in the south of the site were demolished to make room for brick warehouses. In 1944, an explosion destroyed many of the roofs, and in 1955 a fire burned down half the remaining buildings. Today only 58 constructions remain in the world's oldest trading center, which have been partly rebuilt in accordance with the original criteria and painted bright red. They house restaurants and art galleries, and one of them, to commemorate their past, contains the Museum of the Hanseatic League.

16 top This photo shows some of the old houses behind the port. The community in Bergen was exclusively male, and women were only allowed to visit during the summer.

16 bottom left A corner of a merchant's house in the Hanseatic League Museum. The paintings and other precious objects are indicative of the merchant's wealth.

16 bottom right A picture of the kitchens where people would gather after the working day. For safety reasons, fires were forbidden in all other rooms of the buildings.

16-17 Opened in 1976, the Hanseatic League Museum is one of the most beautifully laid out in Europe. It has been carefully reconstructed with original furnishings and fittings. Of particular interest is the store where the salted cod was stored and the Fiskeskrue, the press used to extract cod liver oil.

17 bottom This photo features another room in the museum. In addition to pieces from Bergen's golden period, the display includes one of the most important collections of runic stones in the world plus archaeological finds from the Bergen area.

18 top left and 18-19
The panorama of the
Baroque park at
Drottningholm provides
a view of its perfect

symmetry. This section
stretches for about 2,300
feet from the entrance to
the palace and was
embellished with fountains

and bronze statues by
the Flemish sculptor
Adrian de Vries.
The figure below is
of Hercules.

The Royal Domain of Drottningholm

SWEDEN

ISLAND OF LOVON, STOCKHOLM
REGISTRATION: 1991
CRITERIA: C (IV)

18 top right Rebuilt in 1763, the pavilion is composed of a main body and four lateral buildings. It holds a large number of Chinese and Japanese works of art which were very much in vogue with the aristocracy of the period.

19 top The most outstanding feature of the park is the Chinese pavilion built by King Adolf Frederik for his wife Lovisa Ulrika for her thirty-third birthday.

In 1981, Karl Gustaf XVI of Sweden and his family moved their permanent residence to an island on Lake Mälar, a few miles from the capital. This may have been because a change in the country's constitution during the previous year had limited the monarch to only representative power. With the need for the king to always be at the center of the political life of the country eliminated, the country estate of Drottningholm appeared the ideal solution.

The name Drottningholm, literally "Queen's Island," had its roots in the sixteenth century when King John III built a palace there for his consort Katherine Jagellonica. The building did not last long, having burned to the ground on December 30, 1661, a few months after coming into the possession of Edvige Eleonora, the regent of the young Karl XI. Its reconstruction by Nicodemus Tessin the Elder and, later, his son was supposed to pay tribute to the greatness of Sweden, which had emerged from the Peace of Westphalia in 1648 as one of Europe's leading powers.

The palace marked the triumph of Nordic Baroque. The central part of the building is dominated by a monumental stairway faced onto by magnificent rooms adorned with statues, stuccoes, and frescoes. During the same period, the landscaping of the surrounding land was begun. A Baroque garden was created in the style of Versailles, a place of delights beautified by statues by the famous Flemish sculptor Adrian de Vries.

Drottningholm remained the residence of the women at court until 1744 when it was given to Princess Lovisa Ulrika of Prussia to celebrate her marriage to the heir

LAKE MALAR
STOCKHOLM
DROTTNINGHOLM

20-21 Designed by K.F. Adelcrantz and completed in 1766, the Slottsteater is the oldest theater in the world to have retained its original structure. In 1920, it was equipped with electricity, the ropes for quick scenery changes were replaced, and the nineteenth-century sound system was renovated.

to the Swedish throne, Adolf Fredrik. A golden age began during which the most famous artists and scientists in the kingdom were gathered together at court, one of whom, Carl von Linné, catalogued the royal collection of "natural objects." On Lovisa Ulrika's wishes, some of the rooms were redecorated in Rococo style.

These were the most glorious years of the East India Company and the royal courts of Europe were shot through by an attraction for anything that came from the Orient. To mark the thirty-third birthday of Lovisa Ulrika in 1753, her husband gave her a Chinese pavilion built in Stockholm and – to increase the scenic effect – had it assembled during the night in front of her window. However, within only ten years the wood began to rot and the pavilion was replaced by the Kina Slott, the extravagant blue and gold building that can still be seen today, thanks to the careful restoration work carried out based on the building's original plans.

During the same period, Karl Fredrik Adelcrantz was commissioned to design what today is the best conserved Baroque theatre in Europe. Completed in 1766, the Slottsteater is built from simple materials but to impressive effect. The stage is 66 feet deep, and the sophisticated and perfectly preserved theatrical machinery, built by the Italian Donato Stopani, allowed rapid scenery changes to be made. The stage was equipped with mobile panels able to recreate moving clouds and waves and special effects like thunder, wind, and lightning.

At the end of the eighteenth century, Swedish interest in the theater declined, and little by little the Slottsteater was forgotten. Rediscovered in 1920 by Agne Bejier, a historian of the theater and literature, it was restored to its original glory. The scenery machines were repaired and the ancient backcloths were mended. On August 19, 1922, the curtain was raised once again and the theater began to win back its international reputation for its festivals of works by Haydn, Handel, Gluck, and Mozart. Today, besides being used by the Royal Opera of Stockholm, the theater is a study center for eighteenth-century music and ballet.

20 bottom A cultured and sophisticated queen, Lovisa Ulrika commissioned artist Jean Eric Rehn to decorate the library.

21 top The bedchamber designed by Nicodemus Tessin the Elder for Queen Edvige Eleonora is a perfect example of Swedish Baroque. Finished in 1683, it took a number of Scandinavia's most famous decorators 15 years to complete.

21 bottom The superb stairway that faces onto the Trapphallen is the centerpiece of the royal palace. Its balustrades feature marble statues of Apollo and the Muses by the Italian sculptors Giovanni and Carlo Carove.

The Historic Center of St. Petersburg

RUSSIAN FEDERATION

REGISTRATION: 1990
CRITERIA: C (I) (II) (IV) (VI)

For more than half a century the cruiser Aurora, the historical ship belonging to the Russian navy that is also used as a school, has been anchored in the river Neva in front of the Nachimov Naval Academy in the center of St. Petersburg. As it lay there on the morning of November 7, 1917, it was its own cadets that fired the ship's cannons signaling the start of the assault on the Winter Palace, thus setting in motion the October Revolution. A year later, Lenin moved the country's capital to Moscow and deprived St. Petersburg of the role it had played since the times of Peter the Great.

When he ascended to the throne of Russia at the age of ten, Peter the Great had already witnessed the palace intrigues by which members of his family were gradually removed. By the time he became free of his unwelcome tutors, he also began to dislike the conservative atmosphere of Moscow. A passionate sailor (he had traveled a great deal and worked in a Dutch shipyard), he dreamed of turning Russia into one of the great European powers. He therefore planned to build a new capital on the

islands in the Neva, a river that flows from Lake Ladoga to the Baltic Sea at the eastern end of the Gulf of Finland.

In the summer of 1703 he ordered his army carpenters to build a hut from which he could watch construction progress on Petrogradskaia Storona (Petrograd Island). For six years he lived in two modest rooms with his most precious belongings: a frock coat, a compass, and a rowing boat. Later, the Czarina, Catherine II, had this hut

enclosed in brick walls to honor the memory of the city's founder.

Construction of St. Petersburg began with a large defensive building, the SS. Peter-Paul Fort, on the small Hare Island (Zayachy Island). Initially the walls were made from wood, but later Peter asked Domenico Trezzini to build solid bastions, and the Italian architect placed the two-headed eagle, the emblem of the Romanov dynasty, with Saint George and the dragon on the entrance to the fort. Trezzini was also responsible for the design of the SS. Peter-Paul Cathedral, begun in 1712 and completed in 1733. Massive and finely decorated marble columns, huge

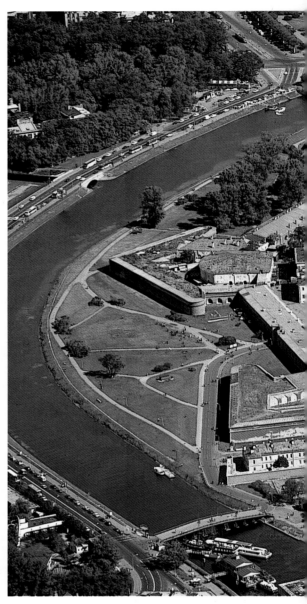

chandeliers, and a polychrome vault surrounded the carved wooden and gilded iconostasis built by Ivan Zarudnyi. In 1725, before construction was complete, Peter the Great was buried in the cathedral, initiating the tradition of the Baroque church being the final resting place of the Romanovs.

1712 was also the year in which St. Petersburg was proclaimed the capital of Russia. Soldiers and manual laborers dug the canals that were supposed to turn the city into the Amsterdam of Russia, and they built the Summer Palace, the czar's first official residence in the city. Trezzini adjusted his creativity to suit the plain Dutch taste of the emperor, designing a two-story palace decorated with bas-reliefs that celebrated the naval triumphs of the czar. Following Peter's early death, the court was returned to the luxury of Moscow during the short reigns of Catherine I and Peter II, but in 1730, Czarina Anna opted for St. Petersburg once more, where she recreated a court inherited from Elizabeth, the daughter of Peter the Great, in 1740.

During her reign, St. Petersburg entered the history of architecture thanks to the contribution of Bartolomeo Rastrelli, who arrived in Russia with his father in the service of Peter the Great.

23 top right The czars in the Romanov dynasty, apart from Peter II and Ivan IV, were all buried in Sts. Peter-Paul Cathedral. Pink and green Corinthian columns, arched vaults, and lovely crystal chandeliers surround the sarcophaguses, made largely from Carrara marble.

22 top right Smolny Cathedral is part of the convent founded by Czarina Elizabeth II. Rastrelli designed the cathedral in 1748 using an admirable fusion of Russian and Italian Baroque.

22 bottom left The elegant gilded spire of the bell tower of Sts. Peter-Paul Cathedral. The commission for this religious building in the Peter-Paul Fort was awarded to the Italian, Domenico Trezzini, in 1712.

22-23 A view of Hare Island (Zayachy Island), the original nucleus of the city founded by Peter the Great. In 1703, the czar had a wooden fort built here that was later replaced, section by section, with a stone fort by Trezzini. An exquisitely elegant Baroque masterpiece, Sts. Peter-Paul Cathedral stands in the center of the island.

ST. PETERSBURG

MOSCOW

23 bottom right Facing onto a canal in Nevsky Prospekt, the Stroganov Palace was built by Bartolomeo Rastrelli in 1753 for the Stroganov family (their cook invented the famous beef dish). Today, it houses the collections of the Museum of the Russian State.

Rastrelli designed buildings in pure Baroque style, including the Stroganov Palace (the residence of Count Sergei), the Vorontsov Palace (long an exclusive military school), and Smolny Convent, which combines Russian architectural tradition with Western taste. However, the masterpiece of this particular blend was the Winter Palace, built between 1754 and 1762. Whereas the interiors have undergone repeated modification, the exterior has retained its original appearance and is a superb example of Russian Baroque.

The Winter Palace was immediately used by Peter III for trysts with his lover, Princess Vorontsova, and this is perhaps one of the reasons why his wife, the German Sophie von Anhalt-Zerbst, instigated a palace plot that ended, after just six months of his reign, in his deposition by the Imperial Guard and assassination. Having usurped the throne and crowning herself as Catherine II, Sophie subjected Russia to tyranny for over 30 years, but during that time gave St. Petersburg some of its most magnificent treasures.

An insatiable art-lover, she bought a huge number of works of art. In the ten years between 1764 and 1774, 2,500 paintings, 10,000 sculpted gems, 10,000 drawings, objects in porcelain and silver, and statues arrived in St. Petersburg. In 1771, having already built the Small Hermitage close to the Winter Palace, she began construction of the Great Hermitage, designed by Yuri Velten, to house her collections. Between 1785 and 1787 she commissioned the Hermitage Theater from Giacomo Quarenghi, and in the mid-nineteenth century the complex was further enriched with the New Hermitage. In 1851, Nicholas I opened the Great and the New Hermitage as public museums; today, with three million objects on display, including some of the most famous works by Impressionist painters, the Hermitage is the largest museum in the world and has the most exceptional collection of paintings, with the possible exception of the Louvre.

25 top One of the Hermitage galleries. Opened as a public museum in 1851 by Nicholas I, it boasts an encyclopedic collection of art works with almost three million objects on display.

25 center left A masterpiece of the genius of Bartolomeo Rastrelli, the broad Jordan Staircase embellishes the Winter Palace. Its name comes from the fact that the royal family watched the ceremony of the Baptism of the Neva from this point, in commemoration of the Baptism of Christ in the Jordan.

25 center right One of the rooms that hold Catherine II's silver collection. An insatiable collector of art, between 1764 and 1774 the czarina purchased 2,500 paintings, 10,000 carved gems, 10,000 drawings, and thousands of statues and works of porcelain and silver.

25 bottom left The immense section dedicated to painting is one of the most visited in the Hermitage. The collection of European art from the Renaissance to the late eighteenth century testifies to the personal and often unconventional taste of the royal family. Nineteenth- and twentieth-century works mainly came from private collections.

25 bottom right The Hermitage Theater was commissioned from Giacomo Quarenghi by Catherine II.

24-25 This photo captures the south face of the Winter Palace, which looks onto Palace Square. The magnificent building is part of the Hermitage complex and is one of the most famous museums in the world. It was built by Bartolomeo Rastrelli between 1754 and 1762. The exterior is embellished with 400 columns and 16 different types of window.

On Catherine's death, the Russian throne passed to her son, Paul I, who had always had a tempestuous relationship with his mother. He detested both her lifestyle and her reign. In constant fear of a plot on his life, he thought he would be safe from his enemies by building the Engineers' Castle, a solid brick building surrounded by a dike, equipped with secret passages and escape routes. In 1801 he finally moved in but it did not prove impenetrable after all and, three days later, he was assassinated in his bed.

His successor, Alexander I, completed construction of the cathedral of Kazan, one of the city's most magnificent churches. Inspired by St. Peter's in Rome, Andrei Voronikhin designed a curved colonnade 364 feet long to hide the direction of the building, which was laid out parallel to St. Petersburg's main street, the Nevsky Prospekt. Supported by red granite columns adorned with capitals and decorated with an elegant mosaic floor, the church contains the

tomb of Mikhail Kutuzov, the Russian hero from the Patriotic War against Napoleon. To celebrate his victory over the French emperor, in 1818 Alexander commissioned the enormous St. Isaac's Cathedral from Auguste de Montferrand. Its construction took 40 years. The Neo-Classical dome, lined with 220 pounds of gold, is visible from the Gulf of Finland, and in order for the marshy land to be able to support the 330,000 tons of the building, the ground was consolidated with thousands of wooden piles.

The city inherited by Nicholas I in 1825 was already shaken by the initial rebellious tremors that were to explode in the October Revolution a century later. The reforms demanded by the people and army were either ignored by the absolutist policies of the czars or answered by bloody repressions, which resulted in pages of passionate literature such as the cutting satire of Gogol and the dramatic novels of Dostoyevsky. But

the court of the Romanovs was more involved in extricating itself from the shackles imposed by the palace than solving the problems of the populace. The architectural wonders along the Nevsky Prospekt, the residences of the nobles and court officers, formed a barrier between the poor section of St. Petersburg and the magnificence of the court. The revolts became more frequent and more violent until they began to result in the loss of important lives. On March 1, 1881, just a few steps from the Field of Mars and Engineers' Castle, Czar Alexander II was killed by a group of insurgents.

His successor, Alexander III, began a period of ferocious repression and had the Church of the Resurrection (better known as the Church of Spilt Blood) built on the assassination spot. With an imaginative juxtaposition of architectural elements, it falls within the tradition of the onion-shaped dome architecture. Inside, the iconostasis, the canopy, and the floors are adorned with innumerable types of material, including Italian marbles, porphyry, Norwegian granite, and jasper. As the last great work in a city created out of nothing that became a triumph of European architecture, including styles from the Baroque to the Neo-Classical, the name of the church was sinisterly prophetic. As soon as it was completed, Nicholas II was forced to abdicate. The new Russia did not spare the Romanovs.

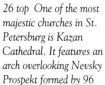

26 top One of the most majestic churches in St. Petersburg is Kazan Cathedral. It features an arch overlooking Nevsky Prospekt formed by 96

Corinthian columns arranged in four rows. Voronikhin's design was inspired by Bernini's colonnade at St. Peter's in Rome.

26 bottom left Designed by Auguste de Montferrand in 1818, the magnificent St. Isaac's Cathedral was built over a period of 40 years. Its gilded dome weighs 33,000 tons and can be seen from the Gulf of Finland.

26 bottom right Decorations in the cathedral include extraordinary ceiling and wall frescoes, many by Karl Bryullov, 14 different

types of marble, and 43 types of precious and semi-precious stones. The interior of the church has a surface area of 43,000 square feet.

27 The Church of Spilt Blood is decorated with gold, marble, mosaics, and enameled ceramic tiles. It was built in 1883 for Alexander III on the spot where his predecessor, Alexander II, was assassinated.

The Kremlin and Red Square
RUSSIAN FEDERATION

With the collapse of the Soviet Union at the start of the 1990's, the President of the Russian Federation, Boris Yeltsin, launched a daring plan to restore the Great Palace to its original splendor. Built between 1838 and 1849 inside the Kremlin (from *kreml*, "fort") by architect Konstantin Thon for Nicholas I, the Great Palace – which cost the huge sum of 12 million rubles – was the former Imperial Palace of the czars and Russian princes until the Russian Revolution in October 1917.

Unable to bear the glorification of czarist Russia, Stalin had some of the most representative rooms of the era demolished between 1932 and 1934, including the rooms of St. Andrew and St. Alexander. In their place, the Supreme Soviet and representatives of the Russian Federation were installed in an area measuring 260 x 65 feet able to seat 3000. Thanks to photographs of the original design found in the royal archive in Windsor Castle in Great Britain, financing of 300 million dollars, and the work of 2500 people, the rooms were completed in 2000 with elaborate stucco decorations and gilded friezes. The Palace once more blazoned the magnificence of the Romanov dynasty.

Leaving aside the Napoleonic ambitions of the czars, it must be said that the Kremlin was for centuries the center of Russia's political and religious life. It was here that the czars, princes, and patriarchs of the Orthodox Church resided, and it was here that the czars continued to be crowned even after the capital was transferred to St. Petersburg by Peter the Great at the start of the eighteenth century. The majestic Red Square that lies in front of the Kremlin was the setting for the military parades that commemorated the October Revolution. And, it was in the Great Palace – despite Stalin's aversion – that Nikita Khrushchev honored Yuri Gagarin on his return from

28 top The red walls around the Kremlin are fortified by large towers. The side seen in the photograph, which faces Moscow, was the first to be built, with construction beginning in the fifteenth century.

28 center The Great Palace and the cathedral are seen here with the walls in the background. Built between 1838 and 1849, the majestic residence of the czars is the largest building in the Kremlin and has a surface area of 484,000 square feet.

28 bottom The gilded domes of the Cathedral of the Annunciation and the façade of the Great Palace stand out against the background of modern Moscow.

28-29 There are four cathedrals in Sobornaya Square, the spiritual heart of the Kremlin. The origins of the Muscovite fort date from the eleventh century, but it was only at the end of the fifteenth, during the reign of Ivan III the Great, that the Kremlin began to take on its present appearance with the construction of the religious buildings and crenellated walls.

29 top The magnificent interior of the small Cathedral of the Archangel Michael, designed by the Italian architect Alvise il Nuovo, features columns and walls entirely covered with frescoes. The remains of Moscow's princes and czars are buried here.

space in 1961, following the first orbit of the Earth by man.

The oldest archaeological finds in the Moscow area date from the Bronze Age, but the first traces of a Slav settlement are no older than the eleventh century. This was the period during which construction of a fortified village was begun on an area that covered no more than 12 acres on Borovickaya hill, a promontory above the confluence of the Neglinnaya and Moskva rivers. In 1147 under the rule of Yuri Dolgoruky, the prince of Kiev, this first village expanded beyond the cramped enclosure, and it was during this period that the city of Moscow was officially founded. It was only in the fourteenth century, during the reign of Ivan Kalita, that the fort began to be considered a separate zone, an administrative nucleus of the town. In 1367-1368, Prince Dimitri Donskoy built a large fortress with white walls and tall towers, and as a result Moscow became known as "the white-walled city."

Between 1485 and 1495, when it was completely rebuilt by Ivan III the Great, Czar of all the Russias, the Kremlin began to take on its current appearance. The white walls were replaced by crenellated fortifications over a mile long along which 20 towers stand at the corners and the various entrances. The civil and religious buildings in the enclosed area (measuring 68 acres) date from different eras and were designed by architects of different nationalities. Some of the works were commissioned from Italian architects such as Marco Friazin, Pietro Antonio Solari, and

Aristotele Fioravanti in the fifteenth and sixteenth centuries.

Entering the Kremlin by the Troickaya Tower, the second-most important, which faces onto Alexandrovsky Garden, the Arsenal, which is home to the Kremlin's military garrison, appears on the left. In front of the building, which was supposed to become a museum of the 1812 Patriotic War during the mid-nineteenth century, there are over 800 cannons captured from the Napoleonic army during that year. Next door there is the Senate, built between 1776 and 1787, which today is the residence of

the President of the Russian Federation. The Palace of Congresses stands opposite these two buildings. Built in 1961 during the Soviet era, it is the only architectural complex in the Kremlin that seems out of place, but fortunately Khrushchev had it built 50 feet below ground level so as not to spoil the view of the other buildings.

Further on, a bell tower, completed in 1600 and, at 266 feet high, the tallest building in Russia at the time, dominates Ivanovskaya Square. At its base stands the "Czar Bell," a masterful bronze work by the founders of Moscow that, at 20 feet tall and

30 top left The large salon on the first floor of the Palace of Facets – the oldest civil building in the Kremlin – has a single square central column, and from this point all the frescoes on the vaults seem to come to life.

30 bottom left A room in Terem Palace decorated with floral motifs. Located next to the Palace of Facets, this building contains the ceremonial thrones and was the property of the reigning family.

weighing 220 tons, is the largest bell in the world. Following a fire in 1737, it fell from its support and broke in two. A century later, it was placed on a pedestal to commemorate the sad event. The nearby "Czar Cannon" also suffered an unfortunate fate: the largest cannon in the world with a 900-millimeter caliber and weighing 44 tons, it was withdrawn from service without ever having fired a shot.

In Sobornaya Square where Moscow's first church once stood, the spiritual and architectural heart of the Kremlin can be found. Constructed by Fioravanti between 1475 and 1479 for Ivan the Great, the Cathedral of the Assumption is the oldest and most imposing temple in the square. This is where the czars were crowned, the most important decrees read, and the metropolitans and patriarchs of Moscow buried. Behind the cathedral stands the small church of the Deposition of the Gown and, to its right, the church of the Twelve Apostles and the Patriarchal Palace. On the other sides of the square can be seen the Cathedral of the Annunciation and the Cathedral of the Archangel Michael, both with onion-shaped domes. Each one contains treasures of Russian iconic art and frescoes by masters such as Andrei Rublev.

Further on appear other palaces such as the Palace of Facets by M. Ruffo and Pietro Antonio Solari. This is the oldest civil building in the Kremlin and is named after the unusual white prismatic facets on its façade. Then, there is the Terem Palace, rebuilt in the seventeenth century by the early rulers of the Romanov dynasty, where a collection of ceremonial thrones is kept, and the Armory Museum, where the treasures of the czars are held and the Russian diamond collection.

30-31 The czars used to receive their guests and advisors in the Gold Room in Terem Palace. Citizens could leave requests for their sovereign in a box in the petition window situated next to the throne.

31 top right The Boyar Room in Terem Palace was named after Russia's feudal lords. Boyars enjoyed great privileges

and met in this room to settle disputes, discuss State administration, and, it is said, to hatch plots against the czar.

31 bottom right A view of the nineteenth-century frescoes on the east wall of the oratory in Terem Palace.

32-33 The nine domes of St. Basil's Cathedral represent the main Orthodox festivals.

32 bottom left Construction of the most famous of Moscow's monuments, St. Basil's Cathedral, was begun by Ivan the Terrible in 1552 to celebrate his victory over the Tatars.

32 bottom right Built completely in brick in accordance with Russian tradition, St. Basil's Cathedral also contains examples of wooden architecture. Inside, outstanding frescoes from the sixteenth century can also be found.

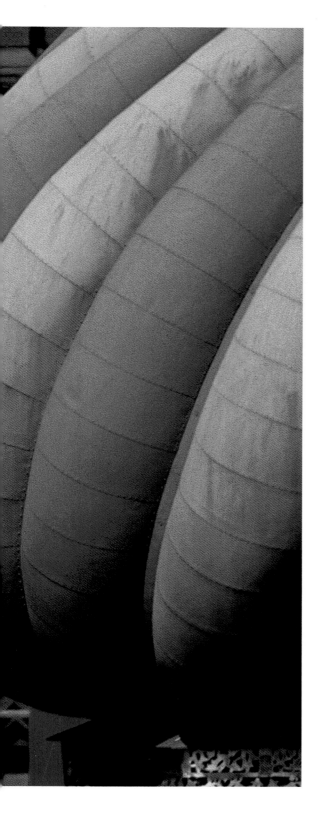

The section of the Kremlin that overlooks Red Square is dominated by Spasskaya Tower (Savior's Tower), built in 1491 by Pietro Antonio Solari for Ivan the Great and named for an icon on one of the walls. In the past, anyone entering the door had to take off their hat in a show of respect for the grandeur of the place.

Just in front of the tower stands the Church of the Intercession (or the Cathedral of St. Basil the Blessed), perhaps the most famous monument in Red Square. The square is not named after the Soviet power but from the term *krasnij*, Russian for "beautiful" and now used to mean "red." It was Ivan the Terrible who began construction of the cathedral to commemorate the taking of Kazan, the capital of the kingdom of the Tatars who had long raided and plundered Moscow. The basilica was designed by the Russian architects, Barma and Postnik, who built it on a plan of eight cylindrical chapels surrounding the ninth and largest, covered by a sloping roof. Each chapel is dedicated to one of the Orthodox festivals.

Completing the perimeter of the square are Neoclassical buildings like the one that has housed Moscow's first large shop, Gum, since 1893. With the collapse of the Soviet Union, traces of the Soviet regime have slowly disappeared. Though Lenin's Tomb is still located in the Senate Tower, recently Red Square has also seen two "old novelties" reappear which had been removed in the 1920's. These are the Church of the Madonna of Kazan and the doors of the Resurrection, which, until 1995, had been moved to allow the tanks to pass during the large military procession held each November seventh.

33 top Outlined against St. Basil's, we see a night view of Spasskaya (Savior's) Tower, which stands opposite Red Square at the most important of the 20 entrances to the Kremlin. The clock bells were heard for the first time in 1625.

33 bottom Red Square (the name comes from the Russian word krasnij, meaning "beautiful") was the main trading area in Moscow. It used to be separated from the Kremlin by a deep ditch. To enter the fort, there were two bridges where Spasskaya and Nikolskaya Towers stand.

Westminster Palace, Westminster Abbey, and St. Margaret's Church

GREAT BRITAIN

LONDON
REGISTRATION: 1987
CRITERIA: C (I) (II) (IV)

34 top The entrance to Westminster Hall. Built in the eleventh century at the time of Richard II for court entertainments, this room is the only part of Westminster Palace to have survived the disastrous fires of 1512 and 1834. Today Westminster Hall – which over the centuries has been a pivot of events in the kingdom – is used for important ceremonies.

34 bottom The Neo-Gothic spires on Westminster Palace. The building contains the Chambers of the Lords and the Commons and was designed by Sir Charles Barry in the early nineteenth century.

Each year, on the official opening of the British Parliament, a deputation of footmen in seventeenth-century costume performs a scrupulous search of the cellars of the Palace of Westminster. This ceremony commemorates the danger faced during the Gunpowder Plot in 1605 in which the Catholic Guy Fawkes and a group of followers attempted to blow up the seat of the Protestant British power.

For British citizens, the religious aspect of the story is an unending one. The history of the Palace of Westminster is 900 years long. Today the building is enormous, with 1200 rooms, 100 staircases, and nearly two miles of corridors, but little remains of the original building that was the principal residence of the English royal family from the middle of the eleventh century, under William I, to 1512, under Henry VIII. In 1512, a fire destroyed most of the original palace, with the exception of the medieval Westminster Hall, St. Stephen's Chapel, and the Jewel Tower, the latter built in 1366 to hold the monarch's private possessions. With reconstruction, the building became the House of Lords, whereas St. Stephen's Chapel was converted to the House of Commons.

The palace was once again reduced to ashes in 1834, but on this occasion, too, Westminster Hall was spared. The design for a new home for the Parliament was the work of Sir Charles Barry who, in tribute to the nearby Westminster Abbey, produced a Neo-Gothic construction. Seriously damaged by German bombing raids in World War II, the palace was restored in 1948-50 following Sir Charles' designs to the letter.

The focus of the complex is the huge octagonal room entered through the principal entrance, St. Stephen's, a masterpiece of Victorian architecture. From here two corridors depart: the north corridor leads to the House of Lords and the south corridor to the House of Commons. The House of Lords was built in 1847. It is an ornate chamber measuring 79 by 46 feet that contains an imposing Neo-Gothic throne on which the Queen sits when she makes her speech at the opening of Parliament each November. The House of Commons, on the other hand, measures 69 by 46 feet and reflects the style of St. Stephen's Chapel. The members sit in rows, the majority party on one side of the hall and the opposing minority party on the other. The center of the room is occupied by the table on which the symbol of royal power, the mace, is placed during parliamentary sessions. Beneath the table, there is a carpet on which two red lines are

34-35 Westminster Palace seen from Westminster Bridge over the Thames. The world's most famous clock tower, Big Ben, stands to the north of the building. The name Big Ben was originally given to the 14-ton bell that has struck the hour uninterruptedly since it was installed in 1859.

36 left Poets' Corner in the south transept, where the most important writers in British history are buried, is one of the most visited sections of the Abbey. The first writer interred was Geoffrey Chaucer, while the body of William Shakespeare, who died in 1616 in Stratford-upon-Avon, was transferred here in 1740. The scandalous life led by Lord George Byron meant that he was only admitted to the Abbey in 1969, over 100 years after his death.

36 center The choir was designed by Edward Blore in the mid-nineteenth century in Victorian Gothic. It stands in the nave of Westminster Abbey, which at 111 feet tall is the highest in England.

36 right The oak coronation throne in St. Edward's Chapel was made in 1300 by Edward I. It is decorated with leaves, birds, and animal motifs, and the back shows the monarch reposing on lions.

37 top The austere Gothic façade of Westminster Abbey. Its towers are 223 feet tall and the whole building covers an area of 31,980 square feet. William the Conqueror was the first ruler crowned here on Christmas Day 1066. The Abbey held 8,300 people on the day of Elizabeth II's coronation in 1953.

37 bottom A detail of one of the many lovely windows in Westminster Abbey, many of which were made over the last two centuries. The set of buildings holds many works of art. The Abbey Museum contains an extraordinary collection of royal effigies.

The Major Town Houses of the Architect Victor Horta

BELGIUM

BRUSSELS
REGISTRATION: 2000
CRITERIA: C (I) (II) (IV)

38 left A triumph of Art Nouveau, Maison van Eetvelde was built in avenue Palmerston in 1895. Although the façade does not betray the daring lines of the interior, Horta established his new architectural style with the construction of this building.

38 bottom right Maison Tassel in Rue Paul Emile Janson was the first house in which Victor Horta broke with architectural tradition and began his journey that led to Art Nouveau.

The old shoe-repairer Pierre Horta must have had a nasty surprise when his favorite son, twelve year-old Victor, was expelled from the vocal instruction course at Ghent Conservatory. It was 1873 and the boy had only just entered the prestigious college. Already all hopes for the future had been dashed.

Like so many other rejections, Victor Horta's was providential, as he was led to begin a course of architecture at the Académie des Beaux Arts where he remained until 1877. Brilliant and restless, after a short stay in Paris he returned to Belgium where he settled in Brussels and found work in the studio of Alphonse Balat, the architect to King Leopold II, and where he remained until 1892. It was with Balat that Horta became interested in the new architectural materials. From his mentor he learned the Neo-Classical forms of the nineteenth century and how to manipulate them. The results were quickly forthcoming for, at the age of just 23, he won the Godecharle Prize for a plan he had presented for the Belgian Parliament.

Horta soon began to receive commissions to design private homes: first at Ghent, then, in 1893, in Brussels, where he began to gather converts from among friends in intellectual circles. One of these was Émile Tassel, an influential collaborator of the industrialist Ernest Solvay. Tassel asked Horta to design a modest house that reconciled the frivolous requirements of his drawing room with the discretion of a grandmother who was almost one hundred years old. In rue Paul Emile Janson, Horta built Tassel the first of his manifesto houses in which he broke with the traditional symmetries of the plan to organize the spaces along a single axis that cut through the whole ground floor of the building. The Neo-Mannerist façade, which reflected the Italian taste of the sixteenth century, relinquished masonry materials in favor of a skeleton made of iron and glass to give the appearance of lightness; it was also given an Egyptian-style entrance topped by a bow-window and flanked by massive brackets on either side. In the spacious reception room, from which stretched a suite of rooms in strict Italian Renaissance tradition, the classical and exotic were harmonized through iron columns built to resemble palm trees in a tropical garden.

BRUSSELS

References to Nature inside the rooms were rendered even more explicit a year later in the Hôtel Solvay, where Horta took advantage of the large garden to bring air in from the outside through a series of pipes. It was in 1895 that the break with classicism took place when Horta produced his first Art Nouveau design. Edmond van Eetvelde, a baron and diplomat recently appointed Secretary of State in the independent Congo, was looking for an architect who combined talent with courage. For him, Horta built a house in avenue Palmerston based on a plan that closely followed the

constructed in iron, which was bent to comply with the decorated windows. Because the lines of the city plan were incorporated into the project, the diagonal corridor that leads to the winter garden is an alleyway that opens out into a square.

Horta's most revolutionary design was perhaps the one he kept for himself when, in 1898, he built his own house at 23-25 rue Américaine. In this building, Horta's stylized decoration reached its peak with his setting of natural forms as though in a theater wing, and the use of transparent materials to better exploit natural light.

modernism for his early works because he broke with nineteenth century styles to introduce Art Nouveau into architecture. On the other hand, his mature works reflected an about-face in his style and a revisionism that led Horta to align himself with conservatism and plunge into futile academism.

In 1944, three years before his death, Horta drew up his will, including in it a spiritual recognition of his master, writing, "What I owe, I owe to the purest (and most personal) of the classical architects, Alphonse Balat."

winter garden in the royal greenhouses designed by Balat. The main section of the house – the reception room – opened onto an entrance in the form of an octagon which stretched for the entire length of the building and was flooded with natural light from the roof. Load-bearing columns, balustrades, and ornamentation were

Maison Horta was perhaps the last of the architect's more innovative projects. In 1902, he suffered a creative crisis that led him to return to more conventional designs and a simplification of lines.

Victor Horta has a double reputation in the history of modern architecture. On the one hand, he is considered the founder of

39 For Maison van Eetvelde, Horta stood glass domes on iron columns, while balustrades and decorations resemble objects from nature. Like other creations by the architect from Ghent, the house was designed to suit the personality and role of its owner.

Palaces and Parks of Potsdam and Berlin

GERMANY

BRANDENBURG, SOUTH-WEST OF BERLIN
REGISTRATION: 1990, 1992, 1999
CRITERIA: C (I) (II) (IV)

40 top A view of the Baroque garden in Sans Souci Palace. Though Frederick II commissioned the work from Georg Wenzeslaus von Knobelsdorff in the mid-eighteenth century, it was the sovereign himself who determined the design of what was to be his maison de plaisir.

40-41 A birds-eye view of Weinberg Hill on which Sans Souci and its six parabolic terraces were built. The Baroque garden and the fountain in the center lie at the foot of the hill.

41 left A lover of music, Frederick II enjoyed entertaining his guests by playing the pianola in the Concert Hall. Superb paintings and furniture decorate this superlative Rococo room.

41 top right Sans Souci's magnificent library is decorated with beautiful stuccoes, gilded bronzes, and a Rococo fireplace. Voltaire himself, the leader of the Enlightenment, filled the library with books.

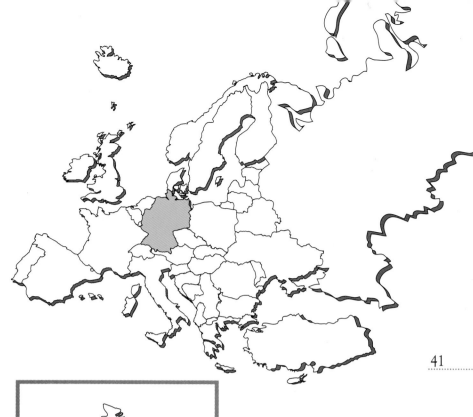

T he son of Frederick William of Prussia, Frederick of Hohenzollern was born in Berlin in 1712. Besides being a strict reorganizer and restorer of the war-ravaged electorate following the Thirty Years War, his father was a devout Lutheran and wanted to educate his son in accordance with the restrained practices he was preparing to impose on his court in order to deal with the huge debts he had inherited from Frederick I. But the century of the Enlightenment was approaching, and the cultured but rebellious Frederick of Hohenzollern was to leave his mark on eighteenth century Europe, partly as a result of his political and military skills, but above all for his progressive views and the intellectual and artistic impetus he gave to his kingdom.

The iron discipline of the palace prompted the young prince to try to escape to the court in Great Britain, but the inflexible authoritarianism of his father cost him two years close confinement at Küstrin where he wrote two works of political philosophy: the *Antimachiavelli and Instruction for the Education of the Hereditary Prince*. In these works, he

countered the reasons of State set out by the Italian writer with his own criteria for creating good government, a moral conception of justice, and the intellectual emancipation of the people.

He came to the throne in 1740, and between 1742 and 1745 Frederick II took advantage of the impressive military resources built up by his father, taking possession of Silesia, the richest of the Hapsburg provinces, thereby winning himself

41 bottom right The Marmorsaal (Marble Room) is the largest room in Sans Souci. Used for court receptions, it is elliptical and crowned by an airy dome.

the nickname Frederick the Great. During this period he also launched his cultural program, commissioning Georg Wenzeslaus von Knobelsdorff to design a summer residence to be built in Potsdam in an area of countryside between Lakes Havel and Glienicke. The first stone was laid on the brow of a hill on April 14, 1745, and the Sans Souci Palace was completed within two years. This came as a surprise because Frederick had held animated discussions with the architect about his idea. Moreover, it was Frederick himself who drew up the plans of the building that was to become a symbol of German Rococo. The king did not want a luxurious or ostentatious palace but a place where he could relax and dedicate himself to art and literary salons.

The north entrance to the single-story palace opens with a hemicycle colonnade onto the Weinbergterrasse, a cascade of six terraces featuring niches and vines, at the bottom of which lies a Baroque garden with a pool and a fountain at its center. The south entrance is decorated by 36 sandstone sculptures that alternate with large windows. Inside, covered by a domed roof, there is the large, oval Marble Room that was used for receptions.

42-43 Filled with statues, grottoes, and artificial ruins, Sans Souci park was the perfect architectural and landscape representation of

Frederick II's intellectual interests. In the background we see the Orangerie inspired by Italian Renaissance villas.

42 bottom Another view of Sans Souci park and one of the ruins. The purpose of these anachronistic

constructions was not merely to be evocative; they were used to hide the water tanks that fed the fountains.

The wings on either side of this room each contain no more than four rooms.

Frederick liked to stay in this intimate and peaceful building from April to October each year, taking long walks and entertaining such guests as the elderly Johann Sebastian Bach and Voltaire. Invited to organize the marvelous cedarwood library decorated with gilded bronze, the French leader of the Enlightenment accepted the hospitality offered him by Frederick II and stayed at Sans Souci from 1750 to 1753. During this period he filled the library with 2200 volumes either

written in or translated into French, but in doing so he endorsed what was increasingly becoming an absolute and intolerant monarchy.

New buildings, grottoes, ruins, the gazebo, and the Chinese tea-house were all built on the grounds. In 1763, the Bildgalerie was built, first under the direction of Knobelsdorff and, later, Johann Gottfried Büring to house 124 paintings by Flemish, Italia,n and Dutch masters such as Van Dyck, Rubens, and Caravaggio.

Clearly satisfied, Frederick charged Büring with the construction of a new and more official royal residence. By 1769, Sans Souci park (which had now been extended to cover 74 acres) also contained the Neuen Palais, the impressive and last symbol of German Baroque. The monumental three-story building is 722 feet long, crowned by an enormous drum dome, and decorated with 428 large sculptures. It contains more than 200 large rooms, an imposing colonnaded court, and official reception rooms decorated with marble and other stones to save what the king called "pointless" transfers to the hated "paternal" city of Berlin. Two buildings facing the Neuen Palais were built to accommodate the staff, the kitchens, and other service rooms.

Frederick the Great died at Sans Souci on August 17, 1786 after reigning for 46 years. The legacy of Great Prussia remained in safe hands even if the architectural taste of his successors was less certain. His nephew, Frederick William II, also wished to put a personal stamp on the site of Potsdam so he had the superb Neuen Garten with the modest Marble Palace laid out between 1787 and

1797 on the banks of the Heiliger See. Inspired by the romantic taste of his wife, he also built a decadent palace on the Pfaueninsel (Peacock Island), which was later transformed into an English garden by his successor Frederick William III.

The road that led backwards to the architectural past was by now clearly laid out and the buildings constructed in nineteenth-century Prussia were obviously influenced by this trend. In 1824, Prince Charles purchased Glienicke Castle, the ancient residence of the Counts von Hardenberg, and had it transformed into Italian Neo-Classical style using fragments from antiquity set in its walls. Two years later, Frederick William III built an entirely new district in the city of Potsdam – the Russian colony named Alexandrovska – for the members of the choir that Czar Alexander I had sent to the court in Berlin.

43 top left A detail of one of the palm-shaped columns that support the arcaded entrance to the Chinese tea-house. Entirely lined with gilded bronze, they have bases and capitals decorated with statues of exotic-looking nymphs.

43 top right Johann Gottfried Büring's design for the Chinese tea-house was inspired by a similar oriental-style pavilion on the estate of Lunéville Castle.

43 bottom Superbly decorated with gilded stuccoes, the Bildgalerie houses Frederick II's personal art collection of 124 paintings by Flemish, French, and Italian artists. Designed in 1763 by Johann Gottfried Büring, it has a two-color marble floor that enhances the perspective.

44 top left The Grotto Room in the Neuen Palais is decorated in a fantastic manner, making use of minerals, shells, and branches of coral.

44 top right Of the 200 rooms in the Neuen Palais, the Marble Room is perhaps the most dramatic. The walls are set with precious panels painted by artists of the French school in the eighteenth century.

44 center Built between 1787 and 1797 by Frederick William II, the Marble Palace is an elegant building of modest size that looks over the Heiliger See.

44-45 A masterpiece of German Baroque, the monumental Neuen Palais is 722 feet long, three stories high, and culminates in an enormous drum and dome. Ostentation was the principal feature of the architectural style.

After coming to the throne in 1840, it was Frederick William IV who made the greatest changes to the garden of delights that Potsdam had by now become. The "romantic king" planned to unite the estate of Charlottenhof, which had been a rural area until 1825, with Sans-Souci Park. With contributions from architects like Schinkel, Persius, and Lenné, he transformed the main building into a small palace in Biedermeyer style with interiors inspired by mosaics from the town of Pompeii. He rebuilt the *orangerie*, turning it into a monumental Classical-Romantic building. But above all, he dramatically changed the farming landscape, turning it into an English garden with vast terraces covered with lawns, small pools, and copses, and he built highly elegant Roman baths, with statues, mosaics, and frescoes.

Under the rule of Frederick William IV, Potsdam was endowed with religious buildings. First came the Friedenskirche (Church of Peace), which is a basilica with a bell tower in early Christian style. In a similar vein is the Church of the Redeemer of Sacrov, which stands on the shore of Lake Havel between the Neuen Garten and the Pfaueninsel.

In the mid-1830's, even Prince William, the younger son of Frederick William III and future Emperor William I, made his contribution. After much hesitation, his father had given him the property of Babelsberg near Potsdam. At the suggestion of his wife, Augusta of Saxe-Weimar, in 1833 William began construction of a Neo-Gothic residence in Tudor style unwillingly designed by Schinkel, who was not in favor of medievalism. The compromise between the architect and the demanding princess resulted in a simply decorated building with clear lines that looked out over the countryside. Once again designed by Lenné in typically Romantic style, the park has twisting paths that lead into openings where unusual buildings stand. One such example is the Matrosenhaus, where the man in charge of the royal boats lived, and another the Gerichtslaube, a tea room built from stone taken from the ancient City Hall in Berlin.

With the exception of the Kaiserbahnhof, the imperial train station built between 1905 and 1908 near the Neuen Palais, the only alteration made to Potsdam during the twentieth century was the Cecilienhof. Built in the Neuen Garten to satisfy the wishes of Emperor William II, it is an unpretentious building resembling an English country house. It was finished in 1916, shortly before the abdication of the emperor, so that it was never inhabited by the imperial family. However, it entered history as the site of the Potsdam Conference of August 2, 1945, when Churchill, Truman, and Stalin decided the sanctions to be placed on the defeated Germany and put an end to the powerful and solid Reich that, two centuries before, had evolved out of the skillful political and military maneuvers of Frederick William I.

The Historic Center of Krakow

POLAND

REGISTRATION: 1978
CRITERIA: C (IV)

At the top of each hour, a trumpeter climbs to the top of the tower of the church of Kosciol Mariacki (St. Mary) in the market square and plays the Marian anthem. The melody, which at one time was played as the gates of the city were opened or closed, is suddenly interrupted, always on the same note, to commemorate the Tatar invasion of 1240 and the moment when the city trumpeter was the first to spot the enemy troops. He was also the first to suffer from their arrival, being shot by an arrow as he blew his instrument to warn the city's inhabitants of the imminent danger.

This unusual tradition is indicative of Krakow's links to its past. The first written evidence of the existence of the city was recorded by a Jewish merchant from Cordoba, Ibrahim ibn Jakub, who in 965 described it as an important trading center that stood below Vavel hill. In the year 1000 the city became an archbishopric, and a castle, cathedral, and various churches in Romanesque style were built on the hill.

The city, which was the capital of the small kingdom of Poland under the Piast Dynasty from the eleventh century, continued to prosper until it was sacked and destroyed by the Tatars. In 1257, reconstruction began and the city was laid out on a new plan that has remained unchanged to the present day. The market square (Rynek), the largest in Europe, was laid out and the city given a new system of fortifications, towers, and gates that was enlarged in later eras.

46 top A view of the impressive Gothic cathedral with its three towers, one of which contains the Dzwon Zymut (Sigismund Bell) cast in 1520.

46-47 This is the view from the Vistula of the Wawel, the hill where Krakow's first medieval settlement was established.

Around the year 1000, the cathedral and a fortified palace were built here. From 1038 on, the palace became the residence of the Polish kings.

47 top left Kosciol Mariacki (St. Mary's Church) in the Market Square is a masterpiece of late Gothic architecture.

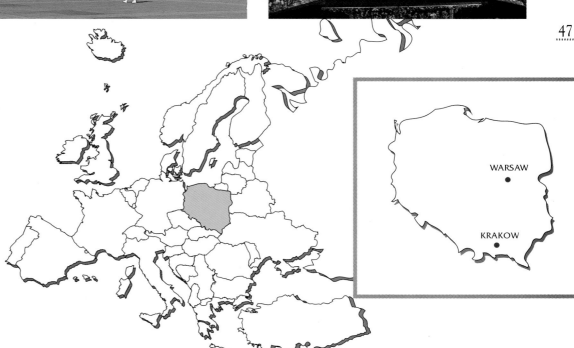

47 top right Kosciol Mariacki holds priceless art works, including the wooden sculpture of the Death of the Virgin (1477-1489) by the German woodcarver Veit Stoss.

47 center The focal point of the royal palace on Wawel Hill is the large cloister onto which most of the official rooms face.

47 bottom right The royal palace is now a museum that holds the Crown jewels and one of the world's most important collections of Flemish tapestries.

48-49 *An aerial view of the Rynek, Europe's largest market square. It is dominated by the Renaissance-style Cloth Palace, which contains shops on the ground floor and the section of the National Museum dedicated to Polish painting.*

48 bottom *The Barbican is Europe's largest fortified rampart. The defensive walls were built in 1498 when the city was at the height of its splendor and capital of Poland. The city was a meeting place for famous humanists and scientists.*

and Lithuania and founded northern Europe's most important royal dynasty, which lasted roughly 200 years.

From the mid-sixteenth century on, Krakow enjoyed a period of great splendor. Under the enlightened rule of the Jagellonic kings, the city was made even more secure with the construction of the Barbican, the largest fortified rampart in Europe, and the city attracted famous humanists, artists, and scientists. Nicholas Copernicus studied there before going to Italy, and Veit Stoss, a master woodcarver, arrived in the city from Nuremberg in 1477 and spent 12 years

carving the immense decorative work, *Death of the Virgin*, from limewood for the altar in St. Mary's church. Three years later, having moved from wood to marble, Stoss sculpted the tomb of Casimir IV Jagellone inside the cathedral and thus began the tradition of the great royal tombs in Krakow.

When Stoss returned to his homeland, the Tuscan sculptors Francesco Fiorentino and Bartolomeo Berrecci were called to the city where, in the cathedral, they created some of the most dazzling examples of Renaissance sculpture outside Italy. In those years, the castle on Vavel hill was also rebuilt and decorated with a collection of wall-hangings ordered from Flanders. However, these were the last years of glory for Krakow: at the end of the sixteenth century the capital was transferred to Warsaw, and Krakow, though retaining its

busy intellectual life, had to adapt itself to the role of a supporting city with the characteristics of a small commercial center.

Another jewel, however, was added to its beauty. At the end of the eighteenth century, Prince Czartorysky returned from a trip to Italy with a unique purchase, Leonardo da Vinci's painting *Woman with an ermine*, which can today be admired in the museum that bears the name of its original owner. This masterpiece, miraculously spared from World War II, has found in Krakow a setting to match its own beauty.

49 left The cloister of the Collegium Maius, one of the oldest buildings in Krakow Academy. The Academy was founded in 1364 by Casimir the Great, the last king of the Piast Dynasty, and was later turned into the Jagellonic University.

49 center right This hall in the Collegium Maius contains old furnishings and paintings.

49 bottom right Another view of the Rynek. In 1899, a monument was raised to Adam Mickiewicz, Poland's best-loved poet, in front of the Cloth Palace.

Krakow's history reached a turning point during the reign of the last of the Piasts, Casimir the Great (1333-1370). As a patron of the arts and sciences, Casimir founded the Cloth Palace, in the center of the Rynek, the church of St. Mary, and two new centers, Kazimierz and Kleparz, which today are two districts of the city. But above all, he established the Krakow Academy, which was later to be known as the Jagellonica University and became Poland's most renowned center of learning. Twenty years later, Casimir gave his daughter in marriage to the Lithuanian Grand Duke, Ladislau Jagellone, who later became king of Poland

The Historic Center of Prague
CZECH REPUBLIC

REGISTRATION: 1992
CRITERIA: C (II) (IV) (VI)

Havel na Hrad, "Havel at the Castle," the citizens of Prague shouted in the exciting days after the fall of the Berlin Wall in 1989 that represented the return to freedom. Vaclav Havel became the first president of independent Czechoslovakia – which became the Czech Republic after its peaceful split with Slovakia in 1993 – and

the tenant of a luxurious apartment in the Hradcany. The site measures 2,800,000 square feet and contains a cathedral, a basilica, a monastery, a royal palace, and a variety towers and courts. It is a city within a city and for more than a thousand years has been the symbol of Prague. It was also, with its labyrinthine layout, a literary inspiration for Franz Kafka, the best-known citizen of Prague throughout the world.

Since Prince Borivoi built a wooden fort on a hill on the left bank of the Moldava in the eleventh century – next to the hill where another, slightly older fort stood, the

Vysehrad – the Hradcany has seen 40 owners come and go and 30 raids and fires. The Hapsburg emperor and king, Rudolf II, lived here, and in 1583 made Prague the capital of his empire. He was known as the "alchemist king" and believed in the philosopher's stone. He built a laboratory in the towers of the castle, where he welcomed guests like the exuberant Milanese artist Giovanni Arcimboldi to turn lead into gold. Then, in 1618, during the period when Jan Hus had been haranguing his fellow-citizens for more than a decade to rebel against the Church of Rome, three Catholic ambassadors were thrown out of the castle windows. This episode has gone down in history as the Defenestration of Prague and marked the

start of the Thirty Years War.

As it appears today, the Hradcany is the result of Baroque restoration undertaken by Empress Maria Theresa of Austria, which was followed, at the start of the twentieth century, by the rebuilding of many of the interiors by Slovakian architect Josip Plecnik, including the lovely Gold Room. The most attractive sections of the complex, however, are much older in origin such as the immense late-Gothic room in the palace, 207 feet long and 43 feet high, which was built between 1493 and 1502, and the Cathedral of St. Vitus. Construction of the cathedral was begun in 1344 by Matthieu d'Arras on the site of a Roman basilica and was not completed until 1929 when the Neo-Gothic west façade was added with two spires 262 feet tall. The overlaying of styles inside also reflects the long span of construction. Next to the splendid Gothic chapel decorated with precious and semi-precious stones and dedicated to St. Wenceslas, one can admire a charming Art Nouveau window by Alfons Mucha.

50 top One of the rooms in the Strahov Monastic Library, which contains one million volumes. The rarest and most precious of these are the first 16 books printed in the Czech language, of which seven are unique. The oldest volume is the ninth-century Strahov Gospel written on parchment with gold uncial characters.

50 center left This is the royal mausoleum in the cathedral of St. Vitus, where several of the most important figures in the history of Bohemia are

buried: Charles IV, Ferdinand I, Rudolf II, and St. Giovanni Nepomuceno.

50 bottom right The large Art Nouveau window by Alfons Mucha in St. Vitus' Cathedral.

51 top A view of the Hradcany (Castle Hill). Still the center of national power, the complex – which covers 2,800,000 square feet – is a city within a city. Its main buildings are St. Vitus' Cathedral, St. George's Basilica, and the Royal Palace.

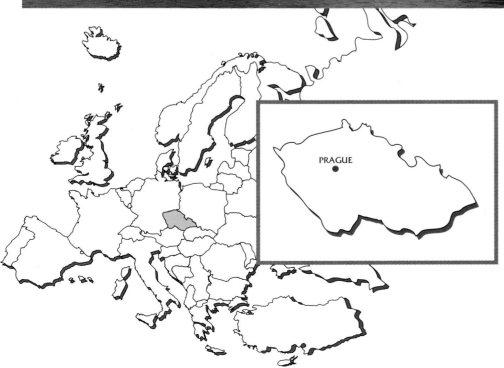

51 bottom The Vladeslas
Room (207 feet long and
43 feet high) inside the
Royal Palace. Built

between 1493 and 1502, it
is considered the masterpiece
of Benedikt Ried. Horse
tournaments were held here.

PRAGUE

As a consequence of commercial expansion, starting in the eleventh century a new community, including many Jewish families, arose on the right bank of the Moldava near the original Prague of the Vysehrad and Hradcany. Called Staré Mesto (Old City), this area achieved the status of a district after 1170 when the Judith Bridge was built (the first stone bridge in Prague), and this gave it the right to build walls and defensive ramparts. The heart of the old city is Strarometske Namesti, the central square dominated by the City Hall and its tower, built in 1364. Half-hidden by the houses to the right of the building, the fourteenth-century church of Teyn contains the grave of the Danish astronomer Tycho Brahe. On the opposite side of the square

stands St. Nicholas' Church, a Baroque masterpiece by Kilian Ignaz Dientzenhofer. Until World War II, Staré Mesto was home to a Jewish community of 12,000 people and still contains several synagogues and the oldest Jewish cemetery in Europe.

In 1257, a new district called Malá Strana ('small part') began to grow below the Hradcany. Heavily damaged by a fire in 1503, today the zone is architecturally harmonious with Gothic and Renaissance churches and civil buildings "bound" together by houses with porticoes built in ornate Baroque. In addition, its tiny alleys, romantic gardens hidden behind the facades, and ancient beer-houses make this the most attractive district in the city and the favorite of the city's bohemians for the

past 100 years. One of the loveliest streets in Malá Strana is the paved Nerudova Ulice lined by richly decorated buildings. Wolfgang Amadeus Mozart lived in one of them for a long time.

When it became part of the Holy Roman Empire, Prague continued to prosper. The Bohemian emperor Charles IV governed it from 1346 to 1378 and planned further physical and cultural development. In 1348, he founded the first university in central Europe and began construction of Nové Mesto (New City), St. Vitus' Cathedral, and the Charles Bridge, which was named after him. Constructed in 1357 to replace the Judith Bridge that was washed away by a flood, it is 1,706 feet long, 33 feet wide, and is

52-53 *A view from above of the elegant façades of the palaces in Starometske Namesti. This attractive square in the heart of the old city contains several of Prague's best-known monuments, which represent 500 years of history.*

53 top *The magnificent astrological clock was placed on the City Hall tower at the end of the fourteenth century. The tower is the most impressive building in the central Starometske Namesti.*

53 center left *The pointed towers of Teyn Church face onto Starometske Namesti. Begun in 1380 in the workshop of Peter Parler, it was completed in the mid-sixteenth century. It contains Prague's oldest baptismal font (1414), the tomb of the astronomer Tycho Brahe, and a series of Baroque paintings by Karel Skreta.*

supported by 16 sandstone arcades. It is said that to protect it from bad weather, the emperor ordered that thousands of grapes should be mixed into the mortar.

The bridge was the place from where Giovanni Nepomuceno, a monk, was thrown into the river in 1393 after being tortured. He was canonized in 1729 and became the most worshipped saint in Bohemia. The cause of his death was the anger of King Wenceslas, successor to Charles IV, to whom the priest refused to reveal the confessional secrets of the king's wife. Before his canonization, a statue of Giovanni Nepomuceno by Jan Brokof was added to the Charles Bridge in 1683. This was the cue for the prominent citizens of Prague, as well as the Jesuits who strongly

53 center right *On the other side of the square stands the church of St. Nicholas. Built in 1732 in Baroque style by Kilian Ignaz Dientzenhofer, it was one of the bastions of the Counter-Reformation.*

53 bottom *A view of the Nerudova Ulice, the street dedicated to the Prague writer Jan Neruda, the author of the Tales of Malá Strana. The street is home to some of the city's oldest beer houses.*

supported the university, to compete in funding other statues of martyrs on the bridge, notably Czechs, Italians, and Spaniards, taking as their model the Ponte Sant'Angelo in Rome.

The center of Nové Mesto and of all modern Prague is St. Wenceslas' Square. Built to be the site of a horse market, it resembles a wide street more than a square (in fact it is 2,460 feet long but only 200 wide) and slopes slightly. Most of the buildings that overlook it were built at the

later in protest against the invasion of the city by the Warsaw Pact troops.

The University is centered on the Carolinum, a building rebuilt in Baroque style with a superb Gothic bow-window. This important cultural institution was joined at the end of the sixteenth century by the Klementinum, the third largest Jesuit college in the world and the second largest monument in Prague after the Hradcany. To build it, it was necessary to demolish 32 houses, St. Clement's Church,

and 160 manuscripts given by Charles to the nearby university, an imperial library was built in 1777. Today the Klementinum contains almost six million volumes, 1,200 papyruses, 6,000 medieval manuscripts, and 3,000 incunabula. In addition to this library, there is the seventeenth-century Strahov monastic library with book rooms described as the most spectacular in the world.

Prague has always been a city of culture. It was here that Mozart composed

start of the twentieth century when Prague was overwhelmed by the wave of Art Nouveau. Of special interest are Casa Peterka at number 12, which now contains the National Museum, and the Hotel Europa, at number 25. This was the square where the revolt in 1968 against Soviet rule began – known as the Prague Spring – and where Jan Palach committed suicide a year

two gardens, and seven farms with all their land. Design and construction of the Baroque masterpiece was the work of Giovanni Domenico Orsi. The chronicles of the era state that in 1696 the Klementinum had 1500 students of which one seventh, coming from poor homes, were provided with free education, board, and lodging. To hold the volumes, books,

his two most famous symphonies, and many citizens of Prague have made a huge contribution to the world of culture. Bedrich Smetana and Antonin Dvorak were important contributors to the musical world, and three outstanding names in the literary world are those of Franz Kafka, Rainer Maria Rilke, and the irreverent Bohumil Hrabal.

55 bottom left An evening view of St. Wenceslas Square with the National Museum in the background. It covers the same area as the old horse market, and consequently looks like a wide, slightly sloping avenue.

55 bottom right The façade of the Grand Hotel Europa in St. Wenceslas Square. Early twentieth-century buildings in Art Nouveau or Functionalist architecture line the whole square.

The Palace and Gardens of Schönbrunn

AUSTRIA

The last important guests to be received in the imperial residence of Schönbrunn were, in 1961, John Fitzgerald Kennedy and Nikita Khrushchev, who met in the Great Gallery of the Hapsburg residence to attempt to put some warmth into the relationship between the West and the Soviet block. Over the centuries the palace had seen other events that had made a deep impression on history, for example, the Congress of Vienna in 1815, when the powers that had defeated Napoleon met to redraw the boundaries of Europe.

Hapsburg property from 1560 on, the Katterburg estate was originally used for farming and consisted of only a small residence with a farm attached. It received its current name when the Emperor Matthias paused to rest during a hunt and named the place where he drank *Schönen Brunnen* (lovely spring). However, the first court summer residence was built there for Eleonora Gonzaga, the wife of Ferdinand II.

It was not until the end of the seventeenth century that Schönbrunn became the epitome of Hapsburg power when, to celebrate the defeat of the Turks after the siege of Vienna, the emperor, Leopold I, invited Johann Bernhard Fischer von Erlach to design a palace that would exceed even Versailles in splendor. Inspired by the villas designed by Palladio, the architect presented his project to the emperor, but the high costs obliged him to be less ambitious. Leopold wanted Schönbrunn to have the character of a family home and to be a mixture between a center of power and a luxurious, but not self-important, residence. The grounds were designed by Jean Trehet in French Baroque style.

The moving spirit of Schönbrunn was, however, Empress Maria Theresa, who raised her 16 children there without neglecting her political duties. Her maternal nature often led her to dispense with court formalities such as the time she took the six-year-old Mozart in her arms in the Mirror Room after his first royal performance.

56 top left The exterior of the Schönbrunn palace and gardens in French Baroque style. The landscape artists Nicolaus Jadot and Adrian van Steckhofen were invited to redesign the park during the reign of Maria Theresa (1740-1780).

56 bottom left The palace seen from the air. It stands in the valley of the river Wien between the Viennese districts of Meidling to the east and Hietzing to the west. The area was originally a hunting reserve but passed into the hands of the Hapsburgs in 1540.

56-57 The magnificent palace was designed by Johann Bernhard Fischer in line with Palladian architecture. The main court (shown here) has a large fountain and pool in the center. Water is a dominant element at Schönbrunn, as testified to by its name, which is derived from Schönen Brunnen (lovely spring).

57 bottom left The superb Neptune fountain with, in the background, the hill with the Gloriette. The Gloriette was designed by Ferdinand Hetzendorf von Hohenberg as the architectural crown of Schönbrunn Park. Built in 1775, its central section and two galleries are formed by eleven arches on Doric columns, and the whole construction is topped by the symbol of the Hapsburgs: an eagle standing on a globe.

57 bottom right The flower gardens at Schönbrunn. The Hapsburgs were fond of nature and wildlife and loved to collect exotic plants. In 1752, the world's first zoological garden was laid out inside the park. In 1881, a greenhouse – the Palmenhaus – was constructed to hold the palms.

SCHÖNBRUNN
(VIENNA)

58 top Decorated between 1769 and 1777 with motifs taken from nature by Johann Bergl, this room is on the ground floor of the palace. The gilded ceramic stove in the form of a tree trunk is a work of art.

58 bottom A room with sumptuous furniture made from carved and painted wood. Unfortunately, Maria Theresa gave away much of the eighteenth-century furniture to her staff because she liked to replace her furnishings frequently.

58-59 Over 130 feet long and 33 feet wide, the Great Gallery was where the court receptions were held. A superb example of Rococo, it has large windows, mirrors, and stuccoes painted white and gold. The ceiling frescoes were created by Gregorio Guglielmi. Maria Theresa and her consort, Francis of Lorraine, are portrayed in the center surrounded by personifications of their virtues.

Under the guidance of the Italian architect, Nicolaus Pacassi, Maria Theresa had the interiors redecorated in sumptuous Rococo styl, with a profusion of mirrors, gilding, frescoes, and boiserie. Nicolaus Jadot and Adrian van Steckhofen laid out the gardens anew and built the Gloriette, the colonnaded building that is the architectural highlight of the park and from whose terrace the whole of Vienna can be seen. Maria Theresa was also responsible for the Neptune fountain and the attractive copy of a Roman ruin adorned with Neo-Classical statues. Here, her consort, the future Francis I of Lorraine, founded the first zoological garden in the world called the Früstückspavillon (the breakfast pavilion) around which the cages were arranged.

As Maria Theresa was in the habit of auctioning or giving away her used furniture to her staff at court, few rooms have retained their eighteenth century furnishings, but one of them, the splendid Yellow Room, has Rococo features and paintings of bourgeois children by the young Swiss painter Liotard.

Also original is the Spartan folding bed that was used for decades by Franz Josef and in which he died in 1916, at the age of 88. The emperor was very stern in character. He would rise at half past four each morning, wash himself in cold water, and then pray like the fervent Catholic that he was. He could have slept next to his beautiful wife, Elizabeth of Bavaria, in the sumptuous blue and white wedding chamber furnished in rosewood, but he preferred to leave luxury to her. Elizabeth was better known as the semi-mythical

Princess Sissi, and so many of her *objets d'art* have survived such as her over-elaborate boudoir where she underwent beauty treatments.

Perhaps Franz Josef was aware of the decline of his empire, but it was his successor, Karl I, who, in the blue Chinese Room on November 11, 1918, was obliged to sign the document renouncing affairs of State. The following day the Republic of Austria was proclaimed and the chapter of Schönbrunn's history as an imperial residence was brought to an end.

59 bottom Some of the rooms in the palace are decorated with enormous wall-paintings of bucolic and hunting scenes commissioned by Maria Theresa. In the Ceremonial Room, the empress wanted scenes that realistically represented important moments in the history of the Hapsburgs.

The Banks of the Seine in Paris

FRANCE

PARIS
REGISTRATION: 1991
CRITERIA: C (I) (II) (IV)

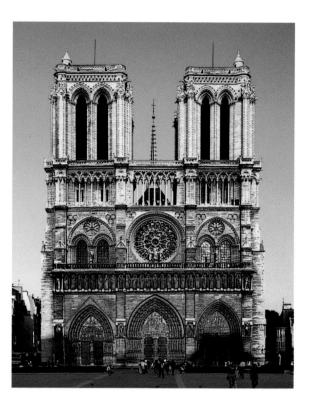

When you come to Paris for the very first time, you get the feeling that you are looking at a single, monumental town-planning scheme: it seems as if the Île de la Cité, the esplanade leading from the Arc de Triomphe to the Louvre via the Champs Elysées and the Tuileries, and even the banks of the Seine to the Eiffel Tower, were created by a single, eclectic mind. In reality, Paris is the outcome of seven centuries of renovation, expansion, and restructuring. Nevertheless, there was indeed one person behind this idea of "cultural" unity: Georges Haussmann. Born in 1809 in a modest home on Rue Faubourg de la Roule, Haussmann was to become the city planner for Napoleon III. As prefect of the *Seine département*, between 1853 and 1870 he transformed the French capital into the famous Ville Lumière, or City of Light.

During the first centuries B.C., the Celtic tribe of the Parisii settled along the banks of the Seine, but a city was not built there until after 52 B.C., when Caesar founded the Roman city of Lutetia. When Julian II (The Apostate) was proclaimed emperor in A.D. 360, the city was renamed "Paris" after its early inhabitants. However, after the fall of the Roman Empire it met with the Viking and barbarian invasions, and it was decimated by epidemics and destroyed by sacking. The Roman buildings were demolished in order to build a walled rampart around the Île de la Cité, where the inhabitants could seek refuge.

Prosperity arrived in the twelfth century with the reign of Philip Augustus. The Île de la Cité, the small island in the heart of Paris set between the banks of the Seine, contains two extraordinary signs of that era, the cathedral of Nôtre-Dame and the Sainte-Chapelle, both masterpieces of Gothic art. In 1163, Pope Alexander III laid the foundation stone of Nôtre-Dame, starting the work that would take 170 years to complete. The cathedral is 427 feet long and supported by flying buttresses, while the pediment is flanked by two towers that are nearly 230 feet tall. Behind the wide transept – topped by the 295-foot-tall spire – there is a carved wooden choir from the eighteenth century that is enclosed by a stone transenna commissioned from Jean Ravy 400 years earlier to shield the services from the noise of the faithful. The interior, with a nave and two aisles, is decorated with paintings and sculptures from different periods. The side chapels hold paintings that the Paris corporations commissioned in the seventeenth and eighteenth centuries from masters like Charles Le Brun. The statue of the Virgin and Child, to whom Nôtre-Dame is dedicated, is next to the transept.

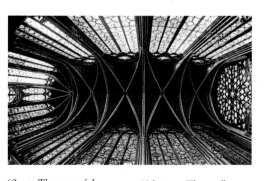

60 top The nave of the cathedral of Nôtre-Dame was completed at the end of the twelfth century. Despite many later alterations, the original style of the nave has been maintained, in particular the hexapartite vault and the massive cylindrical columns of the arches.

60 bottom The smaller chapel in Sainte-Chappelle. The church is one of the greatest works of Western architecture. It was built by Louis IX in 1248 to hold Christ's crown of thorns, a fragment of the Cross, and other precious relics.

61 top The west face of Nôtre-Dame with its three sculpturally decorated portals, the central rose window dedicated to the Virgin, and the two towers. The tower on the right contains the famous bell, Emmanuel.

61 bottom The starred ceiling of the larger chapel in Sainte-Chappelle. Originally reserved for the royal family, the chapel has walls with 15 marvelous windows – separated by slender columns 49 feet high – that illustrate approximately 1,000 religious scenes and subjects.

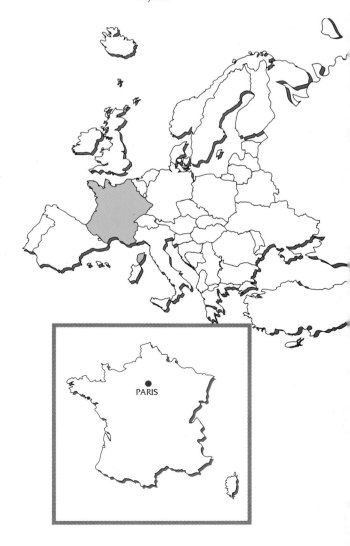

PARIS

In 1248, Louis IX built the Sainte-Chapelle, located near Nôtre-Dame, to hold the relics of Christ, including the crown of thorns the king had purchased from the emperor of Byzantium. The cathedral's lines that stretch up to the sky, the 15 magnificent stained-glass windows of the upper chapel illustrating scenes from the Bible and the Gospels, the enormous rose window, and the carved wooden figures of the apostle earned it the sobriquet of "Gate to Paradise."

Paris was neglected by the French monarchs until Francis I decided that it needed a palace befitting a capital city. As a result, in 1546 construction of the Louvre began, an undertaking that was to span more than three centuries and involve seven different sovereigns. After Francis I, who entrusted to the work to Pierre Lescot, came Queen Catherine de' Medici who had the Tuileries Palace built. Subsequently, Henry IV, Louis XII, Louis XIV (who moved the royal residence to Versailles), Napoleon I, and Napoleon III also left their mark. Despite his love for Versailles, Louis XIV probably had the greatest influence on the construction of the Louvre. Recognizing the stylistic inconsistency of the palace, he asked Gian Lorenzo Bernini, whose fame as an innovator had spread from Italy, to come to Paris to make major changes to the palace. The architect decided to reconstruct the façade but presented plans that were unconvincing. Following the ceremony to lay the foundation stone, Bernini was taken back to Rome and his plans were changed radically. The work was then entrusted to Claude Perrault, who designed the Colonnade enclosing

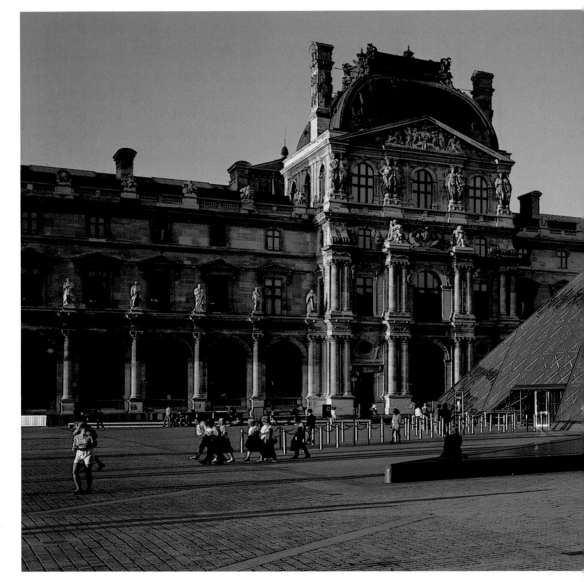

the existing buildings to give the Louvre its magnificent sense of unity.

The seventeenth century was the city's golden age. Between 1671 and 1676, Louis XIV had the Hôtel des Invalides built on the other bank of the Seine to house aged and invalid veterans. Shortly before this, Cardinal Mazarin built the Collège des Quatre-Nations, now the home of the Institut de France and the headquarters of the national academies. Rue Dauphine and Place Dauphine also date from this period, and about 1650 work was

62 top left One of the majestic galleries on the second floor of the Louvre, dedicated to European painting between 1400 and 1900. Naturally, French artists represent almost half of the immense and priceless collection.

62 top right The halls of the Louvre dedicated to objets d'art, furniture, jewelry, clocks, wall hangings, weapons, armor, porcelain, and much else hold a total of 8,000 items. The picture shows a room filled with eighteenth-century French furniture.

62-63 *The Cour Napoléon, the main court in the Louvre, is lined by buildings from the reign of Louis XIII (1610-1654). Restoration work begun in 1981 under François Mitterand was completed in 1989. The famous glass pyramid over the new entrance was designed by the Chinese-American architect, I.M. Pei.*

63 top *A view of the Roman section of the Louvre shows busts and sculptural groups of extraordinary quality.*

63 bottom left *The Dôme des Invalides is a superb church built in 1676 by the Sun King, Louis XIV. The church was intended to hold the remains of the royal family, but after his death, the project was set aside and the building became a monument to the glory of the Bourbons.*

63 bottom right *The interior of the dome in the Dôme des Invalides. Below it lies the crypt where, in 1861, Napoleon's tomb was placed. The dictator's body was brought back from St. Helena to France at the request of Louis Philippe.*

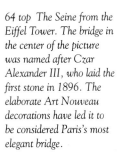

64

64 top The Seine from the Eiffel Tower. The bridge in the center of the picture was named after Czar Alexander III, who laid the first stone in 1896. The elaborate Art Nouveau decorations have led it to be considered Paris's most elegant bridge.

completed to transform the Île de Saint-Louis, southeast of Île de la Cité, into a residential area.

In the middle of the eighteenth century, Louis XV commissioned Jacques-Ange Gabriel to create the Place de la Concorde and build the Military School. Across from this, a broad esplanade, the Champs de Mars, stretched to the Seine and was to be the site of France's most important political celebrations. The French Revolution marked an abrupt pause in Paris' development plans, but Napoleon immediately continued the legacy left by his predecessors. At the time, the *quais* (the banks of the Seine) were dotted with a picturesque jungle of boats, warehouses, and windmills. The emperor regulated river traffic and built stone wharfs, but this was just the beginning of his plans for the city. He built the Madeleine, which was to face an

identical church on the other bank. He had the Place de la Concorde redesigned and laid out the Rue de Rivoli so that it would follow the Seine from the Bastille, the symbol of the Revolution, to Place de l'Etoile. Here, in 1805, following the victorious Battle of Austerlitz, work began on the Arc de Triomphe, one of Paris's most famous landmarks. The great bridges over the Seine, the Pont d'Austerlitz, and the Pont d'Iena, were also built alongside the Pont Neuf in order to better link the two banks of the river.

Napoleon stamped his mark on what was already a large metropolis with a population of five hundred thousands. Nevertheless, it was Napoleon III who, during the middle of the century, ordered the town-planning revolution that would give Paris its immortal charm. One of the reasons behind his decision was his fear that the population, with its penchant for

64 bottom Another view of Place de la Concorde. One of the eight statues that symbolize France's most important cities stands in the foreground. In the nineteenth century, the 3,200-year-old Luxor Obelisk was placed in the center of the square. The Eiffel Tower can be seen in the background.

mass uprisings, could again revolt against its leaders. A city with large squares and broad boulevards would allow him to amass an army to defend the monarchy. Haussmann, who conceived and supervised this new layout, created the route leading from Boulevard Saint-Michel to Boulevard de Sébastopol, reorganized the buildings of the Île de la Cité, transformed the Place du Châtelet, and tore down entire city districts to make room for the main thoroughfares that cross the city.

Following Haussmann's glorious makeover, by the end of the nineteenth century Paris was large and splendid enough to come forward as a world capital. Trade flourished, and European culture chose Paris as its haven. The World Exposition of 1889 was held to commemorate the centennial of the French Revolution as well as the resurrection of the city. For the occasion, a monument was planned in order to celebrate the engineering skills of republican France. Maurice Koechline and Emile Nougier from the Gustave Eiffel Construction Company drew up plans for a nearly 1,000-foot-tall tower to be built at the end of the Champs de Mars – strictly for the duration of the Expo. Nevertheless, people were enraged by the plans. A large group of intellectuals signed a petition in an attempt to stop its construction, but

the Eiffel Tower, with the powerful backing of Gustave himself, was built nonetheless and was inaugurated on Sunday, March 31, 1889. And, there it remained, the emblem of modernity with its 11,000 tons of iron and its intriguing tangle of girders and latticework originally invented simply to stabilize the massive structure.

In more recent years, new and colossal works have been built in Paris, particularly under François Mitterrand, with the buildings housing the National Library, the glass pyramid at the entrance to the Louvre, and the extension of the line of sight from the Louvre to the Arc de Triomphe and on to the enormous Arc de la Défense. These projects have continued the thousand-year tradition of Paris and renewed the grandeur of the City of Light.

66 bottom The Eiffel Tower is probably the most famous monument in the French capital. Opened on March 31, 1889 to celebrate the Exposition Universale in Paris, it was the world's tallest building until 1931 when the Empire State Building was completed in New York.

66-67 From the base of the Eiffel Tower, the view takes in the Champ-de-Mars, which are the gardens that stretch as far as the École Militaire. Originally, they were used for the parades of the school's cadets. This is where the large anniversary celebrations to mark the French revolution are held every July fourteenth.

67 bottom left A section of the Rue de Rivoli. This wide street lined with elegant Neoclassical buildings was laid down for Napoleon in commemoration of his victory at Rivoli in 1797. It connects the Champs Elysées with the Louvre.

67 top right The tensile structure made of glass and steel in the Grande Arche de la Défense was designed in 1989 by the Danish architect Otto von Spreckelsen.

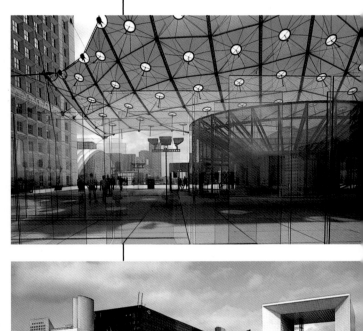

67 bottom right A view of la Défense. Covering nearly 200 acres, it is the largest office area in Europe. Its careful planning also made it an open-air museum of art and contemporary architecture. The Grande Arche was built as a continuation of the axis on which the Arc de Triomphe and pyramid of the Louvre stand.

The Palace and Parks of Versailles

FRANCE

DÉPARTEMENT OF YVELINES
REGISTRATION: 1979
CRITERIA: C (I) (II) (VI)

68 top left Detail of the statue of Neptune in one of the water parterres in Versailles Park.

68 bottom left The Grand Trianon, built in 1687, was Louis XIV's "resting" palace. Its peaceful atmosphere was also appreciated by Marie-Antoinette, the wife of Louis XVI, who designed its gardens.

Thanks to a secret passage that joined the Queen's apartments to those of the King, on October 6, 1789 Marie-Antoinette managed to evade the angry mob, but her salvation was short-lived. The next morning, Louis XVI and his wife were arrested, and four years later, they were both executed.

The palace at Versailles was thus the setting for the tragic, though temporary, end of the French monarchy, overwhelmed by the debts that Louis XV had left to a son who was too young and unprepared to govern. In truth, Louis XVI was already 20 when he took the throne, whereas his most famous predecessor, Louis XIV, who had built the magnificent palace, was only five when he became king. Furthermore, the Sun King was only 23 when the able diplomat Cardinal Mazarin died, and the king decided to reign France only with the help of his trusted advisor, Jean-Baptiste Colbert.

The history of Versailles began at the start of the seventeenth century when the young heir to the throne, Louis XIII, spent long days hunting in the woods and fields around the village of Versailles. As soon as he became king, he took refuge there to avoid the boredom of court ceremony, and he eventually bought the entire Versailles seigniory on April 8, 1623 where he built a small hunting lodge. This stone, brick, and slate building is now enclosed within the majestic body of the Palace and known as the Old Castle.

Louis XIII, however, did not enjoy the peace of Versailles for long. In 1632, he died prematurely and left the throne to his young son Louis, the future Sun King. Having shored up his kingdom by marrying Maria-Teresa, the Spanish Infanta, in 1660, the young king began expanding his father's palace. Under the guidance of the architect Louis Le Vau, two parallel buildings were constructed in front of the existing palace, the interiors were decorated, and the garden laid out. Yet these improvements were not enough to satisfy the ambitious designs of the king, so in 1668, he decided on a second enlargement. Once again he commissioned Le Vau, who wanted to demolish the older building, but the king opposed this and requested that the new palace be built around it like an "*Enveloppe*." It was within this enlargement that the State apartments were created. With the death of Le Vau in 1670, the design of the terrace that overlooks the garden, which was inspired by the architecture of Italian Baroque villas, fell to François d'Orbay.

In 1678, the Sun King decided to make Versailles the symbol of the French crown. He called on a new architect, Jules Ardouin-Mansart, who, in 6 years, built the gigantic wings to the north and south of

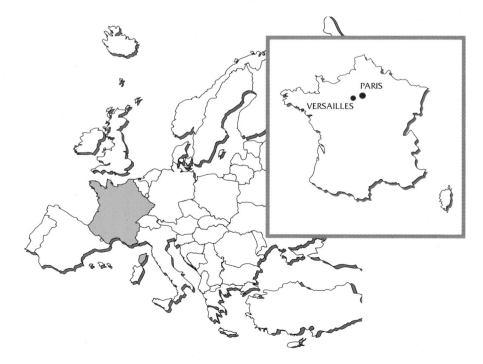

68-69 Versailles palace replaced the Louvre as the official residence of the kings of France on May 6, 1682. With its 700 rooms and wonderful park, it is one of the most famous buildings in the world.

69 top The Apollo Pool is one of the largest bodies of water in the gardens at Versailles. Lying on the main avenue to the palace, it is a huge octagonal basin adorned with a sculpture of the sun god on his chariot by Jean-Baptiste Tuby.

69 bottom Latona's Pool is another of the extraordinary fountains at Versailles, accessible by a large flight of steps. Fountains and running water were one of Louis XIV's favorite amusements.

the palace, the orangerie, the stables, and the large staff buildings. However, his most important contribution was the transformation of the terrace into the famous Hall of Mirrors, which was to become the emblem of the monarchy's absolute power. This marvelous hall is 240 feet long, 34-and-a-half feet wide, and 39 feet high. At one end there is the Salon de la Paix and at the other the Salon de la Guèrre. Seventeen enormous windows looking out onto the garden are faced by an equal number of mirrors made in a Paris workshop, purposefully fitted out by Colbert to rival those in Venice. The arches rest on marble pillars with bronze capitals decorated with roosters and fleurs-de-lis, the symbols of France. Charles Le

Brun was in charge of the Palace decorations and he painted the ceilings personally: 30 pictures framed by stuccoes emphasize the greatness of the Sun King by means of mythological allusions and references to his military and diplomatic triumphs.

On May 6, 1682, Versailles became the official residence of the French court, replacing the Louvre and Saint-Germain-en-Laye. The project to adapt the site required 36,000 workers, but when the Palace was complete, it could host 5,000 guests. A further 14,000 guards and service staff lived in lodgings annexed to the Palace. The gardens were laid out by the landscape gardener André Le Nôtre. Under his direction, 2,000 acres of land

70-71 At 240 feet long and with ceiling frescoes that celebrate the greatness of Louis XIV, the Hall of Mirrors is the symbol of the French monarchy's absolute power. On one side of the hall there are 17 huge mirrors, and on the other, 17 large windows that overlook the park.

70 bottom left In the Salon de la Guèrre, the large medallion carved by Antoine Coysevox celebrates the Sun King's military triumphs.

70 bottom right The Salon de la Paix is named after the painting of Louis XIV. The king asked François Lemoyne to portray him as a bringer of peace to Europe.

71 right Marie-Antoinette was in the queen's bedchamber when revolutionaries broke into the palace on October 6, 1789. Perfectly restored, this room is a perfect example of the splendor with which the royal family surrounded themselves.

were leveled to allow the installation of terraces, avenues, plants, 1,400 fountains, and 400 sculptures.

The extraordinary beauty of the park that lies beyond the Hall of Mirrors cannot be described simply by numbers. Within the grounds, Le Nôtre created dozens of different natural settings joined by avenues that led towards the Étoile Royale. Just behind the Palace lies the Parterre d'Eau, two parallel pools that lead into Latona's Pool and its own Parterre. On the right, to the north, lies the enormous Pièce d'Eau des Suisses, and as

72-73 Two parterres
d'eau decorated with
superb bronze statues lie
right in front of the
central section of the
palace. The pools are
principally ornamental
but they create a highly
dramatic effect by
reflecting the lines of the
building and extending its
architecture.

one heads away from the Palace, there is
Apollo's Pool and after that the Grand
Canal; the latter is a body of water that
covers 57 acres and has a perimeter of over
three miles, and was the site for water
festivals celebrated during Louis XIV's
reign.

The park contains smaller buildings like
the circular marble peristyle designed by
Mansart in 1685, the spectacular Neptune
fountain by Le Nôtre and Mansart, and the
Petit and Grand Trianons. The Petit
Trianon was built in 1762 as a refuge for

Louis XV's frequent trysts and was later
used for privacy by Marie-Antoinette. The
Grand Trianon was built by Louis XIV in
1687 for his not-so-secret meetings with his
favorite, Madame de Maintenon.

The Sun King's day began precisely at
8:30 with his first appointment held in the
Hall of Mirrors at 10:00 a.m. Here he met
commoners who wished to present him
with petitions. Then, at 11:00, he
transferred to the Chapelle Royale,
construction of which was completed by
Robert de Cotte in 1710. Dedicated to

Saint Louis, it has a raised gallery where
the king sat. The nave was occupied by
courtiers and the women distributed
themselves around the side galleries. Built
in both Gothic and Baroque styles, the
Chapelle has white marble interiors with
gilded stuccoes and fine windows. Its
sculpted pillars, frescoed vaults, and mosaic
floor are typical of the early eighteenth
century. After mass, the king returned to
his private quarters where he held the
daily meeting of the Council of State.
After a short lunch in the company of a

the return to the monarchy, the last great innovation was made by Louis Philippe in 1837. The south wing of the Palace was transformed into the Museum of French History, and 194,000 square feet of space were dedicated to celebrating the "*les gloires de la France.*" To complete this immense project, the king commissioned over 3,000 paintings from the greatest painters of the age such as artists of the caliber of Eugène Delacroix. As one wanders through the rooms, the whole of French history unrolls, from the era of the Capetian Dynasty to the mid-nineteenth century.

Versailles is today a symbol of France's

73 top Designed by Jules Hardouin-Mansart with a blend of Gothic and Baroque architectural features, the Chapelle Royale was completed in 1710 by Robert de Cotte.

73 bottom L'Opéra, the court theatre, was built by Jacques-Ange Gabriel during the reign of Louis XV. A complicated mechanical system that raises the auditorium to the height of the stage allowed the theatre to also be used as a reception room.

clutch of courtiers, the king took a long walk in the park and returned at 6:00 p.m. on the dot. This was the time for salon conversation and meetings before dinner and bed.

After the death of Louis XIV in 1715, Versailles was no longer subjected to large scale alterations. Towards the end of the reign of Louis XV, Jacques-Ange Gabriel built the majestic court theater, the Opéra, at the north end of the north wing. Able to hold 700 spectators, the all-wood auditorium provided perfect acoustics. Its

gilded decorations blend harmoniously with the green and pink painted marble. A complicated mechanical device meant that the auditorium could be raised to the height of the stage to allow sumptuous court *fêtes* (parties) to be held. The astounding cost of running the building (10,000 candles would be used on a single gala night) meant that the theater was only rarely used. One of the occasions was the wedding of Louis XVI and Marie-Antoinette in 1770.

Following the French Revolution and

past grandeur, but it still requires a numerous court: eleven curators and three architects to look after the 700 rooms, 67 staircases, and 2,153 windows; 48 gardeners to maintain the park, plant 210,000 new flowers each year, and look after the 200,000 trees; five people to care for the fountains; 18 restorers for the 6,000 paintings, 1,500 drawings, 15,000 etchings, 2,100 sculptures, and 5,000 items of furniture; and, 363 guards to protect this immense artistic heritage that welcomes six million visitors each year.

Mont-Saint-Michel and its Bay

FRANCE

DÉPARTEMENT OF MANCHE, ILLE-ET-VILAINE,
LOWER NORMANDY AND BRITTANY
REGISTRATION : 1979
CRITERIA: C (I) (III) (VI)

Atenth-century manuscript tells how the cult of Saint Michael came to the bay that marks the boundary between Brittany and Normandy. According to the *Revelatio ecclesiae sancti Michaelis*, in the year 708 the Archangel Michael appeared in a dream to Aubert, the bishop of Avranches, touched his forehead with a finger, and ordered him to build a church on the hill known as Mont-Tombe, which stood in the forest of Scissy. This was the period in which the geological phenomenon occurred that caused the subsidence of the land and consequent flooding by the sea, thereby creating the two islands of Mont-Saint-Michel and Tombelaine.

Two centuries later, Duke Richard I of Normandy charged 12 Benedictine monks from Saint-Wandrille with the founding of a monastery where Aubert had built his church of Nôtre-Dame-sous-Terre. In 1023, construction of the abbey's nave was begun with the transept located on the top of the island, and the Benedictines created a community of exceptional spiritual distinction. The mount does not belong to either the land or the sea and is simultaneously threatened and defended by the forces of nature, therefore, it was a perfect refuge for anyone who could reach it. The peace that reigned on the island was propitious for contemplation of the mysteries of the divine.

A part of the abbey was destroyed by fire in 1204 and was replaced by the famous building known as "La Merveille" (The Wonder). It has three floors, is divided into two adjoining sections, and faces the sea to the north of the church. The humblest of the three floors, the ground floor, was where the pantry and refectory reserved for pilgrims were located. The first floor accommodated the dining room used by guests of good standing and the Scriptorium, later called the Knights' Room, in which the monks produced their illuminated codices. On the top floor, the monks' refectory connected with the cloister, which comprised a hanging garden surrounded by arcades supported by columns decorated with floral motifs. The symbolism of the architectural schema is unambiguous. The three floors correspond to the three levels of man: the lowest refers to material drives, the intermediate to erudition and the rational sciences, and the highest signifies communion with God.

Believed to be the earthly representation of the Heavenly Jerusalem, during the late Middle Ages Mont-Saint-Michel became a place of pilgrimage, often inspired by the devotion of the sovereigns, and later became the emblem of French national unity. In 1346, during the Hundred Years War, the English occupied the nearby island of Tombelaine. A brief truce brought peace, but in 1417, they returned to threaten mainland France. In 1426, they tightened their siege of the monastery, which was defended by only 119 knights under the leadership of Louis d'Estouteville. With the help of the monks, the stronghold held out until 1450 when the English abandoned Tombelaine and Normandy was liberated. At the end of the Hundred Years War, the French king, Louis XI, established the Order of the Knights of Saint-Michel and the Archangel Michael was taken to be the patron saint of France. During the long siege, the choir of the church collapsed, and when peace returned, it was rebuilt in the style of Flamboyant

Gothic. With this addition, the abbey became a splendid catalogue of all medieval architectural styles.

In 1790, the monks left Mont-Saint-Michel, which, for the whole of the eighteenth century, had been used by the kings as a political prison. Twenty years later, the mount was officially placed under the

administration of the prisons' authority and was used as a jail for common criminals. The fate of the abbey seemed a sad one, but its existence was vehemently defended by important intellectuals such as Victor Hugo. However, the mount had to wait until 1863 for a decree by Napoleon III that eliminated the prison.

In 1874, Mont-Saint-Michel was registered as a French historic monument and extensive restoration was undertaken that also involved the framework houses in the medieval village that had grown up at the abbey's feet. Three years later a causeway was built to join the island to the mainland so that, for over a century, the tourists who have replaced the pilgrims are no longer required to risk the dangers of the tides.

74 The island has other buildings in addition to the large Benedictine monastery. On the left is Tour Gabriel, the most majestic fortification to be built to withstand the attacks of the English during the Hundred Years War. At the foot of the monastic complex stands the hamlet of framework houses built during the early thirteenth century, the period of Mont's greatest prosperity, when the island was a place of pilgrimage for Christians from all over Europe.

75 top Lit by tall windows, the austere monks' refectory lies to the right of the church and opens into the cloister.

75 center The splendid cloister of the Merveille, with elegant pink granite columns, is considered a masterpiece of thirteenth-century Anglo-Norman Gothic.

75 bottom Now connected to the mainland by a raised road, the island of Mont Tombe (on which the abbey of Mont-Saint-Michel stands) was inaccessible for millennia because of the tides. This extraordinary place lies at the outlet of the Couesnon, the river that marks the boundary between Brittany and Normandy. From afar, it appears suspended between the earth and the sky.

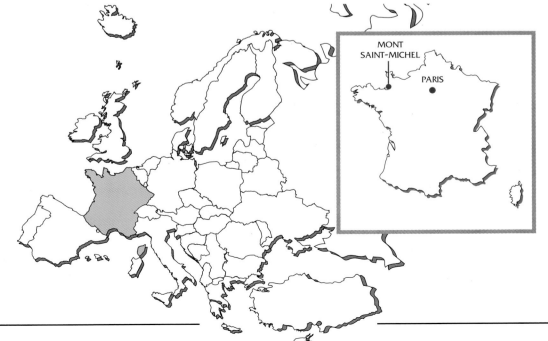

MONT SAINT-MICHEL

PARIS

Venice and its Lagoon
ITALY

VENETO
REGISTRATION: 1987
CRITERIA: C (I) (II) (III) (IV) (V) (VI)

76 top Built to hold the mortal remains of the Evangelist and consecrated in 1094, St. Mark's Basilica is the symbol of Venice. A unique monument in the history of medieval art, it has been adorned over the centuries with Byzantine, Romanesque, Gothic, and Renaissance art. Since 1807 it has been the seat of the Patriarchate, which was transferred here from the cathedral of San Pietro di Castello.

76 bottom The origin of the gilded bronze horses in St. Mark's Quadriga is uncertain. They arrived in Venice in 1204 as part of the booty taken from Byzantium (Constantinople).

A series of large mobile sluice gates have been designed to be anchored to the bottom of the lagoon across the entrances to Chioggia, Lido, and Malamocco. When the level of the Adriatic rises beyond a certain limit, the sluice gates will be raised to prevent the water entering the lagoon. That is a summary of the Moses Project, which, together with other steps being taken for the restoration of Venice, should protect the city and its lagoon from the "high water," the high tides that today strike the city on average 40 times a year.

If global warming raises the sea level as much as predicted, the phenomenon of high water may occur 100 times a year by the mid-twenty-first century, placing an inestimable cultural patrimony in jeopardy. It is inestimable and also unique because, as UNESCO emphasized when defining the entire city as a World Heritage site, the 118 islands on which Venice stands form an extraordinary masterpiece of architecture in which even the smallest palazzo contains works by great masters like Giorgione, Titian, Tintoretto, and Veronese.

Certain sources maintain that Venice came into being on March 25, 421, but this hypothesis is not supported by documentation. However, it is certain that in the middle of the fifth century, with the break-up of the Roman empire, the advance of the Huns under Attila forced many inhabitants from the Veneto mainland to take shelter in the lagoon areas along the Adriatic coast. Remaining in the sphere of the Roman Eastern Empire, the inhabitants of the lagoons obtained a wide degree of independence in 697 when the maritime tribunes sent by Byzantium were replaced by a *dux* (the first Doge), Paoluccio Anafesto.

The decisive moment arrived in 811 when the government under Doge Agnello Particiaco moved the area's administrative center from Malamocco to Rivo Alto (known today as Rialto) in the center of the lagoon. This is conventionally accepted as the moment the history of Venice began. A few years later, two artful sailors smuggled the body of Saint Mark the Evangelist out of Alexandria in Egypt and took it to Rialto where, according to legend, the saint had taken refuge after a shipwreck. The body of the saint was buried in the Doge's chapel in the place where St. Mark's Basilica was later built. The church was consecrated in 1094 on the spot where two buildings had been built to hold and venerate Saint Mark's remains.

In the ninth century, Venetian sailors already enjoyed close relations with the Levant, and the young state had launched a series of military actions against rival ports in the Adriatic. During the early crusades, the plundering of conquered lands allowed the Venetians to accumulate great riches, but their increasing wealth was due more to the city's control of trade throughout a huge area of the Mediterranean. With the Fourth Crusade, Venice's power experienced a sharp upturn in quality. The taking of Byzantium in 1204 marked the conquest of a large part of the Roman Eastern Empire, with the result that the small city of sailors came to dominate islands, ports, and cities throughout the Aegean and Ionian seas. Besides political and economic gains, the sacking of Byzantium also brought Venice the four bronze horses (the Quadriga) that stand on St. Mark's church, the Golden Altar in the same basilica, and the many marble statues that adorn its façade.

77 top The Procuratorie that line the sides of St. Mark's Square are the offices of the nine public prosecutors of St. Mark. Next to the offices is the Clock Tower, built in 1493, at the top of which is the bell struck by two bronze Moors. They are called Moors because of the dark patina that formed on the metal after they were installed.

77 bottom The Ducal Palace was the Doges' residence and the seat of the institutions that governed public life was located. The Palace' current appearance is the result of many modifications made during the fourteenth and fifteenth centuries. To the left, St. Mark's bell tower was rebuilt after collapsing on July 14, 1902.

78 top The famous Pala d'Oro that adorns St. Mark's altar was placed in its current gilded silver Gothic frame in the mid-fourteenth century. The gold tiles are enameled and were probably manufactured in Byzantium between the tenth and twelfth centuries.

78 bottom left The iconostasis in St. Mark's presbytery was crowned by

statues sculpted by Jacobello and Pier Paolo Dalle Masegne in the late-fourteenth century. It is considered a masterpiece of Gothic Venetian sculpture.

78 bottom right The vault in St. Mark's. The five domes imitate the ancient church of Constantinople, and the frescoes that decorate them represent the life of Christ

and the path to man's salvation.

79 The interior of St. Mark's Basilica. Besides extraordinary works of sculpture, the church also

holds a treasury, consisting of 283 pieces of gold, silver, glass, and other precious metals that were largely looted during the sack of Constantinople by the Fourth Crusade.

Venice's greatness was soon rivaled by Genoa, the other great seafaring power in the Mediterranean. The first skirmishes between the two maritime states took place at Tiro. These were followed by over a century of wars in which, on one occasion, Venetians retired to the lagoon when the Genoese landed on the shore near Chioggia.

With the population struck down by the plague in the mid-fourteenth century, Venice was on the point of succumbing, but it managed to hang on. It searched for allies on the mainland and found one in Gian Galeazzo Visconti, the lord of Milan. At the start of the fifteenth century, St. Mark's Republic took the name of the "Serenissima" (The Most Serene Republic) and conquered cities in the Veneto region as far west as Brescia and Bergamo. The city's dominant commercial power led to great wealth that flowed into the coffers of the nobility, who then became patrons of the new schools of art that were flowering throughout Veneto. This period of exceptional prosperity produced painters like Vittore Carpaccio, Giorgione, and later, Paolo Veronese, Titian, and Tintoretto, whose masterpieces adorned the churches and private residences throughout the city.

During the age of this extraordinary artistic vitality, Venice began to lose its predominance. By 1453, the Turks had retaken control of Byzantium, and at the end of the fifteenth century, the French had invaded much of northwest Italy. The discovery of the Americas opened new routes, and national fleets such as those of the Turks and Spanish were gaining the upper hand. Even working at full speed, the Arsenale, the city's shipbuilding yard, was unable to keep up with the new and better organized sea powers.

In 1570, the Turks seized Venetian ships in the Dardanelles and the Bosporus, and then attacked Cyprus. Venice's reaction materialized in the resounding victory at the battle of Lepanto a year later, but by that time the city's fate was already decided. At the end of the seventeenth century, Venice lost Crete too. For a short period it

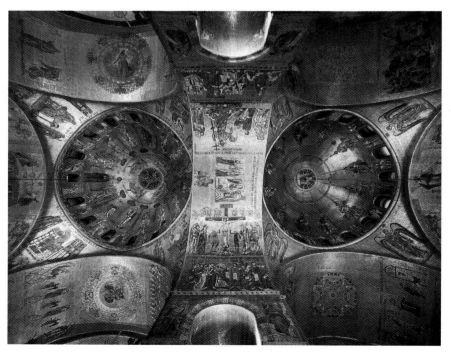

succeeded in taking the Peloponnese, but the region returned to Turkish rule in 1714.

By this time, Venice was alone. Foreign ships crossed the Adriatic without having to pay tolls to the Serenissima and the city's focusing of attention on the Mediterranean had distracted the government from the new routes of world trade. Commerce had definitively shifted to the Atlantic and Indian Oceans with the result that Venice's commercial traffic followed the wane of its military power. However, the city's political and commercial decline coincided with a golden period of art, and the Venetian

advance of Napoleonic troops. In an attempt to play its diplomatic cards once more, the Serenissima chose not to support the rebellion of the cities in the plain of the river Po, but Napoleon imposed harsh conditions on the city nevertheless. Worried only about losing their possessions on the mainland, the Venetian governors accepted the French terms on May 12, 1797, and a few days later Napoleon entered Venice with his troops and sacked it. These were the days that marked the end of the Serenissima Repubblica di San Marco.

palaces were embellished with the magnificent frescoes of Giovanni Battista Tiepolo, Neo-Classical sculpture dawned in the workshop of Antonio Canova, and the theaters were filled with the irony of Carlo Goldoni and the music of Benedetto Marcello. Meanwhile, the increasingly numerous and well-to-do visitors to the city commissioned works by Venetian landscape artists like Francesco Guardi and Canaletto.

While Venice enjoyed its wealth in festivals and banquets as its power declined, Europe was shaken by the

Eight centuries of dominion of the seas and trade had made Venice unique. It is hard to propose any particular view of the city that is more beautiful than the rest, but without doubt the two-and-a-half miles of the Grand Canal are lined with Venice's most famous masterpieces. One begins in St. Mark's Square with the basilica – characterized by an amazing mixture of styles – and the bell tower, which collapsed on July 14, 1902 and was quickly rebuilt; the tower bears marks that record the worst episodes of high water. Next comes the Ducal Palace where the

Doges resided until 1797. The building is separated from the city prison by the famous Bridge of Sighs. Then we have the Procuratie, the porticoed buildings that enclose the square and contained the offices of the nine public prosecutors, the highest Venetian dignitaries after the Doge. The square is bordered on the lagoon side by the Riva degli Schiavoni and faces the island of San Giorgio Maggiore where the church of the same name designed by Palladio stands.

Right at the entrance to the canal there is the church of Santa Maria della

80 bottom right The Signoria (the Doge and his advisors) met in the Sala del Collegio inside the Ducal Palace. Its carved ceiling includes famous paintings by Pietro Veronese and Tintoretto.

80-81 A view of the Sala del Senato in the Ducal Palace, decorated with paintings by Tintoretto and Jacopo Palma the Younger. The 60-member Senate was also known as the "Consiglio dei pregadi" or "Consilium Rogatorium."

81 bottom The church of San Giorgio Maggiore stands on its eponymous island. It was rebuilt between 1565 and 1610 according to a design by Andrea Palladio. Before that time, the church was a fourteenth-century building with a nave and two aisles, and enclosed at one end by old buildings.

82 top The façade of the superb Gothic Ca' Foscari has two splendid eight-arched loggias on the first and second floors. Built for the Giustinian family at the end of the fourteenth century, it became the property of the Doge, Francesco Foscari, in 1453. Purchased and restored by the city, it is now part of the University of Venice.

Salute, then the Accademia, Palazzo Belloni-Battaglia, Palazzo Marcello (where the composer was born), Palazzo Vendramin Calergi (where Richard Wagner died), Ca' Foscari (the headquarters of Venice University), Ca' Dario, Ca' d'Oro, and Palazzo Grassi (where the city's most important exhibitions are held).

Further down the Grand Canal stands the church of Santa Maria Gloriosa dei Frari in which a monumental marble enclosure rings the 124 choir stalls and the sides of the nave are lined by an amazing array of paintings and sculptures. Further along comes Rialto Bridge with its series of shops. It was first built as a pontoon bridge in the ninth century, then rebuilt in stone in 1591 following which it soon became a reference point in the heart of the city.

Even in its most remote areas, Venice does not cease to surprise with its artistic and architectural treasures. Today it is besieged by tourists and threatened by rising water levels, but with the passing of the years, knowledge of the dangers the city faces has resulted in the creation of hundreds of associations around the world whose aim is to safeguard Venice's patrimony.

82 center Despite its
position behind the Rialto
Bridge, the Ca' d'Oro is
one of the most famous
palaces on the Grand
Canal. Built in the first
half of the fifteenth century
by Matteo Raverti and
Giovanni and Bartolomeo
Buon, its name is taken
from the original
decorations in gold leaf,
vermilion, and
ultramarine.

82 bottom right
Ca' Dario is another of the
extraordinary residences on
the Grand Canal. It takes
its name from the
architect, Giovanni Dario,
who designed it in 1487.

82-83 Rialto Bridge, with
its famous shops, was built
between 1588 and 1591
where there had previously
been a pontoon bridge,
later replaced by a wooden
bridge. It took 70 years
before it was decided how
to build the Rialto, and in
the end, the cost reached
the astronomic figure of
250,000 ducats.

83 bottom This splendid
polyptych by Bartolomeo
Vivarini from the second
half of the sixteenth
century is one of the
innumerable works of art
in the church dei Frari.

Piazza del Duomo in Pisa

ITALY

TUSCANY
REGISTRATION: 1987
CRITERIA: C (I) (II) (IV) (VI)

84 top left A detail of the fountain by Giuseppe Vaccà at the entrance to Piazza del Duomo. It shows three putti supporting the coat of arms of Pisa.

84-85 A view of the Duomo and its famous bell tower. Recently re-opened to the public after work to correct its lean, the tower is considered one of the most beautiful in the world for the uniqueness of its architecture.

O n October 16, 1604, Galileo Galilei sent his friend Paolo Sarpi a letter in which he described the basis for the laws of motion. Some claim that the forty-year-old professor of mathematics had discovered those laws by dropping objects from the Tower of Pisa. In fact, Galileo did not have accurate enough timepieces to measure the time of the drop, but more

compelling in the negation of this claim is the fact that he was teaching in Padua at the time. What is certain is that the story was inspired by the lean of the tower.

The bell tower of the Duomo (cathedral) in Pisa had begun to lean long before its construction was completed. Proof of this is given by the inscription above the entrance which commemorates the laying of the first stone on August 9, 1173 by the architect Bonanno Pisano, but just five years later, when builders had not yet finished the fourth level, he resigned from the job. This was due to a subsidence of the ground, inducing the tower lean an inch or so to the

85 top The huge galleried rectangular building borders the area that was once the graveyard. It was built at the end of the thirteenth century on the place where, tradition has it, Bishop Ubaldo de' Lanfranchi spread the earth taken from Golgotha, brought from the Holy Land by ship.

85 bottom left and right Views of the Duomo and Baptistery. The latter is the most impressive building of its kind in Italy. Its circumference is 351 feet and its height, 177 feet.

south, making the architect think he had made a design error.

Work began again in 1275 under the direction of Giovanni di Simone, who added three more levels carefully structured to balance the weight and – in vain – to correct the lean. In 1284, when the tower was only missing the bell housing and the lean had exceeded 35 inches, another sudden interruption was made: Giovanni di Simone died in the battle of Meloria between the seafaring republics of Pisa and Genoa. It fell to Tommaso Pisano to complete the job between 1350 and 1372. The tower stands 184 feet tall, is 51 feet in

diameter at the base, and weighs 16,000 tons. It is decorated with 207 white marble and sandstone columns, 15 of which are at the base, 30 in each of the six round levels, and 12 around the bell-housing. A spiral staircase of 294 steps leads from the entrance, surrounded by two registers of bas-reliefs portraying monsters and animals, to the top floor where the ancient bells are hung.

The tower was the last work to be completed in the square of Pisa's Duomo. The square is called by many the "Campo dei Miracoli" (Square of Miracles), as it was considered a miracle that all the buildings necessary to religious life in the city had been grouped in a single area. The Duomo itself stands next to the tower and is a masterpiece of Romanesque architecture. Built on the site of a pre-existing Byzantine church, construction of the Cathedral of Our

Lady of the Assumption was begun in 1063 under the direction of Buscheto and was consecrated in 1118 by Pope Gelasius II. Despite the duration of the construction and the overlaying of Classical, Byzantine, Ravenna, and Arab style elements, its appearance is one of admirable unity. Its plan is that of a Latin cross, with a transept and egg-shaped dome. The façade, the front extension of the nave and its double-vaulted aisles, and the main apse were built during the second half of the twelfth century.

Originally the interior was to be decorated with large frescoes, but in 1595 a fire severely damaged the building. Fortunately, the generosity of the Grand Duke Ferdinando I de' Medici allowed the cathedral to be restored at a cost of 85,000 scudi, an enormous sum for that period. The three bronze doors and the caisson ceiling were rebuilt, and large paintings were hung on the walls, including those by Antonio Sogliani (a pupil of Raphael) and Andrea del Sarto (from the school of Leonardo da Vinci). The pulpit carved between 1302 and 1311 by Giovanni Pisano was disassembled after the fire. Some parts of it were placed in the Camposanto (cemetery) while others went to foreign museums. In May 1926, this extraordinary marble monument was reassembled and placed once more in the Duomo.

The Baptistery stands in front of the cathedral. It was begun in 1153 by Deotisalvi and completed in the fourteenth century. The magnificent round Romanesque building was later overlaid with Gothic decorations, white marble wall linings, with rows of serpentine stone. The structure is the most impressive of its kind in Italy, measuring 351 feet in circumference and 177 feet tall, with an internal diameter of over 115 feet. The interior is based on a peristyle of four pillars and eight columns

transported from Elba and Sardinia. Here too, the pulpit, by Nicola Pisano, is extraordinary; carved from different colored marbles, it is hexagonal in shape and supported by six outer columns, three of which stand on lions, and by a central column supported by human and animal figures.

The Camposanto lies on the north side of the square. Its buildings were the work of Giovanni di Simone at the end of the thirteenth century. The large frescoes – many of which were damaged in World War II – were begun around 1350 and continued for more than a century. Those that stand out in particular are the "Triumph of Death" and "Universal Judgement," both by anonymous artists. The Camposanto remained the city's burial place until the end of the eighteenth century.

During the last decade, the square was the setting of another miracle. On January 6, 1990, when the lean had reached 17 feet and one inch, the tower was closed to the public for reasons of safety. Three years later, consolidation work was undertaken in which 950 tons of lead were placed at its base and 18 steel cables attached to the first level. Samples of earth and water were taken on the north side so that the subsidence on the other side could be balanced. When the tower had been righted by nine inches, it was reopened to visitors.

The Vatican City and San Paolo fuori le Mura

ITALY

HOLY SEE, ROME
REGISTRATION: 1984
CRITERIA: C (I) (II) (IV) (VI)

On February 11, 1929, the Lateran Treaty, signed by Pope Pius XI and Benito Mussolini, ratified the existence of the sovereign State of the Vatican City, governed by the Pope and completely independent of the Kingdom of Italy. The treaty therefore put an end to the controversy begun on September 20, 1870 when the troops of King Vittorio Emanuele II entered Rome and put an end to the papal state.

In the first centuries of the existence of Rome, the *Ager vaticanus* was a peripheral area that covered the land between the right bank of the Tiber and the Vatican hills, the land as far as the Milvius Bridge to the north, and all of the Gianicolo Hill to the south. Around the first century B.C., these marshy areas were gradually transformed into a residential area where important Roman families built *horti* (luxurious residences). At the time of Augustus, the area was covered by the gardens of Agrippina, and when Caligula became emperor, by a circus – the Gaianum – of which some parts remain in the colonnade in St. Peter's Square.

The history of the Vaticanum changed radically in the fourth century. Emperor Constantine I proclaimed toleration of the Christian religion with the Edict of Milan in 313 and began construction of a church on the place where Saint Peter was supposed to have been buried. Peter had come to Rome with Paul in 42 A.D. to preach the Word of Christ, but the two are thought to have been martyred in 67. Large building works were undertaken so that the new church could be built. The slope of the Vatican hills was leveled, the

burial ground was covered over, and the center of the apse in the Basilica was built right over Saint Peter's tomb. The huge church was built with a nave and four aisles, a wide transept, and a four-sided porticoed atrium but was not completed until 329.

The basilica soon became an important focus of city life. Civil buildings, churches,

monasteries, and hospices for pilgrims began to be built around it. To the south of the city along the Via Ostiense, the large basilica of San Paolo fuori le Mura was constructed, also in the fourth century. Like all early Christian temples, it had an oblong plan, a nave, and two aisles, each of which ended in an apse. Although the original basilica was destroyed in a fire on July 15, 1823, the

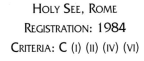

88 top Designed by Carlo Maderno in 1629, San Lorenzo's Chapel in San Paolo fuori le Mura is also known as the Chapel of the Choir. The wooden stalls were remade in 1928 according to a design by Guglielmo Calderini.

88 bottom San Paolo fuori le Mura is a Benedictine abbey that stands on a former site of Christian churches from the first centuries A.D. It was destroyed by fire on the night of July 15, 1823, and the reconstruction – which lasted more than a century – was completed in 1931 with the installation of the monumental bronze central door.

reconstruction was in full respect of the original, though little remained of the original structures. A fifth century mosaic decorates one side of the triumphal arch that separates the apse from the nave. The apse mosaics of Christ with Saints Peter, Andrew, Paul, and Luke were Venetian from the thirteenth century. The *Confessio*, the tomb in which Saint Paul is said to be buried, lies below the altar.

89 top left The basilica of San Paolo fuori le Mura was built between 1831 and 1854 with a nave and four aisles. Pasquale Belli designed the reconstruction on the same plan as the original. The ceiling is decorated with the coats of arms of the popes that contributed to the costs of reconstruction.

89 top right The chapel of the Most Holy Sacrament in San Paolo fuori le Mura was built in 1725. Its fame comes from the twelfth/thirteenth-century mosaic of the Virgin and the thirteenth-century Crucifixion attributed to Pietro Cavallini, whose remains are buried in the chapel.

88-89 In the twelfth and thirteenth centuries, San Paolo fuori le Mura enjoyed a period of spiritual and economic prosperity. This was the period in which the lovely mosaic that decorates the apse was installed by the best mosaicists from Venice.

ROME AND THE VATICAN CITY

While Rome survived through the dark ages of the barbarian invasions, a new popular district arose around St. Peter's. Between the eighth and ninth centuries, with the consent of Charlemagne, Pope Leo III decided to protect the area by building an encircling wall with only one entrance at Castel Sant'Angelo. Upon the death of the pope, however, the walls were pulled down by the Romans, and in 846 the city was sacked by the Saracens who devastated the Christian places of worship. It was Leo IV who once more protected the Vatican with new walls, and

from that moment on the district was considered to be independent. Nonetheless, the popes continued to live for centuries in the Lateran District of Rome. The first to reside in the Vatican was Nicholas III in 1277, who also set about strengthening the city walls. Before the Vatican was to become the permanent residence of the papacy, however, the Church moved its court to Avignon, which led in turn to the "Babylonian captivity" of the pope by the French monarchs.

During the fourteenth century, the

Vatican became run down, and in the fifteenth Constantine's basilica was falling into ruin. In 1452, Nicholas V planned restoration work, which was put into the hands of Bramante 50 years later by Julius II. In 1506, the first stone was finally laid in the new church. The St. Peter's that was to rise from the ruins of the former church was designed to be the beacon of Christianity. To build the immense basilica – the largest religious building in the world with its nave measuring 611 feet and dome 448 feet tall – took more than a century to build, and the project involved

90-91 St. Peter's basilica and its square surrounded by the unusual elliptical colonnade were designed by Gian Lorenzo Bernini in the mid-seventeenth century. The obelisk in the center of the square was brought from Egypt by the Roman emperor, Caligula, and raised in the square on September 10, 1586.

the greatest engineers of the Italian Renaissance and Baroque periods. Bramante was succeeded by Raphael, Antonio da Sangallo the Younger, Michelangelo, and Carlo Maderno, who completed the façade in 1614. Inside, there are eleven marble-lined chapels, five altars, and innumerable works of art, many of which were recovered from the original basilica; the rest were commissioned from artists during the sixteenth and seventeenth centuries.

The interior is dominated by the papal

altar that stands below the dome. Made from a simple slab of marble taken from Nerva's Forum, it was designed by Michelangelo though he did not live to see it completed at the end of the sixteenth century during the pontificate of Clement VIII. The magnificent gilded-bronze canopy above the altar was designed by Gian Lorenzo Bernini and stands on spiral columns 66 feet tall. All around, the basilica is adorned with superb works of art. First and foremost is the white marble sculpture of the Pietà by Michelangelo, which stands in a side

91 top Built between 1624 and 1633, the colossal bronze canopy designed by Bernini weighs 81,400 pounds. It stands over the papal altar below the dome of St. Peter's and is the largest bronze monument ever built.

91 bottom The Pietà was begun by Michelangelo when he was just 22 years old. Today it is one of the most famous sculptures in the world. Commissioned by the Vatican legate of the French king Charles VIII, it was supposed to be completed within one year and to be placed in the St. Petronilla Chapel, also known as the Chapel of the French Kings.

90 bottom The original Basilica of St. Peter in the Vatican was built between 324 and 329 by Constantine over the tomb of the Apostle on the former site of Caligula's and Nero's circus in which he was crucified. The current basilica was begun in 1506 during the pontificate of Julius II according to a design by Donato Bramante.

chapel near the Holy Door and was finished by the artist in 1499 when he was just 25 years old. Other works by Bernini include the throne of St. Peter in the apse on the right side of the basilica and the monuments dedicated to popes Urban VIII and Alexander VII. The latter was his last work, completed in 1678. Bernini was also the architect of the vast square in front of the basilica, which is faced onto by St. Peter's modest parvis. Designed between 1656 and 1667, the square is enclosed by a curved colonnade and, at its center, has the Egyptian obelisk moved there in 1586 by Sixtus V.

Next to the basilica stand the Vatican palaces, designed as residences for various popes. The first papal palace was built in 1198 for Innocent III, but the structures were ornamented during the Renaissance. In 1473, Sixtus IV had the Sistine Chapel built. At the end of the century, Innocent VIII commissioned Bramante to build the Belvedere, and this was later subjected to a number of enlargements, particularly during the eighteenth century. These palaces represent an enormous artistic heritage: the Sistine Chapel is decorated by frescoes by Botticelli, Perugino,

Ghirlandaio, and of course, Michelangelo, who painted the extraordinary "Last Judgement" behind the altar in 1541. In the four year period between 1508 and 1512, he concentrated on the ceiling where he painted a cycle containing more than 300 figures in episodes taken from Genesis and other books of the Old Testament. During the same period, Raphael was decorating the four rooms in the private apartments of Pope Julius II. The work was commissioned by Julius to renovate the rooms where his predecessor and rival, Alexander VI, had lived. It took 16 years and Raphael did not live to see it finished.

In the mid-eighteenth century, with the

92-93 It was Pope Julius II della Rovere who commissioned Michelangelo in 1508 to paint the ceiling of the Sistine Chapel. In four years, the Florentine artist produced an astounding pictorial cycle showing episodes from Genesis and the Old Testament.

93 top and center Two details from the ceiling of the Sistine Chapel illustrating episodes from Genesis. At the top, the Creation of Adam; in the center, the Expulsion from Paradise.

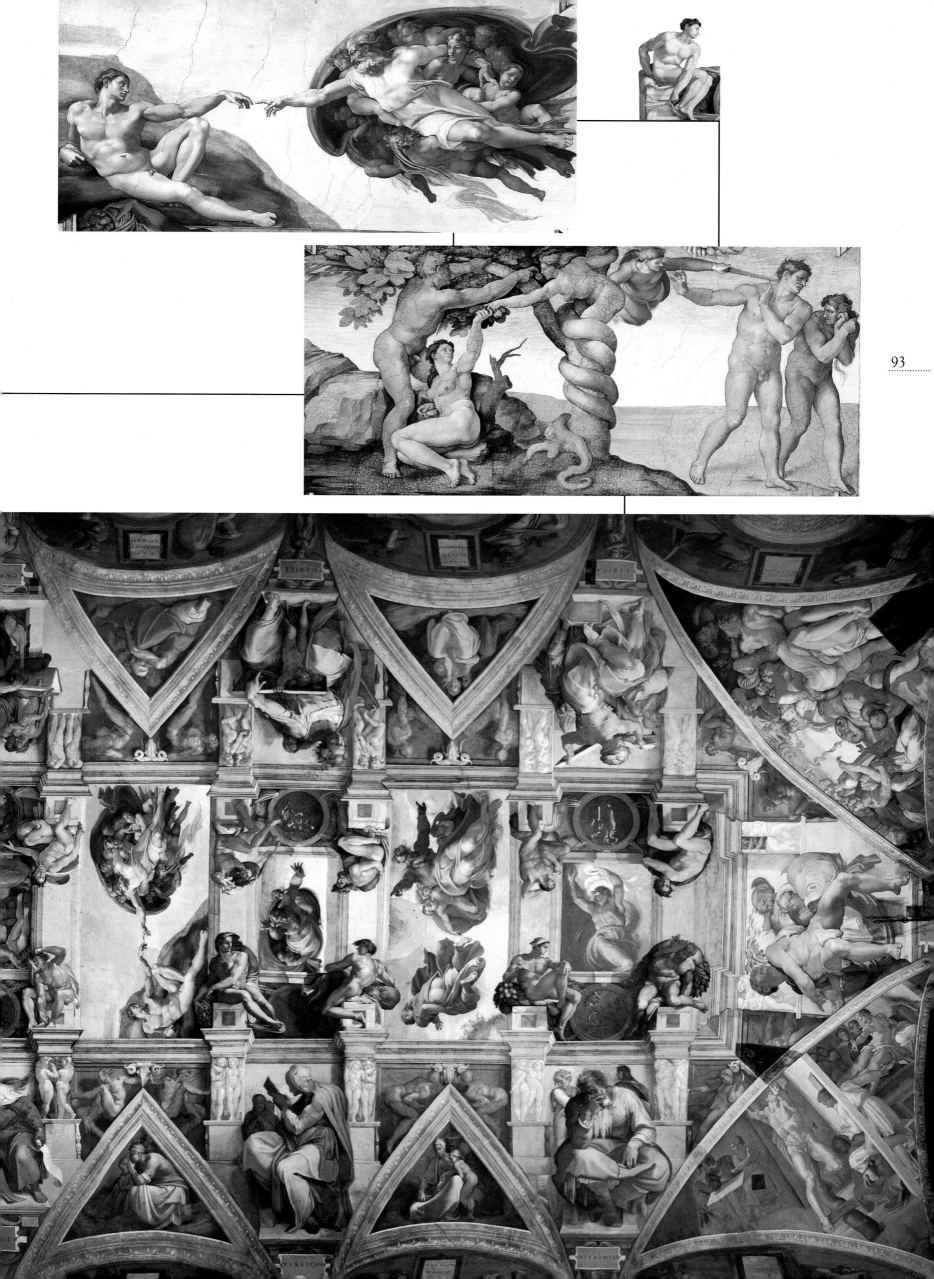

94 *The room containing the fresco of the "Fire in the Borgo" was the last in the Vatican to be supervised personally by Raphael, who only painted the lunette that shows the fire in the Roman district. Perugino painted the vault, shown here, in 1508.*

94-95 *The Sala Regia was built after the sack of Rome in 1527 and decorated with large frescoes by Giorgio Vasari and other Mannerists. The relief stucco ceiling was the work of Perin Del Vaga, completed in 1549 during the pontificate of Paul III.*

95 top left *The Chiaroscuri Room – with the wooden carving of the Flagellation – was decorated by pupils of Raphael and used by the Pope as a bedroom.*

95 top right *The Court of the Pinecone is named after the large bronze pinecone in the niche above the landing of the staircase. Found in Agrippa's Baths, the pinecone used to decorate a fountain. The bronze work, "Sfera con sfera" by Arnaldo Pomodoro, stands in the center of the court.*

95 bottom *The richly frescoed ceiling in the Map Gallery. The name comes from the 40 maps that show the regions of Italy and the possessions of the Church.*

foundation of the Sacred Museum and the Museum of Pagan Antiquities, the popes opened their collection of sacred treasures to the public. The first collections to be exhibited were the Greek and Roman antiquities, then, from 1837, works of Egyptian, Assyrian, and Etruscan art. Although most of the Vatican Museum is dedicated to Greek and Roman art, the popes during the Renaissance period commissioned artists like Raphael, Beato Angelico, and Pinturicchio to decorate the walls, and their frescoes are unquestionably considered part of the masterpieces on display.

The art gallery contained a small but extraordinary collection of paintings with works by Leonardo, Raphael, Titian, Domenichino, and Caravaggio. There is also a collection of modern art that was begun by Paul VI in 1973 and which includes works by Georges Braque, Paul Klee, and Edvard Munch and ceramic works by Pablo Picasso.

Flanked by the two large courts of the Belvedere and the Pigna, the Vatican Library holds an extraordinary collection of texts with over 1.6 million ancient and modern printed works, 8,300 incunabula (65 of which are on parchment), 150,000 illuminated manuscripts and archive papers, and 100,000 prints. In addition to these are the extensive collections of the secret archives that contain letters, codices, and declarations that encompass the history of the Catholic Church.

Parc Güell, Palau Güell, and Casa Milá

SPAIN

Barcelona, Catalonia
Registration: 1984
Criteria: C (i) (ii) (iv)

As winter approached, Eusebi Güell y Bacigalupi, a rich businessman in the textile industry, a huntsman, and a lover of Wagner, headed for the Passeig de Gracia in Barcelona to buy a pair of gloves. Having reached the shop, he remained impressed by the attractiveness of the window. He entered and asked who was responsible for such an imaginative display. Eusebi Güell, naturally, forgot to buy his gloves, but he made a much more important purchase that was to mark a turning point in the history of architecture. The window-dresser turned out to be a recent graduate from the University of Barcelona. He came from Reus, near Tarragona, and his name was Antoni Gaudí

96 top Detail of a fountain in which the water spurts from the mouth of a dragon. Gaudí designed a water system for Palau Güell, and some of the oddest forms in the park hide valves and faucets.

96 bottom The entrance to Parc Güell. What was actually completed was only a small part of the original project. The client intended the complex to become a garden city with 60 detached houses situated at the gates of Barcelona.

y Cornet. Thus began a relationship between a patron and artist that was to be one of the most successful creative associations in history.

After a few minor commissions, in 1886 Güell asked Gaudí to design him a house in the city center on a small plot of land in Calle Nou de la Rambla. Just 34 years old, the architect built his patron his first masterpiece. The heart of the Palau Güell is the central reception room that

rises three floors. It is topped by a dome, inspired by Arab architecture, with small holes to give the impression of a night sky. Swept away with enthusiasm, Gaudí oversaw every detail of the project; he made the lamps, railings, and gates by bending wrought iron into improbable shapes, designed the furniture, and dreamed up a roof on which fairy-tale chimney pots covered with pieces of ceramic sprouted like mushrooms.

This visionary design was talked about by all of Barcelona, and Gaudí made his triumphal entry into the most important drawing rooms, receiving praise and commissions. With the passing of time, he perfected his style and, during that period, began his most famous work, the Sagrada Familia, which, more than a century later, has not yet been completed. In 1900, Güell once more commissioned Gaudí with what was to be his most original work.

96-97 Some of the domes in Parc Güell. Color is the distinctive element in this extraordinary development. Most of the architectural elements are lined with majolica fragments that were found in the waste area of a ceramics factory.

97 top right Another architectural detail in the park. For the businessman Eusebi Güell y Bacigalupi, Gaudí also designed the equally imaginative Palau Güell.

97 bottom left What is most striking throughout the park is how luxuriant it is, both in terms of vegetation and architecture. Antoní Gaudí's outlandish figures were inspired by natural forms.

97 bottom right An attractive passage in Parc Güell featuring Doric-inspired columns.

98 top Casa Milá is better known as la Pedrera (stone quarry). It has a surface area of 10,760 square feet and stands on the corner of Passeig de Gracia and Calle Provenza in the central district of Eixample.

98 center Gaudí also designed the monumental fireplace in the dining room of Palau Güell in his typical style.

98 bottom The large central salon seen here in Palau Güell is three floors high and topped by a dome in which Gaudí put small holes to give the sensation of a starry night sky.

99 The façade of the Pedrera. The undulating rhythm of the projections and recesses resembles sand dunes. In the building, the slight link with Catalan Modernism is represented by the cast iron inserts of the load-bearing columns and balconies, which have also been twisted into bizarre shapes.

The intention of the client was for Parc Güell to be a huge neighborhood/garden in an isolated area on a hill that overlooks Barcelona. The site was to have 60 plots, each of which was to be built with a single family home. The villas were in fact never constructed, but Gaudí laid out the street design made up of five elements: a main street, an avenue, a square, streets for vehicles, and paths for pedestrians. At the entrance there was to be a sort of Greek temple with Doric columns and ceramic rosettes that hung from the ceiling. The whole park is populated with fantastic creatures and splashes of color because Gaudí covered everything with small pieces of ceramic that had been thrown out as waste by a ceramics factory. The style was represented best by the wavy balustrade/bench that bounds the large panoramic terrace.

In 1906, Pere Milá Camps, another successful Catalan businessman, commissioned Gaudí to build a block of apartments on a plot measuring nearly 11,000 square feet on the corner of Passeig de Gracia and Calle Provenza. Here the brilliant architect let his imagination run wild: the house he built was made of stone sculpted into wave-like forms that seem to expand and contract with life. The load-bearing structure is made from wrought iron girders and vaults supported by brick and metal architraves. The construction of the façade was carried out somewhat like a ritual. Gaudí worked on rough sketches, then the blocks of stone were brought to the site to be cut, shaped, and laid in place. At this point he would modify the curves and shapes as the feeling took him. To passers-by, the street increasingly resembled a stone quarry, la pedrera, which

is the name Casa Milá has always been known by in Barcelona. The final touch came with the addition of the roof on which the chimneys were given the appearance of masked warriors.

Due to delays caused by the architect's exuberance, construction lasted four years. When it was completed, the enthusiastic client, Pere Milá, moved into the first floor of the building. His wife, Señora Rosario, did not appreciate Gaudí's somersaults of the imagination but put on a good face. Casa Milá was Gaudí's last civil building as, from that time until his death in 1926, he thought of nothing other than the Sagrada Familia. After his death, the Señora Rosario took advantage of the situation to transform the entire first floor of "The Pedrera" into an elegant but banal apartment in Louis XVI style.

The Cathedral, the Alcázar, and the Archivo de Indias, Seville

SPAIN

After two years of patient siege, on November 23, 1248, Ferdinand III of Castile forced the Moors in Seville to surrender and he made his triumphal entry into the city. The Catholic king found a beautiful city strongly characterized by the Islamic architecture of the flourishing region of al-Andalus. The return of the Christians also marked the return of their religious ceremonies, and as there were no churches to perform them in, the archbishop blessed the Almohad mosque that been built just 50 years prior.

It was necessary to wait until 1401 for construction of a cathedral to begin. Founded on the site of a former mosque, the cathedral measured 381 by 249 feet, with a nave, four side aisles, and 25 chapels. Known as the *Magna Hispanensis*, it was the second largest church in the world after St. Peter's. It took 100 years to complete the structure and more than 300 for the internal decoration to be finished. After the discovery of the New World by Christopher Columbus (whose body is buried here), the riches that flowed into Seville allowed the cathedral to be adorned with large windows, *retablos*, and magnificent paintings by artists such as Murillo, Zuburán, Pedro de Campaña, and Goya. Besides its many paintings, other artistic masterpieces in the cathedral include the high altar dating from 1482, considered the most intricate in Spain, and the impressive, elliptical Chapter Room.

The cathedral has nine doors. The main one, Puerta Mayor, is on the west side; the north door, the Puerta del Perdón, is a perfect example of *mudejár*

style and incorporates elements of the original Almohad mosque. *Mudejár* is the result of the syncretism of Islamic and Christian architecture, and the term was originally used to define Muslims who decided to remain in Spain after the Reconquest, though without converting to Catholicism (the word is derived from the Arabic *mudayyan*, which means "one allowed to stay"). The Puerta del Perdón leads into the Patio de los Naranjos (Court of Oranges), a garden laid out under Islamic criteria (it includes a fountain for performing ablutions). Similarly, the Giralda, an elegant minaret built between 1172 and 1195, was transformed into a bell tower and given two bells at the end of the

100 left Masterpieces by Goya, Murillo, and Zuburán are kept in the extraordinary elliptical dome of the Chapter Room.

100 right The sarcophagus of Christopher Columbus (1890) in the cathedral is supported by figures representing the kingdoms of Castile, León, Aragon, and Navarre.

MADRID

SEVILLE

100-101 This aerial view of the historic center of Seville embraces the three monumental complexes under the protection of UNESCO. In the center, the cathedral with its famous Giralda, the minaret that was built in 1198 and later turned into a bell tower. To the right there is the Alcázar and, in the background to the left, the building that holds the Archives of the Indies.

101 bottom left The elaborate columned vault of the Capilla Mayor. Access to the chapel is gained through a large grill beyond which lies the largest retablo in the Christian world.

101 bottom right The Patio de los Naranjos next to the cathedral, along with the Giralda, is what remains of the earlier Moorish building. In the center of the patio stands the fountain Muslims used to perform their ritual ablutions.

102 top Azulejos and elaborate stucco work decorate the Ambassadors' Room with its three symmetrical horseshoe-shaped arches. This is one of the most dramatic rooms in the Alcázar.

102-103 A picture of the Alcázar from the top of the Giralda. Originally, this was the site of the palaces built for the Almohad rulers. In 1346, after the Reconquest, Pedro I ordered their restoration in accordance with his own tastes to create a magnificent royal residence.

102 center Inside the Alcázar, the apartments of Charles V are embellished by spirited sixteenth-century azulejos and large wall hangings.

102 bottom left A view of the patio that leads to the magnificent apartments built in the first half of the sixteenth century by Charles V in the Alcázar.

102 bottom right A room in the Archivo General de Indias, created by Charles III in 1778. Housed in what was originally the Lonja, the merchants' loggia, it holds roughly 40,000 documents relating to Spanish holdings overseas from the time of the discovery of America to the independence of various states.

sixteenth century.

Opposite the cathedral stands the Alcázar, the fortified palace built in 913 by the Almoravid caliph, Abd el-Rahman III, which was transformed into a royal residence by Pedro I "the Cruel" in 1350. The modifications he made represent the height of *mudejár* style in Seville, but Pedro was not the only one to make alterations on the building, and now it comprises various styles that include Renaissance and Neo-Classical. The same mix is to be seen in the gardens, for example, Charles V's sixteenth century pavilion, which combines Moorish elements with statues of classical mythological figures, humorous hydraulic

objects typical of the Italian Renaissance like an organ that spouts water, and the eighteenth-century Jardín Inglés, in the landscaping style of the British Isles.

All trade in Seville took place in front of the Alcázar, between the steps of the cathedral and the Patio de los Naranjos, until 1572 when Archbishop Don Cristóbal de Rojas y Sandoval sent an indignant letter to King Philip II, who immediately initiated construction of a Lonja (a loggia for merchants) that faces onto the same square. The architect responsible was Juan de Herrera, who had designed the royal monastery of San Lorenzo de El Escorial. The building is square with a dual-colored façade softened by pillars and vaults.

Less than a century later, however, the commercial fortunes of Seville began to decline. In 1660, the building was converted to house Murillo's school of painting and then slowly left to fall into ruin. The idea of using it to house all the Spanish documents relating to the Indies was approved in 1778 by Charles III. Restoration of the Lonja, renamed the Archivo General de Indias, was completed in 1789. Today it holds about 40,000 documents divided into 16 sections, and includes handwritten letters by Christopher Columbus, nautical and land-registry maps, and even the request by Miguel de Cervantes for a shipload from the Indies.

The Cultural Landscape of Sintra

PORTUGAL

REGISTRATION: 1995
CRITERIA: C (II) (IV) (V)

"Palaces and gardens stand amongst high, craggy hills, waterfalls, and precipices, [along with] the monasteries on splendid heights [and] a distant view of the sea and the Tago, combining the wildness of the western Highlands with the greenery of southern France." Thus the 21-year-old George Byron described the wonders of Sintra in a letter to his mother. It mattered little that he had not seen either the Highlands or Provence, yet his words were a faithful portrait of this semi-mountainous area, not far from Lisbon, that looks out onto the Atlantic from Cabo da Roca, the westernmost point in Europe.

Byron had withdrawn here in 1809 to write *Childe Harold's Pilgrimage*, the epic poem, some of which describes the landscape of Sintra. Considered during the Romantic age as "the Eden of Europe," Sintra was the destination of the rich and noble of every nationality for the summer period. The origin of Sintra, however, is much older.

Its geographical position and the picturesque views from the Sintra mountains aroused the interest of the Moors who, in the eighth and ninth centuries, built a fort there known as the Castillo dos Mouros. Conquered in 1147 by Dom Alfonso Enriques, the castle remained a residence of the Portuguese royal family until the fourteenth century when it was abandoned, later to be restored during the Romantic age.

At that time, Dom Joao I ordered the construction of a palace in Chao da Oliva, what today is the historic center of Sintra and probably the site of an earlier Moorish building. Sintra's Gothic touch,

taken up in many other Portuguese buildings, was the work of another king, Dom Manuel, after whom the style Manueline was named. Renovated mostly during the Renaissance, today the Paço Real complex features extravagant architectural forms such as the two conical chimneys above the kitchens that have become the symbol of Sintra. The palace attracted a circle of artists and men-of-letters, and according to tradition, this was where Luis de Camões gave the first public reading of his poem The *Lusiads*.

In the centuries to come, the Portuguese royal family made Sintra their *buen retiro* (favorite country residence).

104 top The style of the Paço Real is predominantly Gothic, though a Moorish influence and extravagant Manueline forms can be identified. The most evident feature is the two cone-shaped chimneys over the kitchens.

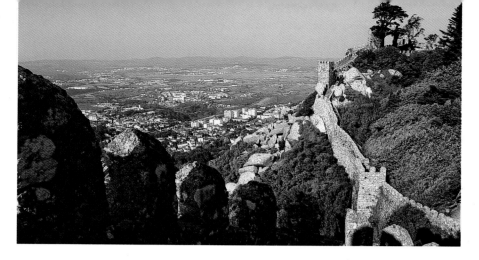

105 top The ramparts of the Castillo dos Mouros, the first building constructed in the area. The Moors built the fort in the eighth and ninth centuries, but when it was conquered by Dom Alfonso Enriques in 1147, it became the residence of the Portuguese royal family until the sixteenth century.

104-105 The Sala das Armas is the most dramatic in the Paço Real. Its walls are lined with azulejos and the barrel-vaulted ceiling is decorated with the coats of arms of 72 Portuguese noble families.

105 bottom The Sala dos Cisnes is named after the elegant swans that decorate the ceiling. On the first floor of the Paço Real, it is one of the plainest rooms.

106 top The lovely Sala do Trono in the Palácio Queluz was designed by the architect Jean-Baptiste Robillion. The mirrors hung on all the walls increase the sense of spaciousness. Silvestre Faria Lobo carved their gold-leaf wood frames.

106-107 Though smaller, Palácio Queluz is often compared to Versailles. Jean-Baptiste Robillion and the Dutch gardener José Van der Kolk designed its gardens, filled with statues and fountains, according to French tastes in the eighteenth century.

107 top Detail of the elegant statue of a sphinx in the Queluz garden. The garden was designed for the royal family to relax in with cages for exotic birds, and pools and fountains inhabited by black and white swans.

In 1747, Dom Pedro bought the country estate of the Marquis of Castelo Rodrigo and built the Palácio Queluz there, an elegant building surrounded by a park adorned by Rococo statues, a navigable canal decorated with *azulejos*, a pavilion designed by the French architect Jean-Baptiste Robillion, and fountains, one of which, the Fonte de Neptuno, has been attributed to Gian Lorenzo Bernini.

Perhaps Sintra's most surprising building is the Palácio da Pena. Situated high on the rocky peaks of the Sintra mountains, it arose from the ruins of the

107 bottom The marvelous statuary group of the Fonte do Neptuno stands in front of the main entrance to the Palácio Queluz. The sculpture has been attributed to the Italian master, Lorenzo Bernini.

108 top *The entrance, crowned by towers, to the Palácio da Pena. This unusual building was designed in 1839 by the German baron, Ludwig von Eschwege, for Ferdinand II of Saxe-Coburg. Ferdinand is immortalized as a battling horseman in a statue on the hill opposite the palace.*

108 bottom *Detail on the Palácio da Pena showing a threatening deity from Hell. Much of the decoration both inside and outside was made using concrete.*

Jeronymite monastery of Nossa Señora da Pena, built in the sixteenth century to celebrate the deeds of Vasco da Gama. The palace was commissioned by Ferdinand II of Saxe-Coburg in 1839 for his wife, Queen Maria II of Portugal, from Ludwig von Eschwege. The architect created a magnificent concoction of domes, ramparts, passageways, and decorations partly inspired by Ludwig II's castle in Bavaria and partly by the works of Schinkel in central Europe.

Besides the royal residences, Sintra is also the site of churches, monasteries, and aristocratic *quintas*. One of these is the astounding Victorian residence of Monserrate. Its history began in 1793 when William Beckford, the richest self-made Englishman of the period, rented the estate and began to decorate its interiors and gardens in his refined personal taste. Half a century later, Monserrate was bought by another Englishman, Sir Francis Cook, who rebuilt the house taking his inspiration from the Mogul palaces of India.

With the opening of the railway between Lisbon and Sintra in 1887, the delights of this area became accessible to one and all, but notwithstanding the prod towards progress, the romantic charm of the place has remained unaltered.

108-109 *A panoramic view of Sintra shows the Palácio da Pena looking like a fairytale castle. It resembles Ludwig's castle in Bavaria and is an orgy of kitsch. It blends Gothic and Manueline styles with the triumphal architecture of Schinkel in Germany.*

109 bottom left *The quinta of Monserrate is a splendid residence whose name is linked to two eccentric figures: the first was the English writer William Beckford, who lived here from 1793 to 1799 and made it an* arcadian retreat; the second was the magnate Francis Cook who lived here about 50 years later. He renovated it in Asian-inspired Victorian taste and beautified the garden with tropical plants and all the conifers known at that time.

109 bottom right *The Salão Nobre is decorated in Romantic-Eclectic style. This is one of the plainest interiors in the Palácio da Pena, built on the site of a monastery founded to celebrate the sighting of Vasco da Gama's fleet on his return home.*

110 top left The entrance court at the Budavári Palota (Royal Palace). The buildings now house four museums, the most important of which are the National Gallery of Hungary and the Budapest History Museum.

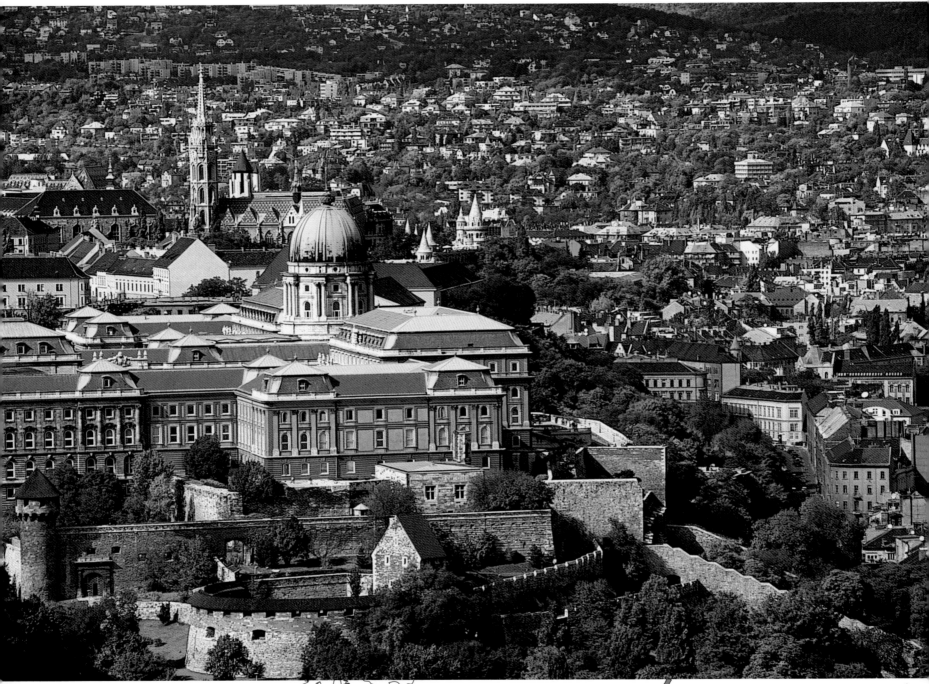

110 top right The south rampart in the original medieval fort in Buda. Buda is the hill that rises about 200 feet above the Danube River on the right bank.

● BUDAPEST

Budapest, the Banks of the Danube and Buda Castle

HUNGARY

BUDAPEST
REGISTRATION: 1987
CRITERIA: (II) (IV)

At the end of the nineteenth century, when the Austro-Hungarian empire had a strong influence over international affairs, Budapest enjoyed a moment of glory. Gustav Mahler and the young Béla Bartók performed at the Academy of Music, and Art Nouveau buildings sprang up like mushrooms in the residential areas. The city was illuminated at night by an electric lighting system, and in 1896 continental Europe's first underground train system was opened. The occasion being celebrated was the thousandth anniversary of the Hungarian state, but the city's history went back further than that.

The first settlement on the Gellert hills named Ak Ink, meaning "rock rich with water," was built by the Celts in the first century B.C. At the start of the Christian era, it became the capital of the Roman province of Pannonia Inferiore with the name Aquincum, but it was soon invaded by the Huns. After the Hun empire was dismantled, it was the turn of the Gepids, the Lombards, the Avars, and other Germanic and central Asian peoples. The Magyars first appeared around the ninth century and settled their own capital at Esztergom; later, in the thirteenth century, they moved it to Obuda, (the Roman Aquincum) near Pest, a trading town inhabited by Germanic and Hungarian peoples.

In the mid-thirteenth century, following the invasion of the Tatars, King Béla IV began construction of the royal palace and fortified walls on a terrace elevated about 200 feet above the right bank of the Danube. This side of the river could be more easily defended than Pest, which was situated on a plain. Buda, which grew up around the fort on the hill, was the third city founded in that area, and it soon grew. The country's second university was established there in 1395 and, in 1473, the first Hungarian book, *Budai krónika* (*The Chronicles of Buda*) was printed.

The political, economic, and cultural capital, Buda enjoyed its greatest splendor in the late fifteenth and early sixteenth centuries when it was visited by travelers from all parts of Europe. At the start of the sixteenth century, the city's ramparts were strengthened, but they could not withstand the Turks, who succeeded in taking the city by cunning. The Ottoman occupation marked a long period of decline and came to an end in 1686 after a long siege. Having lost almost all its inhabitants as a result of the hostilities, Buda was relegated to the role of a small provincial city in the Hapsburg Empire until the mid-nineteenth century.

110-111 A view of the city with Buda Hill and the royal palace in the foreground. Built in the thirteenth century and seriously damaged in the bloody battle for independence against the Turks, the palace was enlarged in the eighteenth century and renovated in Neo-Baroque style in 1890.

111 top right The Baroque fountain dedicated to Mattia Corvino, the enlightened ruler and general who reigned over Hungary in the second half of the fifteenth century. With an army of 30,000 mercenaries – known as the "Black Army" – he was able to halt the advance of the Turks.

111 bottom The entrance to the Royal Palace from the Fishermen's Rampart. Note the bronze equestrian statue of King Stephen the Holy, the legendary founder of Hungary by Alajos Strobl.

Having also been seriously damaged during the Nazi occupation, Buda's appearance today is composed of a variety of styles. Its streets – dominated to the north by the Fort and its residential district, and to the south by the royal palace – are lined with Gothic, Renaissance, and Baroque buildings. The Turkish domination is also seen in buildings like the Király public baths, built between 1566 and 1570, later enlarged with Neo-Classical wings.

The city's most interesting building is the Church of Our Blessed Lady, also known as the Matthias Church because it

112 top An imposing Neo-Gothic building in the historic district of Várhegy Hill on the right bank of the Danube. The river cuts through the city for 17 miles.

contains the armor of Matthias Corvinus who reigned from 1458 to 1490. The history of this church is one of suffering, like that of the city: the first religious building was raised on this site in the thirteenth century but was soon replaced by a Gothic cathedral that was never completed. During the Ottoman era, the building was converted into a mosque, and during the siege of 1686 the tower and roof collapsed. Reconstruction included Baroque elements, but in the nineteenth century, the Gothic building was rebuilt following excavation of the remains of the medieval church. Especially interesting are the Neo-Gothic bell tower and the south door; the latter was frescoed with a scene of the "Death of the Virgin" and the interior enlivened with stucco-work and paintings with ornamental motifs.

Behind the church stands the Fishermen's Rampart, in a style somewhere between Neo-Gothic and Neo-Romanesque, from where one can admire the whole city. Its name is taken from the district over

which it looks, where the fishermen used to live, and from the fact that a fish market was held there in ancient times because the placid waters of the Danube that separates the two halves of the Hungarian capital flow nearby.

Shortly afterwards the stubbornness of the aristocrat István Széchenyi proved useful: blocked on the east bank while the funeral of his father was being held on the west bank, he spared no effort until finally the river was crossed by a bridge. Thanks to him, in 1848, the Széchenyi Lánchid, a magnificent chain bridge, was completed, and for the first time, the two banks of the great river were joined.

112 center The façade of the Church of Our Lady, better known as the Church of Mattia because the crown that belonged to Mattia Corvino is kept there. Built around 1260 in Gothic style, it has had its vicissitudes. During the Turkish occupation, it was used as a mosque and, in 1873, the building was restored and altered by the architect Frigyes Schylek.

112 bottom Fishermens' Rampart. Built in sandstone in the nineteenth and twentieth centuries in a style somewhere between Neo-Romanesque and Neo-Gothic, the bastion is decorated with statues of medieval heroes and towers in the shape of a helmet, which symbolize the Magyar tribes.

112-113 View of the Danube and Pest. In the center, there is the famous Bridge of Chains, also called Széchenyi Lánchid after the ambitious person who commissioned its construction in 1839 from the English engineer Adam Clark. The left bank of the river is dominated by the huge Parliament building designed in the late nineteenth century in Oriental Neo-Gothic by the architect Imre Steindl.

113 top left Detail of an old house in Buda, with a shrine showing Mary and Jesus.

113 top right An imaginative decoration on a Jügendstil palace in the Várhegy district. There are many examples of this eclectic style that flourished in the late nineteenth and early twentieth centuries. Odon Lechner was Hungary's greatest architect in this style.

Mount Athos

GREECE

CHALCIDIAN PENINSULA
REGISTRATION: 1988
CRITERIA: C (I) (II) (IV) (V) (VI);
N (III)

The Greek Constitution of 1927 contained an appendix dedicated to Mount Athos in which it defined the independent nature of the monastic community that lives there, the relationships between it and the State and Church, and the administrative responsibilities and hierarchical relations within the community itself. The document confirms that Mount Athos depends on the Ministry of Foreign Affairs for political questions and on the Patriarch of Constantinople for religious ones, thereby sanctioning the peninsula's semi-autonomous nature that comes from a

During the classical era, the place was cited in the works of Homer, Herodotus, and Strabo before it fell into Roman hands.

The date of the first religious settlement there is uncertain, but records exist of monks and hermits on the northernmost promontory of the Chalcidian Peninsula – dominated by Mount Athos at 6,690 feet high – since the eighth century. It is known that a delegation of monks was present at the Ecumenical

long history of independence.

In mythology, Athos was a giant Thracian who attempted to hurl an immense boulder at Poseidon, but the rock slipped from his fingers and formed the mountain that has taken his name. Another myth says that Mount Athos, also known as *Aghion Oros* (holy mountain), was requested as a gift from Jesus, who had been shipwrecked there while visiting Lazarus.

Council of 843 called by the Byzantine empress, Theodora. And in 885, Emperor Basil issued an edict that officially recognized Mount Athos as an area governed exclusively by monks and hermits who had chosen to pass their lives in prayer and contemplation.

At the end of the ninth century, the community was already sizeable. The monks lived ascetically in makeshift shelters and without any general organization with the

114 Detail of a fresco in the Katholikon in Iviron Monastery. Dating from the sixteenth century, it was probably the work of the Theban artist, Frangos Katelanos.

114-115 Founded in the late tenth century by hermits from what is today Georgia, Iviron Monastery stands on a rocky promontory overlooking the sea. Besides the Katholikon, 16 other chapels face onto the monastery's main court, one of which contains the miraculous icon of the Virgin Mary.

115 top left Frescoes in Iviron Monastery. The iconography and dating suggest that artists from the Cretan school, influenced by Hellenistic art, worked here.

115 top right Dedicated to the Nativity, Simonopetra Monastery was named after Saint Simon who lived on Mount Athos in the mid-fourteenth century. With seven stories, it is the largest of the monastic buildings in the area.

116 top A view from the top of the Great Lavra Monastery. Founded in 963 by Saint Athanasios with the help of Emperor Nikephoros Phokas, it is the earliest of the monasteries on Mount Athos and the only one not damaged by fire.

116-117 The entrance to the church of the Great Lavra, with frescoes from 1535 by the Cretan, Theophanis Strelitzas. The artist admirably combined forms from Hellenistic art with iconography strictly linked to Orthodox Christianity.

exception of the Monastery of Kolobou founded in 872 in Ierissos. At the end of the next century, the destiny of Mount Athos was altered with the arrival of Athanasios, a monk from Trebisond. The son of a well-to-do family, he embraced poverty but took advantage of his friendship with Emperor Nikephoros Phokas to build the Great Lavra, the monastery that is still at the heart of the community. The central church, the Katholikon, with the chapels dedicated to Saint Nicholas and the Forty Martyrs, is still the site of the refectory, the kitchen, and the library. The monks' cells are distributed throughout the four wings that surround the monastery.

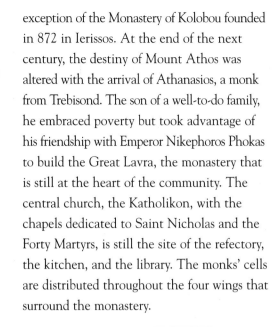

Athanasios did not have an easy life. The hermits most inclined to private meditation objected to the advent of an organized monastic community, but the emperor agreed with Athanasios, and in 971, he issued an imperial bull, the *Tragos*, that laid down the first rules to be followed on Mount Athos. With the support of Byzantium, at least 40 monasteries were built by the fourteenth century, despite pressure from the Roman Church for the reconciliation of the Catholic and Orthodox faiths.

The peninsula's prosperity was about to end, however. When Constantinople fell to the Turks, Mount Athos passed under Ottoman influence, which lasted 400 years. The Turkish sovereigns never changed the law but imposed increasingly large taxes on the monasteries, with the result that the number of monks gradually declined and aid had to be asked from the Russians, Wallachians, and Moldavians. With the independence of Greece in the nineteenth

century, Mount Athos became a destination for monks from all over eastern Europe, in particular, Russians. They established themselves in 1875 in the large monastery known as Aghios Panteleimon, characterized by the onion-shaped domes that were typical of the Orthodox Church in czarist Russia.

Today Mount Athos includes 20 monasteries inhabited by 1,500 monks. Their architecture is a curious mix of styles created by continual additions and rebuilding that has gone on since the Byzantine epoch. Each monastery is composed of a maze of buildings huddled against one another and a sequence of chapels, each of which has a particular function. Few, however, of the original frescoes have survived. Those in the Great Lavra are from the thirteenth century, and there are fragments of mosaics dating from the eleventh in Vatopedi Monastery. The heads of Saints Peter and Paul frescoed in the refectory were painted just a little later. Each monastery has its icons, some dating back to the Byzantine period, and the libraries are filled with important Greek and Slavic manuscripts.

Despite the unceasing changes in fortune suffered by the monasteries, the natural appeal of Mount Athos still attracts mystics from all over Europe, and the strict rule still survives that prohibits women from all of the peninsula, so that the monks can remain far from temptation.

The Historic Areas of Istanbul

TURKEY

PROVINCE OF ISTANBUL
REGISTRATION: 1985
CRITERIA: C (I) (II) (III) (VI)

On May twenty-ninth each year, Istanbul celebrates the conquest of Byzantium by the Ottomans and, consequently, the conversion from Christianity to Islam in 1453. It is said that Sultan Mehmet II, who in honor of the occasion was given the title "Conqueror," thanked Allah for having guided him in the taking of what he called "the greatest and most splendid city in the world."

Accounts of the grueling siege of Byzantium feature many dramatic turns of events and astonishing acts of heroism, plots, betrayals, and ruses. For example, it was suggested to transport the Ottoman ships over land to a bay to the south of the city so as to surprise the Byzantines who, in order to protect the Golden Horn from the north (logically the only route available), had stretched an iron chain across the Bosporus. A decisive fact in the taking of the city was the "largest cannon in the world" that created large breaches in the walls. The weapon was sold to Mehmet by a Hungarian mercenary who had, in fact, arrived on the shores of the Bosporus as an ardent supporter of Christianity hoping to offer it to the Byzantines. But the power of money was more persuasive than that of his faith, and having understood that the Byzantines could not afford it, he turned to the wealthier Muslims.

The greatest and most splendid city in the world was at that time little more than a ruin ravaged by debt, depopulation, and general, wide-spread decline since its capture by their supposed Christian friends in the Fourth Crusade. But the crusaders, instead of continuing east to wrest Palestine and Syria from the infidels, found it more convenient to sack Byzantium of its treasures and to hold it in check for more than half a century.

After three days of looting in the districts that had provided resistance (this was traditional Ottoman practice), Mehmet entered the church of Hagia Sophia. It is said that, before passing through the heavy entrance doorway, he covered his head with ashes as a sign of respect for the extraordinary building,

which was the largest basilica in Christendom at the time. Yet his respect did not prevent him from converting it into a mosque, thus putting an end to over 1,000 years of tradition. Today Hagia Sophia has become a historic monument and has lost its religious significance, but upon entering it, one cannot ignore the symbolic importance of this magnificent building that was constructed by Justinian between 532 and 538 in celebration of the glory of God and to restore the grandeur of the Roman Empire.

Also known as the Church of Holy Wisdom, Hagia Sophia stands on the site of an earlier basilica (destroyed during a revolt) built during the age of Theodosius that, in turn, had been built over the remains of the Acropolis from the Hellenistic period. Construction of Hagia Sophia was commissioned from two Greek architects – Anthemius of Tralles and Isidore of Miletus – who conceived the structure as a synthesis between early Christian basilicas and imperial palaces. To build the dome, which was at that time a challenge to the laws of gravity not yet fully conquered, they used hollow bricks made from particularly porous, light clay that they imported from Rhodes. To decorate the interiors, where precious materials were used, Justinian ordered a sequence of mosaics that became the object of disputes between the Church and the Byzantine State for their very splendor. The former claimed that the realistic images that shone with gold were impious and wanted them to be replaced with more ascetic versions. The governors of the state, however, supported by the people of the city who formed large, admiring crowds around the building, won out against the wishes of the Church. Despite surviving this battle, many of the mosaics were destroyed by the iconoclasm of the Muslims. Of those that remain (restored following the removal of a layer of lime applied by the Ottomans), the most important are the one known as the Deisis (Christ between the Virgin and Saint John the Baptist on the south gallery), Christ

118 top The face of Christ in the mosaic in the eastern gallery in Hagia Sophia. When they were produced in the sixth century, the decorations in the basilica were considered impious by representatives of the Byzantine Church for the quantity of gold and precious materials they used.

118 bottom The interior of Hagia Sophia, also referred to as the Church of Holy Wisdom. The picture shows the imperial cloister and the central dome, which has a diameter of 105 feet.

119 The grandeur of Hagia Sophia seen from an aerial view. When Sultan Mehmet II conquered the city in 1453, the basilica was converted into a mosque and remained that way until 1932. Since then, the Turkish state has withdrawn its religious status and made it a museum.

ISTANBUL

ANKARA

120 top Built between 1459 and 1465, Topkapi Palace was the symbol of the Ottoman empire for almost 400 years. In keeping with Islamic tradition, the palace consists of a number of pavilions laid out around an equal number of courts.

120-121 The bulk and six minarets of the Sultan Ahmet Camii Mosque are visible from a great distance. The mosque was built in 1609 near the equally imposing Hagia Sophia.

121 top Süleymaniye Camii overlooks the Golden Horn. It was designed and built by Sinan between 1550 and 1557.

Pantokrator above the third door, and the portraits of the saints in the upper galleries that were originally reserved for women.

To the Ottomans, Hagia Sophia was both a model and a challenge. To build a mosque that equaled it in magnificence was a categorical imperative from the time of Mehmet II, but it took 100 years of Muslim rule over the city before this goal was achieved. Sultan Suleyman the Magnificent commissioned his janissary and military genius Sinan to build a mosque dedicated to the ruler himself to be built in a dominant position over the Golden Horn. Sinan had previously overseen consolidation and restoration works in Hagia Sophia and had become obsessed by the building. To demonstrate his capacity to "outdo the Greeks," between 1550 and 1557 he produced a massive domed building, the Suleyman Camii, that is surprisingly geometrical and features a perfect balance between light and shade and elegantly minimalist decoration. At the corners of what was to become the symbol of Ottoman Istanbul (and which earned Sinan the nickname "the Turkish Michelangelo"), there are four slender minarets.

The Hagia Sophia's second rival, the mosque of Sultan Ahmed Camii, was built at the start of the seventeenth century facing the former Christian church. Better known as the Blue Mosque, the forms of the domed building are extraordinarily harmonious. Its name is derived from the blue majolica tiles manufactured in the city of Iznik that entirely cover the walls of the mosque.

Istanbul has many other monuments from the Ottoman period, the most important of which are Topkapi palace,

121 center left Sultan Ahmet Camii is better known as the Blue Mosque due to the 20,000 blue majolica tiles made in the city of Iznik that completely cover its walls.

121 center right A richly decorated room in the Topkapi harem. Over the centuries, many western travelers have been fascinated by this mysterious place. It is said that, at the time of Mehmet II, 688 odalisques lived here. The most famous woman in the harem was Roxelana, the powerful concubine of Suleyman the Magnificent.

121 bottom The entrance to Sultan Ahmet Camii. Note the gilded arabesques and the enormous hanging light typical of Turkish mosques.

the Great Bazaar with its han (caravanserai), and the city's dozens of mosques. UNESCO's attention, however, is focused on the more ancient monuments from the age of Constantinople and Byzantium, which are in need of more extensive restoration. Their importance lies in their contribution to the revelation of the spirit of a city that, over its long history, has seen many great civilizations flourish and pass. Above all, the city has always

managed to rise from its ashes, changing name in the process, from Constantinople to Byzantium to Istanbul, with each new version more magnificent than the former.

A perfect example of this continuity, and a warning for the governors, was the ancient Hippodrome (horse-racing track), which today is covered by the huge esplanade that lies between the Hagia Sophia and the Blue Mosque, and below which lies the most famous of the many cisterns built to guarantee water supplies during a siege. The Hippodrome was built on Constantine's orders and included a Greek column that had been raised in front of the Temple of Apollo at Delphi that Constantine had transported to the new city in 330. The place quickly became a meeting point in the city, a role that it still plays. During the Byzantine epoch it was used for chariot races, the results of which often caused riots that had a political fallout and could lead to the destitution of the emperor. Many centuries later, in 1826, during the troubles that marked the decline of the Ottomans, the Hippodrome was the setting of the famous massacre of the Janissaries by Mahmud II.

Another important indication of the history and power of the city is the elaborate defensive system built in the fifth century to protect it from the mainland. It comprises 96 towers, 13 gates, and a further eleven gates protected by lookout bastions. The walls were knocked down once by the Crusades and later by the powerful Hungarian cannon belonging to Mehmet II, but they were then kept in perfect condition until the nineteenth century when, having become redundant, they were left to fall into ruin. Restoration work was begun in 1980 and has been the source of bitter argument as it has not been faithful to the original design.

Istanbul has experienced enormous demographic growth in the last few decades and is now a metropolis of ten million inhabitants with uncontrolled urban development. Many ancient architectural treasures have been surrounded by ghetto areas and their

safeguarding is now a desperate task. One such example is the twelfth-century monastic complex of Christ Pantokrator, which contains three churches decorated with refined mosaics and was the resting place of the Byzantine emperors for more than 200 years. Following the Ottoman conquest, the complex was turned into a Koranic school and then a mosque with the name Zeyrek Camii. Still used for Muslim worship, it is considered by UNESCO one of the hundred sites at risk throughout the world.

122 left An Egyptian obelisk stands in the center of the Hippodrome, an area now covered by the esplanade between Hagia Sophia and the Blue Mosque. Originally 197 feet tall, it broke during transportation. The same esplanade contains a column from Apollo's Temple in Delphi.

122 right Probably built during the reign of Emperor Constantine, the Yerabatan Saray (the basilica's water tank) is the largest of the city's ancient water storage containers. The container stands on 336 Corinthian columns and could hold 2,825,000 cubic feet of water.

122-123 Stuffed with carpets and other goods, this is one of the main galleries in the Great Bazaar. The entire complex contains more than 5,000 shops.

123 top left Built in the fifth century during the reign of Theodosius II, Constantinople's walls measure 21,820 feet in circumference. Now in ruins, they are at the center of a much-debated restoration project.

123 top right This is the Monastery of Christ Pantokrator. Empress Irene founded its church in the twelfth century.

The Ancient City of Damascus
THE ARAB REPUBLIC OF SYRIA

ADMINISTRATIVE DISTRICT
OF DAMASCUS
REGISTRATION: 1979
CRITERIA: C (I) (II) (III) (IV) (VI)

It has been said that every man of culture must feel that he is the son of two homelands, his own and Syria. This country has been the setting for the birth of agriculture, the alphabet, the three great monotheistic religions, philosophy, trade, and the art of diplomacy. Damascus even contends with Aleppo for the title of the world's oldest city. Nonetheless, recent excavation has brought to light an older urban center, Hama, exactly halfway between the two great cities. The debate remains open.

Dimashq-ash-Sham, or *Sham* – as it is known to its inhabitants – gets its name from Noah's eldest son who, according to the Bible, settled here after the Flood. The first written reference to the city has been found at Mari, on the Euphrates, engraved on a clay tablet during the Neolithic period, and a papyrus document proves that Damascus traded with Egypt as early as the ninth millennium B.C.

These fragments do not indicate who the governors of Damascus were during those remote epochs, but it is certain that, in the second millennium B.C., the city

was the capital of the kingdom of the Aramaeans, who had been chased out of their lands after the Assyrians landed on the Phoenician coast of Syria. After a 30-year period under the control of the Babylonian king, Nebuchadnezzar, in 538 B.C. the city was conquered by Cyrus, the king of Persia, who made it his capital. However, it was under Alexander the Great in 333 B.C. that Damascus became the heart of an immense empire that stretched from the eastern Mediterranean to Afghanistan.

64 B.C. signaled the beginning of Damascus' golden age with the arrival of the Romans. They built a magnificent city on the foundations of earlier versions and it soon became one of the empire's ten most important centers. The Roman trading aristocracy was composed of Damascenes, who formed the commercial bridgehead

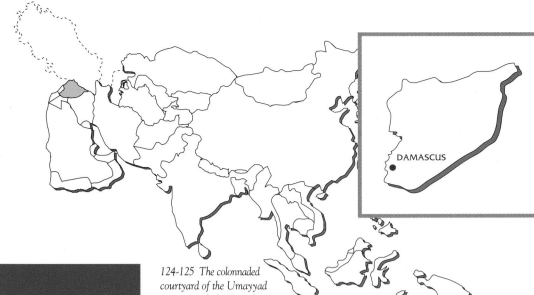

124-125 The colonnaded courtyard of the Umayyad mosque with the Bait al-Hal (Treasury) in the foreground. This octagonal construction was used for storing valuables. For reasons of security, it stands on eight Corinthian columns taken from Roman temples.

125 center left An overall view of the Umayyad mosque surrounded by the buildings that comprise the Suq al-Hamadiyyeh.

125 center right In the center of the huge prayer hall in the Umayyad mosque stands the marble monument erected in the nineteenth century on the site where, according to tradition, the head of St. John the Baptist was buried. John the Baptist is numbered among the holy men of Islam.

between Europe and the East at the time. The swords and fabrics produced in Damascus were sought after in even the remotest of regions.

In A.D. 34, as Saul of Tarsus, a Roman dignitary better known as Paul, was traveling on the road that brought Damascus so many riches, he was blinded by a dazzling vision, as a result of which he converted to the new Christian religion that was creating such turmoil in the empire. Because of the convergence of the sacred and the profane in the city, within a century the power of the bishop of Damascus grew to be second only to that of the Patriarch of Antioch.

The Roman empire was replaced by the Byzantine version in A.D. 395, but the real

stretch from the Atlantic to the Indus.

Today the old city of Damascus, enclosed by high walls, is an extraordinary mix of Umayyad, Roman, paleo-Christian, and Byzantine remains that were combined to a surprising degree. For instance, the center of the Umayyad city was the Great Mosque; this stood on the site of a church dedicated to Saint John the Baptist, which had been built over a Roman temple dedicated to Jupiter, which in turn occupied the site of an earlier temple dedicated to the Aramaic god Hadad.

To glorify the power of the dynasty, in 705 Caliph al-Walid ibn-Abdul Malik began the construction of a new building. The work cost the fabulous sum of eleven million gold *denari*, lasted ten years, and required 1,200 laborers. The austere walls give no indication that the interior is one of the grandest glorifications of the power of Allah. The Gate of Paradise (the main entrance to the Great Mosque) leads into a huge court ringed with columns. Originally, mosaics covered well over 48,000 square

feet, lining all the outer walls, but in the catastrophic fire of 1893 most of these were lost. However, enough remains to indicate the quality was only equaled by the mosaic art in Santa Sofia in Istanbul or the basilicas in Ravenna. The Byzantines were accustomed to producing figurative works and their art was so perfect that the caliph devised a way to avoid the Islamic principle of not reproducing human figures and works. He decided that the decorations on the walls of the Great Mosque would represent the "City of God," with the result that gold and 30 shades of green were used to contrast the lapis lazuli and aquamarine of the rivers of Paradise.

Al-Walid also appreciated Roman

124 top The west tower (al-Garbiyya minaret) was built by the Mameluk sultan Qait Bey in 1488 in Egyptian style.

124 bottom Byzantine artists produced the mosaics on the south wall of the Umayyad mosque. Despite the destruction of many of the decorations over the centuries, this is one of the largest mosaics in the world. This particular mosaic shows the gardens of Paradise.

turning point for Damascus was to come after nearly 1,000 years of western rule when the troops of the Umayyad caliphs arrived in Syria from the Arabian peninsula and made mass conversions, at times forcibly, to yet another recently-created religion: Islam. The powerful new rulers were astounded at the city's beauty and made it the first great capital of the Muslim world, which, only a century later, was to architecture and ordered that the columns in the temple of Jupiter be used in the construction of the mosque. They can be seen with their Corinthian capitals supporting the octagonal structure covered with luminescent mosaic tiles known as the *Bait al-Hal* (Treasury) where the Damascenes used to keep their valuables and documents.

Syncretism between Islam and Christianity is evident in the presence of the Saint Paul and who was later canonized, is of great symbolic value to Christians. A few ancient houses belonging to Jews survive near the streets where Christians still live.

In 750, the honor of being the Islamic capital was transferred from Damascus to Baghdad when the Umayyads were overthrown by the Abbasids. Nonetheless, Damascene architecture continued to be used as the model for the construction of by a high vaulted metal structure, like most of the city's souks. Passing by the remains of a Roman arch, one comes to the Great Mosque, and then enters a tangle of alleyways. These contain many *hammam* (public baths) and *khan* (caravanserai), including the large and magnificent one built in *suq al-Bizurieh* (the spice market) by Assad Pashà al-Azem, the governor of Damascus in the mid-eighteenth century. He

tomb of Saint John the Baptist in the prayer room, and in the fact that one of the minarets is dedicated to Jesus. Muslims believe that on the Day of Judgment, Christ will descend to Earth by placing his foot on this massive tower.

Damascus is one of the four Islamic holy cities and it is said that a prayer recited in the Great Mosque of the Umayyads is worth 10,000 elsewhere. The bodies of famous individuals are conserved in mausoleums and mosques, like that of Saladin, the holy man and army leader who defeated the Crusaders in the twelfth century, and that of Saida Ruqqaya, the granddaughter of the Prophet worshipped by Shiites.

The humble underground church of Ananias, the ascetic who gave refuge to Arab cities in Andalusia, Cordoba in particular, and the roses of Damascus, for example, were used in Granada as a decorative motif in the Alhambra. After a long period in which trade prospered, the city grew weaker during the Crusades and in 1400 was sacked by the Mongol troops led by Timur, as known as Tamerlane.

In 1516, the Ottomans arrived and remained in power until the end of World War I. Under the Turkish empire, Damascus was enhanced with magnificent buildings and enjoyed a second golden age. Lovers of beauty and earthly pleasures, the Ottomans restored the Great Mosque and turned the city into a flourishing commercial center.

Little has changed inside the walls since that time. From Bab al-Faraj, the main gate, one enters the Souk al-Hamadiyyeh covered was also responsible for the construction of the Azem palace, an enchanting residence built around a series of flower-filled patios and home to the Museum of Arts and Traditions where thousands of objects are displayed in boiserie-lined rooms.

This was the building that inspired the construction by Ottoman nobles of houses that sing a hymn of joy. Two of these, Bait Siba'i and Bait Nizam, have been returned to their original beauty with the restoration of frescoes, wood carvings, stuccoes, and marbles. Upon entering, it is easy to understand the words of an anonymous Damascene poet who claimed that the city's houses were made with mud, water, wood, straw, colors, stone, marble, glass, poetry, and love.

126 left The Mausoleum of Saida Ruqqaya was built in the nineteenth century in Persian style in honor of the Prophet's granddaughter, who is worshipped by the Shiites. The tomb of the young martyr is a place of pilgrimage for hundreds of thousands of women.

126 right Built in 1196, the tomb of Saladin, the hero of Islam, was neglected for centuries until 1898 when Kaiser Wilhelm II had it restored as a tribute to the Ottoman sultan, Abdel Hamid II.

127 top Built in the mid-eighteenth century, Bait Azem was the splendid residence of the Ottoman governor in Damascus. Its magnificent interiors and patios have been converted into a museum for popular arts and traditions.

127 bottom left These are the elaborate multicolored marble decorations of the walls and the fountain in one of the iwan (rooms) in Bait Nizam, one of the loveliest and best conserved Ottoman houses in the Old City.

127 bottom right Bab Sharqi (the East Gate) is the oldest existing monument in Damascus. It is the only one of the seven or eight gates built in Roman times to have retained its original form.

Jerusalem and its Walls
ISRAEL

JERUSALEM DISTRICT
(SITE PROPOSED BY JORDAN)
REGISTRATION: 1981
INSCRIPTION IN THE LIST OF WORLD HERITAGE
SITES IN DANGER: 1982
CRITERIA: C (II) (III) (VI)

In 1947, the United Nations passed a resolution defining Jerusalem as a *corpus separatum* that did not belong to either Israel or Palestine. Over half a century later, however, the parties involved – often using weapons rather than diplomacy – have yet to agree on the status of the city, which stands as the symbol of a seemingly endless conflict. Jerusalem's registration in UNESCO's list of World Heritage sites in 1981 was followed by its inscription a year later on the list of World Heritage Sites in Danger. In addition to the direct effects of Arab and Israeli extremism, Jerusalem also suffers from unbridled urban development, the negative effects of tourism, and negligence toward its monuments. Its status as "everyone's city" is by definition unfortunately turning it into

"no one's city."

Jerusalem is considered the holy city of the three great monotheistic religions, Judaism, Christianity, and Islam. For Jews, it is the site of Abraham's sacrifice. For Christians, it is where Christ was crucified and resurrected. According to Muslims, the prophet Muhammad ascended into heaven from this city.

Although Jerusalem currently looks like a modern city, the Old City – an area of less than one-half of a square mile circled by 39-foot-high walls two and a half miles long – bears witness to its troubled history spanning 5,000 years.

Founded by the Canaanites in the third millennium B.C., Jerusalem forcefully earned its place in eternity in about 1,000 B.C. when the biblical King David conquered the city and King Solomon built the Temple there. In 586 B.C., King Nebuchadnezzar devastated it, destroying the Temple and sending the population into exile in Babylonia. Fifty years later, the Persian king, Cyrus the Great, conquered Babylonia and allowed the Jewish population to return to Jerusalem and rebuild the Temple. The Persians held the city until 333 B.C. when Alexander the Great added Palestine to his empire, only to lose it a few years later to Ptolemy I of Egypt.

In 198 B.C., the Seleucid king Antiochus III conquered Judea – of which Jerusalem was a part – and made it one of Syria's tributaries until the Judeans rebelled against their rulers. The Temple was re-consecrated in 168 B.C. and the city prospered, led by the Jewish dynasty of the Maccabees until the Roman conquest in 63 B.C. Jerusalem was rebuilt under Herod, the sovereign installed by Rome, but power was still exercised by the Roman governors, and it was one of these, Pontius Pilate, who authorized the crucifixion of Christ.

From then on, the Jews repeatedly attempted to break away from Roman rule. Following the revolt in A.D. 70, the second Temple was burned, and after the revolt in 135, the Jews were banished from Jerusalem. During the fourth century, the Christian religion was legalized in the Roman world and Jerusalem became an important place of pilgrimage. Many

128 bottom left Bab al-Rahmeh (the Golden Gate) is cited by all the ancient texts of the three monotheistic religions. For Jews, it is where the Messiah will enter Jerusalem; for Christians, it is where Jesus entered the city for the last time; for Muslims, it is the Gate of Mercy through which the just will pass on Judgment Day.

128-129 A view of Jerusalem with the Dome of the Rock in the foreground. As a result of a continually growing population (now roughly 700,000), mass tourism, and the interminable Palestinian-Israeli conflict the fragile and ancient equilibrium of the city is at serious risk.

129 top The labyrinthine old city that lies within the two-and-a-half-mile-long walls contains over 100 streets and more than 1,000 shops.

129 bottom Suq Khan az-Zait is the most crowded street in the Arab quarter of Jerusalem and the most densely populated area of the old city.

JERUSALEM

churches were built, including the Holy Sepulcher, the site of the resurrection of Christ.

With the exception of the brief Persian rule between 614 and 628, the city was governed by the Romans and, upon Rome's downfall, the Byzantines. In 638, it was conquered by the Arabs, who built the Dome of the Rock over the site of the Temple. Despite this affront, the Jews, Christians, and Muslims continued to live together peacefully until 996 when the Fatimid caliph al-Hakim began to persecute the non-Muslim population. Christian Europe responded swiftly, embarking on a campaign to regain the city, and after an extended siege, the victorious Crusaders entered Jerusalem in 1099. Nevertheless, a little less than a century later Saladin returned the city to

Islamic domination. Under the Ayyubids, Mamlukes and Ottomans, Muslim rule continued until the British occupation in 1917, and Jerusalem remained the capital of Britain's mandate over Palestine until 1948. The plan to internationalize the city failed with the Six-Day War between Egypt and Israel in 1967, and the rest is a painful part of history.

The walls of the Old City, built by the Ottomans at the end of the sixteenth century, circle an area divided into three districts: the Hebrew quarter, the Muslim quarter, and the Christian quarter that includes an area for Armenians. In addition to the colorful souk and white stone houses, there are numerous religious buildings that have survived destruction and transformation, revealing the plurality of Jerusalem's religious life. Among these,

the Wailing Wall, the Holy Sepulcher, and the Dome of the Rock are the sublime symbols of the three monotheistic religions, and they expression a powerful cultural and political identity.

The texts of the Jewish mystics indicate Mount Moriah, along the western section of the wall, as the center of the universe. This was where Abraham, the patriarch of the people of Israel, prepared to sacrifice his son Isaac. This was also where Solomon built *Beth-El*, the Temple, to hold the tablets of the Ten Commandments. When the second Temple was destroyed in A.D. 70, it was commemorated by what the Jews refer to as *Ha-Kotel Ha-Ma'aravi*. This was the wall built by Herod and later incorporated into the Ottoman fortification. For centuries, the "Chosen People" have come here day and night to

130 top left, center and right The Wall is more famously known as the Wailing Wall because the Hebrews here came to weep when the second Temple was destroyed in A.D.70 following a popular rebellion. Believers place prayers written on slips of paper in the cracks in the wall.

130 bottom The tradition of making a pilgrimage to the Wall began during the Ottoman era when the buildings in the Old City huddled almost up to the wall, leaving only a narrow space for prayer. The Arab district in this area was demolished in 1967 during the Six Day War.

131 Ha-Kotel Ha-Ma'aravi (the Wall) was built by Herod in 20 B.C. to contain the embankment on which the second Jewish temple stood. Today, the Dome of the Rock, practically a symbol of the difficult co-existence of Islam and Judaism, stands just beyond the Wall.

weep over the fate of the Temple, leaving folded notes with their innermost prayers and confessions to God in the cracks between the stones.

Overlooking the Wailing Wall is the *Qubbat as-Sakhrah*, or the Dome of the Rock, the oldest masterpiece of Islamic art. Its construction, which lasted from 685 to 691, can be considered a political act. The caliph Abd al-Malik built it to affirm his supremacy over rival sultans from the Arab peninsula. Interpreting the seventeenth *sura* of the Koran to suit his needs, he identified the site of the ruins of the Temple of Israel as the place where Muhammad ascended into heaven. Thus, an extraordinary building was constructed around the rock bearing the prophet's footprint. Rising from a stone platform are two concentric colonnades, the first octagonal and the second circular,

supporting a dome with a diameter of 66 feet and a total height of 98 feet. The interior is richly decorated with mosaics of geometric, calligraphic, and floral motifs, the oldest of which were made by Byzantine craftsmen. The mosaics cover an area of 13,800 square feet. Following the conquest of Jerusalem, the Crusaders consecrated it for Christian worship and on top of the dome they mounted a golden cross that was later removed by the Ottomans. In the sixteenth century, Suleyman the Magnificent decorated the dome and the exterior walls with 45,000 faience tiles in blue, the color of the sky and thus of infinity, and gold, the symbol of Allah's power. In the early 1990's, King Hussein of Jordan paid homage to the third most important site of Islam by covering the entire dome of the *Qubbat as-Sakhrah* with sheets of pure gold.

132 top left Two concentric colonnades, one octagonal and the other circular, support the 66-foot-high dome of the mosque.

132 top right The dome of the mosque was lined with sheets of pure gold at the start of the 1990's by King Hussein of Jordan, whose family is directly descended from the prophet Muhammad.

132 bottom Underneath the Dome of the Rock is the sacred rock on which Abraham prepared to sacrifice his son, and from which Muhammad ascended to heaven to take his place next to Allah.

132-133 Built between 685 and 691 by Sultan Abd al-Malik, the Qubbat as-Sakhra (Dome of the Rock) is the earliest masterpiece of Islamic art. To affirm the supremacy of Islam, the sultan ordered his architects to use the rotunda of the Holy Sepulcher as a model.

133 top Suleyman the Magnificent decorated the outer walls and the vault of the Dome of the Rock with 54,000 blue and gold majolica tiles, which represent the color of heaven and the power of Allah.

134 top The court that leads to the Church of the Holy Sepulcher is lined on the left by the Chapel of the 40 Martyrs, the Greek Orthodox Chapel of St. John, and the Chapel of St. James. The façade of the church was built during the Crusader era in the twelfth century.

134 bottom The Church of the Holy Sepulcher. Surrounded by houses, the church has practically been suffocated by Jerusalem's urban sprawl.

The Church of the Holy Sepulcher is located further away from the sacred Jewish and Muslim sites, at the end of a road that is traditionally indicated as the Via Dolorosa, where the Passion of Christ took place. Emperor Hadrian built a temple dedicated to Venus here. It is said that the mother of Emperor Constantine came to Jerusalem in 326, found the Holy Cross here, and ordered that a church be built on this site. To avoid copying the structure of pagan temples, the model of the basilica, a civil building used for meetings and trade, was chosen. The Church of the Holy Sepulcher was repeatedly destroyed, but its current form, which dates to the era of the Crusades, is a faithful copy of the first Constantinian church. The *Rotunda*, which has a diameter of 131 feet, is the accepted site of the crucifixion, burial, and resurrection of Christ. Another basilica, with galleries and colonnaded courtyards, was built over it. Representatives of the six Christian Churches take turns each day to keep watch over Christianity's most sacred complex.

In addition to these mainstays of the three monotheistic religions, each corner of the Old City contains monasteries and churches of the different Christian cults, including St. Anne's, built over the site of the Virgin's home, as well as synagogues, Talmudic colleges, mosques, and civil buildings from the Mamluke and Ottoman periods. Nevertheless, the most astonishing and moving sights are the throngs that flock here from all over the world, bearing a message of peace for the Holy Land.

135 top left The Katholikon, the Greek choir in the Holy Sepulcher, contains representations of all six faiths of the Christian religion.

135 top center The Altar of the Virgin stands on the site of Calvary where the Crucifixion took place.

135 top right The Unction Stone, at the entrance to the Holy Sepulcher, is said to be where the body of Jesus was anointed once he was taken down from the Cross.

135 bottom left The Rotunda, 131 feet in diameter, is believed to cover the place of the Crucifixion. The many chapels added over the centuries have contained the remains of people who have played an important role in the defense of the Holy Sepulcher such as the Crusader kings Baldwin I and Goffredo of Buglione.

135 bottom right Christ Pantokrator is frescoed on a vault in the Church of the Holy Sepulcher.

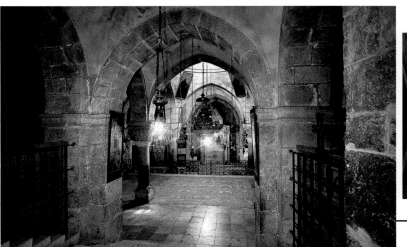

136 top Once the
symbol of the power of
the Safavid empire,
Meidan Imam (Royal
Square) measures 1,640
feet by 591 feet. It is

lined by the Royal
Mosque, Sheikh
Lotfollah mosque, Ali-
Qapu royal palace, and
the entrance to the city's
Grand Bazaar.

136-137 The superb
central court of the Royal
Mosque. The eivan
(portals) and porticoes
decorated with turquoise
and gold majolica tiles are

reflected in the large
pool. Built in the early
seventeenth century, the
Royal Mosque marks the
apotheosis of Persian
architecture.

137 top right The
interior of the Royal
Mosque is lined with
elaborate floral motifs
and calligraphic
decorations by the artist

Ali Reza Abbassi. From
the city of Tabriz and of
Safavid origin, he was the
best-known artist of his
time in Persia.

Meidan Imam in Isfahan

IRAN

PROVINCE OF ISFAHAN
REGISTRATION: 1979
CRITERIA: C (I) (V) (VI)

E sfahan nesf-é jahan, meaning "Isfahan is the center of the world," was the phrase on the lips of everyone who visited the city in the seventeenth century, impressed as they were by the magnificence of its buildings and extent of its commercial activity. Yet, this marvelous city was created in just 30 years by an ambitious ruler who had successfully made use of the services of two mercenaries.

For all of the sixteenth century, the Safavid Dynasty, which had reigned over Persia for 150 years, watched its territory shrink at the hands of Ottoman troops. This situation continued until Sir Anthony Sherley and his brother Robert knocked at the door of Shah Abbas I. The two English adventurers had offered to the European courts to undertake diplomatic exploits – in return for payment and honors – to provide the Safavids with support against the Ottomans. Moreover, the pair offered to initiate the Persians into the "magical" powers of a new invention, gunpowder, and to teach them to build cannons. An agreement was reached with the result that, in less than two years, Shah Abbas was able to win back much of Persia.

Having entered Isfahan in triumph in 1598, the ruler decided to make the city his new capital and he began to construct buildings to celebrate its greatness. Using the modest Turkish palace as the basis, he had the six-story Ali Qapu, the royal palace, built looking onto the ancient esplanade of Nagash-e-Jahan that measured 1,640 by 490 feet. On the east side of the square, which he renamed Meidan Shah but that was later to become Meidan Imam, he began construction of the Royal Mosque (*Masjed e-Shah* or *Masjed e-Imam*).

The building was completed in 1628, one year after the death of Shah Abbas I, and is considered one of the greatest examples of Persian art. It has been estimated that its construction required 18 million bricks and 472,500 blue and turquoise majolica tiles to cover its surface. It had been the tradition to use monochromatic tiles on which motifs were carved at the moment of application, but Shah Abbas was impatient to see the finished effect and ordered the process to be accelerated by laying tiles already decorated with floral motifs, known as *haft rangi* (seven colors).

The entrance gate stands 89 feet tall, and it is topped by a superb dome and flanked by two round minarets. To keep the entrance to the mosque on the same axis as the square and, at the same time, to allow the *mihrab* to face Mecca, the architect, Abu'l Qasin, "rotated" the complex by 45 degrees. The complex includes several vestibules, the great domed prayer hall, and the Koranic school, all arranged around a colonnaded court.

In 1602, Shah Abbas had another mosque built, this time on the west side of Meidan Imam, dedicated to his father-in-law Sheikh Lotfollah, a famous Shiite theologian. More modest in size and with no minarets (as it was built for the exclusive use of the royal family), it rivals *Masjed e-Shah* in

137 center A view of Isfahan includes the two minarets of the Royal Mosque and, in the background, the mosque dedicated to the Shiite theologian Sheikh Lotfollah. Though the building is small, the dome, decorated with arabesques, rivals that of the Royal Mosque for beauty.

137 bottom The only surfaces inside the Royal Mosque not to be covered by majolica tiles are the pillars in the prayer hall. The immense complex contains several Koranic schools.

the refinement of its majolica tiles and structure. On the north side of the square stands the magnificent entrance to the Qeyssarieh, the city bazaar. In order to give a fresh boost to trade, Shah Abbas I invited Armenian merchants and conceded privileges to English and Dutch representatives of the East India Company.

The two mosques, the royal palace, and the bazaar form a harmonious whole as a result of the elegant portico that encloses them on the four sides of the square, the pivot around which Shah Abbas I's power revolved. Although he won himself a position of importance in the context of Persian art, sadly he is also remembered for his cruelty. In order to introduce the Shi'a doctrine and Farsi language into Persia, he had followers of the rival Sunni doctrine massacred. And he was so afraid of plots on his life that he had his eldest son killed and two younger ones blinded so that they could not reign after him.

Consequently, he was succeeded by his granson, Shah Safi I, who also passed into history for his systematic elimination of all claimants to the throne, including his mother. He was in turn succeeded by Shah Abbas II, a child of only ten, who, a virtual prisoner of advisors and tutors, marked the decline of the Safavid Dynasty and Isfahan. At the start of the eighteenth century, the city was put to the sword by the Afghans, and in 1736 the capital of the country was moved to Mashhad.

138 top left A detail from a floral decoration in polychrome faïence on a blue background.

138-139 A view capturing one of the two minarets in the Royal Mosque and the dome of the Sheikh Lotfollah Mosque. The majolica decorations of each were produced using the heft rangi (seven colors) technique.

139 top A richly decorated interior of Sheikh Lotfollah Mosque. The mosque was built between 1602 and 1619 for Shah Abbas I and dedicated to his brother-in-law. It was for the exclusive use of the royal family.

139 bottom Sheikh Lotfollah Mosque. The superb pishtaq (portal) has a vault decorated with geometric motifs that imitate stalactites. This type of decoration was derived from Umayyad and Abbasid architectural styles.

The Taj Mahal

INDIA

140 center Designed to represent the paradise of Allah, the gardens in the Taj Mahal combine Mogul, Persian, and Arab styles. The huge pool that runs down the center symbolizes the Kawthar, the celestial pool of abundance mentioned in the Koran.

140 bottom The Chowk-i-Jilo Khana is the building at the entrance to the site. Built from red sandstone, it is purely Islamic in style in the middle but flanked by Hindu-style temples. Calligraphic decorations on sandstone and white marble line the walls.

140-141 The traditional view of the Taj Mahal at dawn. It stands 246 feet tall on a platform 187 feet square and has a minaret at each corner that leans slightly outwards for reasons of perspective.

It took 20 years and 20,000 workers, both men and women, to construct the Taj Mahal, India's most famous building. A town called Mumtazabad, modern Taj Ganj, was founded a short distance away from the enormous construction site in order to accommodate the workers. A thousand elephants plied the route between Makrana mine in Rajasthan and Agra to transport the enormous blocks of white marble. The nearby city of Fatehpur Sikri supplied 114,000 cartloads of red sandstone, and its inhabitants were employed for years in firing the bricks that were used to support the structure of the building.

According to a Persian chronicler from the seventeenth century, the decorations in the Taj Mahal required the purchase, for outrageous sums, of lapis lazuli from Afghanistan, turquoise from Tibet, crystal from China, jasper from the Punjab, onyx from Persia, agate from the Yemen, coral from the Arabian Sea, and chalcedony from Europe. It was the task of the merchants in Jaipur to procure diamonds, both those in Gwalior magnetite and those in Baghdad cornelian.

All of this was paid for in cash by one man, the Mogul emperor Shah Jahan. He was an immensely rich man who bore the title "king of the world" and, between 1627 and 1666, ruled over a territory that stretched from Kandahar in the west to Assam in the east, and from the plateau of Pamir in the north to the plain of Deccan in the south. No Indian ruler had ever governed so vast an empire, but even for him the expense was not indifferent. Despite that, he did not tax his people even one rupee during the 20-year construction project: for him, the Taj Mahal was a "personal endeavor."

This extraordinary monument - defined by Rabindranath Tagore, the greatest Indian poet of the twentieth century, as "a teardrop on the face of eternity" - is probably the greatest and most tangible gift of love that any man has ever given to a woman. Shah Jahan had it built to hold the remains of his beloved Mumtaz Mahal so that her memory would be honored for ever.

Although Mumtaz Mahal was not his only wife (the emperor had a harem of 5,000 concubines), she was the only one he married for love rather than for reasons of state, as was the custom of the time. The daughter of a high Persian dignitary born Arjumand Bano Begum, in honor of her beauty she was nicknamed Mumtaz Mahal, meaning "chosen one of the palace," by her father-in-law Jehangir the day after her wedding on March 27, 1612. Until her death in 1631, she and Shah Jahan were inseparable. He never ceased to court her and cover her with fabulous jewels. She assisted him, with grace and intelligence, in matters of state and even accompanied him to war. They had 14 children, the last of which, born in a tent near a battlefield in the Deccan, cost her her life.

Legend has it that, with her last breath, Mumtaz Mahal made Shah Jahan promise to build the most beautiful tomb in the world for her. True or not, the emperor had no peace until the Taj Mahal was completed.

Once he returned to Agra, the emperor

purchased a plot of land on the banks of the river Yamuna that was to have two purposes. The first was to accommodate a tomb (*rauza*), the second was to become a place of pilgrimage (*urs*) during the ceremonies that marked the anniversary of the death of Mumtaz Mahal.

Over the centuries, many hypotheses have been made as to who was the architect of the building. There are those who believe that it was the work of the Venetian Pietro Veroneo who, according to documents of the period, was in the service of the emperor during the two decades of its construction. However, it seems highly improbable that an Italian, even a contemporary of Gian Lorenzo Bernini, could have conceived a monument that so perfectly weds Indian and Persian styles. Finally, experts are inclined to believe that

the design was the joint product of the best oriental minds of the time.

The complex of the Taj Mahal is entered through a red sandstone gateway 98 feet tall, historiated with verses from the Koran in elegant script. Two small temples in Hindu style stand at the sides. From here the view of the mausoleum opens. The magnificent construction stands 246 feet tall on a square platform that measures 187 feet long on each side. A minaret 154 feet tall stands at each of the four corners, built to lean slightly outwards for reasons of perspective and also so that, in the event of an earthquake, they would not collapse onto the central mausoleum. The enormous dome of the Taj Mahal is topped by a bronze pinnacle 30 feet high and was once covered entirely with gold. It was probably designed by Ismail Effendi, who was called

from Istanbul where he had built splendid buildings for the Ottoman sultans.

The Taj Mahal is a miracle of engineering. The perimetrical walls support a weight of nine tons per square foot, while the dome weighs over 13,000 tons alone. The marble-covered structure is supported by arches reinforced by bricks, wooden poles, and bands of iron driven into the platform. A system of wells protects the site from flooding by the river Yamuna, which was deviated from its natural course so that it flows past the building, providing it with a further dimension of beauty, particularly in the morning when the Taj Mahal is reflected in its waters. Apart from its technical excellence, the extraordinary art of the mosaicists, jewel cutters, and engravers who embroidered the surfaces with elegant floral decorations makes the mausoleum an unparalleled masterpiece. What strikes the observer most forcefully are the harmony and symmetry of the Taj Mahal and the complex as a whole.

The mausoleum is flanked by two identical red sandstone buildings, built in pure Mogul style and each topped by eight domes. The one on the left, which faces Mecca, is a mosque. The opposite one, called "*jawab*," meaning "the response," was designed as a welcoming area for pilgrims. In the center is the *char bagh*, the Persian style garden designed as a reflection of paradise. Filled with fountains, it too is perfectly symmetrical and characterized by the number four and its multiples. It is a square divided into four parts and originally had sixteen flowerbeds, each of which contained four hundred plants.

The only element that breaks the symmetry of the Taj Mahal is the tomb of Shah Jahan himself. Inside the mausoleum, in the huge room lined with niches and decorated with semi-precious stones, mosaics, and carvings in the marble, lie two false tombs: the one in the center is that of Mumtaz, and the one to the left that of the emperor. While he was still alive, the room was covered with carpets and adorned with candlesticks and precious objects. The asymmetrical layout is repeated in the actual tombs of the royal couple, situated in a chamber below the room. The reason for this imbalance in the mausoleum is that Shah Jahan lies here against his will. The emperor wanted another tomb to be built

for him in black marble, identical to the Taj Mahal, on the other side of the Yamuna, and for the two buildings to be connected by a solid gold bridge. However, upon Shah Jahan's death, his son Aurangzeb - who ascended the throne after having organized the assassination of half his family - did not consider the project important, and had his father placed beside his mother.

The era of Shah Jahan marked the apogee of the Mogul empire, which, from his death onwards, was pulled apart by internal struggles and went into inexorable decline. In addition, even the Taj Mahal was the target of continual plundering. The silver entrance gate was melted down and replaced by a copper one, and many of the precious stones were stolen. After their arrival in India, the British replaced the gold lining of the dome with a copper one.

The Anglo-Indian writer, Rudyard Kipling, called the Taj Mahal "the ivory gateway through which dreams pass," and many of his British compatriots considered it the eighth wonder of the world. Notwithstanding this, there were even those who proposed demolishing it and selling the parts to embellish English country houses.

With India's independence, the monument has undergone continuous restoration and has been returned to its original glory, but the toxic fumes put out by the nearly 200 foundries in Agra are seriously putting the white marble at risk.

143

143 top right Details of narcissi, tulips, and roses made from marble and precious and semi-precious stones. The gems were imported from all over Asia and Europe and cost enormous sums.

143 bottom right A view of the Taj Mahal from the river Jamuna. While it was being built, Shah Jahan had the river deviated so it would flow past the complex. His intention was that he would be buried in an identical building made from black marble on the other side of the river, but his successor, his son Aurangzeb, cancelled the project for economic reasons.

142-143 A side view of the Taj Mahal. Each side has large arched recesses called pishtaq *with façades decorated with floral motifs and verses from the Koran glorifying the Muslim paradise.*

143 bottom left The interior of the mausoleum with the lacework marble enclosure around the two empty tombs of the emperor Shah Jahan and his beloved wife Mumtaz Mahal. The rulers' actual tombs lie in a crypt below the perimeter of the balustrade.

The Forbidden City
CHINA

144

The authorities of the People's Republic of China renamed it Gu Gong (Palace Museum), but for the rest of China the most grandiose complex of buildings – covering nearly eight million square feet and containing 9,999 rooms in the center of Beijing – in this enormous country is and always will be Zijin Cheng, the Forbidden City.

Death was the penalty for anyone who, without permission, dared to pass through the gates of the sumptuous residence that was home to the 24 emperors of the Ming and Qing dynasties. For these rulers, the Forbidden City was a gilded prison because,

owing to their status as "sons of heaven," they were not allowed to mingle with ordinary mortals. How it was possible to govern such a vast empire from that padded world is a question that does not find a ready response. Probably all the complicated ceremonies, luxuries, and vices in which the rulers spent their days provided a means for distracting their attention away from the power struggles among the army of eunuchs, emissaries, ambassadors, and ministers who governed the Middle Kingdom.

In 1407, at the start of the fifth year of his reign, Yong Le, third emperor of the Ming Dynasty, began construction of the Forbidden

City. To complete it, 14 years and one million workers were required. Of these, 100,000 were the best craftsmen in the empire. The stone used in the platforms of the pavilions and the bas-reliefs was quarried at Fangshan just outside Beijing. To aid in its transportation, wells were dug every 160 feet beside the road so that, during freezing conditions in winter, water could be flung onto the surface to form ice, thus allowing the blocks of stone to slide more easily. The much-appreciated camphor wood used in the columns came from the southern provinces of Yunnan and Sichuan. To fire the tiles of yellow majolica (the imperial color), kilns were built a short

distance from the building site. The lime used to cover the perimeter walls – smooth, 28 feet thick at the base, and 22 feet thick at the top – was mixed with red pigments, sticky rice, and egg whites to make it more solid. In the pavilions, bricks were used for the flooring so that the sound of footsteps was more pleasing. With the exception of the platforms and tiles, the rest of the buildings were made from wood, and this of course has meant that many of them have been lost in fires so that a large percentage of those seen today date from the eighteenth and nineteenth centuries.

The Forbidden City is divided into two parts, one designed for the functions of government and the other residential. The complex lies north-south with the imperial buildings, bearing names associated with Confucian philosophy, all facing south along the axis. Perfectly symmetrical along the sides are the service buildings where the concubines, domestic servants, and approximately 200,000 eunuchs lived.

The main entrance to the Forbidden City, the Wumen (South Gate), is 117 feet tall. It is topped by five pavilions and has five archways. The center one was for regular use only by the emperor, by his wife on their wedding day, and by students on the day they received their diploma after passing their exams at Confucian school. The central pavilion above the gate was where the emperor dictated the laws which were then taken by emissaries to the Ministry of Rites, where a copy was made for each province in the empire.

Having crossed this monumental threshold, one enters a large court where the Golden Waters run. This is a river crossed by five bridges corresponding to the number of virtues in Confucianism. From the Taihemen (Gate of Supreme Harmony guarded by two bronze lions) one enters a court so large it can hold 100,000 people, the Taihedian (Pavilion of Supreme Harmony). This is the most impressive building in the entire city and, at 123 feet tall, was the highest in Beijing during the Ming and Qing dynasties. A symbol of imperial power, the main room, adorned with 72 columns decorated with motifs of dragons and clouds, was where state ceremonies were held and where the sovereign received homage on his birthday.

144-145 Covering a surface area of 183 acres, the Forbidden City was the residence of 24 emperors of the Ming and Qing dynasties. The 9,999 rooms were built between 1407 and 1421 by a million laborers. It is the largest residential complex in the world.

145 center left The large court where one arrives after entering through the Wumen (the main entrance) is crossed by the Golden Waters River. Its five bridges symbolize the virtues of Confucianism.

145 center right The bronze statues of a crane and a tortoise – symbols of longevity – stand on either side of the Pavilion of Supreme Harmony. A lid on the shell of the tortoise covered a hollow where incense was once burned.

145 bottom right The main room in the Pavilion of Supreme Harmony is the largest in the palace and the emblem of imperial power. It was used as the setting for state ceremonials.

144 top left According to Chinese tradition, the tops of many pavilions are decorated with wenshou (animal-like motifs). At the top of the roof of the Pavilion of Supreme Harmony there is a deity riding a phoenix, followed by other mythological animals.

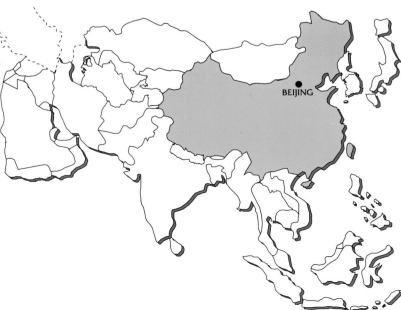

BEIJING

The side rooms were used for audiences and storing documents. One of these rooms, the Wenyuange (Pavilion of Literary Inspiration) was where the Sikuquanshu was held; with 36 volumes, this is oldest and largest encyclopedia in the world. In front of the Taihedian stand two enormous bronze vases, the only ones remaining from all of those that lined the perimeter of the building; they were filled with water to be used in the event of a fire. Another fire-prevention measure was represented by the bronze statues of five-taloned dragons inside, each weighing four and a half tons, which were supposed to encourage rain.

The Baohedian (Pavilion of the Conservation of Harmony) was the second most important building in the complex. Built in 1420 and rebuilt in 1625 and 1765, it combines elegant architecture with a surprisingly sophisticated hydraulic engineering system. A complicated system of drainage channels ensured that, on rainy days, water would gush from the mouth of each of the 1,412 marble dragons' heads on

the perimeter columns. The pavilion was used to hold court banquets.

Access to the residential section was marked by a horizontal marble stele 54 feet long, decorated with dragons playing with a pearl, an imperial symbol seen throughout the Forbidden City. The first residential

buildings are the Qianqinggong (Palace of Heavenly Harmony) and the Kunninggong (Palace of Terrestrial Tranquillity). In the first, built in 1420 as a private apartment for the emperor but later turned into a reception room, there are four enormous mirrors, which were very rare and precious during that period. It was in this building, in 1722 and 1785, that the emperor offered the Banquet of the Thousand Ancients to which people over 60 years of age were invited from all the provinces in the empire.

In the Kunninggong – the only example of Manchu architecture in the Forbidden City – it was customary for the emperor to spend his wedding night. The wedding chamber has walls painted red and decorated with the ideogram of double happiness. The *kang* (brick beds with a built-in heating system) are still in place. Next to the chamber is the room in which, each day, sacrifices to the gods were made.

Further on, one comes to the

146 top The entrance steps to the Baohedian (Pavilion of the Conservation of Harmony) are decorated

with a marble stela 52 feet long and ten feet wide. It weighs over 275 tons and is decorated with motifs of dragons and clouds.

146 center left Qianqingmen (the Gate of Heavenly Harmony) is the main entrance to the inner palace. During the Qing

Dynasty, the emperor, seated on a throne at the center of the gateway, would hear his advisors and render his decisions.

146 center right Qianqinggong (the Palace of Heavenly Harmony) was built in 1420 as a private apartment for the emperor but was later turned into a reception room. The imperial throne stands in the center of the room, surrounded by large mirrors and fine decorations.

146 bottom A detail of the stairway to the throne in the Palace of Heavenly Harmony. Note the superb carved balustrades and the incense burners that perfumed the emperor's rooms.

147 Two solid bronze lions guard the Gate of Heavenly Harmony, each of which has a decorated sphere under one paw to symbolize the power of the emperor and the unity of the lands he ruled.

148 bottom right and 149 right In addition to 20 or so buildings, the Imperial Garden was decorated with many lovely bronze sculptures featuring fantastic creatures or exotic animals, like the lion and elephant in this photograph.

149 left The Pavilion of Rain and Flowers in the Yuhuayuan (Imperial Garden) was built in 1417 during the Ming Dynasty. The imperial family's private garden covers an area of three acres.

148-149 Built during the Ming Dynasty and then rebuilt by the Qing emperor, Yong Zheng, the Yangxingdian (the Palace of Spiritual Nourishment) was an important building in the Forbidden City as it was here that the heirs to the imperial throne learned the duties of government.

148 bottom left One of the entrances to the Imperial Garden where the Duixiushan (the Hill of the Collection of Beauty) was built. This was a small man-made hill from where it was possible to view the entire complex.

Yuhuayuan (Imperial Garden). It covers 129,000 square feet and is filled with attractive nooks and delicate buildings for the imperial family's leisure. Standing in front of the main pavilion is a pine tree that is thought to be 400 years old. It is a symbol of the harmony between the emperor and empress.

Of the other buildings in the residential section, the Yangxingdian (Palace of Spiritual Nourishment) stands out for its historical significance. This contained the private apartments of the emperor and it was here that on February 12, 1912 Emperor Pu Yi abdicated following the coup d'état by Sun Yat Sen, but was given permission to live in the Forbidden City until 1924.

A short distance away, the Xiliugong (the Six Western Palaces) was where the concubines lived, and they are still furnished with the original items from the late Qing Dynasty. The adjacent Ningshougong (Pavilion of Tranquil Longevity) was built in 1689 as a scaled

down replica of the Forbidden City and holds a collection of 100,000 paintings. The Leshoutang (Palace of Joyful Longevity) contains a one-ton jade sculpture and an extraordinary mat measuring seven feet one inch by four feet seven inches that is woven from very thin strips of ivory. Among the many treasures on display, there are Ming jewels and furniture, Tibetan reliquaries, and silk paintings.

Many of the objects that belonged to the emperors were stolen by Sun Yat Sen's army and now form the nucleus of the National Museum of Taipei in Taiwan. In an attempt to replace them after the Maoist revolution, the administrators of the Forbidden City gathered precious objects from all over China. Above the main entrance to the complex they placed a giant picture of Mao Zedong; he smiles at the people and faces the symbol of modern Chinese power, Tiananmen Square.

The Historic Monuments of Ancient Kyoto

JAPAN

ISLAND OF HONSHU, PREFECTURE OF KYOTO
REGISTRATION: 1994
CRITERIA: C (II) (IV)

150 top Constructed before the capital was moved to Kyoto in A.D. 794, Kamowake-ikzuchi (Kamigamo Temple) was built to worship the guardian spirit of the powerful Kamo family.

150 bottom The large statue of the Buddha Amithaba in the Pavilion of the Phoenix in Byodoin Temple is surrounded by 52 wooden sculptures of bodhisattva playing instruments and dancing.

Around the year 1600, the powerful *shogun* family, the Tokugawa, began to transfer political power from Kyoto to Edo, though Kyoto (the name means "capital city") remained the seat of imperial power until 1868 when Emperor Meiji moved the Dajokan (Great Council of government administration) to Edo; this city then took the name of Tokyo (western capital).

The city of Kyoto, which lost its role as the political and economic center of Japan, had been founded eleven centuries earlier as a result of the subtle diplomatic shifts that took place between the great empires of the East. Piqued by the beauty of the capital city, Chang'an (present-day Xi'an), of his Chinese rival, the Japanese emperor, Kanmu, decided to move his court from Nagaokakyo to a new city that he decided to build in the region of Yamasiro. Thus, in A.D. 794, Heiankyo, or more simply, Kyoto, was established along three sides of the mountains in the south of the island of Honshu.

The layout of the city over nine square miles was an exact imitation of the Chinese capital, with a grid of streets that divided the city into more than 1,200 districts of identical size. Closed off by an embankment that was supposed to offer the city protection, its great southward-facing Rashomon gateway opened onto the main street, the Suzaku. The imperial palace stood at the far end of this street. The complex did not just contain the emperor's residence, but was also the seat of the government and related buildings. The original plans for Kyoto had included space for two markets, one for the craftsmen and the other for the merchants. Noble families were conceded plots of land in accordance with their rank. This first attempt at urban planning formed the basis of the city for the entire Heian period, until the end of the twelfth century, and it is still visible in the pattern of the streets, even though Kyoto suffered fires and battles that destroyed it almost completely.

The city still has elements dating from its foundation such as Shimogamo Temple, dedicated to the city's patron deities. It is said that the site of the city had been discovered by two gods, Kamo taketsu-no-mikoto and Tamayori-hime, who were worshipped in the 53 buildings that constitute the temple. Dating from even

150-151 Built as a civil building at the end of the tenth century, Byodoin Temple was transformed into a sanctuary in 1052. It centers on the Ho-oh-do (Pavilion of the Phoenix), which is a reproduction of the heavenly palace of Amithaba in the Pure Land.

earlier than the Heian era is Kamigamo Temple. This temple was built in an zone of gardens and includes an area located between the first and second *torii* (the characteristic doors in Japanese temples) where thoroughbred horses to be used in sacred ceremonies were raised.

The most important legacies of the Heian period are the Byodoin and Daigoji temples. The first was built on the west bank of the river Uji and was the residence of a noble who, in 998, donated it to the functionary Fujiwara-no-Michinaga. After the latter's death in 1052, his son wished to turn it into a place of worship in memory of his father. The beautiful Ho-oh-do (Phoenix Room) features a reproduction of the heavenly palace of Amithaba in the Pure Land; its side corridors have roofs adorned with two phoenixes whose wings are spread ready for flight. Inside, the large statue of the Buddha Amithaba is surrounded by 52 images of *bodhisattva* dancing and playing musical instruments. Partially reconstructed after the sixteenth century, Daigoji Temple boasts a five-story pagoda that was completed in 952 and is the oldest monument in Kyoto to have survived intact.

151 top right Comprising more than 100 pavilions, Daigoji Temple is dominated by a five-story pagoda built in 952 by Emperor Murakami, which is the oldest monument in the city. Most of the other buildings date from the sixteenth century.

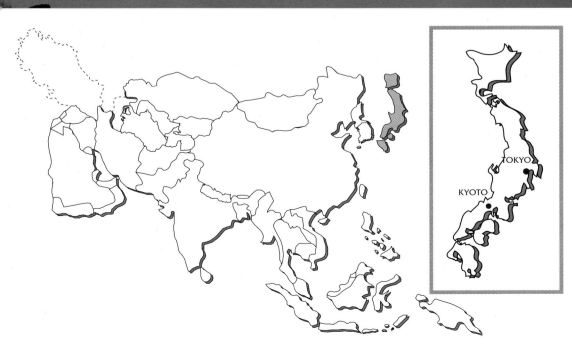

151 bottom right A detail of the elaborate carvings on the roof of the pagoda in Daigoji Temple. During the Onin War in the fifteenth century, the other buildings of the temple were destroyed in two fires.

The Toji (Temple of the East) also dates from the foundation of the city and was built in 796 to bring down divine protection on the city. Kiyomizu Temple was built two years later on the initiative of an influential general on the spot where the hermitage of the ascetic Enchin had stood. Hieizan Enryakuji Temple was founded in 788 by the Buddhist monk Saicho, who

gathered a religious community around him. Lastly, Emperor Uda ordered the construction of Ninnaji Temple, later known as Omuro Palace, in 888. The people placed in charge of the building were monks from the imperial family, and this tradition lasted until the Meiji Dynasty. However, all these buildings have suffered serious damage over the centuries, and most of them are the result of wide-ranging rebuilding.

The Heian period also saw the flourishing of extraordinary cultural centers in Kyoto that laid down the foundations for Japanese poetry, literature, and religion. In

905, the emperor ordered Ki-no-Tsurayuki to compile the *Kokin-waka-shu*, a collection of classical poems that indicated the way for works like *The Tales of Genji*, *The Happy Prince* (the first novel in history), and *The Pillow Book*. This was an intimate diary in which Shei Shonagon, a female courtier, described her amorous encounters. Two Buddhist cults, the Tendai and the Shingon, developed respectively in the Enryakuji and Toji temples.

The eras of the Kamakura (1185-1333), Muromachi (1333-1573), and Momoyana (1573-1598) dynasties were times of civil wars and cultural upheaval. The Zen, Jodo, Jodo Shin, and Nichiren schools of Buddhism made their first appearance. Kozanji Temple was built during the Kamakura period on the mountainside by the monk Myoe in a place suited to contemplation. Saihoji Temple (Temple of the Mosses) was built for the 120 species of moss that grew on its walls and roof. The temple also included Zen gardens in which rocks and sand were set out in harmonious balance. In 1339, Tenryuji Temple was built by the Zen master Muso Kokushi for Kyoto's first *shogun*, Ashikaga Takauji. The building was supposed to honor the memory of Emperor Godaigo and was founded on the site of a former imperial residence. Its garden lay behind the Hojo, one of the buildings in the complex, and was designed with pools of water surrounded by flowerbeds, integrating aristocratic traditions with Zen style, in which the forms and colors of the garden alter with the seasons.

The Muromachi period saw the

152 top left Founded in 796, the Toji (Temple of the East) was built to supplicate the gods to protect the new capital. At the end of the Heian period (twelfth century), the Buddhist Shingon cult flourished.

152 bottom left According to legend, in 778 the monk Enchin built a small chapel where, 20 years later, Kiyomizu Temple would later stand. Shogun Iemitsu Tokugawa rebuilt many of the buildings standing today during the period 1631-1633.

152 top center A recurrent motif in oriental figurative art, this dragon is part of the Todoroki Torii, one of the entrances to Kiyomizu Temple. Lined with copper, the sculpture is also a fountain and water jets from the creature's mouth.

152 top right In addition to its main pavilion and an elegant three-story pagoda, Kiyomizu Temple comprises beautiful gardens.

152-153 Completed in 1603 and renovated in 1626, Nijo Castle consists of two buildings, Honmaru and Ninomaru, the rooms of which are decorated with paintings and carved wood panels.

construction of Rokuonji Temple with a golden pagoda in 1397, the Jishoji Temple with a silver pavilion that contains the statue of the venerable Avalokiteshwar, and Ryoanji Temple with a rock garden in 1450. This was the period in which Kyoto developed arts like Noh theater, tea ceremonies, and *ikebana*, the art of flower arrangement developed by Ikenobo Senkei in 1462 to adorn the home of a noble family.

The Onin War (1467-1477) resulted in destruction for much of the city, and the following century was marked by

same brutal expedient as his predecessors: the physical elimination of all rival claimants. In the few short years of his rule, Hideyoshi began the transfer of the temples that had survived the destruction to the Teramachi District of the city. This project was continued by Iesayu, who also completed construction of the massive Nijo Castle. Completed in 1603, the castle was where most of the important events until 1867 took place, when the *shogun* Tokugawa Yoshinobu restored administrative power to the imperial family. Nijo Castle has two sections, the

to Tokyo, the Edo period (from 1600 to 1868) was marked by peace and stability, and Kyoto flourished once more as a cultural and commercial center. The *shogun* Tokugawa Iemitsu rebuilt many buildings, including Kiyomizu Temple between 1631 and 1633. In 1644, he built Japan's largest pagoda in Toji Temple; it has five stories and stands 187 feet high.

Fortunately spared from the bombing raids of World War II, Kyoto remained an island in twentieth-century Japan. To celebrate its 12 centuries of existence in 1994, large festivals in seventeenth-

internecine struggles from which the Momoyama clan emerged victorious. In 1573, Oda Nobunaga took power, followed by Toyotomi Hideyoshi and Tokugawa Ieyasu. The last of the three succeeded in restoring stability using the

Honmaru (main building) and the magnificent Ninomaru Palace. Decorated in Momoyama style, both buildings feature sophisticated architecture and superb ornamentation.

Despite the transfer of political power

century costume and events that commemorated the history of the city were organized. Entering one of the tea rooms marked by the slow rhythm of tradition, one gets the feeling that Tokyo never became the country's capital.

The Medina in Fez

MOROCCO

FEZ
REGISTRATION: 1981
CRITERIA: C (II) (V)

In 1921, the French General Lyautey issued a circular that prohibited non-Muslims entry to mosques or places of Islamic study in Morocco. The document summarized directives that had been part of the institutional treaty of the French protectorate, signed on March 30, 1912. Although visitors are not allowed to enter sacred buildings to admire the beauty of their decorations, they may at least enjoy the appeal of the Medina in Fez, with its intricate labyrinth of roughly 1,000 alleys, where the colors, smell, and sounds remind one of the age in which the city was the capital of the Moroccan empire.

At the eastern end of the fertile Saïss plain, ringed to the south by the foothills of the Atlas mountains, Fez was founded in 789 by Moulay Idris I, a sultan who was able to boast direct lineage from the Prophet Mohammed. The name of the city comes from the word *fas*, the Arabic word for the gold and silver hoe given to him to mark the place where the city would stand. It was his son, Idris II, who made Fez the capital of the Idrisid dynasty in 809. A decade or so later, the sultan accepted 8,000 Muslim families into the city that had fled from the Umayyad sultanate in Cordoba; they settled on the right bank of the Oued Fez, the seasonal river that crosses the valley. In 825, Jews and Berbers arriving from Kairouan in modern Tunisia took their turn and occupied the left bank of the river.

At the time, the two settlements, each enclosed by high walls, led separate lives. The Cordovans built the Mosque of Al-Andalus on their bank, in the Hispanic Islamic architectural style, while the foundation of the Mosque of Al-Qarawiyin

on the other bank was, surprisingly, inspired by a woman, Fatima, the daughter of a trader from Kairouan. A *madrasa* (Koranic school) – today considered to have been the first university in the West – was soon annexed to the mosque of Al-Qarawiyin. Over the following one hundred years, both communities prospered and other mosques, public baths, markets, and *fonduk* (caravanserai) were built.

In 1055, Fez fell under the rule of the Almoravids who moved the capital to Marrakech, but they were overthrown a century later by the Almohads. In trying to win the goodwill of the people, the Almohad sultans demolished the walls of the two separate communities to build a new one, fortified by *birj* (defensive towers), around both of them.

The advent of the Almohads marked the start of the commercial success of the city and its development as a religious and cultural center. They enlarged Al-Qarawiyin Mosque so that it could hold 20,000 worshippers and built a huge court surrounded by columns similar to the Alhambra in Granada. They also decorated the mosque by covering it with white and blue *zellij* (majolica tiles). Under the leadership of Sultan Youssef Ben Tachfine, the city was also provided with an elaborate water system so that, by

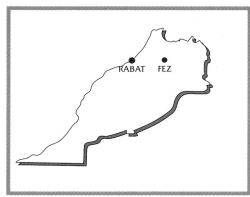

154-155 Fez el Bali, the original nucleus of the city, was founded in 789 by Sultan Moulay Idris I at the eastern end of Saïss plain. Seen from above, Fez medina is striking for its uniform and compact layout.

154 top The court used for ablutions in al-Qarawiyin mosque. Founded in 859 by Fatima ibn Muhammad from Kairouan, it was enlarged in 956 and again in 1135. It is the country's largest mosque and is still an important centre of Islamic studies.

154 bottom The roofs of al-Qarawiyin covered with green majolica tiles. This enormous religious complex includes a library that contains over 30,000 ancient volumes.

155 top The birj (defensive towers) of Fez' walls date from the twelfth century. They were built by the Almohad sultans to replace the ninth-century fortifications. Originally the city was divided in two settlements, one inhabited by the Jews who fled from Cordoba, and the other by the Berbers from Kairouan.

155 center right One of the large entrances to the Medina that indicate the importance of the city throughout the centuries and the skill of the Moslem architects during the late Middle Ages.

155 bottom left The entrance to al-Andalus mosque, built in the ninth century. The architecture and decorations are typical of the Moorish style in Spain.

the end of the twelfth century, the mosques, *madrasa*, and most of the houses had running water.

In 1250, the Marinid dynasty took power and moved the capital back to Fez, but the walls were by then too restricting to accommodate the civilians and troops that arrived with the new rulers. This led to the construction of Fez el Jedid, "New Fez," which in turn led the original city (what is now the Medina) to be known as Fez el Bali, "Old Fez."

With the rise to power of a new dynasty at the start of the sixteenth century, the Sa'adi, Fez's continuing development

suffered a pause until 1666 when it entered a second period of prosperity under Sultan Moulay Abdullah. The traders in the Medina formed corporations controlled by a *mohtasseb*, and the *fonduk* and the markets were divided into sections based on the goods they sold, a system that is still in use in what has become the largest market in North Africa, Medina del Maghreb.

Bab Bou Jeloud is the gate decorated with majolica tiles – green ones in tribute to Islam and blue ones that celebrate the color of the city – that leads into Fez el Bali and signals the start of the Talaa Kebira (the Great Street), lined by Almohad

buildings. The alleys that head off from this street lead to the various souks, where shops of potters, fabric sellers, cobblers, spice sellers, and most typical of all, the tanneries and leather dyers can be found.

Although the arrival of the French in Morocco brought the definitive transfer of the capital to Rabat, they insisted on preserving the historical importance of Fez as a spiritual and intellectual center. They forbade the construction of new buildings in the Medina and began a program of restoration still active today in which the crafts and trading traditions for which the city is famous are safeguarded.

156 The elegant stone and wood decorations in a palace built during the Merinid era in the heart of the Medina in Fez el Bali.

157 top left The Fonduk en-Nejjarin ('Palace of the Carpenters') built during the Merinid dynasty. It was one of the caravanerais where traveling merchants stayed.

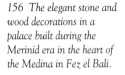

157 top right One of the souks in the alleys next to Talaa Kebira, the main street in the largest medina in the Maghreb. In 1666, the merchants in the Medina formed regulated guilds.

157 bottom left A detail of the Bab Bou Jeloud. Decorated with green (the color of Islam) and blue (the color of the city) majolica tiles, it leads into the madrasa of the same name and Talaa Kebira.

157 bottom right Fez is famous throughout the world for its tanneries. The coloring vats usually stand on the terraced roofs of the hide-treatment workshops.

The Ancient City of Ghadames
LIBYA

AL-HAMADAH AL-HAMRA
REGISTRATION: 1986
CRITERIA: C (V)

A Tuareg legend says that the name Ghadames comes from Arabic and that it refers to the misadventure that occurred when a caravan accidentally left some of its food supplies behind. When it was time to prepare the meal the next day, someone remembered

back to earliest civilizations. The first settlements in the area were formed roughly 10,000 years ago as the Paleolithic age gave way to the Neolithic, when the Sahara was still a fertile plain. The Ain al-Faras spring was the source of a large oasis that measured about 185 acres and which became a stopping-place on the caravan route that linked the Sudan with the Mediterranean. Its importance grew from 19 B.C. on when the Romans founded the city of Cidamus there, which remained under their control for several centuries. A fairly large garrison was stationed in the oasis during the third century, and, in the fourth and fifth, during the Byzantine empire, a bishopric was founded.

The Arab conquest led by Sidi Uqba in 667 during their sweep across North Africa marked the beginning of Ghadames' greatest period. Just a few decades later, Ghadames became a major link in the Arab world, which soon extended as far as the Atlantic. An important trading town from the eighth century on, Ghadames was laid out around a central square and the large Jami' al-Atiq and Yunus mosques, two of the oldest in Libya. Both are transversal

158 left The narrow streets in Ghadames oasis. The urban center is built around a majlis (square) where the ancient Jami al-Atiq and Yunus mosques stand.

having left the provisions in the place where "yesterday's lunch" (*ghada ams* in Arabic) had been eaten.

In fact, the history of the magnificent oasis in the highlands of al-Hamadah al-Hamra – where the borders of Libya, Algeria, and Tunisia meet – dates right

158 right Many of the buildings in Ghadames are whitened with lime and have external walls with sharp triangular points. The significance of these architectural details is still unknown.

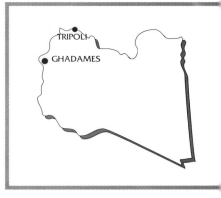

in plan, with, respectively, two and three aisles parallel to the *qibla*.

The most notable aspect of Ghadames, known as the Pearl of the Desert, is its layout and the original, harmonious architecture of the city. Its isolation at the northern edge of the great desert encouraged unique city-planning solutions; to protect the city from the torrid summer heat and winter cold, the narrow, winding streets of the oasis were covered with buildings, thereby transforming the city into a single tangle of private buildings and common areas.

158-159 A view of Ghadames. The ancient artesian spring known as Ain al-Faras ('Spring of the Mare') makes the existence of the 75 hectare oasis and its roughly 25,000 palms possible.

159 top The ajard (entrance) to a typical house in the oasis. Next to it on the ground floor is the tali ni ajard (storeroom) and another service room.

Built from mud, clay, and palm trunks, the houses in Ghadames had three floors, each with its own function: near the entrance on the ground floor, there were two service rooms; the *tamanat* on the first floor, illuminated by a large skylight, was house's main living space, and this was surrounded by other rooms connected to it by various flights of steps; the upper floor, reached from the *tamanat*, consisted of terraces that were used for the kitchen and the women's area.

The traditional houses in Ghadames have survived until the modern era though the oasis has suffered various tribulations over the past century and a half. In 1860, once the prosperity of the trans-Sahara trade routes came to an end, Ghadames passed under the dominion of Tripoli. Later, during Italy's rule over Libya, it offered fierce resistance to the Europeans, but fell in 1924, ten years after it had first been besieged. In 1940, it came under French control and experienced its

most difficult years. Heavily damaged during World War II, it was contested until 1951 when Tunisia accepted its cession to Libya.

During the 1950s, it was provided with electricity but its fate was already decided by the fact that there was no longer enough water to go around. Women carried water from the wells to the mosque and were obliged to remove used water. Ghadames' final abandonment by its inhabitants began in 1982.

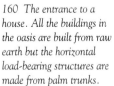

160 The entrance to a house. All the buildings in the oasis are built from raw earth but the horizontal load-bearing structures are made from palm trunks.

161 top The streets in Ghadames closely connect with the houses. Together the two elements form a unique (internal) urban fabric that has developed over the centuries to improve living conditions in the Saharan climate.

161 center left The streets in the oasis are between 8 and 10 feet in width and run beneath decorative arches or living spaces.

161 center right The main living area in Ghadames' houses is the tamanat. It is 13-16 feet high, fairly cubic in shape, and is surrounded by rooms on different levels connected by stairways.

161 bottom Ajurer (kitchens) in Ghadames are on the top floor of the house, the one reserved for women. They face onto a terrace that give access to the nearby houses.

Islamic Cairo

EGYPT

CAIRO GOVERNORATE
REGISTRATION: 1979
CRITERIA: C (I) (V) (IV)

The people of Cairo claim that Khan al-Khalili, the city's largest bazaar, built in 1392, played a pivotal role in the discovery of America. They say that Christopher Columbus' caravels set sail to open a new trade route in order to break the monopoly that Cairo, then governed by the Mameluks, held on the spice markets throughout the known world.

This may be an exaggeration, but ever since it was founded, the city's importance has reached beyond the boundaries of Egypt and even of the African continent. Today, with its immense urban area and a population of 15 million, al-Qahirah, the city's name in Arabic, meaning "victorious," is Africa's largest metropolis. It is so important that the Egyptians themselves refer to it simply as *Masr*, or "Egypt."

Contrary to what one might think, given that the Egyptian civilization dates from the dawn of known history, Cairo is a relatively young city, officially founded in only A.D. 969. Before then, three towns stood on the site of al-Qahirah along the banks of the Nile. Clustered in an area of four square miles, they are now part of the Islamic heart of Cairo. The first, al-Fustat, was little more than a military encampment established in 641 by Amr, the first Arab to govern Egypt.

The little city flourished under the Umayyad caliphs until 750 when it was conquered by the Abbasids, who founded al-Qatai on the other bank of the Nile. In 870, the Abbasid caliph ibn Tulun rebelled against Baghdad's power and proclaimed himself the king of Egypt, founding the Tulunid dynasty and, with it, the new city of al-Qata'i. In 879, he ordered a mosque built in his honor, which is the largest and oldest building of its kind in Egypt. It has a simple plan, with a fountain for ablutions that forms the heart of the entire complex. It has survived to the modern day virtually unaltered, despite the addition of a splendid *mihrab* decorated with mosaics from the Mameluk era, and the restoration work done by the Ottomans. The prayer room covers five naves along the side facing Mecca, and there are two naves on the opposite side. It has sycamore panels carved with writings from the Koran.

A little more than thirty years later, the Abbasids avenged the insurrection of ibn

Tulun by destroying the royal palace and the legendary gardens of al-Qata'i and re-establishing al-Fustat as the seat of power. Nevertheless, Abbasid Egypt was in chaos by this time, while a new dynasty, the Fatimids, had risen to power in what is now Tunisia. Legitimated by the fact that they were the direct descendents of Fatima, the daughter of the Prophet Muhammad, the Fatimids headed east to conquer the Arab world and spread the true doctrine, the Shi'a. The Fatimids appointed Gawhar, a former slave from Sicily who had become their most courageous general, to lead the expedition to conquer al-Fustat.

The first monument built by Gawhar honored the Shi'ite doctrine. The mosque of al-Azhar, dedicated to Muhammad's daughter Fatima Az-Zahra', was inaugurated in 972. An Islamic school was annexed to it shortly after, and the first lesson was held in 975, making al-Azhar one of the oldest universities in the world. At approximately the same time, following the decline of Baghdad and the Spanish *reconquista* of Cordoba, the universities in both these

162 top Decorative tiles on the outer walls of Ahmed ibn-Tulun Mosque, built in 879 by the Abbasid caliph of the same name.

162-163 Al-Azhar Mosque. Dedicated to Fatima, the daughter of the Prophet, it was built in 972 by the Shi'ite sovereign, Gawhar, and soon included a Koranic school that was to become one of the most important universities in the Islamic world.

163 top right The porticoed court of ibn-Tulun mosque with, in the center, a large building for devotees to perform their ablutions. It is the oldest building of its kind in Egypt.

163 top center The portico in Taybesir madrasa. Situated in the university complex of al-Azhar Mosque, it was built in 1309 and is surrounded by the library building.

163 bottom center The interior of al-Azhar Mosque. The architectural features of the complex have been repeatedly altered over the centuries and thus reflect the influence of all the dynasties that governed Cairo.

CAIRO

164 top left The domes of Mohammad Ali Mosque, designed by Yousef Bushnaq and built between 1830 and 1857 in Ottoman style by Mohammad Ali Pasha, the governor of Egypt.

164 top right The interior of Mohammad Ali Mosque, commonly called the 'alabaster mosque' because of its extensive use of the material, excavated in Beni Suef, in the prayer hall.

164-165 The Citadel is the superb fortified complex built by Saladin between 1176 and 1183 to protect the city from the Crusaders. Since then, the fort has never been without a military garrison. The walls are 32 feet high and 9 feet thick.

165 top Built by Caliph el-Aziz and his son, el-Hakim, between 990 and 1013, el-Hakim Mosque is the second largest Fatimid mosque in Cairo. It has been used as a confinement for Crusader prisoners, as stores for Napoleonic troops and as a school during the presidency of Gamal Nasser.

cities were closed, and as a result men of learning from the entire Muslim world flocked to Cairo. By the end of the eleventh century, 10,000 students had attended al-Azhar, and since then it has never lost its role as a beacon of Islamic culture. Over the centuries, it has also become the driving force behind all of Egypt's political and social changes.

From an architectural standpoint, the modern-day al-Azhar, located in the heart of Islamic Cairo, is a superb palimpsest of all the cultural styles and influences that have passed through Egypt. Five minarets dotted with small balconies and elegant bas-reliefs tower over it, and it has six entrances. The main one, Bab el-Muzayini, or Barber's Gate (because the students had to shaved here before they could attend the university), dates from the eighteenth century. From here, a small courtyard leads to the Aqbaughawiya Madrasah, built in 1340 and now used as a library. Bab el-Qaitbay, on the other hand, leads to the largest courtyard, which is lined with patios dating from various periods. The patios reflect the names and decorations of the areas in the Islamic world from which the students and teachers came.

The Mosque of al-Hakim, built between 990 and 1013, also dates from the Fatimid era. Despite renovation work done during the Mameluk period, it still has its original marble walls and exquisite stuccowork. It is also of great historic significance because it was commissioned by the founder of the Druse sect. The mosque of al-Aqmar (the Grey Mosque) is an elegant stone building whose entryways feature stalactite decorations. This mosque as well as some of the loveliest gates to the city, such as Bab

el-Nasr and Bab Zuwaylah, were built at the end of the eleventh century.

Nevertheless, Fatimid domination was waning by this time. At the beginning of the twelfth century, Egypt had become the battleground for the conflict between the Crusaders and the Seljuks, the new Islamic power that had come down from the steppes of Central Asia. Led by Nureddin, in 1168 the Seljuks conquered Cairo. The new ruler died the next year and the leadership of the city was taken over by a young commanders, who was destined to become one of the most important figures in medieval history: Salah-ad-Din, better known as the cruel Saladin.

Despite the reputation attributed to him by the Christians, as a ruler Saladin promoted coexistence between the peoples of Cairo, and he embellished the city with new architecture. His Citadel, whose only "flaw" is that part of it was built with stone blocks taken from the pyramids, is one of Cairo's treasures. Its walls are 33 feet high and ten feet thick, and the buildings inside demonstrate Saladin's military genius. They include a cistern that is 285 feet deep and could guarantee an almost unlimited reserve of water in case of siege. The complex was subsequently expanded to add a royal palace and stables, which could house 4,800 horses.

In 1182, Saladin left to defend Palestine and Syria, but he never returned to Cairo. Most of the members of his army and his court dignitaries were former slaves or prisoners of war who had converted to Islam. As a result, they won the trust of the Seljuks and became very influential in the government. They were referred to as Mameluks and, following the death of Saladin's successor, they inherited the rule of Cairo in 1249. They ruled as absolute

165 bottom left Bab Zuwayla marks the southern boundary of Fatimid Cairo. The city did not have proper fortifications until 1087 when Badr ad-Din el Gamali decided to build a defensive wall with three large gates. It design was commissioned from Syrian architects.

165 bottom right One of the five minarets in al-Azhar Mosque seen against the background of the city. Today Cairo has fifteen million inhabitants and is the largest city in Africa.

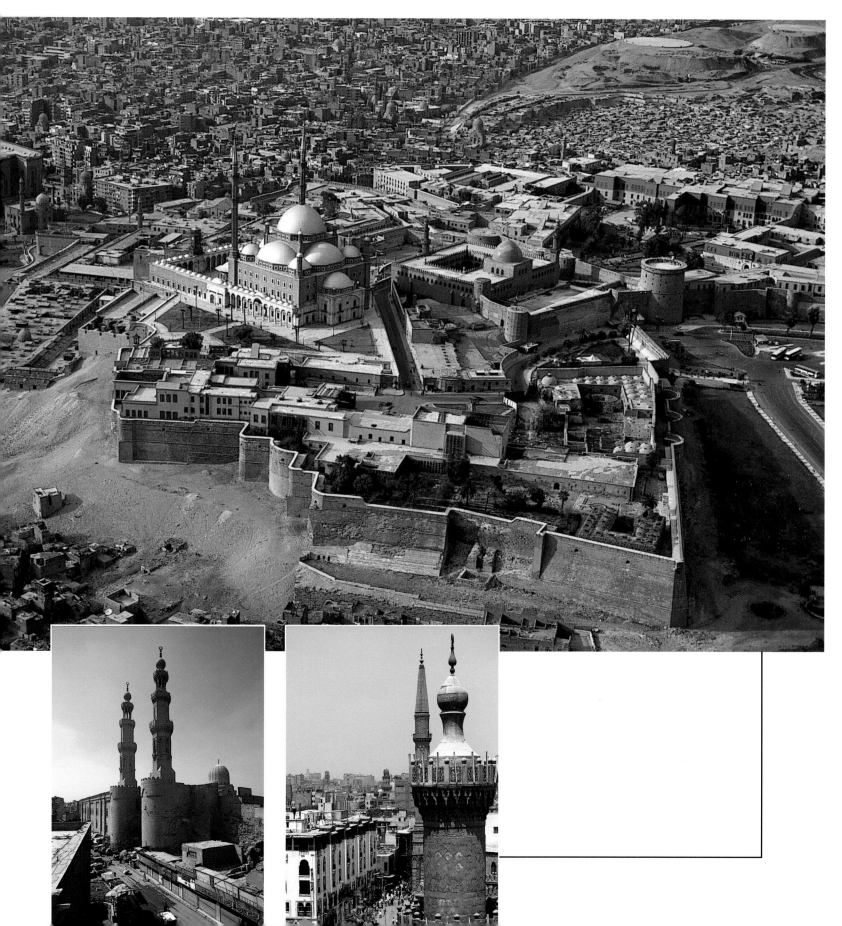

166 top right Some of the tombs of the Mameluke rulers. The Mamelukes were the freed slaves that took power on the death of Saladin's grandson.

166 bottom left Stylistically, Sultan Hassan Mosque and its madrasa is considered the most unitary and harmonious monument in the city. Built in 1256 for Sultan Hassan bin Mohammad bin Qala'un, it was designed so that each of the four Sunnite sects had its own school, though sharing the building with the other three.

monarchs until the end of the fifteenth century, further embellishing Cairo with mosques, public and residential buildings, *hammam* (public baths), theological schools, caravanserais, markets, and fountains. The complex that best epitomizes typical Mameluk architecture is the Qala'un Mosque complex, which includes a mosque, a madrasah (Koranic school), a mausoleum, and a *mauristan* (hospital), which remained open until 1920. Noteworthy mosques include the fourteenth-century Aqsunqur, better

known as the Blue Mosque because of its blue and turquoise ceramic tiles from Iznik, and the fifteenth-century al-Mu'ayyad, or Red Mosque, which has elegant marble decorations set with ivory and mother-of-pearl.

Cairo reached its apogee during the Mameluk era, becoming the crossroads for trade between East and West. The opening of the trade route via the Cape of Good Hope in 1488 marked the end of Egypt's monopoly, and it also coincided with the defeat of the Mameluks by the Ottomans, who ruled Egypt until the

166-167 The unusually Rococo domes of Haush al-Basha are one of the many marks left by the Mamelukes on the city, along with mosques, public buildings, Koranic schools and caravanserais.

167 top The city's southern cemetery is where the Mameluke tombs lie, in Haush al-Basha. The Mamelukes governed the city from the mid-thirteenth century to the end of the fifteenth.

early nineteenth century.

The city's tradition of trade continues to thrive, as demonstrated by its numerous markets, particularly Khan al-Khalili. The excellent craftsmanship of Cairo's residents, who are highly skilled at jewelry-making, glassblowing, wood carving, and embroidery, can be seen behind the walls of El-Ghuri Wakala, one of the city's most intriguing buildings, built as a hotel for merchants from Asia, Africa, and Europe.

167 bottom right This is el-Mu'ayyad (the Red Mosque) situated near Bab Zuwayla and built between 1415 and 1420 by Sultan Mu'ayyad. Inside, the walls are completely lined with geometric patterns made from polychrome marble.

167 center right The Mameluke ruler el-Mansur built the Sultan Qala'un complex along Sharia el-Muizz, a street | *in Fatimid Cairo, in 1284. It was the first example of the Syrian architectural style that was to typify the Mameluke era.*

The Statue of Liberty
UNITED STATES OF AMERICA

NEW YORK
REGISTRATION: 1984
CRITERIA: C (I) (VI)

168 left Donated to the United States to celebrate the centenary of its independence in 1776, the Statue of Liberty was not in fact inaugurated until October 28, 1886.

On the night of July 3, 1986, thousands of people were present in the New York harbor to watch a fireworks display that cost two million dollars. It was a large sum, but negligible compared to the 87 million that had been spent on restoring the Statue of Liberty to celebrate its centenary. Nonetheless, the return to the original splendor of what has been the symbol of America for nearly one hundred and twenty years was well worth the expense.

The idea to create a work of sculpture that symbolized the brotherhood of France and the United States in their battle for liberty began to torment Frédéric-Auguste Bartholdi in spring 1865, when the Confederate troops surrendered at the end of the Civil War. In 1871, the artist crossed the Atlantic to present his project to the President, Ulysses Grant. In the end it was decided that, to celebrate the centenary of American independence, the work would be unveiled on July 4, 1876, and the American government would further contribute with the creation of the pedestal.

Alas, the forecasts were optimistic. The economies of the two countries were not in good shape, and for several years the finances stagnated, until Joseph Pulitzer (after whom the journalistic prize is named) launched a campaign to collect funds through the columns of his newspaper, *The World*, with a series of blistering editorials that invited all Americans to participate in the venture. In 1884, the Statue was finally completed, and a year later, when the base had been prepared, the 350 pieces of copper of which it was composed were sent across the Atlantic on the French frigate Isère.

On October 28, 1886, on Bedloe Island, right in front of the port of New York, "Freedom enlightening the world" was

inaugurated by President Grover Cleveland, more than ten years later than had been planned. It stands 151 feet high (305 feet and weighs nearly 30,000 tons if the cement pedestal is included), and is formed by a central steel pylon designed by Alexandre Gustave Eiffel that provides the load-bearing structure. The copper skin, weighing 34 tons but only 2.37 millimetres – under one-tenth of an inch – thick, is hung on this central support system and has a tormented history. In order to create the largest metal statue ever built, Bartholdi made models on ever larger scales, some of which are preserved in the Statue Museum inside the base. In order to forge the face of Liberty, the French sculptor chose his mother as his model, but the pose tired her too quickly during production of the work, so Bartholdi went out into the streets of Paris in search of a young woman whose facial features resembled those of his mother. He met Jeanne-Emilie Baheux de Puysieux who, after finishing her task as model, became the sculptor's wife.

Starting from the base of the Statue of

Liberty, it is necessary to climb 354 steps to reach the crown, the highest point open to the public, from where one has a superb view of the bay of New York. The crown is one of the most symbolic sections: its seven points represent (or so it is interpreted) the seven seas (the Arctic, Antarctic, North Atlantic, South Atlantic, North Pacific, South Pacific, and Indian oceans), or perhaps, the seven continents (North and South America, Europe, Asia, Africa, Australia, and Antarctica). The windows in the crown are supposed to represent the 25 natural minerals of the Earth. The torch (rebuilt in 1986 and lined with 24 carat gold) that the woman holds in her right hand represents the light that Freedom brings, and the tablet she carries in her left hand bears the date of American independence, July 4, 1776, in Roman numerals. The figure's toga commemorates the Roman republic, the first democratic "experiment" in history, and the broken chain at her feet symbolizes the victory over slavery.

Built within the walls of Fort Wood, which stood on Bedloe Island to protect New York port, the Statue of Liberty was first administered by the United States Lighthouse Board, then responsibility was passed to the Department of War, and finally in 1933, to the National Park Service. In 1956, the island was renamed Liberty Island.

A strange fact is that no one ever saw the statue with her original copper color; rapid oxidation of the material meant that when she reached New York she had already turned a very dark brown, almost black. Twenty years later, she turned her characteristic green, the color that signified the hope of a new life for entire generations of immigrants who went to America in search of fortune.

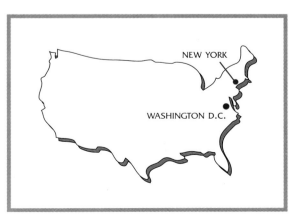

168 right Standing in the court of Fort Wood on Bedloe Island, at the mouth of the Port of New York, the statue is placed on an eight-point star that contains the Immigration Museum.

169 left Many elements of "Freedom Enlightening the World" (the official name of the monument) are symbolic.

The torch, covered with 24-carat gold, represents the light that accompanies Freedom, and the toga she wears commemorates the Roman Republic, the first national experiment in democracy.

169 top right The tablet that Liberty holds in her left hand bears the date July 4, 1776, Independence Day in the United States.

NEW YORK

WASHINGTON D.C.

Pueblo de Taos

UNITED STATES OF AMERICA

TAOS VALLEY, NEW MEXICO
REGISTRATION: 1992
CRITERIA: C (IV)

170 top Taos Valley, through which flows a tributary of the Rio Grande of the North, is still a wild region today. The Pueblos Indians built several villages in this area starting in the early thirteenth century, and the Pueblo de Taos that exists today dates from 1350.

170 bottom Most houses in Pueblo de Taos have hornos for baking bread in front of them. These are round ovens that are clearly of Arab derivation, the design of which was brought to North America by the Spanish in 1540.

Each year at the end of August, the Pueblo de Taos initiation ceremony is held at the Blue Lake. It is a required rite if one is to be admitted to the religious life and political positions of the community. For the Pueblo Indians of Taos Valley, through which a small tributary of the Rio Grande runs to the north, the lake was the origin of the native population living in the New Mexico and Arizona region. In a 1970 decision that represented a turning point in the reconciliation between the United States and the remaining indigenous population, the Federal government returned to the Pueblo tribe the sacred lake, high up on the mountain, that dominates the valley in which they live.

Indications have been found of primitive human settlements in the valley from 5,000 years ago, but the first occupants of whom there exists solid evidence are the Anasazi Indians – the "Ancients" – who lived in the region around the ninth century A.D. Little is known of their civilization, but it is certain that they lived in shelters dug in the ground before the era in which the Pueblo buildings were built. The village of Pueblo de Taos, a few miles north of the modern city of Taos, was built in the mid-fourteenth century.

The first Europeans to set foot in Pueblo de Taos were, in 1540, the *conquistadors* led by Hernán Alvarado, who was later followed by Franciscan missionaries. Thanks to the goodwill of the Spanish king, Philip II, the Pueblo Indians were allowed a certain degree of autonomy, and the communities lived in relative peace until the end of the century. During this period, the baked brick constructions of the Pueblos felt the Spanish influence and, indirectly, that of the Arab architecture that dominated the south of the Iberian peninsula. The Pueblos had known the technique of baking bricks for centuries, but it was only then that they began to use wooden moulds to give their bricks a regular shape and to build circular ovens for baking bread that were clearly Arab in nature.

In the seventeenth century, the Spaniards made their presence felt more strongly, and in 1680 the Pueblos rebelled but were put down in 1692. The following century brought a large number of agricultural settlers to New Mexico and saw the founding of self-sufficient farms near the local villages. The closure of Spanish settlements gave the Pueblos a certain degree of isolation that allowed them to continue their traditions and the spirit of independence that they still embrace. When Mexico won its independence from Spain in 1821, friction soon sprang up between the new country and the fur traders who traveled the long distance from the East Coast. These "mountain men" – symbolized in the collective unconscious by Daniel Boone and the backwoods image of the politician Davy Crockett – lived side by side with the Indians, learning their hunting techniques and adopting their customs. They also fought beside them when defending the villages of the sedentary Pueblos against the attacks of the

170-171 All the buildings in the village are made from adobe – a mixture of mud and straw – which is formed into bricks and lined with mud. Though it requires maintenance after every rainy season, the material holds warmth during winter and cool during summer.

nomadic tribes of the plains such as the Navajo and the Apache. The expansion of the United States westwards culminated in the 1846 war after which the province joined the United States' Territory of New Mexico, which included Arizona. These were the years that Kit Carson fought in the Civil War, defending the flag of the Union that flew over Pueblo de Taos.

The arrival of the "intruders" did not end there, and in the 1870's the Gold Rush occurred, which brought new inhabitants in search of fortune into the valley. Then, at the start of the twentieth century, it was the turn of the artists; Ernest Blumenschein and Bert Phillips were the first of a "colony" joined by intellectuals like painter Georgia O'Keeffe, photographer Ansel Adams, psychoanalyst Carl Jung, and writer D.H. Lawrence.

Notwithstanding the many outside influences, the architecture and culture of the Pueblo de Taos community have survived, and today the village is one of the oldest settlements on American soil. The Pueblos maintain their sovereignty over the land through the Governor of the Tribe and the Tribal Council. Their economic independence is ensured by flourishing craft and tourist industries.

171 bottom The church of San Francisco de Asis is one of the most interesting constructions in Pueblo de Taos. Since the end of the nineteenth century, artists and avant-garde intellectuals have been interested in the primitive architecture of the village.

TAOS   WASHINGTON D.C.

The Historic Center of Oaxaca

MEXICO

STATE OF OAXACA
REGISTRATION: 1987
CRITERIA: C (I) (II) (III) (IV)

172 top The porticoes in the zócalo, where the inhabitants of Oaxaca meet. Behind, note the Plateresque-style façade of the Iglesia de la Compañía de Jesús, built by the Jesuits in 1579.

172-173 Evening in the Alameida di Plaza de la Constitución, or zócalo, overlooked by the cathedral. Oaxaca's most important religious building is not the most impressive architecturally. Built in 1574, it underwent substantial alterations over the next four centuries, thereby losing its stylistic unity.

A colonial house in Calle García Vigil in Oaxaca is home to a museum in honor of Benito Juárez, the city's favorite son. Elected President of Mexico in 1858, Juárez – a Zapotec *indio* of humble origin who was educated by Franciscans in his own home – has passed into history for his resistance against social prejudice, the overwhelming power of the Catholic Church, and from 1862 on, against the invasion of the French. His motto, "*El respecto al derecho ajeno es la paz*" (peace is respect for the rights of

others), soon became a symbolic expression for all liberals who fought for the democratization of the country.

Since its beginning, Oaxaca was a city to which Olmec, Zapotec, and Mixtec Indios migrated and then mixed peacefully with the Spanish *conquistadors*. In the area today, there are still 16 different ethnic groups that speak roughly 150 dialects. Every July, the Guelaguetza is celebrated, a colorful festival in which the indigenous groups dance and exchange gifts as a sign of mutual respect.

In 1521, after the conquest of Tenochtitlán, Hernán Cortéz sent troops under his lieutenant, Francisco Orozco, towards Huaxyacac, as the city was then known. It was the most important town in the valley situated at an altitude of 5,250 feet and surrounded by hills. Although Orozco had sent Cortéz a letter stating he was against the occupation of the area (it had no precious metals and was inhabited by highly combative Indios), Cortéz wanted the situation checked in person. Orozco fell in love with the natural beauties of the place and succeeded in reaching an agreement with the natives. On April 25, 1532, the king of Spain approved the founding of the city and conferred the title of Marqués del Valle

de Oaxaca on Cortéz.

The layout of the city was designed by Alonso García Bravo, the architect of the Escorial who had also planned the structures of Mexico City and Veracruz. At either ends of the *zócalo* (one of Mexico's loveliest squares), construction began on the headquarters of Spanish power and on the cathedral (on the site of a Zapotec temple in honor of the dead).

The city's main streets fanned out from the square, and according to the planner, portrayed the balance between sacred and profane. What is unusual is that it was never necessary to build a city wall, and, in fact, Oaxaca was left relatively free to get on with its own business. Crops grown in the surrounding area were maize, wheat, coffee, and sugarcane, the latter used to provide the court in Spain with sweet delicacies. This was also where it was discovered that a red tint could be extracted from cochineal, a wheat parasite, which could be used to dye fabrics.

Shortly after the founding of the city, the Dominican monks arrived who began to construct religious buildings. The Spanish

173 left The city's main pedestrian street, Calle Macedonio Alcalá, is lined with the old houses of the Spanish notables. Some of these have been turned into museums and art galleries.

173 right The brilliant colors and elaborate wrought iron railings distinguish the façades of typical colonial-style houses in Oaxaca's historical center.

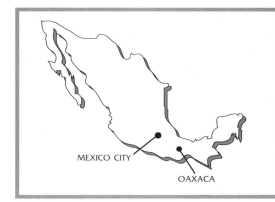

MEXICO CITY

OAXACA

Baroque is harmoniously combined in Oaxaca with indigenous traditions and the city's churches and elaborate decorations represent the best of Mestizo architecture in Mexico. Construction of the cathedral dragged on until 1733, but more magnificent and extravagant is the Iglesia de Santo Domingo. The late sixteenth-century façade is made from finely sculpted stone and is flanked on either side by a bell tower. The interior is lined with hundreds of pounds of gold. The high altar and the decorations on the walls and ceiling illustrating biblical scenes are all extraordinary. On the choir's lower wall, a gilded stucco bas-relief illustrates the genealogical order of the Dominican Order in the form of a vine. Attached to the church is a large monastery that today holds the Regional Museum. One of its displays contains a collection of Mixtec gold objects found in a tomb during excavation of the nearby archaeological site of Monte Albán.

Other fine examples of Baroque architecture are the Basilica della Nuestra Señora della Soledad and the Iglesia de San Felipe Neri. The latter was used as a barracks during the Mexican Revolution and was restored in 1920. It was redecorated with the addition of Art Nouveau elements, a touch that is also to be seen in the elegant Teatro Macedonio Alcalá, near the city square. The porticoes of the zócalo are the heart of the busy life of the city.

Many writers and artists have illustrated the beauties of Oaxaca. Friedrich Nietzche wanted to retire there, and Aldous Huxley and Italo Calvino both stayed in the city. Its atmosphere today resembles that of the novels of the father of magical realism, Gabriel García Márquez.

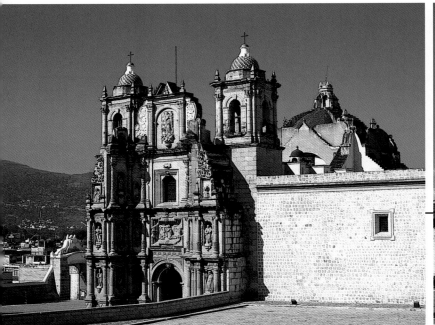

174 top left Consecrated in 1697 to the Virgen de la Soledad, Oaxaca's patron saint, the Basilica is one of the city's most resplendent examples of Baroque architecture. Inside, the image of the Virgin is venerated for its miraculous powers.

174 top right The imposing façade of the Iglesia de Santo Domingo has a central section 85 feet tall and two towers 115 feet high. The domes are covered with azulejos. The plainness of the exterior is in stark contrast to the exuberant Baroque decorations inside.

174 bottom The main entrance to the Teatro Macedonio Alcalá. Officially opened on September 15, 1909, it also functioned as a casino for its first 50 years. The interior is decorated in grand Empire style.

175 top The interior of the Iglesia de Santo Domingo is one of the best examples of Mexican Baroque and covered with hundreds of pounds of gold. Like the vault, the high altar is extraordinary, decorated with medallions depicting biblical scenes and Dominican martyrs.

175 bottom The façade of the Iglesia de Santo Domingo has a bas-relief of St. Dominic and St. Hippolyte supporting the church, onto which the image of the Holy Spirit is descending.

Trinidad and the Valle de los Ingenios

CUBA

PROVINCE OF SANCTI SPÍRITUS
REGISTRATION: 1988
CRITERIA: C (IV) (V)

S itting in the shade of the patios in the old colonial houses painted blue, yellow, and pink, the old people of Trinidad like to tell the story handed down through the generations of the city's happiest day. It took place in 1850 when a ship loaded with French furniture berthed in the nearby port. The cargo had been ordered by Conde de Brunet to furnish his newly-constructed home in Plaza Mayor. All the mule-owners in Trinidad were hired to carry the precious load along the path that connected the port to the town. In the evening, everyone gathered in the square to celebrate the arrival of mirrors with

Trinidad that, four years later, Cortéz sailed to conquer Mexico. Yet Trinidad remained a hideout for smugglers until the end of the eighteenth century, when a number of landowners emigrated there from Haiti following the uprising of the slaves and the burning of the sugarcane plantations.

In the eyes of the new arrivals, the Valle de San Luis near Trinidad – dominated by the Escambray massif and made fertile by the Río Agabama – was a perfect place to grow sugarcane. The idea was particularly attractive as the price of sugar had risen sharply with the closure of the Haitian refineries. Thus, the initiative of the French, copied soon after by the Spanish, led to the establishment of 50 or so Ingenios (plantations with sugar mills) within 20 years across the 107 square miles of the Valle de San Luis. It is estimated that 2,800 *macheteros* slaves worked there cutting the 4,400 tons of cane necessary to produce 770 tons of sugar-loaves, 1,000

177

176 bottom This splendid patio is part of Casa Brunet, which was owned by a rich family of sugarcane barons. In 1974, the building was turned into the Romantic Museum.

177 top The large number of perfectly conserved colonial houses makes Trinidad one of the loveliest places in the Caribbean.

177 bottom left A room in the Romantic Museum, opened in 1974 in a lovely two-storey house built for the Conde de Brunet around 1840.

176-177 A street in the center of Trinidad, flanked by brightly-painted houses from the colonial era. In the background, the bell-tower of the Iglesia de San Francisco de Asís.

magnificent gilded frames, four-poster beds, and Limoges porcelain.

Today these treasures and other objects from Trinidad's aristocratic mansions are displayed in the Museo Romantico in the former Casa Brunet, and they perfectly represent the era in which this small town in central Cuba was the flourishing territory of the sugarcane barons.

In fact, the history of Trinidad began in the early days of the Spanish colony when, in 1514, Captain Diego Velázquez founded a base there for the expeditions to be made throughout the New World. It was from

barrels of *aguardiente* (firewater), and 1,000 barrels of molasses each year.

Made rich by the profitable trade, the landowners of Trinidad competed to build magnificent mansions embellished with flower-filled patios and decorations made from carved wood, wrought iron, and stucco. In 1817, construction of Cuba's largest cathedral began, the Iglesia Parroquial de la Santísima Trinidad, which, thanks to its splendid architectural features and altar, greatly overshadowed the Iglesia del Convento de San Francisco de Asís, built a century earlier.

177 bottom right A symbol of the Valle de los Ingenios, the Manacas-Iznaga tower was built at the start of the nineteenth century. It was used to monitor the work of the macheteros in the sugarcane fields. It stands 43.5 meters tall and has 184 steps.

178-179 *Facing onto Plaza Mayor, the Iglesia de la Santísima Trinidad is Cuba's largest church. It was built in 1892 in Neo-Classical style on the site of a sixteenth-century church. Its wooden altar substituted the traditional marble version.*

179 *top left Some of Trinidad's old houses have been turned into museums. The* Architecture Museum can be seen in the 1738 house that belonged to the Sánchez Iznaga family of landowners.

179 *top right Another street in the colonial center of the city. In the eighteenth century, an entire district in Trinidad was inhabited by pirates. Their houses can be seen in what is now Calle Ciro Redondo.*

The sugar production industry flourished until the start of the twentieth century when the land began to become less fertile and the importance of Trinidad started to diminish with the construction of the port in nearby Camagüey.

The richest period of Trinidad's history is marked by the city's buildings that were either assigned to the common people – probably descendants of the slaves who had performed the backbreaking work in the plantations – after the Cuban revolution or turned into museums. Those buildings that stand in what is referred to by all as the Valle de los Ingenios represent what was the most important agricultural complex in all of the Caribbean. The structures number 77, of which eleven were the homes of the plantation owners, three are the ruins of sugar mills, and the rest are warehouses, machine rooms, and *bohíos*, the huts where the *macheteros* lived.

The best preserved buildings are those on the plantation called Ingenio Manacas-Iznaga, which was the largest and most productive until 1857. Here, the tren *jamaiquin* still works, so named because the railway was brought to Cuba from Jamaica, which was a British colony at the time. For a while the train was used to transport the cane juice to the mills for refining. This plantation is also the location of the Torre de Manacas-Iznaga which was built at the start of the nineteenth century to allow the plantation owner to watch his slaves at work. This was the first building in the valley to be declared a national monument, and it has since become the symbol of the valley.

178 *top A view of Trinidad city center. The first Spanish settlement in San Luis valley dates from 1514 when Captain Diego Velázquez founded a base there to explore the New World.*

178 *center and bottom Two of the fourteen rooms in the Romantic Museum that contains nineteenth-century furnishings and decorations that belonged to the rich landowners of the city.*

180 Situated in the
Pelourinho district, the
Igreja do Rosário dos
Pretos was built by slaves
in Baroque style in the
eighteenth century. They
mostly worked at nighttime
and used smuggled
materials.

SALVADOR DE BAIA

BRASILIA

The Historic Center of Salvador de Bahia

BRAZIL

BAHIA STATE
REGISTRATION: 1985
CRITERIA: C (IV) (VI)

181 top left The colonial houses in Praça da Sé in the heart of the city. The square is named after the Sé da Bahia, one of Latin America's most magnificent churches, which was built in 1533 and demolished four centuries later.

On the evening of December 31 each year, the image of Senhor bom Jesus dos Navegantes is carried to the Igreja Nossa Senhora da Conceição. To celebrate the arrival of the new year, the next morning it is accompanied from there by dozens of boats in a sea procession to the Igreja Nossa Senhora da Boa Viagem, packed to the rafters, where it is kept until the following year. Although this rite was inherited from a Portuguese tradition, it should not be surprising that Salvador de Bahia begins the new year with a ceremony that is both religious and marine in nature because these are the two elements that have always determined the lifestyle of the city.

Salvador is the capital of the state of Bahia in northeast Brazil. It stands on the Baía de Todos os Santos, the huge and peaceful bay named by the crew of Amerigo Vespucci on their arrival there on November 1, 1501. A few years later, a ship under the command of Diogo Álvares was wrecked there, and he was given shelter by the Tupinambá tribe who lived on the coast. He married the daughter of Chief Taparica and ended up by playing a decisive role when the king of Portugal, João III, gave orders that a city should be built in the bay.

In 1549, a fleet carrying more than 1,000 colonists left European shores under the command of captain Tomé de Souza. When they arrived on the shores of the Baía de Todos os Santos, they were welcomed with all honor by Álvares and the local populations. This was the beginning of Salvador de Bahia, the capital of the new colony, and Tomé de Souza was bestowed with the title Governor of Brazil.

After half a century the city had 1,600 inhabitants and traded sugarcane, tobacco, and cotton. A little later, the profitable trade in slaves began, which through the mixing of South American natives, Portuguese colonists, and African slaves made Bahia a multiethnic city. Such sudden prosperity naturally attracted the attention of foreigners who prepared expeditions to conquer Bahia.

181 center right The Baroque altar of the Igreja do Convento do Carmo. Founded in the seventeenth century, the complex unites great architecture with important events linked to Brazilian independence.

181 bottom left The majestic main façade of the Municipio, the former residence of the governors, is crowned by a dome.

Bahia was the capital of Portuguese America until 1763 when the monarch decided to move the capital to Rio de Janeiro.

181 bottom right Bahia Port. On the left is the Elevator Lacerda, the massive elevator installed in 1868 to facilitate access to the upper part of the city.

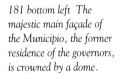

182 top The cloister of the Convento de São Francisco decorated with blue and white azulejos. The Franciscans arrived in Bahia in 1587 but had to wait a century before they were provided with land to build a monastery.

182 bottom A view of Pelourinho shows its colonial houses dominated by the twin bell towers of the Igreja Nossa Senhora de Conceição. The name of the district means "whipping place" because the slaves were bought and sold there.

First came the Dutch of the East India Company, who ruled the city in 1624-1625. Once peace returned, Bahia became a repository for the new treasures coming from the gold and diamond mines in the interior. The rich Portuguese dignitaries began to build themselves magnificent houses and Baroque churches. By 1763, the city had grown enormously, numbering 60,000 inhabitants of every caste and nationality, but then the Portuguese monarch decided to move the capital south to the equally prosperous city of Rio de Janeiro. This marked the start of a slow decline for Salvador de Bahia which did

not halt even with independence from Portugal in 1822.

The city is famous for the beauty of its colonial architecture. The greatest evidence of its European past in the lower part of the city can be seen in the remains of the fortifications built to protect the important port and the Mercado Modelo where goods arrived. On the top of the hill, on the other hand, there is the large Igreja do Nosso Senhor do Bomfim, dedicated to the patron saint of the city. Daily life in Bahia for the most part takes place in the upper section, which is linked to the port by an elevator originally built in 1610 by Jesuits to lighten the work done by slaves. Today no trace remains of the first apparatus but the Elevator Lacerda, a massive steam-driven, iron piece of equipment installed in 1868, can still be seen. The upper section of Bahia contains not only the houses of the nobility and merchants but most of the city's churches. Legend has it that there were 365 at one time, one for each day of the year, bearing witness to the strength of religion in a city where Catholicism was often united with the animist beliefs of the African slaves to form the syncretistic cult of Candomblé.

The loveliest church is undoubtedly the Igreja de São Francisco, the walls and altar of which are completely covered with gold leaf.

Nearby lies the ancient quarter of Pelourinho, an impressive cluster of seventeenth and eighteenth-century buildings. The name Pelourinho means "place of the whips" because it the slaves were bought and sold here. Today the old slave market, in Largo do Pelourinho, is the site of the Fundação Casa de Jorge Amado, in honor of the great Brazilian writer who lived in a nearby hotel during his university years.

183 top left Situated in the square of the same name, the Igreja de São Francisco was built between 1708 and 1723 in exuberant Baroque. It is considered the loveliest church in Brazil.

183 top right The Igreja do Nosso Senhor do Bonfim is dedicated to the patron saint of the city and is the best-loved church in Bahia. Located in the Cidade Baixa, it was completed in 1722 and has a Rococo façade decorated with Portuguese azulejos.

183 bottom The best example of Portuguese Baroque in the world, the interior of the Igreja de São Francisco is a celebration of jacaranda wood decoration entirely covered with gold leaf.

Ancient Civilizations
introduction

From Ayutthaya and Chichén-Itzá to Carthage, Petra, Machu Picchu and Rapa Nui (Easter Island): the brief history of human civilizations is dotted with cultures that have enjoyed periods of extraordinary success, perhaps creating empires and then declining – sometimes slowly, sometimes suddenly – before disappearing.

These nations were often defeated by enemy powers, as in the case of the Khmers, who built the majestic Angkor temple complex in the heart of the Cambodian forest, close to the shores of the Tonle Sap, and dominated all of modern Cambodia from the 9th to the 15th century, before falling to the neighboring Siamese. The same is true of Carthage, Rome's intrepid adversary on the opposite shore of the Mediterranean Sea, defeated by Scipio Africanus and subsequently razed to the ground by the armies of Scipio Aemelianus in 146 BC. The same destiny was shared by the great Roman Empire itself several centuries later, when it was overrun by barbarian invasions.

However, other civilizations met a different end. The Mayan Empire, for example, may have broken up due to a sudden change in climate, which drove the population toward other latitudes. And it is certain that the inhabitants of Rapa Nui were the victims of their own prosperity, which caused their civilization to collapse between the 15th and 16th centuries. They exploited their environment's scarce resources down to the very last tree and ended up being decimated by internal struggles, leaving only the moai – the gigantic, enigmatic stone statues that populate the island – and *rongorongo*, the only written language of the Pacific area.

About a quarter of the UNESCO World Heritage forms a trail that that winds across the history of ancient civilizations, commencing in those places where man took his first steps, such as the Awash and Omo Valleys in Ethiopia, or the fossil sites of Swartkrans, Sterkfontein and Kromdraai, in South Africa, where examples of hominids have been discovered that date back to 3.5 million years ago. These are chronologically followed by the sites in which art was born, with the rock paintings of the Kakadu National Park in Australia, the Tadrart Acacus sites in Libya, and the Vézère Valley in France, which includes the Lascaux Cave that has earned the nickname of the "Sistine Chapel of Paleolithic Art." The trail continues, across the Neolithic sites where humankind started to forge metals and create modern societies, until reaching cultures closer to our own: from Mesopotamia and the ancient Egyptians to the Greece of Athens and Delphi, and Rome, before progressing to the Asian and Mesoamerican civilizations.

Only a few traces of certain cultures remain, while others have left behind extraordinary monuments, testifying to their technological skills and wealth, and enabling us to reconstruct the progress of civilization over the millennia. In this selection of these precious areas of memory, an important part is thus inevitably dedicated to the Egyptian, Greek, Roman and great Pre-Columbian civilizations. From the pyramids and the Acropolis to Pompeii, the Imperial Forums in Rome, Palenque and Tikal: these peoples have left us such an extensive and magnificent legacy that it is impossible to limit it to a few brief mentions. However, an overview of the great cultures could not fail to feature the extraordinary testimonies left by Buddhism, from India to China, or Mesa Verde, a unique complex of Pueblo Indian dwellings.

The modern world developed out of these peoples and their civilizations, and their very distant and diverse histories, and it is only their remaining traces that enable us to continue to preserve the memory of our origins.

185 The face of an apsara *(a creature that cheered the divine palaces of the Khmer rulers) emerges from the elaborate decorations at Angkor Wat in Cambodia. Here, Hinduism and Buddhism overlapped in the twelfth and thirteenth centuries, coexisting for a long time.*

Stonehenge and Avebury

UNITED KINGDOM

COUNTY OF WILTSHIRE, WESSEX, ENGLAND
REGISTRATION: 1986
CRITERIA: C (I) (II) (III)

186 An aerial view of
Stonehenge, the most
famous and mysterious
megalithic site in the world,
built between 3100 and
1600 BC. Myths and
folklore aside, today not
even the scientific
community is able to
provide unequivocal
explanations of its purpose
and use.

AVEBURY

LONDON

STONEHENGE

W ho built Stonehenge? Over the centuries, dozens of legends have flourished and all kinds of serious and not-so-serious hypotheses have been put forward. Was it the Celts, the Saxons, the ancient Egyptians, the Romans, or the people of Atlantis? Then again, perhaps people from outer space? Or – as is claimed by some – were the stones placed "strategically" by a group of fanatical British in search of new forms of spirituality in 1968 at the height of Beatlemania?

The answer is no, at least to the last idea. The first written reference to Stonehenge dates back to 1135. In his *History of the Kings of Britain*, Geoffrey of Monmouth claimed that the stones were brought from Africa to Ireland by a tribe of giants, and then made to fly from there across the sea by Merlin the magician, where they were then mounted on Salisbury Plain in homage to King Arthur. However, the Druids, the priests of the Celtic people, have always claimed their forebears were responsible for the construction. Until 1985, the ancient order of the Druids used to visit the monument, dressed in white tunics and carrying harps and trumpets, to celebrate initiation rites on the summer solstice.

Not even the scientific community is in a position to give unequivocal answers regarding the world's most famous megalithic site. In the most recent study, published in 2003 by the gynecologist Anthony Perks in the *Journal of the Royal Society of Medicine*, it was suggested that the ring formed by the stone blocks represented the female sexual organ through which the Earth Mother– the main divinity during the Neolithic era – gave birth to the plants and animals. However, this was met by a chorus of protests and was refuted in writing by David Miles, the archaeologist who has been director of the site for years.

Whoever was responsible for Stonehenge (the name is derived from an ancient Anglo-Saxon word meaning "hanging rocks"), the monument was constructed in three phases between 3100 and 1600 BC. In the earliest phase, a circular earthwork was raised measuring roughly 100 yards in diameter; it was bounded by a dike and, a short distance away, by a ring of 56 holes that were once filled by an equal number of wooden poles. These holes are known as Aubrey Holes after the person who first described them in 1666. In the second phase, around 2550 BC, the first stones appeared. Called "bluestones," they are the smallest stones on the site, despite the fact that they each weigh about five tons. They were transported – first probably by sea, then up the river Avon, and finally across land – the 236 miles to Salisbury Plain from quarries in Pembroke in southwest Wales. During the third phase, which started around 2100 BC, Stonehenge was given the structure seen today, composed of megaliths each weighing about 30 tons. They were brought from the hills of Marlborough, about 19 miles away. These blocks from the Eocene epoch are called *sarsen*, a word meaning "foreigner" in the ancient language of Wessex.

The outermost element in the Stonehenge site is an avenue about 650 yards long lined on either side by dikes that run parallel at a distance of 25 yards from one another. The avenue leads to the Heel Stone, another sarsen that, during the summer solstice, projects its shadow to the exact center of the site. Further along, the avenue leads to the circular earthwork. At its entrance is the Slaughter Stone, whose name was given by the red marks in the rock from iron "melted" by the rain over the millennia. From here, the central part of the site formed by concentric megalithic structures can be seen. The external ring is composed of 30 sarsens of which 17 are still in place; they stand 13 feet high and are connected to one another by a series of architraves held in place by mortise-and-tenon joints. Ten feet away from this circle, there is another ring, this time of 60 bluestones (many of which have fallen or are broken), standing nearly seven feet high. At the center of the two circles stands a massive horseshoe-shaped structure (today incomplete) consisting of five trilithons, the tallest of which stands 23 feet tall, each formed by two standing stones supporting a horizontal one. Finally, a modest horseshoe of bluestones rings the so-called Altar Stone at the center, though this does not have the drainage system typical of

187 top This view shows the circle of sarsen stones, the enormous blocks that were transported to Stonehenge 3,000 years ago from the hills of Marlborough 19 miles away.

187 bottom A detail of the five massive triliths (two uprights and an architrave) that stand in a horseshoe shape inside the ring of Stonehenge. The tallest measures 25 feet 6 inches in height.

altars in sacrificial temples built elsewhere during the same period.

The fame and dramatic nature of Stonehenge obscures the fact that Wiltshire boasts many Neolithic sites, such as Silbury Hill (the largest prehistoric burial mound in Europe), West Kennet Long Barrow (the largest chamber grave in England), and Avebury. This last site is the largest stone circle in the world, covering an area of roughly 28 acres. At one time it was formed by an earthwork exactly one mile in diameter, which enclosed a circle of 98 stones (27 of which are still in place). Like the large ones at Stonehenge, they also came from the Marlborough Downs. Avebury has several megaliths of huge size, including the Swindon Stone weighing 66 tons, and the Devil's Chair, which was named after a popular belief that it was possible to make the devil appear there if you ran around the stone 100 times counterclockwise.

Although scholars agree that Stonehenge and Avebury were places of worship, there are innumerable speculations overlaid on this certainty relating, for example, to the remarkable astronomical coincidences of its layout. It is not clear if the site could have been an *ante litteram* observatory for the study of the heavens, as many claim, nor whether it was simply a calendar to mark the events of the seasons, such as sowing and harvesting the grain. Some go further, claiming that it was used to forecast eclipses, although it was utterly improbable that the ancient people of Stonehenge had such advanced knowledge.

Unless – and here another theory enters the picture – Stonehenge was designed by an individual from a more advanced culture who arrived at Salisbury Plain to teach the locals the knowledge required to erect the megaliths. Moreover, this person would have had to return regularly over the period of 1,500 years during which the monument was built. Nevertheless, this is a theory that is only good for those who believe in extraterrestrials and flying saucers.

The Painted Grottoes in the Vallée de la Vézère

FRANCE

AQUITAINE, DORDOGNE
REGISTRATION: 1979
CRITERIA: C (I) (III)

The climb up the hill overlooking the village of Montignac on the left bank of the Vézère River in the Dordogne was supposed to be nothing more than a fun outing for Marcel Ravidat, Jacques Marsal, Georges Agnel, and Simon Coencas. Instead, it turned out to be one of the most famous archaeological discoveries of the twentieth century.

It was September 12, 1940 and the four boys, armed with only a dim flashlight and their natural sense of recklessness, decided to climb into the pit left by a fallen tree in the middle of the wood. Sliding down a heap of stones that had filled the entrance to a cave, they suddenly found themselves in a wide opening that today is known as the Great Hall of the Bulls. The rock paintings in the Great Hall of the Bulls are probably the most outstanding examples of Paleolithic art in the world. They cover about 200 square feet on both walls that curve over to form a vault in an

almost circular ravine, and consist of three groups of animals: horses, bulls, and deer.

Amazed at the incredible works of art that they had found, the boys told their teacher, and news of their discovery ended up in the school newspaper. From that moment on, archaeologists began to arrive in Lascaux, starting with Abbot André Glory, who was to spend more than a quarter of a century meticulously copying

all the incisions. It took this much time because the Lascaux Cave continues for over 110 yards into the depths of the mountain and includes at least seven more areas with significant paintings. On the left, the Painted Gallery is the natural continuation of the Great Hall of the Bulls, featuring zoomorphic figures that cover as much of the walls as in the cave's vault, consequently nicknamed the French

"Prehistoric Sistine Chapel." To the right, there is the Lateral Passage, followed by the Main Gallery, and then the Chamber of Felines, which is the most internal of the decorated areas. A side passage leads to the Chamber of Engravings and then the Shaft of the Dead Man, which, besides the wall paintings, was found to contain a vast range of handmade objects. They included 21 finely worked lamps made from rough stone, 14 bone spearheads, a painter's "palette," thanks to which it was possible to study the pigments used by Paleolithic artists, and eight mineral agglomerates from which the pigments were extracted.

Overall, there have been almost 1,500 incisions catalogued on the walls and vault of the grotto, which were painted around 17,000 years ago according to some, or 15,000 according to others. Whichever it was, they represent the apex of Paleolithic rock painting, widespread throughout the Dordogne region during the period of the Magdalenian culture between 18,000 and 11,000 years ago. In just the Vallée de la Vézère, 147 prehistoric sites and 25 painted caves have been found, which have made it possible to reconstruct features of the lifestyle of *Homo sapiens* during the phase immediately preceding the introduction of farming.

The marvels of Lascaux, however, have been inaccessible to the public for around 40 years now. Already by 1955, due to the excess of carbon dioxide in the air, the first traces of deterioration in the paintings were noticed, and some years later, the first worrying green stains produced by algae and mosses started to appear. In consequence, André Malraux, the French Minister of Culture, decided to close the grotto on April 20, 1963.

Once the causes of environmental contamination had been eliminated, the paintings at Lascaux returned to their original state, however they have remained closed forever to the public. In 1980, the authorities decided to create a

190 top A bull with huge horns on a wall at Lascaux.

190 bottom left The rock paintings in the apse of the Hall of the Bulls are considered some of the best examples of Paleolithic art in the world.

190-191 Galloping cattle and horses animate the interior of the Hall of the Bulls.

191 top and bottom To paint the almost 1,500 figures in the caves at Lascaux (bottom, the so-called "Chinese horse"), the people of the Paleolithic era used 12 pigments, ranging from pale yellow to black.

complete replica of the grotto, which they did with great accuracy and the use of materials that allowed the colors, incisions, and even the granular quality of the original rock to be perfectly reproduced. Lascaux II opened to the public in 1983.

In 2001, a new threat to the paintings in the original grotto was identified: colonies of bacteria and fungi were found on some of the rocks and cave floor, which had to be treated with fungicides and antibiotics. The problem has been solved but concern remains about the fragility of the biological environment of this extraordinary legacy from the dawn of civilization.

PARIS

VÉZÈRE

The Pont du Gard

FRANCE

PROVENCE
REGISTRATION: 1985
CRITERIA: C (I) (III) (IV)

In 1958, extreme flooding of the Gardon River caused enormous damage to the area of Nîmes in Provence. The modern railway bridge that crossed the river near Remoulins was literally swept away, but the Pont du Gard a little upstream, which had been standing for 2,000 years, stood impassively before the turbulent waters. Once the emergency had passed, everyone rejoiced for the wellbeing of the bridge built by the ancient Romans (this monumental construction receives more than two million visitors a year and is France's secondmost important provincial tourist attraction after Mont-Saint-Michel), though twentieth-

century engineers could not but feel they had been "beaten" by their ancient colleagues.

Historical documents attribute the design of the Pont du Gard as well as the entire aqueduct that carried water from the *Ucetia* spring (modern Uzès) to Nemausus (Nîmes) to no less than Marcus Agrippa, the son-in-law of Augustus. Known for his engineering skills, Agrippa visited Gaul in 19 BC and soon began work on the colossal hydraulic project.

Probably completed during the reign of Trajan (AD 98–117), the aqueduct follows a U shape 30 miles long, 22 of which run underground, with a total difference in height of just 56 feet. What is most striking is not the length of the aqueduct but its extraordinary precision: from the spring to the huge cistern (called the *castellum* by the Romans) situated in what was then the outskirts of Nîmes, the water ran down a constant slope of just 21.5 inches per mile. From the *castellum*, ten canals departed to supply the baths, public buildings, and houses of roughly 50,000 inhabitants with water. Thus, they were each allocated approximately 106 gallons per day, a quantity considered sufficient even by modern standards. It has also been calculated that the construction of the aqueduct cost 30 million sesterces, the equivalent of fifty years pay for 500 officers of the Roman legions.

The symbol of the magnificence of the entire construction is the Pont du Gard. Majestic, yet elegant and almost delicate, it is a little over 330 yards long and stands 157 feet high over the river in three orders of arches. The lowest order has six arches that vary in width from 52 to 70 feet and supports a road that was widened for carriages in the mid-eighteenth century. The second order has eleven arches, and the top one, over which the water canal passes, has 35 small arches. The bridge was made from stone dense with fossil concretions quarried locally. Its yellowish hue blends perfectly with the surrounding landscape of green hills and vineyards. The blocks each weigh 6.6 tons and were assembled without mortar with surprising precision.

The continual habitation and constant development of this corner of Provence have been providential for the safeguarding of the bridge. The first

PARIS

PONT DU GARD

restoration project was carried out during the reign of Napoleon III, and the most recent, which have only just ended, cost 30 million euros, most of which financed the construction of a visitors' center. The reinforcement of the Roman monument entailed the replacement of 390 cubic yards of stone, roughly five percent of the entire structure.

192 This frontal view of the Pont du Gard reveals the harmony of the three orders of arches. The bridge is the second-largest tourist attraction in provincial France after Mont-Saint-Michel.

192-193 Majestic yet elegant and almost delicate, the Pont du Gard is about 325 yards long and rises 157 feet above the water.

The yellowish stone harmonizes perfectly with the landscape.

193 bottom An aerial view of the Roman bridge, built as a section of the aqueduct that carried water 30 miles to Nemasus (Nîmes). It was designed by Marcus Agrippa, Augustus's son-in-law, around 19 BC and completed during the reign of Trajan.

The Roman Monuments of Arles

FRANCE

194

*S*pectators in the Arena at *Arles* by Vincent Van Gogh – today in the Hermitage Museum in St. Petersburg – is a magnificent painting. The warm colors and impetuous brushstrokes give a sense of anxious expectation and overwhelming passion, the same emotions, in fact, felt by the spectators at the *corrida*. In 1888, when it was painted, the amphitheater in Arles had only been restored about fifty years prior. After centuries of looting, it was turned into a fort and then a residential area for the poor, before being returned to its original vocation, a setting for cruel spectacles. Built between AD 90 and 100, it is elliptical (measuring 149 yards along its longest axis and 117 along its shortest), formed by two orders of 60 arches each, and can hold 24,000 people. The arena proper is separated from the cavea by a high wall that was built to protect spectators from the wild beasts used in the games. This superb construction is not the only one to survive from the city's Roman period. Colonized by veterans of Julius Caesar's Sixth Legion, Arles – or rather *Iulia Arelate Sextanorum* – was in 49 BC a small town on the left bank of the Rhone River inhabited by peoples of Celtic-Ligurian and Greek origin. Much closer to the sea then than it is now, the city soon established a flourishing economy and adopted an ambitious urban development plan. Covering 100 acres, it was enclosed within a defensive wall. The section of the road leading to Marseilles was used as a *decumanus*, whereas the *cardus* and other streets were traced out to create a grid. The construction of a theater for 10,000 spectators (today restored and back in use) and the forum date to 40–15 BC, during the reign of Octavian Augustus. The forum lay around the sanctuary of the Genius Augusti, which was surrounded by porticoes resting on crypto-porticoes.

Following a period of economic stasis from the second to mid-third century AD, Arles experienced a sort of renaissance thanks to the expansion of its textile industry and the skill of its chiselers, who were famous throughout the empire for their production of sarcophagi. In the fourth century, when

194 top The thick round walls of the amphitheater at Arles are characterized by round arches alternating with rectangular cornices and towers. They surrounded the castrum built by Julius Caesar to garrison his legions during consolidation of the conquest of Gaul.

194 bottom Unlike the Colosseum in Rome, the underground rooms in the amphitheater have survived pretty much intact with their original covering. As with similar structures, the rooms were used to store the stage machines.

194-195 Arles' spectacular amphitheater is the most important Roman monument in Provence. Built between 90 and 100 AD, over the centuries it has been looted, turned into a fort, and even become a residential area.

he was elected emperor, Constantine decided to settle there and so awarded the city the appellative *Gallula Roma*. A monumental program of construction and expansion was undertaken to make Arles a worthy imperial residence; of what remains of the emperor's palace, today it is possible to see the baths and the crypto-porticoes beneath the Augustan sanctuary. Restored by Constantine, the crypto-porticoes consist of two galleries of arches 100 yards long. In one of these, the bases of two granite columns have been found bearing an inscription mentioning the monuments built by the emperor to beautify the city and the names of the people who oversaw the works.

PARIS

ARLES

195 bottom The elegant
theater was built during
the principate of Octavian.
Founded by the Celts,
Arles was colonized
by the Romans, who
endowed it with
monuments and
named it Iulia Arelate
Sextanorum.

The Roman Monuments of Merida

SPAIN

PROVINCE OF BADAJOZ,
REGION OF ESTREMADURA
REGISTRATION: 1993
CRITERIA: C (III) (IV)

196 One of Merida's greatest treasures is the austere bridge over the Guardiana; this is the longest Roman bridge to have survived to the present day. Built towards the end of the first century AD, it has 81 arches and measures 866 yards long in its entirety.

196-197 The amphitheater in Merida was inaugurated in 8 BC on the occasion of the circus games. It could hold 14,000 spectators and was divided into three orders.

The Puente Lusitania was inaugurated in Merida in 1991. This slender structure across the Guadiana River is the pride of the residents, and not just because it was designed by Santiago Calatrava, one of the most famous contemporary architects. It is but the most recent manifestation of Merida's special relationship with bridges, which began when the first stone of a bridge was laid, thus marking the city's foundation.

of resistance to the expansion of the Roman Empire as far as the western edge of the known world.

The new colony built itself an aqueduct to bring water from the Proserpina Spring north of the city. It was 908 yards long, up to 80 feet high, and crossed the Albarregas River. Although today more than half of its arches have been destroyed, the grandeur of the structure is as evident as the elegance of the colors of the granite blocks and bricks with which it was built. The bridge over the Guadiana was built at the same time as the aqueduct. It has a span of 866 yards that is supported by 81 arches of an average height of 39 feet above the river level. Besides being the main means of reaching Roman Merida, from the sixteenth century on the bridge became a junction on the Via de la Plata, the road along which the Spanish transported the silver shipped from their American colonies to the state coffers in Madrid.

Soon the city flourished, and in 15 BC Marcus Agrippa (Augustus' son-in-law), arrived to preside over the celebrations held to mark the foundation of the Roman *provincia* of Lusitania, of which Merida was the capital. On this occasion, Agrippa inaugurated the theater that could hold 6,000 spectators and which had a cavea divided into three orders of seats for the different social classes. The amphitheater, which could seat 14,000 spectators and had been completed some years earlier, was used to stage gladiator fights, and together these buildings marked the start of a series of monumental constructions that were to

197 bottom left 1,750 yards long, the San Lazaro (or Rabo de Buey, "bull's tail") Aqueduct crossed the Albarregas River to carry water from underground springs into the city.

In the year 25 BC, Publius Carisius, a legate of Emperor Augustus, reached the banks of the Guadiana. The surrounding area was fertile, numerous fresh-water springs flowed in the nearby hills, and there was an abundance of granite. These resources were enough to decide the foundation of the *Colonia Augusta Emerita*. It was populated by veterans of the Fifth Alaudae and Tenth Gemina legions, which had been victorious against the Cantabrian and Asturian peoples that represented the last pockets

197 bottom right The Los Milagros Aqueduct is 908 yards long and 82 feet high. It was built in two stages between the end of the first century BC and the third century AD. It carried water to the city from the reservoir known as Lake Proserpina.

MADRID

MERIDA

make Merida the "*speculum et propugnaculum Imperii Romani.*"

Owing to the interest of the emperors of the Claudian dynasty, in the first century AD the city came to accommodate a garrison of 90,000 soldiers and witnessed a rapid growth of the economy in all of Roman Spain. The forum was paved with marble, and the Temple of Diana and a huge elliptical circus, able to seat 30,000, were built. The temple was the city's primary religious building and stood at the junction of the *cardus* and *decumanus*. Despite its name, it was dedicated to the imperial cult, which was determined by the discovery of a statue of the Genius Augustii and a sculptural group of Aeneas, Anchises, and Ascanius.

Merida reached its peak in the second century AD under Trajan and Hadrian, both natives of Spain. During this period, numerous patrician villas were built and decorated with mosaics – many examples of which are held today in the archaeological museum – or existing buildings were enlarged. The city's population also grew thanks to the arrival of troops from the North African provinces. These soldiers brought with them a new religion linked to the cult of Mars. Thus, from AD 155, Merida became one of the centers of Mithraism, as is demonstrated by the many bas-reliefs found in the city portraying the god fighting a bull. In fact, the Spanish passion for bull-fighting later originated in Merida.

198 top left and right The large mosaic floor of harvest scenes (right, a detail) is the most interesting feature in the Roman House of the amphitheater. This is a notable example of a patrician residence from the late imperial age, and is arranged around a central patio embellished with a peristyle.

198 bottom Located in the center of modern Merida, the temple of Diana (built between the late-first and early-second centuries AD) is a superb peripteral, hexastyle building in granite whose base measures 45 by 24 yards.

198-199 Built in 15 BC
by Marcus Agrippa as a
tribute to the city designated
the capital of Lusitania,
Merida's Roman theater
could seat around 6,000
spectators.

199 bottom A panther
hunt in a fourth-century
AD mosaic panel in the
National Museum of
Roman Art. The museum
has an extraordinary
collection of mosaics,
sculptures, and frescoes
from Merida's Roman
villas, plus many objects
from the necropolis
discovered during
construction of the museum
itself.

Ancient Rome

ITALY

PROVINCE OF LAZIO
REGISTRATION: 1980, 1990
CRITERIA: (I) (II) (III) (IV) (VI)

*P*anem et circenses, "bread and games": this was the basic formula of which Juvenal wrote in his AD 81 *Satire* that allowed the Roman rulers to maintain control of the masses. Distribution of food and working public baths on the one hand and gladiators, exotic animals, sports competitions, and theatrical performances on the other: these were the tools the emperors used to divert the discontent of the people.

Rome was the first true metropolis known to the world. With a million inhabitants, perhaps a million and a half, a complex city layout, and a natural setting that placed severe limitations on rational planning, the city already suffered problems of traffic and overcrowding as in modern-day metropolises, but with the added perils of poor hygiene, the ever-present risk of fire, and a lack of public order.

Consequently, it is hardly surprising that the emperors tried to distract the populace from their daily grind. When Juvenal wrote his caustic sentences, the most famous of the Roman monuments dedicated to games had only just been inaugurated. Commissioned by Vespasian and opened by Titus in AD 80, the Colosseum (or Flavian Amphitheater) stood 158 feet high, had four levels, was 205 yards across, and could seat 50,000 spectators. Three and a half million cubic feet of travertine and 330 tons of iron were required to build it. The first level was 34 feet six inches high and was decorated with Doric half-columns; the second was 38 feet ten inches high and was given Ionic columns; the third was 38 feet high and had Corinthian columns. The top level was made of brick and was given a system of poles that anchored the

velarium, a huge awning that sheltered the spectators from the sun.

Founded in 753 BC in the area of the Palatine Hill and surrounded by a number of villages, by the end of the eighth century BC Rome was one of the most important settlements in the Mediterranean. Under Tarquinius Priscus and Servius Tullius, the first public works were undertaken, with the construction of roads, squares, systems for drainage and water provision, and even the first street paving (625 BC), which can still be seen in the area of the Imperial Forums. From 509 BC on, the city was run by a system of republican government and, in the space of a few centuries, it became the capital of an empire. Victorious in the Punic wars in the third and second centuries BC, Rome became the uncontested ruler of the Mediterranean.

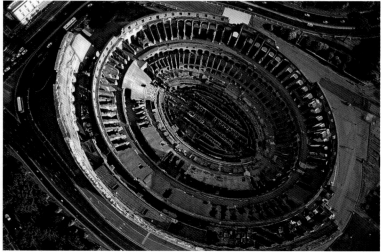

ROME

200 top Ritual in origin, the munera gladiatoria developed into cruel public games in 105 BC. This fourth-century AD mosaic shows different types of combatants with their real or "professional" names.

200 bottom left and right The Colosseum or, more properly, the Flavian Amphitheater, was built in five years between AD 75 and 80 but only received its fourth architectural order some years later during the reign of Domitian. The emperor's and priests' rostra were on opposite sides of the structure's shorter axis. The aerial view shows the complexity of the animal stalls and storerooms on the level under ground.

201 The Roman Forum stretching towards the Colosseum: the most evident characteristics are the well-preserved temple of Antoninus and Faustina and the basilica of Maxentius (left), and the three surviving columns from the temple of Castor and Pollux.

The city monuments that have survived until the modern day, however, were all built to embellish the *Urbs* during the imperial age. The Forums were the heart of imperial Rome. Built to celebrate the greatness of the city and used to house administrative functions, they were constructed in an area that had been used for gladiatorial combats. There were five forums in all: Caesar's Forum, Augustus's Forum, the Forum of Peace, Nerva's Forum, and Trajan's Forum. Their construction marked the transition of Rome from a republic to an empire. Treading the same path as Julius Caesar, all the most important emperors wished to leave a mark of their own passing, resulting in a collective site that is one of the richest and most fascinating archaeological areas in the world.

Covering an area of 175 yards by 85, Caesar's Forum was a rectangular plaza lined by a dual colonnaded portico. At the far end stood the temple of Venus *Genetrix* (Venus the Begetter), which Caesar built to commemorate his victory in the battle of Pharsalus. Constructed to provide the Forum with greater importance, the temple was one of the most striking examples of political self- acclamation.

To make space for his own Forum, a little further north, Augustus had to buy up a large number of private houses in

nearby Suburra. Inaugurated in 2 BC, the new forum was adorned with gigantic statues, including one of the emperor that was 56 feet tall and stood against a wall built to protect the Forum from fires. At the back of the plaza there was a gigantic temple dedicated to Mars Ultor (Mars the Avenger), the god of war, also in imitation of Caesar's Forum. Large grooved columns supported a triangular tympanum bearing images of Mars, Venus, Aeneas, and Romulus along its sides.

Both Vespasian's Forum, or the Forum of Peace, and Nerva's Forum were less spectacular. The former was a monumental square flanked by the *Templum Pacis* (Temple of Peace), built between AD 71 and 75, to celebrate the peace after the Civil Wars. Nerva's Forum – also known as the Transitorium as it lay in the narrow space between the forums of Augustus, Caesar, Vespasian, and the Republican Forum – had been begun by Domitian but was only inaugurated in AD 98 by Nerva, the succeeding emperor, who named it after himself.

The most majestic forum was built by Trajan to commemorate the Roman victory in Dacia in AD 105. To have it constructed he did not hesitate to remove a section of the Quirinale, where the Trajan Markets were built alongside the steep side of the hill. Trajan's Column was placed inside the forum and inaugurated on May 18, 113. It is made from massive blocks of marble that were hollowed out to create a tomb for the emperor in its base and a spiral staircase that leads to the top. A long spiral frieze on its exterior is carved with 2,500 figures illustrating the two Dacian campaigns.

Columns were raised all over ancient Rome to celebrate military victories. In 176, Marcus Aurelius began to build a monument to commemorate his own victories against the Germans. It was completed in 192 and stood 100 Roman feet high (equal to about 96 modern feet), becoming a total of 138 feet tall if the statue of Saint Paul that Pope Sixtus V had placed on the top in 1589 is considered. Marcus Aurelius' column is composed of 28 drums of marble placed one atop the other and is decorated with a spiral bas-relief that winds around the column 21 times. Inside there is a spiral staircase with 203 steps that climbs up to the statue. Of the other monuments under the aegis of UNESCO, one of the most majestic and best conserved is the Pantheon. Built by Marcus Vipsanius Agrippa in 27 BC and rebuilt by Hadrian between AD 118 and 125, it is the result of the combination of a circular building, a hemispherical dome, and a colonnaded rectangular pronaos. A circular wall over 100 feet high supports the drum, and at the center of the dome there is an oculus 30 feet across that provides the interior with light. In 609, Pope Boniface IV transformed the building into a church, and today it is the site of the tombs of Raphael, Vittorio Emanuele II, Umberto I, and Margherita of Savoy. Nor should the funerary monuments be forgotten. Augustus's Mausoleum is truly impressive, begun in 28 BC after having defeated Antony and Cleopatra. With a diameter of roughly 285 feet and a height of 144, is has a cylindrical body lined with blocks of travertine at the center of which a doorway is preceded by a short flight of steps. On either side of the entrance, two pillars bear bronze tablets engraved with the *Res Gestae*, the emperor's autobiography. From the entry *dromos*, two round corridors were accessed that then encircled the burial chamber. At the center of the chamber there is a cylindrical nucleus lined with blocks of travertine around which the entire construction is focused. Equally remarkable is Hadrian's Tomb, construction of which was begun in AD 121. Today it has become Castel Sant'Angelo, located near the Vatican. Originally, it consisted of a square base on which the cylindrical body of the building we see today stood. This cylinder is 69 feet high and 210 in diameter. A second, smaller cylinder rose from the center in which Hadrian's ashes were placed. Higher up, where the angel bearing a sword now stands, there used to be a chariot drawn by four bronze horses that transported an effigy of the emperor towards the heavens. This has been just a brief summary of the monuments listed by UNESCO as justification for the ancient city's inclusion in the list of World Heritage sites.

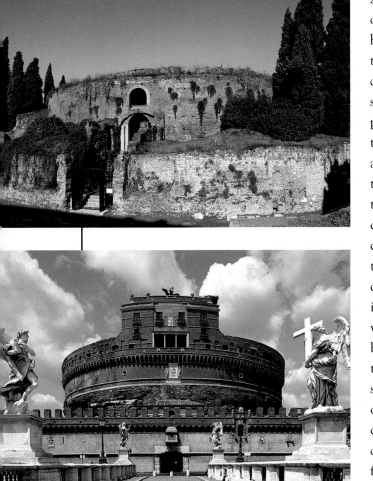

204 top and 204-205 Augustus' Mausoleum, built in 28 BC, holds the ashes of the first emperor of Rome and of some of his relations and descendants. Despite the various uses the building was put to in the imperial era (fort, quarry, theater until 1936), it has still partially retained two of its three levels.

204 bottom Back in the imperial age, Hadrian's Tomb – now Castel Sant'Angelo – already performed the defensive functions that were to characterize its future. It even provided refuge for popes during times of tumult.

205 bottom left Coffers lighten the perfect hemisphere of the Pantheon's dome. The building is lit naturally through the 30-foot oculus that symbolizes the sun.

205 bottom right The Pantheon is one of the most daring and well-proportioned buildings in the world. It has survived in spite of the human and natural cataclysms that have always beset Rome. The concrete of which the dome is made is mixed with lighter and lighter material as it progresses towards the oculus.

206 top left Part of a two-tone mosaic, this figure of Eros riding a dolphin decorated the floor of a room in Caracalla's Baths, which at one time were the most magnificent in Rome.

206 top right Different wall paintings remain in the surviving rooms of Nero's Domus Aurea. Construction began in AD 64 but its delights were not long enjoyed by the emperor, who committed suicide in AD 68.

However, the incredible legacy left by the imperial age to the Eternal City would require many more pages. Just some of the buildings worth mentioning are Caracalla's Baths and the gigantic Circus Maximus, which could seat 350,000 spectators after Trajan had it rebuilt in the second century AD Not to be forgotten, there are recently discovered ancient sites like the Domus Aurea (Nero's magnificent residence) and the tombs along the Appian Way. The excavations carry on: Rome continues to yield more of the wonders of its ancient greatness.

206 center The indelible outline left by the Circus Maximus harks back to Rome's early centuries, to the kingdom of the Etruscan king, Tarquin. It was the setting for horse races from the fourth century BC to the sixth century AD, and it could hold 250,000 spectators.

206 bottom The Octagonal Room in the Domus Aurea was the focus of Nero's immense residence (it can only be visited today by booking). After the emperor's death, everything was done to take it to pieces and reuse the materials in other buildings, thereby dissipating his memory.

206-207 The human figure disappears among the magnificent rooms of the empire's most splendid baths. Built by Caracalla, the complex included hot- and cold-water pools, shops, libraries, massage rooms, beauty-treatment rooms, and gardens.

207 bottom Of the 323,000 square feet of wall paintings in the Domus Aurea, 1,200 have been restored. In part, the paintings have survived because the rooms were buried back in the Roman era beneath other monumental structures, and were thus filled with rubble.

Pompeii, Herculanum, and Oplontis

ITALY

PROVINCE OF NAPLES, REGION OF CAMPANIA
REGISTRATION: 1997
CRITERIA: C (III) (IV) (V)

"A black and dreadful cloud bursting out in gusts of igneous serpentine vapor now and again yawned open to reveal long fantastic flames, resembling flashes of lightning but much larger... Soon afterwards the cloud... began to descend upon the earth, and cover the sea...." This short passage from one of the letters sent by Pliny the Younger to Tacitus described the catastrophic eruption of Vesuvius. When it occurred on August 24, AD 79, Pliny was still a boy; he was staying at the villa at Cape Misenum on the coast of Campania with his uncle, Pliny the Elder. Since early morning, the rumblings of minor earthquakes and the sinister smell of sulfur had persuaded the famous, elderly naturalist to take to the sea in an attempt to reach Pompeii and Herculanum where he would be able to observe and annotate the "terrible prodigy" from a closer viewpoint.

Together with many thousands of others, Pliny the Elder died in the eruption, but his nephew transcribed his notes, which today represent the most vivid account of the hecatomb that struck the magnificent cities on the Campanian coast. Vesuvius had begun to make its voice heard some days before and the inhabitants of Pompeii had hurriedly celebrated the *Vulcanalia*, the sacrificial rites to ingratiate themselves with the god of fire that lived in the bowels of the earth. Some decided to leave the city,

but most were surprised by the deafening rain of pumice discharged from the mountain. And when, on the morning of August 25th, the volcano hurled a burning cloud of ash and small stones into the air at a speed of over 60 mph, there was no longer any means of escape. The two cities that had been the pride of the ancient Romans, places of relaxation and amusement for the patrician families, were buried beneath a blanket of ash 20 feet deep.

Founded by the Samnites in the sixth century BC over an earlier "mixed" settlement of Greek, Etruscan, and indigenous origins, Pompeii passed into Roman hands in 80 BC when the general Publius Cornelius Sulla established the *Colonia Cornelia Veneria Pompeianorum* there. The city, which stood on a plain overlooking the sea at the mouth of the Sarnus River and was surrounded by fertile fields, was soon embellished with public and private buildings, most importantly the temple dedicated to Venus. During the reigns of the emperors Augustus (27 BC–AD 14) and Tiberius (AD 14–37), it underwent a "frenzy of construction." Then, in AD 62, a violent earthquake struck the entire area around Vesuvius. This was so large that, 17 years later when the volcano erupted, Pompeii, Herculanum, and the villas all along the coast were still in a phase of reconstruction.

During the rule of the Bourbon monarchy, removal began of the thick layer of ash, thus revealing the cities exactly as they had appeared in AD 79 and providing the modern world with a fascinating snapshot of life in the Roman era. Temples, baths, houses, urban and rural villas, theaters, streets, aqueducts, shops of all kinds, and even brothels are now visible in their entire original splendor. In Herculanum, the town closest to the volcano, even wooden furniture and foods have been conserved.

208 bottom A tragic mask hangs over a naturalistic scene in the House of Venus Marina. Ironically, in AD 79, this beautiful domus, one of the least known in Pompeii, was being restored at the time of the eruption.

208-209 In this aerial view, the well-preserved cavea of the Great Theater is seen to be slightly oriented towards the northwest, perfectly in line with the cardus maximus and Vesuvius.

209 top left Painted during Nero's reign (the last years of Pompeii), this portrait of the baker Terentius Neus and his wife, now in the Archaeological Museum in Naples, was hung in the tablinum of the house named after the man.

209 top right "Sappho" is the conventional name given to this painting, though it probably was of an imaginary person. Writing was not a common pastime among Roman women.

209 center Apollo the archer, in the southeast corner of the blackened ruins of the temple dedicated to the god: an attempt may have been made to save the original of this statue (today in the National Museum in Naples), which was found outside the building.

209 bottom The fountains were often decorated with busts from which jets of water spurted. One of these, the face of a woman holding a cornucopia, gave the name to the Via dell'Abbondanza (in the photograph), one of the main streets in the city.

ROME

POMPEII
HERCULANUM
OPLONTIS

210 top Marble pools and a cupid in a peristyle in the House of the Vettii, which still has almost all its original furnishings.

210 bottom The oecus (the "room" cited by Pliny and Vitruvius) in the House of the Vettii is decorated with theatrical views and mythological illustrations, all of which were created with an extraordinary sense of volumes and perspective.

210-211 Alexander the Great (bareheaded on the left) prepares to hurl his spear beneath the disconcerted gaze of Darius. This famous mosaic is in the House of the Faun.

Excavation of Pompeii has extended over 109 of the 156 acres of the city and revealed a series of buildings of great historical and artistic value. There are temples (the most important being the Temple of Isis, built by Popidius Ampiatus, a freed slave who became the richest man in the city), the forum, baths, and a great number of superb private homes. The House of the Faun, named after the bronze statuette found standing in the middle of the *impluvium* (a basin that collected rainwater in the main courtyard), covers an area of 3,600 square yards. Built after the earthquake of AD 62 over a previous building, it is the most impressive of the houses in Pompeii. Its various frescoed rooms are arranged around two atria and two gardens with a peristyle. The superb sculptural and mosaic decorations, like the outstanding floor mosaic portraying the battle between the Persian king Darius and Alexander the Great, can now be seen in the archaeological museum in Naples. Typical of the houses of the nobility are the wall paintings in the style of "illusionistic realism," which are paintings of buildings and, sometimes, mythological figures meant to give rooms the impression of greater spaciousness.

211 bottom The Vettii were a rich family of freedmen who moved to Pompeii in the early years of the first century AD. The house named after them was restored after the serious earthquake of AD 62, the first serious warning of the imminent catastrophe. The new frescoes were executed in the Fourth Style, which was characterized by fantastic, almost ethereal motifs. This was the case with these cupids producing perfumes and, at the center, two characters grinding the ingredients.

212 top Traditional themes linked to the myths of Mars and Venus (left in the illustrated composition) make up the frescoes in the tablinum in the house of Marcus Lucretius Fronto. This name appears several times on walls recommending that he be elected to the construction magistracy.

212-213 The Villa of the Mysteries gets its name from the pictorial sequence that illustrates the various phases of an initiation rite into the Dionysiac "mysteries". The initiates of this practice, which was based on preferences different from that of the public religion, were bound to silence. Sileni, satyrs, maenads, and demons with whips populate a cycle that was already famous in antiquity.

Frequent in the gardens of houses of this kind are magnificent fountains, often adorned with sculptures.

These features are also found in the villas. In Pompeii, the most impressive is the Villa of the Mysteries, a luxurious residence that was also a *villa rustica* dedicated to agricultural production.

213 top A simple marble table today furnishes the atrium of the House of Fronto, with the impluvium visible in the foreground and the tablinum in the background. The house was cleared of ash in 1900 and immediately fitted with a roof to protect the paintings as they were gradually returned to the light of day.

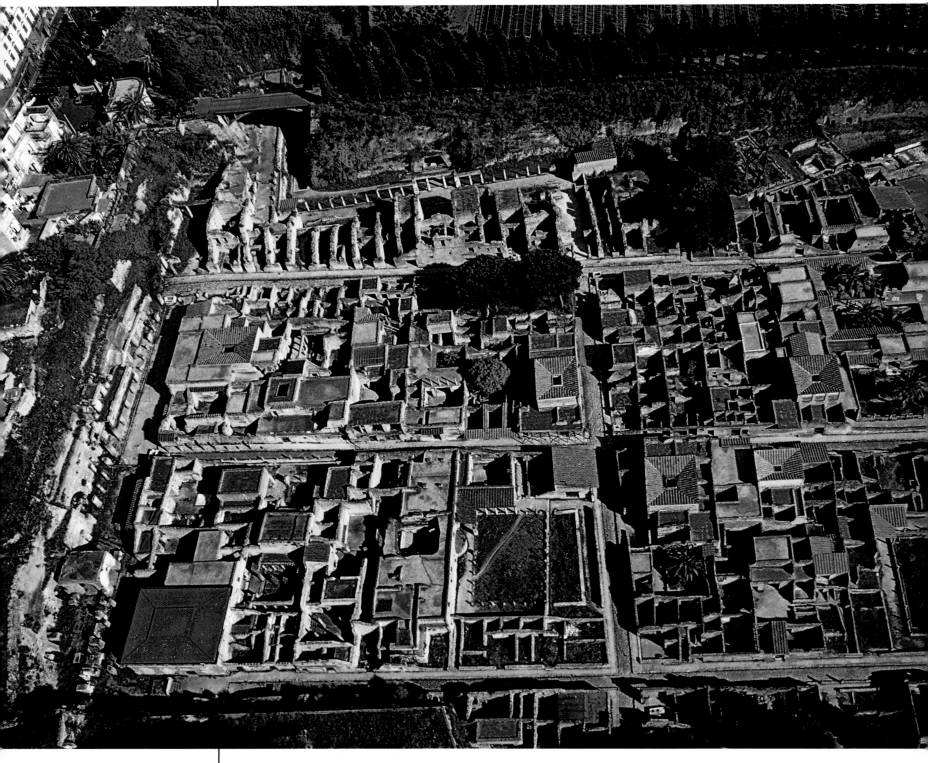

214 top left A nymphaeum is visible in the background of the triclinium of the House of Neptune and Amphitrite, as well as a lovely polychrome mosaic (right) from which the house gets its name.

214 top right The Collegio degli Augustali is decorated with paintings in the Third Style. It was dedicated to the cult of the emperor and was administered by six men appointed for the period of one year. The divinization of Augustus was made official by Tiberius a few years before the eruption.

214-215 *This aerial view covers the entire excavation zone of Herculaneum. At top right there are the suburban baths, in the opposite corner the Collegio degli Augustali, and, in the center foreground, the city baths. Unlike Pompeii, Herculaneum was submerged beneath mud and volcanic detritus.*

215 top *A bust and a marble pool can be seen in the half-light of the suburban baths. The vestibule is illuminated by a light-well over the arcades.*

215 bottom *The House of the Deer, built between AD 55 and 70, is one of the largest in Herculaneum. The city buildings are very well preserved, particularly above ground. Together they formed a small town about one third the size of Pompeii, with roughly 5,000 inhabitants.*

The exceptionally fine Villa of the Papyruses, on the other hand, can be seen at Herculanum, where there is also a basilica, baths complex with annexed *palaestra*, and a theater that seated 3,000 spectators. Built on a series of terraces sloping down towards the sea, the Villa of the Papyruses boasted a 72-yard-long swimming pool, a 100-yard-long 40-yard-wide peristyle decorated with mosaics, 50 bronze statues, and 20 marble ones. Believed to have belonged to Appius Claudius Pulcrus, a man of culture and a friend of Cicero, this villa has been named after the important discovery inside its library of 1,758 papyruses bearing texts of the Epicurean philosopher Philodemus of Gadara.

Another two extraordinary residences are found at Oplontis, three miles from Pompeii where the modern town of Torre Annunziata stands. The first is a perfect example of a "villa of *otium*" (leisure) and is attributed to Poppea Sabina, the second wife of Emperor Nero. Enormous and magnificent with a very elegant baths area, it was built in the first century AD and enlarged during the reign of Claudius. The second villa, known as the "Villa of Lucius Crassius," was a residential complex with an attached farm that produced agricultural products and sold wine. At the moment of the eruption 54 men took refuge in the farm's storerooms, and of their bodies, like so many other people who died in Pompeii and Herculanum, archaeologists have been able to take casts by pouring liquid plaster into the hollows and cavities in the petrified ashes left by their disintegrated bodies. Today brought "back to life," even in the expressions on their faces and folds of their clothes, they are perhaps the most horrible and fascinating relics of that fateful day.

Cilento and the Vallo di Diano with the Sites of Paestum and Velia

ITALY

Province of Salerno, Campania
Registration: 1998
Criteria: C (III) (IV)

Lauded by Virgil and other Roman poets, the roses of Paestum were for a long time more famous than its temples. In the drawings of Piranesi, they can be seen lush and blooming against the background of the ruins, and descriptions of them are found in Goethe's *Journey in Italy*. In 1802, the traveler Johann Gottfried Seume even set out on foot from distant Lipsia inspired by his desire to smell their intoxicating perfume.

The fertile plain on which Paestum stands is bounded on one side by the warm Tyrrhenian Sea, and, on the other, by the green hills of the Cilento, and boasts a climate and flora of extraordinary charm.

It was the landscape, abundant water, and proximity to the sea that, since remote times, brought the area of the Cilento and the flat strip of land referred to as the Vallo di Diano to play a fundamental role in the development of Mediterranean civilization. Inhabited since the Neolithic era, the zone had been colonized by Anatolic-Aegean populations before when, in the seventh century BC, people from Thessaly founded Poseidonia, the city that was renamed Paestum in 237 BC following the arrival of the Romans.

Linked to the myths of Odysseus and the sirens, Jason and the Argonauts, and the battle between the god Heracles and the Centaurs, Poseidonia grew to be rich and impressive, as attested to by the rose-colored limestone temples that have survived to this day in exceptional condition. The earliest building is the Basilica, a name that was attributed to it in the eighteenth century by archaeologists working for the Bourbons during the first excavation operations, though it was actually a temple dedicated

216 left The temple of Neptune (460 BC), the largest and best-preserved building in Paestum, was originally dedicated to Hera. It features six columns along the façade and fourteen on the longer sides. Its construction reflects great expertise, which can be noted in aspects such as its overall harmony.

216-217 The basilica, on the right side of the picture (the temple of Neptune is on the left), is the oldest monument in Paestum (circa 550 BC). Its name originated in the eighteenth century, when archaeologists mistakenly interpreted the temple, which was actually dedicated to Hera, as a civic building of the Roman era.

217 top The temple of Ceres, or the Athenaion, was built on the highest point in the city. Built around 500 BC, it is of great architectural interest as it merges two styles, the archaic Doric and the Ionic.

to Hera. Built in Doric style in the mid-sixth century BC, its tapered columns, whose shafts are fuller at the middle and whose capitals are decorated with leafy crowns, are miraculously still in intact. Aligned with the Basilica, the Temple of Neptune, or the *Poseidonion*, is the largest and best conserved of Paestum's buildings. Built between 460 and 450 BC

ROME

PAESTUM
VELIA

217 bottom The Romans arrived in Paestum in 273 BC and only partially modified the layout of the city. It was the Romans who built the amphitheater, shown here in an aerial photograph, as well as the temple dedicated to Jupiter, Juno and Minerva.

218 top The slab covering
the Diver's Tomb is now
displayed in the National
Archaeological Museum of
Paestum. Archaeologists
agree that the delicate

painting of the nude young
man, in the act of diving,
should be interpreted as a
symbolic representation of
the sudden transition
between life and death.

218-219 and 219 bottom
The lateral slabs from the
Diver's Tomb depict a
banquet. A comparison of
this convivial scene with
highly similar ones, found on
Attic pottery, has made it
possible to date the tomb to
about 475-470 BC.

in Doric style, its majesty and style are reminiscent of the Temple of Zeus at Olympia. On the far side of the remains of the Amphitheater and civil buildings lies the *Athenaion*, renamed the Temple of Ceres, which dates back to 510 BC and owes its lighter and more elegant proportions than the other two temples to its blend of Doric and Ionic styles.

In the fourth century BC, the Greeks of Poseidonia came to coexist with the Lucanians and Etruscans, with the result that the different cultures slowly merged. The Lucanians were responsible for the construction of a massive quadrilateral defensive wall with smoothed corners. The Etruscans were responsible for the tombs in the vast necropolis that lay outside the city limits, discovery of which was made in 1968. Of these, the most interesting is the Tomb of the Diver, named after the famous painting on the ceiling slab of a young man about to dive from a springboard.

The city's contact with Rome in 273 BC led to the construction of the Italic Temple, which was dedicated to the triad of Jupiter, Juno, and Minerva.

Despite its name change, the city remained essentially autonomous for a long time, as did the nearby city of Elea, or Velia. Excavations of Velia are still in progress but much of the city was lost during the Middle Ages when the Normans used the stones of its temples to build a castle. Nevertheless, Velia preserves the memory of those glorious times when it was the birthplace of the philosophers Parmenides and Zeno, during that ancient period when the culture of Magna Grecia was the universal culture of the Mediterranean.

220-221 The presence of a place of worship in Delphi, visible here almost in its entirety, was documented as early as the Mycenaean era. However, the first sanctuary of the oracle was built at the beginning of the eighth century BC.

220 bottom The Omphalos or "navel," the stone that marked the center of the earth, was the sacral heart of Delphi. Though quite ancient, the stone at the local museum is not the original one, which was lost centuries ago.

221 left The work of Polymedes of Argos, who sculpted it between 610 and 580 BC, this kouros (over 6 and a half feet tall) in the archaic Doric style is one of a pair of statues portraying Kleobis and Biton, the two pious sons of one of Hera's priestesses. However, according to another interpretation they represent the Dioscuri. Found in the sanctuary of Apollo in 1893, the kouroi are now at the Museum of Delphi.

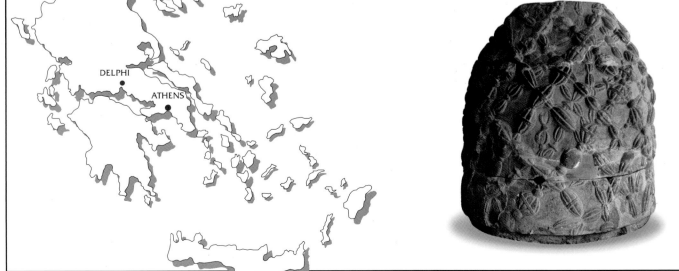

221 top right Used for the Pythic Games, which were second only to the Olympic Games, the stadium at Delphi was built in the fifth century BC and was restructured in the second century AD at the expense of Herod Atticus. The stone terraces and monumental entrance were added at this time.

Delphi
GREECE

PREFECTURE OF PHOKIS, STEREÁ ELLÁDA
REGISTRATION: 1987
CRITERIA: (I) (II) (III) (IV) (VI)

221 bottom right From the cavea of the theater at Delphi, which had 35 rows of seats, spectators could watch the paeans, stagings of Apollo's battle against Python, as well as ritual dances in the god's honor.

The legend of the origin of the most important religious site in ancient Greece begins with two eagles set free by Zeus in the antipodes of the world; the place where they met – later called Delphi – was where the king of the gods placed the Sacred Stone (the *omphalos*) that marked the center of the world. It was here that the goddess Gaea and her son, the serpent Python, dwelt until Apollo, enchanted by the beauty of the place, left Mount Olympus to take possession of it, defeating the serpent in order to do so. From that time on, Apollo lived in Delphi for nine months of the year, imposing on himself the other three months as a period of exile for having killed a rival. During his stay at Delphi, he spoke to humans through his oracle, the Pythia.

Passing from legend to history, the earliest evidence of a place of worship here dates back to the Mycenaean age, though the construction of a sanctuary to accommodate the oracle was not built until the eighth century BC. Authors from Greek and Roman literature such as Pliny, Plato, Aeschylus, Cicero, and Strabo all left behind abundant descriptions of the site and the prophecies that were announced there. Generals, colonizers and even simple citizens afflicted by problems of health and money, consulted the Pythia. The oracle's responses were also recorded in mythological stories, the most famous being that of Oedipus, who was told he would kill his father to marry his mother, and who tried, in vain and by all means possible, to evade his destiny.

The visible remains of the Temple of Apollo are those of a fourth-century-BC Doric building that was built over another, much older building. At the center of both was the *adyton* (prohibited area) where the Pythia sat holding an olive branch. According to tradition, the oracle – a woman who could be young or old, aristocratic or common, the only requirement being that she had to be a native of Delphi – fell into a sort of trance and received inspiration from sweet-smelling fumes emerging from a crack in the ground. After centuries of debate, the recent discovery of traces of inebriating gas coming from a geological stratum beneath the archaeological site has proved the veracity of the ancient Greek and Roman sources.

Although the site is still very beautiful, Delphi is but a shadow of what it was during its period of greatest splendor, or until the year AD 191 when it was conquered by the Romans. Until that time, it had been visited by people from around the Mediterranean basin who brought gifts to give thanks to Apollo and his oracle. High quality objects found during excavation can be seen in the museum next to the site, but little remains of the many buildings, votive temples, and 3,000 statues that lined the Sacred Way leading to the Temple of Apollo. The only building that archaeologists have been able to reconstruct is the Treasury of the Athenians, dating back to the end of the fifth century BC, which was built following the victory over the Persians at the battle of Marathon (490 BC). The ruins of the black and white marble Altar of Chios (fifth century BC) are clearly distinguishable in the Ionic Stoa of the Athenians (478 BC) as well as the two monumental fountains from the early

222 left The Sphinx of Naxos (at the Delphi Museum) honors the oracle and was donated by the islanders towards the middle of the sixth century BC. It has a woman's face and the body of a winged dog.

222-223 This view of the Marmaria, the "marble quarry," shows the tholos, the sanctuary of Athena Pronaia (fourth century BC), and the remains of a previous temple of Athena, presumably constructed towards the end of the sixth century BC.

223 top left Built in about 380 BC, the tholos was partly rebuilt in 1938. Its functions are unknown, but given its refined overall elegance it was indubitably an important building, possibly a sanctuary dedicated to Gea.

223 top right The Stoa of the Athenians was built in 479 BC to house the booty from the naval battle of Salamis, which marked a dramatic defeat for the Persians.

Roman period that adorned the fountain of Castalia, where pilgrims purified themselves before proceeding to the oracle. Also of great interest, as well as being better preserved than the religious buildings, are the theater (fourth century BC, but rebuilt by the Romans in the imperial age) and the stadium that was built in the fifth century BC to hold the Pythian Games (second in importance only to the Olympic Games) and remodeled in the second century AD by Herod Atticus. Once they had conquered Delphi, the Romans were more interested in its wealth and sporting fame than its religious value, though oracles were allowed to continue dispensing prophecies there for another two centuries. However, in AD 393, the Roman emperor Theodosius abolished the "vile rites and pagan games," marking the demise of the site forever.

224 top The Archaeological Museum of Delphi houses much of the rich statuary from the site, as well as valuable works from the treasuries and sanctuaries, and "secondary" objects like this gold button, which came from a ceremonial garment.

224-225 A splendid example of mature Archaic art, the bas-relief on the treasury of the Siphnians is decorated with representations of the gigantomachy, or the war the Olympian gods waged against the Giants. The treasuries housed the "tenths," tributes the Hellenic city-states paid to Apollo.

225 top left A griffin of Asiatic origin decorates this small votive plaque, held at the Delphi Museum. The local museum was inaugurated in 1903 but was expanded a number of times; a new hall was added in 1974 to house gold and ivory objects.

225 top right This natural-sized head made with the chryselephantine technique – using gold for the garments and ivory for the flesh – probably portrays the god Apollo.

The Acropolis in Athens
GREECE

ATTICA
REGISTRATION: 1987
CRITERIA: C (I) (II) (III) (IV) (VI)

226-227 The area was first settled during the Neolithic period, and in the Mycenaean era the Acropolis was a fortified citadel. During the sixth century BC the tyrant Pisisatrus started the work that would ultimately give the Acropolis its monumental layout. The view is dominated by the Parthenon, or temple of Athena Parthenos.

226 bottom Shown here is
the western side of the
Parthenon, which was built
between 447 and 432 BC.
The originals of the three

statues from the west
tympanum, depicting the
contest between Athena
and Poseidon, are now at
the Acropolis Museum.

227 bottom Three young
hydriaphoroi (water-
bearers) carry their
hydriae on their left
shoulders, in a detail from
the north frieze of the
Parthenon. As a whole,

this section depicts a
sacrificial procession.
Some of the blocks, which
average 4 feet in length,
are housed at the Acropolis
Museum, while others are
at the British Museum.

Sublime wisdom in times of war and peace was the characteristic of Athena, the goddess of the most splendid and powerful city in Greece. According to myth, she was victorious over her brother Poseidon in the struggle to possess Attica, which she then consigned to king Cecrops, having appeared to him in all her magnificence on the top of the hill on which the Acropolis was to be built. On that occasion, she offered him the gift of an olive tree, as opposed to the gift of a horse – an efficient instrument of war –, which had just been offered by Poseidon. The king's wisdom led him to accept the apparently modest symbol of hard, honest work and the oil trade that was related to it, but, above all, of the peace and justice that were necessary for the city to progress.

Although the construction in the seventh century BC of the temples dedicated to Athena, Zeus, Artemis, Heracles, and even the defeat of Poseidon was attributed to this legendary event, the site on which they were built – the steep rocky hill which was to become the religious heart of the Athenian *polis* that today dominates the chaotic capital of Greece– had in fact been inhabited since the Neolithic period, and the Mycenaeans had built a fortified citadel on the spot. The first to give the Acropolis a monumental appearance was the tyrant Peisistratus in the sixth century BC, the same leader who instituted the Panathenian Games, held in August every four years in honor of the goddess Athena. One hundred years later, after the interlude in which the Persians invaded Athens and placed their own idols on the Acropolis, the ruler Cimon commissioned the architect Kallicrates to design a magnificent temple dedicated to Athena Parthenos.

The year 449 BC marked the point at which the Acropolis was to be transformed into the most extraordinary and beautiful architectural complex in the Classical world. It would represent the meeting point between philosophic conceptions, ethical and religious values, political will, and the technical skills of the proud Athenian *polis*. There were two main personalities behind the development: Pericles, the city leader personifying Athenian democracy, and Phidias, his close friend, who may have been the greatest sculptor in history.

Construction of Kallicrates' temple dedicated to Athena Parthenos – universally known as the Parthenon – had suffered an interruption but was completed under the direction of the architect Ictinus. He turned the original plans into an extraordinary Doric octastyle peripteral temple in which every measurement, proportion, and form was simply the translation into stone of the arithmetical, geometric, and philosophical theories of Pythagoras and Plato. Even today, the numerous techniques incorporated to influence the observer's perspective and create optical illusions to harmonize and mitigate individual

ATHENS

elements of the monument are astounding.

In addition to the architectural expertise of the construction, the decoration of the Parthenon, completed by Phidias his skilled workshop – the greatest masters of the era – transformed the monument into what has been rightly described as an "experiment in perfection." Unfortunately the gigantic statue of Athena executed by Phidias in ivory and gold using the chryselephantine technique has been destroyed, and a good part of the friezes that adorned it can no longer be admired *in situ* as they are scattered among the museums of Europe, in particular the British Museum in London. However, when one is standing beside the Parthenon, the imagination easily relocates the sculptural masterpieces on the pediments of the temple. They were originally painted in bright colors and portrayed the birth of Athena from Zeus's head and the contest between the goddess and Poseidon for supremacy over the city.

Carved decorations on the 92 metopes (41 of which are still in place) depict allegories of the struggle between Good and Evil, such as the war between the Greeks and the Trojans (an epic image

evoking the still-smoldering conflict with the hated Persians) and battles against Amazons, centaurs, and giants. The absolute masterpiece of Phidias was the Ionic frieze in the *naos* (the abode of the goddess Athena inside the temple) depicting the long and solemn procession of Athenian citizens during the Panathenian festivities. The astounding plasticity of the figures, the richness of the details down to the thinnest garment, and the care lavished on individual jewels, hairstyles, facial expressions, and gestures, which provide an immediate understanding of the psychology of the various figures in the procession, demonstrate Phidias' exceptional awareness of the human figure, both physically and philosophically.

With the Parthenon almost complete, in 437 BC Pericles inaugurated construction to provide the Acropolis with a worthy entrance, harmonizing proportions, elegance, and stateliness. The challenge was enormous but one that another great architect, Mnesicles, accepted enthusiastically. Construction was concluded in record time – just four years. The splendid *propylaea* were the result of this project, devised by Mnesicles with an

228 top The Porch of the Caryatids, on the south side of the Erechtheum, was built in the Ionic style in about 420 BC. Five of the six original graceful caryatids, which have been attributed to Alcamenes, are now at the Acropolis Museum; the sixth one is at the British Museum in London.

228 center The east façade of the Erechtheum is decorated with six elegant Ionic columns. According to tradition, it was built over the site of the contest between Athena and Poseidon, which decided who would be the patron of the city. Nearby is the olive tree said to be sacred to Athena.

228 bottom Built in the Ionic style by the architect Kallicrates towards the end of the fifth century BC, the little temple of Athena Nike is an amphiprostyle building, meaning that it has a rectangular layout, with two columned porticoes on the short sides.

228-229 *This view shows the southeast corner of the Erechtheum, with the Porch of the Caryatids clearly visible. Constructed in the Ionic style in about 420 BC, the building was divided into two parts to worship the two chief deities of Attica, Athena and Poseidon-Erechtheus.*

229 top *The Propylaea, monumental pylons at the entrance to the Acropolis, were designed by Mnesicles and built between 437 and 432 BC; they include a central structure and two lateral ones. The north wing was the Pinakotheke and its walls were decorated with frescoes and painted panels.*

230 top The theater of Herod Atticus faces south over the modern city in the southwest corner of the Acropolis. Still used for important theatrical performances, the building was donated to the city by the famous patron of the arts, man-of-letters, and Sophist of the second century AD. Herod Atticus was the consul for Antoninus Pius and gave lessons in rhetoric in Athens.

230-231 The cavea of the theater of Dionysios Eleuthereus (fifth century BC) stands on the southern slopes of the Acropolis, the southeast corner of which is seen in the background. This theater was the most famous in the Greek world and took its name from the Great Dionysia, a dramatic festival held in honor of the god of music.

230 bottom Beyond the ruins of a portico of the Roman agora, the octagonal Tower of the Winds dates to the first century BC, the late Hellenistic age. It had two functions: inside there was a water clock and outside there were relief decorations portraying the winds (still partially visible). A weathervane on the top of the roof indicated the direction of the wind, identifiable by the relief to which it pointed.

231 top Seen here from the interior, this propylaeum was the principal west entrance to the Roman agora. There are few traces of the agora today, but it was a large complex: porticoes on four sides and shops on three bounded an area of about 10,000 square yards.

231 bottom left The Hephaisteion (temple of Hephestus) is also known as the Theseion as the body of the hero Theseus was supposely buried there. Theseus's remains were found in the fifth century BC by the politician and general Cimon on the island of Skiros, where he fought the Persians. The temple is famous for its excellent condition and is unique in that it still has its original roof.

"ascending" perspective that perfectly overcame the problem created by the "contrast" with the Parthenon. The elegant colonnaded structure with porticoed wings lines a steep flight of steps, emphasizing the sacredness of the Acropolis. A dozen or so years later, Kallicrates was once more called on to design a small, elegant, and original temple dedicated to Athena Nike to be constructed on a rocky spur beside the *propylaea*. It was decorated with allegories of Victory by an excellent but unfortunately anonymous pupil of Phidias' school.

The last building to be raised on the Acropolis, at the end of the century, was the Erechtheum. The temple stands to the north of the Parthenon near the sacred olive tree that was traditionally recognized as being the gift of Athena to the city, but

the city's atmospheric pollution.

Despite the decline of Athens, the Acropolis continued to be venerated for a long period, and not just for its religious significance. To the Romans, the Acropolis was a museum representing the essence of the philosophy, politics, and aesthetics of ancient Greece. In other words, it was a model for Rome to follow.

In later epochs, the Parthenon was transformed into a Byzantine church and later a mosque, but it and the other buildings on the Acropolis have survived the darkest eras almost unharmed. The first wound suffered by the Acropolis occurred in 1687; at the time, the Turks, who had turned the ancient temple of Athena Parthenos into a munitions store during the Venetian siege of the city, occupied

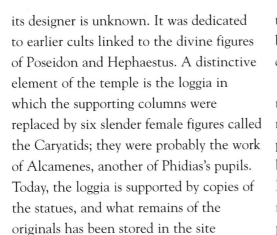

231 center right and bottom right Perhaps representing a triton, this colossal but fragmentary statue (top) was found near Agrippa's Odeon. The building stood opposite the Stoa of Attalus (at the bottom of the photograph) and was restored to seem a contemporary building. Today it houses the Agora Museum.

its designer is unknown. It was dedicated to earlier cults linked to the divine figures of Poseidon and Hephaestus. A distinctive element of the temple is the loggia in which the supporting columns were replaced by six slender female figures called the Caryatids; they were probably the work of Alcamenes, another of Phidias's pupils. Today, the loggia is supported by copies of the statues, and what remains of the originals has been stored in the site museum safe from the damage caused by

the hill. The Venetians fired an incendiary bomb, causing a tremendous explosion and destroying a section of the temple.

The most serious attack on the monument took place at the start of the nineteenth century and was apparently peaceful in intent. Perhaps for love of beauty or perhaps for envy, Lord Elgin, the British ambassador in Constantinople, removed Phidias' masterpieces from the pediments and shipped them back to England.

Mycenae
GREECE

DISTRICT OF ARGOLIS, PELOPONNESE
REGISTRATION: 1999
CRITERIA: C (I) (II) (III) (IV) (VI)

"**E**xultant, I announce to Your Majesty that I have discovered the tombs that, according to tradition, belong to Agamemnon, Cassandra, Eurymedon, and their companions. In the tombs, I found immense treasures, which alone would make the finest of museums famous." This was the message sent by Heinrich Schliemann to king George I of Greece on December 6, 1876. The German archaeologist was in a state of extreme excitement: he had only begun to excavate the site of Mycenae three months earlier and had already achieved phenomenal results supporting his intuition. He had followed to the letter the indications given by Pausanias (the Greek geographer of the second century AD) who had identified Mycenae as the city of the Achaeans, the people that declared war on Troy, as narrated by Homer in *The Iliad*.

That day Schliemann had held in his hands a marvelous gold leaf mask, which he had found in one of the tombs. "I have seen the face of Agamemnon!" he exulted. Though he was considered by many a coarse autodidact and a shady figure embodying the worst characteristics of a tradesman, Schliemann had the undoubted merit of opening up a new world to archaeological studies and paving the way to an understanding of the most important civilization in Greek prehistory, one that flourished between the sixteenth and twelfth centuries BC.

The exact location of Mycenae had been known, in fact, for thirty or so years. Part of the cyclopean walls between 20 and 26 feet thick that run for nearly a mile and the stately, monumental Lion Gate (named after the two stylized animals carved in bas-relief on columns supporting the triangular architrave) had been found on a flat area between two mountains in Euboea in

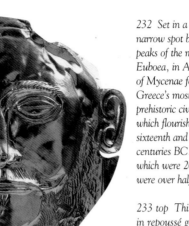

232 Set in a desolate and narrow spot between two peaks of the mountains of Euboea, in Argolis, the city of Mycenae founded one of Greece's most important prehistoric civilizations, which flourished between the sixteenth and twelfth centuries BC. Its walls, which were 20-26 feet thick, were over half a mile long.

233 top This death mask in repoussé gold is also known as "Schliemann's Agamemnon," due to the fact that the Greek archaeologist discovered it on December 6, 1876 in Tomb V of Grave Circle A in Mycenae. Dating from the second half of the sixteenth century BC, it is now at the National Archaeological Museum in Athens.

233 bottom A noblewoman is portrayed in this fresco fragment from a Mycenaean palace. It is now at the National Museum in Athens.

Argolis. Yet, Schliemann was not interested in the walls or gate and did not even consider the ruins of the royal palace, places of worship, houses, or granaries of importance. He dug large trenches through them, ruining important archaeological data from the middle and late Mycenaean periods. However, he did discover Grave Circle A (with 19 graves) inside the city wall, and Grave Circle B (with 25 graves, of which 14 were royal tombs) just outside the Lion Gate. Grave Circle B included the grave Schliemann believed to be that of Agamemnon.

The two complexes date back to the fifteenth and sixteenth centuries BC respectively. Some are shaft graves dug out of the rock, and some tumulus graves. Inside, he found jewelry, masks,

234 top The tholos (a round or pseudo-ogival domed structure) of the tomb of Clytemnestra, one of the nine beehive tombs in Mycenae, dates from the end of the fourteenth century BC.

234 center left and bottom right The most beautiful royal Mycenaean tombs (top, the treasury of Atreus; bottom, the tomb of Clytemnestra) are preceded by a long dromos, or sacred way.

234 center right Mycenaean dwellings are not well preserved, perhaps due also to Schliemann's work. In searching for the necropolis, he dug wide trenches through them.

234 bottom left The great ramp, which also had sections of steps, led from the Lion Gate to the royal palace of the Atrids.

235 Framed by four colossal monoliths, the Lion Gate consists of a flat triangle with two stylized lions sculpted in bas-relief on opposite sides of a column. Somber and severe, the gate represents the height of Mycenaean architecture.

and vases made from gold and silver, decorated mostly with abstract motifs; there were also fragments of clothing and goods from far away places like Nubia, Anatolia, Syria, and Mesopotamia, demonstrating the high level of civilization and wealth achieved during the Mycenaean period.

Carried along on a wave of enthusiasm, and using the Homeric myths as his "guide," Schliemann undertook a new excavation in Argolis in 1884, helped by Wilhelm Dörpfeld, in which he unearthed the lost city of Tiryns, which, in *The Iliad*, was ruled by king Diomedes. Tiryns boasted extraordinary walls, nearly 800 yards long and up to 26 feet thick, that enclosed cells and corridors. Inside the walls, he found a vast royal palace and a city laid out in a manner linking it indissolubly to Mycenae from the earliest days of the Mycenaean civilization.

To the visitor, the ruins of Mycenae and Tiryns do not have the same charm as more refined and "recent" archaeological areas in Greece, but for archaeologists they are of fundamental importance to understanding the subsequent Hellenic civilization, offspring of the earlier Mycenaean one. And, even if they do so through gritted teeth, they are obliged to thank that "visionary" Schliemann.

236 left The tombs of
Grave Circle A have
yielded a variety of
everyday objects, such as
this long pin in silver and
gold, found on the body of
a woman buried in Tomb
III.

236-237 Grave Circle A
contained six royal tombs
that were between about 3
and 13 feet deep, enclosed
in a double circular wall.
There were 19 bodies
buried in them and the
funerary treasures found
there included nearly 31
pounds of gold.

236 bottom Far less elaborate than "Agamemnon's Mask," this specimen dates from the fifteenth century BC and is now preserved at the National Archaeological Museum in Athens.

237 bottom left A lion-hunting scene in gold and silver decorates the blade of this bronze dagger, discovered in Grave Circle A. The work dates back to the sixteenth century BC.

237 bottom right Found in Tomb IV of Funerary Circle A, Nestor's Cup, 5.7 inches high, features handles ending in two animal figures that look as if they are either biting the edge or drinking from the cup.

The Megalithic Temples of Malta

MALTA

Various localities on the islands
of Malta and Gozo
Registration: 1980, 1992
Criteria: (IV)

It was in 1913 that the Maltese archaeologist Themistocles Zanmit heard the curious complaints of a farmer regarding the presence of huge rocks in his field near Paola. When he went to see, he found he was looking at the megalithic temple of Tarxien. Ten years earlier, another fortuitous circumstance had revealed the entrance to another extraordinary hypogean temple, that of Hal Saflieni. On that occasion, workers excavating a well had had to interrupt their digging when they came across a layer of rock that hid, they later discovered, three underground chambers. Excavated in the rock as much as 6,000 years ago, the chambers contained a chamber that had probably been used as the ceremonial room, and a series of catacombs found to contain almost 7,000 graves, amulets, statuettes, vases, and other objects.

At the start of the twentieth century, Malta and Gozo figured prominently in the interest of many experts, in particular British scholars, who set about performing a series of digs, attracted by the puzzle of the many megalithic monuments scattered across the two islands. Some of these were even older than Stonehenge, having been built between 4,000 and 2,500 years ago by a people that had probably reached the islands from Sicily, though their civilization later disappeared completely, perhaps at the hands of conquerors or an epidemic. Even today, only hypotheses can be made about the culture and fate of the people responsible for the temples. They were a peaceful people (no defensive works or weapons have been found at any of the sites, not even rudimentary ones) whose livelihood was based on agriculture; they owned domestic animals and developed remarkable skills in their production of handcrafts. As for their "spiritual life," the discovery of a great many statuettes, both large and small, of the Mother Goddess, a figure common to all the Mediterranean area, indicates that they practiced cults linked to fertility.

It is not yet possible to determine whether the priests of the cult were men or women, or whether the priests were the heads of the community or simply performed a ceremonial role. The main temples on Malta – Tarxien and Hal Saflieni, Hagar Qin and Mnajdra, Skorba and Ta' Hagrat, Tal Qadi and Bugibba – as well as the Ggantija

238 top left One of the entrances of Tarxien in the village of Paola. This enormous complex was discovered by chance in 1913 by the Maltese archaeologist Themistocles Zanmit.

238 bottom left This looks like the lower section of a colossal effigy of the Mother Goddess at Tarxien. The many images linked to the cult and the remains of animal sacrifices demonstrate that the megalithic temples on Malta and Gozo were temples.

238 top right Known as the "Sleeping Woman of Malta," this terracotta statuette was found in the hypogean temple of Hal Saflieni. It is one of the most refined images of the Mother Goddess, who was associated with the cult of fertility throughout the Mediterranean.

238-239 Of the megalithic monuments on the island, Tarxien represents the highest point of artistic expression by the early Maltese people. The decorations on the stones are inspired by nature: dominant motifs are spirals and fish.

239 top left Only an aerial view allows the observer a complete understanding of the megalithic complex of Tarxien. Covering 5,000 square yards in all, most of its structures date back to 3000-2500 BC, but its earliest nucleus was built around 3600 BC.

239 top right One of the rooms inside Hal Salfieni. Excavated from the rock starting about 6,000 years ago, the rock tomb is formed by a large and probably ceremonial chamber and catacombs in which the remains of roughly 7,000 people have been found.

GGANTIJA

LA VALLETTA
HAL SAFLIENI
TARXIEN

MNAJDRA
HAGAR QIN

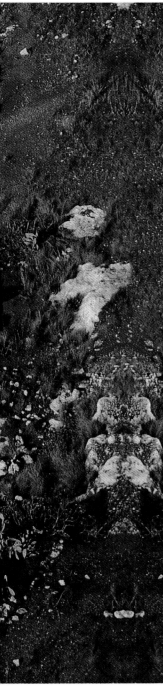

complex on Gozo were built in pairs, a short distance from one another, suggesting to scholars that they may have been used respectively by male and female priests. Each of the megalithic complexes was built with a half-dome roof and it is thought that animal skins furnished the rest of the covering.

Despite their enormous size (Tarxien covers 5,000 square yards), the temples –built on a cloverleaf plan– have a central chamber just 16 feet across and ten feet tall. This means that no more

240 bottom left Dug out of a massive monolith, this entrance to one of the temples at Hagar Qin is called the "Gate of the oracle." The complex was built in several stages between 3600 and 2700 BC.

240 bottom right Although the megalithic complexes of Malta are very large, the chambers dedicated to worship did not allow many people inside at the same time, to be suggesting that the rites were not open to the people.

241 top One of the passages that leads to the ceremonial chambers at Hagar Qin. Little or nothing is known of the Maltese Neolithic people, nor of their demise, which may have been due to war or epidemic.

240 top Hagar Qin, situated on a plateau in the south part of Malta. There is no evidence that the temples had a stone roof, and it is supposed that they were covered by a canopy made of animal skins.

240-241 A view of Mnajdra, Malta's oldest temple, built around 4000 BC. Note the cloverleaf plan that was characteristic of all the megalithic complexes on the island.

than a dozen people could enter at one time, which suggests that the people did not indulge in rituals. Traces on the walls, however, indicate that the chamber was entirely lined with ocher-colored stucco featuring spiral decorations and pictures of animals painted with great artistic skill.

In some temples, the central chamber contains a niche (called the

"niche of the oracle") in the wall opposite the entrance that the sunlight enters on the days of the equinox. Many of the megaliths stand in positions aligned with the sun, suggesting to some that history's first calendar may reside on Malta. This could even make Malta the next place to become fashionable among New-Age enthusiasts.

241 center In the archaic Maltese language, Hagar Qin means "standing stones" and takes its name from these menhirs on the edge of the complex. Each one weighs about 70 tons.

241 bottom The temple of Ggantija on the island of Gozo. According to an ancient legend, this mysterious place was the abode of a giantess with superhuman strength named Qala.

Carthage
TUNISIA

DISTRICT OF TUNIS
REGISTRATION: 1979
CRITERIA: C (II) (III) (VI)

242-243 Of the Antonine Baths, today only their base remains, where the storerooms and furnaces for heating water were located. The thermal salons were found on a raised floor supported by giant columns. One of the columns, visible on the right in the photo, has been reconstructed in recent years. It is almost 50 feet tall and crowned by a Corinthian capital.

In 218–217 BC, the young Carthaginian general, Hannibal, crossed the Alps at the head of an army of 38,000 soldiers, 8,000 cavalry, and 40 or so elephants. His plan was to attack the heart of his enemy, conquer Rome, and take over control of the Mediterranean. The first battles were fought on the Trebbia River, at Lake Trasimeno, and at Cannae and seemed to support Hannibal's strategy, but once arrived at the gates of Rome, he delayed because his army was tired, with the result that the enemy had time to reorganize, thus carrying the conflict back to Africa. In 204, after fifteen years of uninterrupted warfare, Scipio the African inflicted a very heavy defeat on the Carthaginians at Zama and the city of Carthage was obliged to surrender.

The history of Carthage is mostly famous for the episode when its troops challenged the hegemony of Rome in the three Punic Wars, but the city dates back to at least six hundred years earlier, officially from 814 BC. Legend has it that Carthage was founded by Dido, who escaped from Tyre after Pygmalion, her brother, killed her husband in order to take the throne. In reality, it was probably a group of exiles who, after unsuccessfully trying to take the Phoenician city, built a new settlement on the coast of what is today Tunisia.

Few ruins actually remain of Punic Carthage, destroyed first by the Romans and then definitively by the Arabs around AD 700. The most interesting are found on Birsa Hill where the acropolis stood, which was ringed by defensive walls at the time. A few graves have been found there but none of the public buildings and houses survived the conquests. Some ruins mark the sanctuary of Tophet, the place used for sacrificial burials, where there was a temple dedicated to the Phoenician gods Baal and Tanit. To these gods, the children of the Carthaginian noblemen were immolated. Identified in 1921, a number of stelae have been unearthed that have helped in part to understand the customs of the era. A pool beside the sea a little to the north of the city is all that remains of the two large ports – mercantile and military – that had made Carthage great.

From the Roman era there is more to see, such as the vestiges of the large baths of Antoninus built between AD 146 and 162. Today, it is only possible to see the base, which was the location of the servants' rooms and the furnaces for heating the water sent to the baths on the

244 top and 244 bottom left Nearly seven feet in diameter, the monolithic support columns of the Antonine Baths must have weighed over 70 tons. One of the capitals – recently discovered – is over three feet tall and weighs over four tons.

244 center left Hailed as one of the most majestic in the Roman world, the amphitheater in Carthage was famous as far as the extreme reaches of the empire for its battles between beasts and gladiators, well

before it became a site of martyrdom for thousands of Christians. Admired until the Middle Ages for the elegance of its arches, it was gradually stripped bare by stone scavengers. Today, only a few remnants remain, hidden among the green of the pine trees.

244 center right Hadrian's theater, a mighty structure that has preserved its elegance intact, still hosts an international music, song, and dance festival, held between July and August.

244 bottom right A mosaic portrays a horseman against the background of a luxurious palace with tropical vegetation found on the hill of Borj-Jedid. The slopes of this rise are still today yielding remains belonging to various periods, among which some Punic-era graves.

245 The terrace of the House of the Aviary is covered by a vast floor, originating in another residence, that features an alternation of square mosaic panels, portraying horses and their riders, with others in marble. Of the original 98 pieces, 62 have been preserved.

upper floor, in turn supported by columns almost seven feet in diameter, each of which weighed 70 tons. One of these columns has been reconstructed in recent years and reaches a height of 49 feet, whereas the vault of the *frigidarium* (which is being rebuilt) should be over 66 feet high. A short distance away is the basilica of Damus el-Karita, the name of which is probably a distortion of the Latin Domus Charitatis, where Saint Augustine preached between 399 and 413.

The amphitheater was used to hold

shows featuring gladiator battles and fights between wild animals. It was famous throughout the Roman world and was celebrated as being one of the largest amphitheaters in the empire, but today it is only just visible among the pine trees as most of the stone blocks were taken away over the centuries and used to construct other buildings. Northeast of the amphitheater, there is a series of gigantic cisterns that provided the main water source for the city in the Roman period. Very little remains of the theater built by

Hadrian or of the temples and houses of the ancient Mediterranean power.

Fortunately, memory of the city's greatness is preserved in the collections of the national museum, housed in the White Fathers Seminary next to the cathedral of Saint Louis built by the French in 1890. The museum has vases, sculptures, inscriptions and ceramics discovered during excavation; these are the last tangible remains of Carthage – whether Punic, Roman or Arab – and the vestiges of a lost empire.

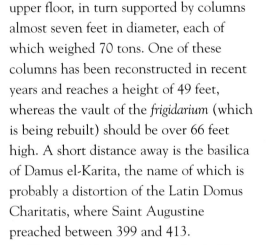

Sabratha

LIBYA

DISTRICT OF ZAWIA
REGISTRATION: 1982
CRITERIA: C (III)

Although Italo Balbo, governor of Italian Libya during the 1920s, did not pass into history for his talent as a military planner or administrator, anyone who loves ancient times will be grateful to him for having restored the theater in Sabratha to its past splendor. Enchanted by the beauty of the ruins, Balbo drew abundantly on the coffers of the Italian state to sponsor a colossal operation of excavation and restoration.

The archaeologists Giacomo Giusti and Giacomo Caputo were commissioned to authentically rebuild the largest theater in Africa, which was constructed in AD 190 for the emperor Commodus. With a stage almost 50 yards long, the auditorium could seat 5,000 spectators and measured just over 100 yards across. Lining the back of the stage was an amazing *frons scenae* composed of three semi-circular niches and a triple order of 108 Corinthian columns made from differently colored marbles with elaborate decorations on the capitals. Also magnificent were the high reliefs in the niches carved with dance scenes, mythological figures, and allegorical celebrations of the relations between Rome and Sabratha.

Nevertheless, the theater was not the only marvel in Sabratha. This port city in Roman Tripolitania – founded by Punic colonists in the fourth century BC – enjoyed a period of great wealth between AD 138 and 210 thanks to the export of African animals and ivory to Rome. During that golden century, Sabratha saw the construction of monumental buildings in marble and stucco-lined sandstone. One of these, standing in a magnificent position overlooking the sea, was the Temple of Isis, whose cult had

spread from Egypt to the Roman cities and who was worshiped as the protectress of sailors. Others were the Capitolium, the Sanctuary of Serapis, the Temple of Liber Pater, and the building referred to as Mausoleum B. Also rebuilt by the Italian archaeologists, this last monument features a pyramidal roof and merged Punic, Egyptian, Hellenistic, and Roman architectural elements. Particularly outstanding are the high-relief decorations on the metopes, bounded by lions supporting ten-foot-high male figures. Though many statues and mosaics have been destroyed or moved to the museum at the border of the archaeological area, the public buildings, such as the Forum, Curia, and the three

246 top and bottom The border of the theater's stage is decorated with a series of niches and panels, with bas-relief and high-relief figures representing divinities, dancers, thespians, and historical scenes attesting to relations between Rome and Sabratha.

246 center The imposing theater, the most important in Roman Africa, was built by Emperor Commodus around AD 190. The structure was returned to its original splendor thanks to a skillful restoration project dating back to the era of the Italian colonization of Libya.

246-247 The elegant frons scaenae of the theater of Sabratha recalls the façade of a royal palace. 148 feet long, it features a triple order of 108 Corinthian columns in different-color types of marble with elaborate decorations on their capitals. The sides are closed in by the versurae, or "angles" where the rectilinear line of the stage connected to the cavea.

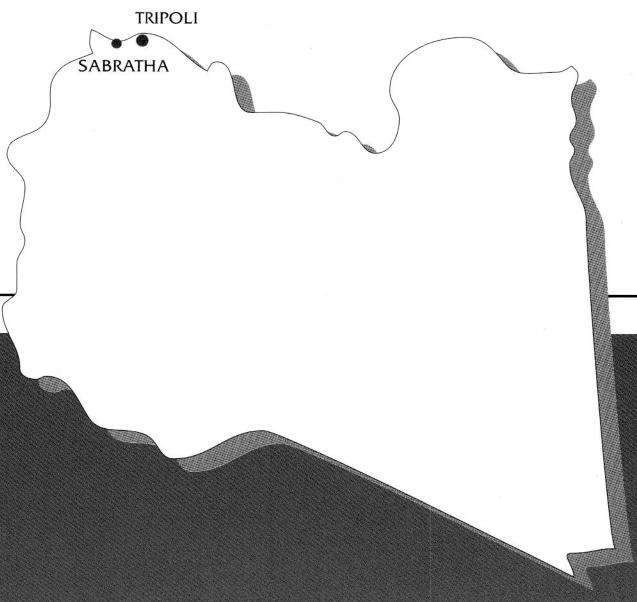

elegant baths complexes, still exude an aura of magnificence.

The decline of Rome in the third century AD also marked the decline of Sabratha, which, in any case, was struck by an earthquake in 365. The city had to wait almost two centuries before it reacquired any importance under the Byzantines, when the defensive walls and superb Basilica of Justinian were built.

In fact, Sabratha already had a basilica (today only the foundations remain), which had been a law court and a place of worship for the cult of the Roman emperors in the first century AD, before being transformed 300 years later into a Christian church.

In AD 158, the building had been the site of an event that resounded throughout the Roman world. It was there that the trial of the philosopher Apuleius was held, accused of having used magic powers to seduce and marry a rich, old widow in order to inherit her money. The author of the *Golden Ass* defended himself in person: his summation lasted four full days, at the end of which he was exonerated. This masterpiece of oratory, later transcribed, not only brought great fame to its author but remains a precious source for understanding daily life in Sabratha in the second century AD.

248 top Although lacking its head, thanks to the symbols and the richness of its clothing, it was possible to attribute this figure to the emperor Titus. The sculpture is held in the Museum of Sabratha, full of Punic artifacts as well.

248 bottom left Not far from the outstanding main theater, the amphitheater of Sabratha was erected between the end of the second century and the beginning of the third. In addition to its spacious cavea, it features intact the corridors by which beasts entered the arena.

248 bottom right A panoramic view of the residential area along the sea. Thanks to its favorable position, since the Phoenician era Sabratha prospered on maritime trading in African goods.

248-249 In a magnificent position overlooking the sea, the temple of Isis features two rows of columns and a part of its podium. The building, in a decentralized position, was partially excluded from the wall enclosure raised in the fourth century.

249 bottom left The columns of the temple of Isis, carved in rather poor-quality local sandstone, still feature part of the abundant plastering used in efforts to protect the monuments.

249 bottom right Almost double natural proportions, this bust of Jupiter, possibly part of a statue from the capitolium, is one of the highlights of the Museum of Sabratha.

250 top left An octagonal pool opens in the middle of the lovely mosaics decorating one of the main rooms in the sumptuous baths near the sea. From here, a splendid view of the coast and the ruins of the warehouses of the city's ancient port can be enjoyed.

250 top right The god of the ocean, with his thick green beard and a crown of fruit on his head, is portrayed in this octagon from a mosaic adorning a room in the seaside baths.

250 center A meeting place for the senatorial class, the curia of Sabratha still contains a good number of its columns, on which rested Corinthian-order capitals in white marble. The building faces the forum, the hub of city life.

250 bottom This supple marble statue portrayed a naiad, a nymph considered to be the protector of fresh-water springs. It once adorned one of the numerous fountains in Sabratha.

250-251 A view of the ruins over which Mausoleum B looms. The funerary monument has a pyramidal roof and mixes Punic, Egyptian, Hellenistic, and Roman stylistic elements. Extraordinary features are the high-relief decorations on the metopes, framed by lions that support male figures 10 feet tall (now in the Sabratha Museum).

251 top This refined mosaic panel portrays a Christian saint and dates back to the era of Sabratha's revival during Byzantine times. The important mosaic, like others found at the site, is held in the Sabratha Museum.

Leptis Magna

LIBYA

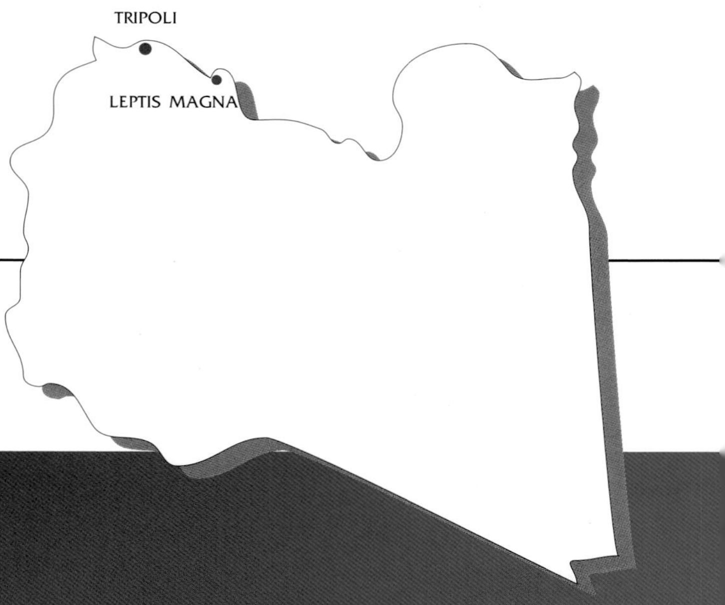

TRIPOLI

LEPTIS MAGNA

DISTRICT OF AL-KHOMS

REGISTRATION: 1982

CRITERIA: (I) (II) (III)

252-253 One of the livelier places devoted to business and trade in the Roman Empire, the market at Leptis Magna consisted of a series of octagonal kiosks, porticoes, workshops, and a majestic central pavilion.

252 bottom Decorated with Corinthian columns and precious marble bas-reliefs and about 66 feet tall, the Arch of Septimius Severus was built at the intersection of the cardus and decumanus in AD 203, on the occasion of the emperor's fifty-seventh birthday.

253 top A staircase and an arch lead into the area of the fruit and vegetable market. The excellent-quality sandstone used in the construction of the main monuments in Leptis Magna came from the Ras el-Hammam quarry, about a dozen miles south of the city.

The son of rich merchants of Punic origin, Lucius Septimius Severus, born in the city of Leptis in AD 146, was sent to Rome to study when he was still a boy. At that time, he was a "true African" and spoke Latin badly. Nevertheless, in the space of a few years, his stubbornness, courageous temperament, and eloquence got him noticed by the imperial court. His rise was rapid and took him straight to the top, being made emperor in 193. He waited ten years before returning home to Leptis, which was given the title *magna* in his honor. He did everything in his power to make it great. He had the magnificent triumphal arch bearing his name built at the entrance to the city, surrounded by four fountains decorated with columns and bas-reliefs. He then entirely rebuilt the port and joined it to the center of the city by means of an impressive colonnade, inaugurated an elegant *nymphaeum*, and had a huge forum built surrounded by a forest of columns and decorated with Medusa heads. The most outstanding construction, however, was the Basilica (completed by his son Caracalla), which featured a 100-foot-tall main hall and was decorated everywhere with elegant reliefs of nymphs, acanthus leaves, grapes, and pomegranates.

If truth be told, Leptis was already a magnificent city. It had 80,000 inhabitants and was known throughout the empire as the "pearl of Africa." As had happened to Septimius Severus, the city flourished upon coming into contact with Rome. Founded by Phoenicians from Tyre, it had for centuries been under the rule of the Carthaginians, but this state of affairs ended in 146 BC when the Romans defeated their historic rival across the sea and took possession of the city. It became the most important city in Tripolitania, and later the entire province of Africa. Thanks to its port and the skill of its merchants, Leptis got rich by trading gold, ivory, ebony, slaves, and wild animals for the games in the circus. The expansion of the wharves and markets was matched by construction of increasingly impressive civil and religious buildings. These were financed by the families of the merchant class who competed in importing the loveliest

marbles and most skilled artists and decorators. The wealthy Hannibal Tapapius Rufus amazed his fellow citizens by sponsoring the construction of the Theater – adorned with statues, it may have been the jewel of the city – and the Market, which had two elegant octagonal kiosks at its center surrounded by a

253 center Bounded by pink-granite columns, the palaestra of the luxurious baths commissioned by Emperor Hadrian was inaugurated in AD 127 and stood in the forum. The complex lies near the stream in Wadi Lebda, from which the water required for the baths was channeled.

253 bottom Sixty-nine feet wide and still impeccably paved, the decumanus maximus led to the port. The route was marked by the monumental Arch of Septimius Severus and the more modest arches of Tiberius (AD 37) and Trajan (shown in the photo), erected in AD 109-111.

254 top The extraordinary Severan Forum, separated from the basilica by a tall sandstone wall, covers an area of 328 by 197 feet. Originally, it was constructed with precious materials: green cipolin for the arches, Egyptian pink granite for the columns, and bright white marble for the floor.

254 center The inscription on the portico of the forum praises Lucius Septimius Severus. Lucius, born in Leptis in AD 146, was elected emperor at 47 years old, and after a decade returned to the city, which received the title of "Magna" in his honor.

multitude of counters for goods to be displayed. The Flavini family, on the other hand, were responsible for the construction of Leptis' most unusual building, an immense amphitheater dug out of the ground on the seashore.

Even before the advent of Septimius Severus, other emperors had judged Leptis worthy of particular attention. Hadrian had provided it with a magnificent baths complex, two large temples facing the port, and a city wall. Further back in time, Nero helped to protect the port with the digging of a

254 bottom Once an ornament on the portico, this is one of about 70 medusa heads that today rest on the open ground of the new Severan Forum, now badly stripped. In the sixteenth century, the French consul Claude Lamaire brought back 200 columns and decorative marble pieces with him to France.

254-255 The grandiose Severan Basilica was initiated by Septimius Severus and completed, in AD 216, by his son Caracalla. Later, in the sixth century, the building was transformed into a Christian church by Justinian.

255 bottom left In this detail, two capitals resting on pink-granite columns in turn support the winged griffins on the only remaining piece of the pediment, which faces the apse of the Severan Basilica.

255 bottom right Rendered even more vivid by the warm light of the sun, the decorations on one of the columns in the north apse of the Severan Basilica portray numerous mythological characters, gods, and demigods among acanthus leaves and bunches of grapes.

dike, but this worsened the port's operations as it impeded the currents and caused the port to silt up gradually.

The mistake made by Nero's engineers occurred just as Leptis was reaching its greatest splendor, and marked the first, although immediately almost imperceptible, inkling of its decline. Around the year 250, with the end of the Severian dynasty, it quickly lost prestige and business dropped off. The end came in 365 when, along with all the cities of Tripolitania, it was destroyed by an earthquake.

Under Diocletian and Constantine, the city may have seen a glimmer of light shortly before the end. Nonetheless, perhaps having received a presage of the disaster, a treasurer buried 100,000 coins to the west of the city, during the rule of Constantine. Discovered in 1981, this haul was the most sensational numismatic find from the ancient world. Today some of these coins are on display together with other treasures in the museum next to the lovely archaeological site of Leptis Magna.

256 top A forest of columns faces the port of Leptis Magna. The city was founded between the seventh and sixth century BC by Phoenicians from Tyre, who chose the site because there was an inlet providing the only safe landing point on the tract of coast between Alexandria and Carthage.

256 bottom left, right, and 257 bottom right The Museum of Tripoli holds some statutes from the theater of Leptis. From left to right, there is Athena with a Corinthian helmet, lance, and shield at her feet, a nymph, and a portrait of Marcus Aurelius. All the sculptures date back to between the first and second centuries AD.

256-257 Situated in a panoramic position, the theater in Leptis was, and still is, one of the most magnificent in the Roman world. Its construction between the first and second centuries AD was financed by the merchant Hannibal Tapapius Rufus, an influential member of the city aristocracy.

257 bottom left A portico of columns with Corinthian capitals, accessible via an archway, surrounds a thermal bath in Leptis Magna. On its short side, narrow steps that "facilitated" entering the water can be noticed inside the pool.

Memphis and its Necropolis. The Pyramids from Giza to Dahshur

EGYPT

GOVERNORATE OF GIZA
REGISTRATION: 1979
CRITERIA: C (I) (III) (VI)

In the beginning, there was *Inbw-hdj*, or "white walls," which probably referred to the appearance of the fortified palace, though it was but a part of the city that most likely lay in the area now occupied by the town of Abusir. Later, the name was changed to *Hwt-ke-pth* after one of its temple enclosures, from which the Greek name *Aigyptos* was derived, and finally the modern version of Egypt. However, the most suitable name may have been *Ankh-tawy*, which more or less meant "the place that links the two lands." Located at the apex of the Nile Delta, at the

confluence of the commercial routes joining the East and West, the ancient city is best known today as Memphis, which is derived from *Mennefer*, the name of the pyramid built by the pharaoh Pepi I. *Mennefer* was transformed into the Copt *Menfe* and then the Greek *Memphis*.

Memphis was the royal residence and capital of Egypt during the proto-dynastic period and the Old Kingdom (3100–2184 BC), and for at least another two millennia, it was one of the most populated and famous cities in the region. Indeed, Herodotus, Strabo, and Diodorus Siculus all described its magnificence in

their writings. Modern evidence of its greatness, besides the few remains of the city itself excavated at Mit Rahina and Saqqarah, is found in the enormous necropolises stretching for 19 miles along the edge of the desert on the west bank of the Nile. In addition, there are the pyramids of Helwan, Dahshur, Saqqarah, Abusir, Zawyer el-Aryan, Abu Rawash, and of course, Giza. According to William Matthew Flinders Petrie, a nineteenth-century British archaeologist, Memphis must have measured about seven miles long by four miles wide and lain around the temple of Ptah in the area of the modern city of Mit Rahina. Ptah was the principal god of the city at the start of the dynastic period, if not earlier, and the first temple built in his name may rest hidden beneath a knoll called Kom el-Fakhry. Of the more recent temple, built during the reign of Ramses II, only the western section has been excavated, which is formed by a massive pylon and a colonnaded hypostyle room. Remains of foundations nearby indicate the presence of an earlier temple attributed to Thutmosis IV (Eighteenth Dynasty, 1419–1386 BC). The grandeur of Memphis begins to become apparent a little to the west, where the field containing the pyramids of Dahshur lies at the southern tip of the necropolis. A point of reference is the pyramid of Snefru, the founding father of the Fourth Dynasty who was pharaoh from 2630 to 2606 BC, and whose reign marked the transition from stepped pyramids to smooth-faced constructions. At Dahshur, pharaohs of the Twelfth Dynasty, Amenemhat II, Amenemhat III, and Sesostris III built another three pyramids. Next to the royal tombs are two groups of noble tombs,

called *mastabas*. They are rectangular with their sides slightly inclined and composed of two rooms: the burial chamber and a chapel. Buried in them were the princesses Iti, Khnemt, Itiwert, and Sitmerhut, all daughters of Amenemhat II, and other members of the families of the Twelfth-Dynasty pharaohs. Further north at Saqqarah, the entire history of Ancient Egypt can be embraced in a single site. It covers the period from the first unbaked brick *mastaba* of Menes, the legendary pharaoh of the First Dynasty considered the founder of Memphis, to the Greco-Roman period. The tombs of the royal families,

258 The awesome "Red Pyramid" at Dahshur was named for the color of the granite at its core. It was built by Snefru, a pharaoh of the Fourth Dynasty. Standing 345 feet tall, it is the third largest pyramid after those of Khufu and Khafre.

258-259 Djoser's funerary monument at Saqqarah is the most complete example of a stepped pyramid. Its concept was derived from the overlaying of simple, ancient "bench tombs," called mastabas.

259 top The foundations of the funerary temple of Sahura, the second king of the Fifth Dynasty, precede what remains of the king's funerary temple at Abu Sir. Originally the monument was a "true" pyramid, i.e. with smooth rather than stepped sides.

259 center The imposing nucleus is all that remains of Snefru's pyramid at Meidum. Begun as a stepped monument, it was later fitted with smooth sides.

CAIRO

MEMPHIS - GIZA

nobles, and high dignitaries of the First Dynasty run along the east edge of the desert plateau. Dominating Saqqarah is the stepped pyramid of Djoser, the oldest of the 97 known Egyptian pyramids, which was built in the middle of the twenty-seventh century BC and surrounded by temples and buildings used to celebrate the royal jubilee. There are at least 13 other royal pyramids at Saqqarah, of which the most notable are those of Sekhemkhet (the successor to Djoser in the Third Dynasty), Unas and Teti (Fifth and Sixth dynasties, twenty-fourth century BC), Pepi I (Sixth Dynasty, ca. 2300 BC), and

259 bottom With the Twelfth Dynasty, the era of the pyramids came to an end. The funerary monument of Senusret, shown here, at Illahun was never completed due to the king's premature death, and it later collapsed completely.

260 top left Bearers carry offerings in the tomb of Ti, a supervisor of the pyramids and sun temples at Saqqarah, and chief hairdresser at court.

260 top right The nobleman Ptahotep faces his own name in finely carved hieroglyphs on a wall in his mastaba at Saqqarah. The meaning of the name is "(the god) Ptah is pleased."

Didufri (Fourth Dynasty, 2583–2575 BC) in the northernmost area of the necropolis. To the north of Djoser's pyramid lies the largest area of non-royal tombs from the Old Kingdom, besides an unknown number of more recent graves. There are hundreds worth mentioning, either because they were of people of a particular rank or because of their architectural, structural, or decorative aspects. Recently archaeologists in the field have found new leads for excavation.

260 bottom On the great mastaba at Saqqara, Mereruka, on the right, is portrayed with his mother and his wife, sculpted in small size at his feet, whereas he appears with one of his two sons on the left.

261 The vizier Mereruka advances towards the offerings' table standing on a stepped dais. The tombs of the great dignitaries, as was customary, stood near the pyramid of the king they had served. In this case, the pharaoh was Teti.

262 top Enormous, gradually overlapping blocks of granite form the Great Gallery at the heart of Khufu's pyramid. This extraordinary passage is 154 feet long and 28 feet high.

Further north there are the most famous monuments, those that the Ptolemies (the Macedon governors of Egypt that took power in the fourth century BC) wished to see included as one of the Seven Wonders of the World. They are the pyramids of Giza built by Khufu, Khafre, and Menkaure, the three pharaohs of the Fourth Dynasty that governed Egypt for almost all of the twenty-sixth century BC. In fact, the Giza plateau (which lies about 130 feet higher than the plain and from which the greenery of the Nile Delta can be seen) had already been used as a necropolis since the proto-dynastic period, but it was with these three pharaohs that the royal tombs reached their greatest glory. Construction of the pyramid of Khufu (*Cheops* in Greek) required 35 years of work and two and a half million blocks of stone weighing between two and 75 tons each. It originally stood 481 feet four inches tall and its square base measures 755 feet nine inches on each side. Today, after

millennia of being worn away by erosion, it still stands 452 feet ten inches high. The entrance lies at a height of about 56 feet where a narrow corridor enters the rock and continues for more than 110 yards inside the monument to the first chamber. This was where the pharaoh was to be laid in the first plan, but in fact, to reach his real burial chamber, it is necessary to take an ascending side corridor 35 yards from the entrance that leads up to a junction. From here, one passageway leads to an intermediate chamber referred to as the Queen's Chamber, whereas the Great Gallery – almost 160 feet long and 28 feet high – leads to the pharaoh's real place of burial. Here, in a chamber measuring about 33 feet by 16, stands Khufu's simple granite sarcophagus. Khafre (*Chephren* in Greek) built his funerary monument just a little to the south of his father's. It measures 689 feet on each side and, being more inclined, reached a lower height of a little over 470 feet.

262 bottom The steep angle of the sides of Khufu's pyramid (51° against the 45° of Snefru's, the first "real" pyramid to have survived without collapsing) gave it an overall height of 482 feet as opposed to its 456 feet today.

262-263 It is not know for certain why Menkaure's pyramid is so small in comparison to the "giants" of Giza, but probably construction of the earlier two was so demanding on the nation that it could not be repeated.

263 bottom left These large niches in a wall inside the pyramid of Menkaure, the fifth pharaoh of the Fourth Dynasty, may have been used for offerings.

263 bottom right The burial chamber of Khafre is roofed with sloping slabs of pink granite: this placement made it possible to redistribute the enormous weight of the upper part of the pyramid, which would have crushed an empty room with a flat roof. On the left wall, the budding invasion of archaeologists at the beginning of the 1800s is heralded in the triumphant words etched by Belzoni as he made his discovery in 1818.

To the side of and downhill from Khafre's pyramid, two temples are found in a better state of conservation than those of Khufu. To the west is the enigmatic and gigantic sculpture of the Sphinx, about 180 feet long and 66 high. It was carved out of a single block left remaining from the quarries used to provide the materials for Khufu's pyramid. Unique in Egypt, its date oscillates between the reign of Khufu and Khafre, though it was almost certainly attributable to the former. In the symbolism of Ancient Egypt, the sculpture represented the pharaoh in whom the strength of wild animals combined with the intelligence of man. The last of the pyramids built at Giza was that of Menkaure (*Mycerinus* in Greek), the son of Khafre, on the remaining space on the south side of the plateau. At just 343 feet per side and a height of 213 feet four inches, and with a layout of burial chambers the same as that of Khufu's pyramid, it marked the last of the colossal funerary monuments of the Fourth Dynasty. The temples also feature a simple layout and were ornamented with fine statuary made from a variety of materials. With these constructions, the era of the great pyramids closed forever.

Ancient sources provide us with almost no information on the techniques used to construct the three monuments, but it is probable that they were assembled using many small ramps to transport the blocks of stone up heights of 80 to 100 feet and these were then combined to form a single ramp for the higher sections of the construction. However, any theory is pure speculation. What is certain is that the pyramids of Giza are the only wonder of the ancient world to have survived until the present day almost unaltered and to have raised astonishment and admiration for 4,500 years. Even the great Napoleon, on the eve of the battle of Giza, admonished his soldiers saying, "from the tops of these pyramids, 40 centuries of history gaze down upon you."

264 top The identity of the king portrayed on the Sphinx is unknown: it was once believed to be Khafre, due to the monument's connection to the ramp of his pyramid, but more recently some experts have associated its construction with Khufu.

264 bottom A vast sanctuary lay in front of the Sphinx, built in various stages as part of Khafre's burial complex. The ramp that ran up to this pharaoh's pyramid can be seen bottom right.

265 The inconsistent stratification of the rock that forms the Sphinx is revealed in the different colors of its parts. The head is darker and the most resistant section, whereas the paws seem well preserved but are in fact "artificial," having been lined with limestone that is easily restored or replaced.

Ancient Thebes and its Necropolis

EGYPT

GOVERNORATE OF QENA
REGISTRATION: 1979
CRITERIA: C (I) (III) (VI)

About 420 miles south of Cairo, where the Nile River rounds a tight bend and is lined by a low range of mountains, tourism is certainly not a novelty, nor is the uncontrollable desire of visitors to leave a sign of their passage on the monuments and works of art. In Thebes - the capital of the Egyptian dynasties during the New Kingdom, from

1570 to 1070 BC - the scrawls of the tourists have also become a piece of history. The first to pass through were Greek and Roman travelers during the Ptolemaic age, and they left at least 2,000 graffiti scribblings on the walls of the tombs of the pharaohs in the Valley of the Kings. In addition to these, there are messages in Phoenician, Cypriot, Lycian, Coptic, and other languages. All of these are proof that the greatness of Egypt was already legendary before the start of the Christian era.

The ancient Greek writers Pausanias, Strabo, and Diodorus Siculus described Thebes – *Waset* to the Egyptians – as a city of marvels, so the richer inhabitants from the other side of the Mediterranean ventured to Egypt to admire the magnificent temples, spectacular Colossi of Memnon, and the endless necropolis of the Valley of the Kings. It was the opinion of Diodorus that "the tombs do not leave to posterity the possibility of producing anything more beautiful."

Today, Luxor, the city that stands on the left bank of the Nile on the site of the ancient capital, in an area inhabited for at least 250,000 years, is the most extraordinary open-air museum in the world. A few miles north of the modern city stands the temple of Amon-Ra at Karnak, consecrated to the sun god, one of the most important in Ancient Egypt. Built around 1900 BC by Sesostris I, a pharaoh of the Twelfth Dynasty during the Middle Kingdom, it did not cease to expand and change until the fourth century AD. Each pharaoh wanted to leave his own mark because the temple of Amon-Ra reflected the Ancient Egyptians' conception of the world. Its structure was spread along two axes: the east-west axis mirrored the trajectory of the sun, which symbolized the divine nature of things, whereas the north-south axis ran parallel to the course of the Nile and was linked to the territory and the function of the sovereign, in which the pharaoh represented the fusion of everything divine and human and whose existence ensured the prosperity of the kingdom.

Further south, in the heart of the city on the east bank of the Nile, stands the temple of Luxor, built during the reign of Amenhotep III (1386–1349 BC) and connected to Karnak by a long paved processional way (*dromos* in Greek) lined by sphinxes. A stretch of this can still be seen in front of the temple. Also called the "southern harem of Amon," it was started by Amenhotep III but concluded by Ramses II.

According to accounts on papyruses, the cult of Amon in the Great Temple at Karnak had no fewer than 20,000 priests. Once a year, on the occasion of the feast of Opet, the priests removed the statue of Amon from its shrine and carried it in procession to the temple of Luxor on a simulacrum of a boat made from gilded wood.

266 top The colossal statue of Ramses II stands in Luxor Temple.

266 bottom The Great Hypostyle Hall in the temple of Karnak contains 134 sandstone columns divided into 16 rows that staand in an area of 53,800 square feet. The shafts in the central nave stand 79 feet tall.

CAIRO

THEBES

266-267 Sixteen centuries (from roughly 1950 to 350 BC) were needed to build the extended temple of Amon-Ra at Karnak. On the left, towards the river, stands the pylon built by Ramses II and Horemheb; in the foreground, beside the sacred lake and Hatshepsut's eighth pylon, lie the ordered foundations of granaries and temple storerooms.

267 top left The ruins of the temple of Luxor stand a few yards from the Nile east side of the "bank of the living." The Great Colonnade (center), built by Amenhotep III, was once enclosed by a parallelepiped building.

267 top right The pylon of Ramses II is flanked by two colossi of the pharaoh. It leads to the temple of Luxor (Ipet-Resit or "Residence of the South" to the Ancient Egyptians) where the statue of Amon was carried once a year during the great Opet festival held in the season of the flooding of the Nile.

On the other side of the river, as though to underline the distance between the government of the divine world represented by the priests of Karnak and the government of the earthly world, Amenhotep III built his palace. Of all those belonging to the pharaohs, this is the one that has survived in the best condition. Like other residences in Egypt, it was built from mud bricks (which is why so many of them have been lost). It was not only home to himself and his queen Tiy, but also the 317 Hittite concubines he received as a gift for having married a Hittite princess. Malkata (the palace's Arab name) was also the pharaoh's administrative center, and nearby a village developed where the craftsmen and servants who served the pharaoh lived.

A mile away stand the Colossi of Memnon, the two gigantic quartzite statues of Amenhotep III that are each 75 feet tall and weigh a thousand or so tons. They stand at the entrance to the original funerary temple of the pharaoh. Here, at the foot of the limestone cliff of Deir el-Bahari and behind the first majestic temple, another 14 "temples of the millions of years" stand in line. These are the funerary temples of 14 other pharaohs, including Ramses II, Amenhotep II, and Seti I to mention the most famous. They were built to last for eternity so that the pharaohs could always be remembered by their subjects.

Nevertheless, today as in antiquity, the fame of Thebes is owed principally to the

269 center The ruins of the "migdol" (a kind of tower borrowed from Mesopotomian architecture) in Medinet Habu lie in front of the pylon and ceremonial palace of the temple of Ramses III, the last great Egyptian pharaoh, who lived roughly a century after the illustrious Ramses II.

269 bottom The portico that faces onto the second court of the temple of Ramses III is in excellent condition. It is supported by papyriform columns carved entirely with reliefs and painted. On the right, the pharaoh receives the homage of the god Atum "the Whole."

Valley of the Kings and, to a lesser degree, the Valley of the Queens, the two necropolises located on the other side of the cliff. Between the two stretch the civilian necropolises incorrectly called the "Tombs of the Nobles." This is a complex of 500 graves that can be distinguished from the royal tombs by their architecture and the modesty of their decoration.

The Valley of the Queens contains between 75 and 80 tombs from the Eighteenth, Nineteenth, and Twentieth dynasties in which not only the wives but also the children and family members of the pharaohs were buried. They include the tombs of Queen Titi of the Twentieth Dynasty, young Khaemwese, the fourth son of Ramses II, and Amenhikhopeshef, son of Ramses III. However, the most famous of all, and considered one of the most beautiful in all of Ancient Egypt, is unquestionably that of Nefertari, the favorite wife of Ramses II. The walls and ceiling of the tomb are completely covered with scenes in which the queen, "the most beautiful of all," dressed in a white garment and gold crown adorned with vulture's plumes, is accompanied by Egyptian gods and goddesses.

270 top left The goddess Ma'at accepts offerings from Nefertari (not visible). The queen died before her husband, Ramses II, but nothing is known of her demise. After being honored with monuments like the Small Temple at Abu Simbel, she disappeared from recorded history.

270 top right Ta Set Neferu, "Place of the royal children," lies southwest of the Valley of the Kings. At first it was the burial place of the princes and princesses of the Eighteenth Dynasty, but over time, queens like Nefertari (Ramses II's principal wife) were also buried there.

270-271 A ceiling adorned with a myriad of stars on a blue background covers the magnificently decorated burial chamber of Nefertari, "House of Gold." In the background, facing north, the door that led to the "abode of Osiris," the god who oversaw resurrection, can be seen.

271 top Nefertari makes food offerings to Atum and Osiris (left), the god who rose from the dead, shown here as a mummy with green flesh. The provisions include the bodies of decapitated oxen and loaves of bread.

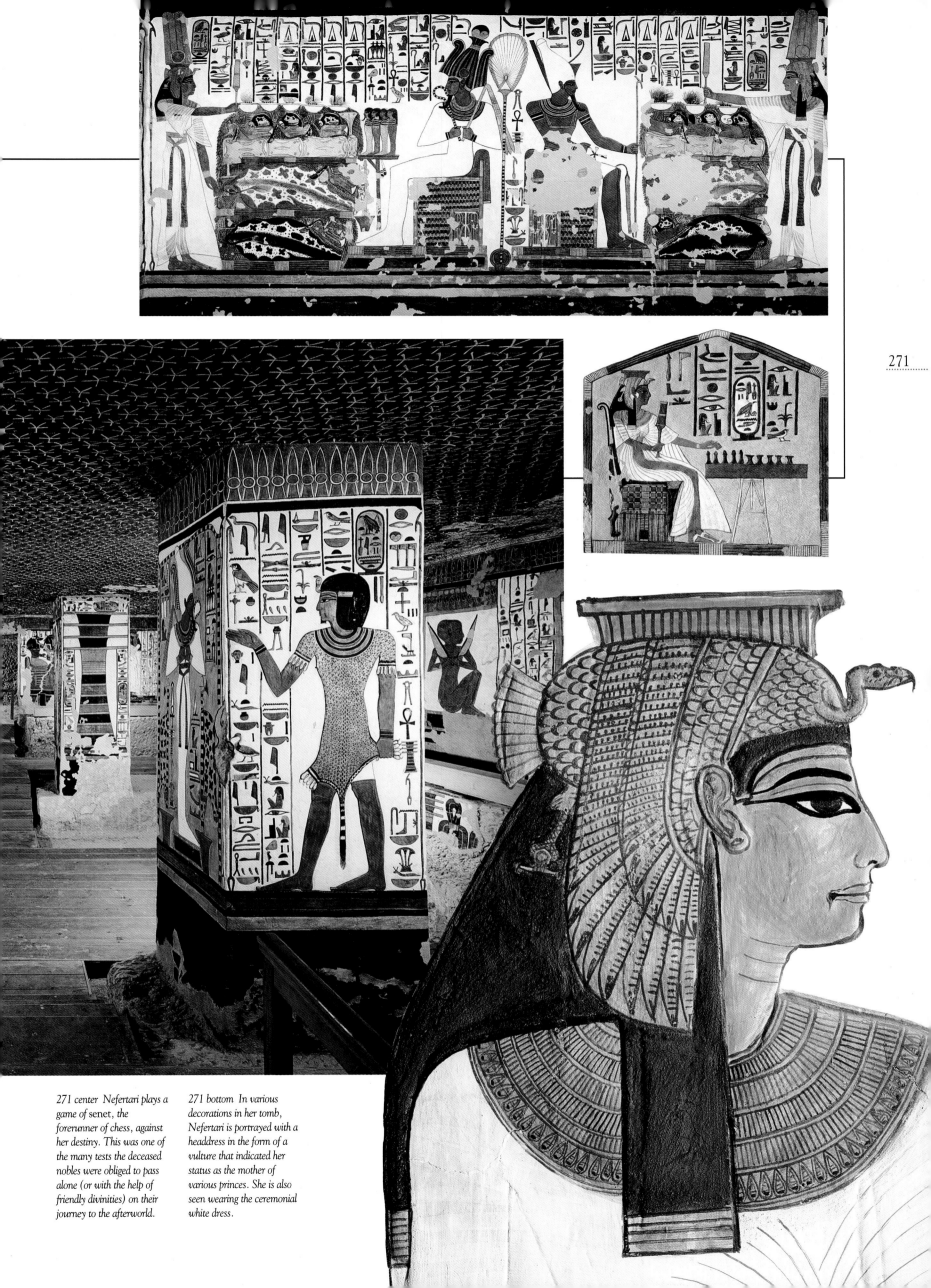

271 center Nefertari plays a game of senet, the forerunner of chess, against her destiny. This was one of the many tests the deceased nobles were obliged to pass alone (or with the help of friendly divinities) on their journey to the afterworld.

271 bottom In various decorations in her tomb, Nefertari is portrayed with a headdress in the form of a vulture that indicated her status as the mother of various princes. She is also seen wearing the ceremonial white dress.

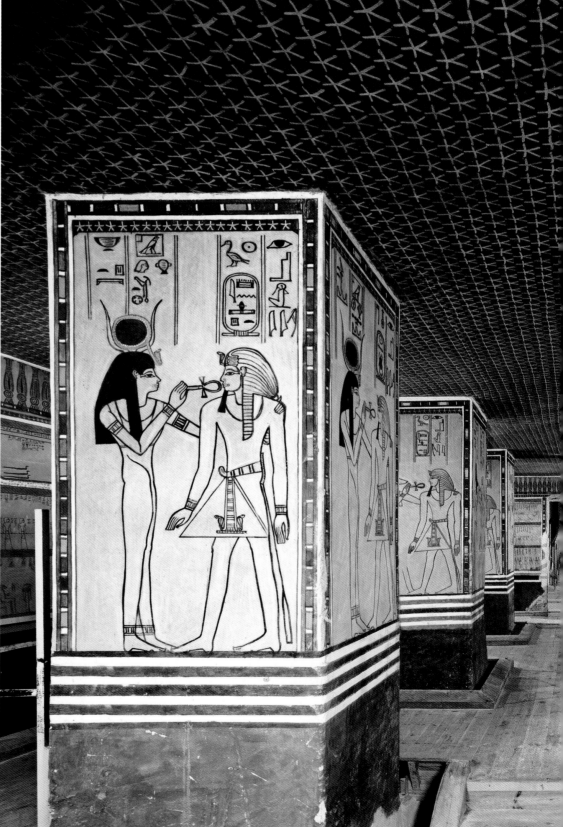

The Valley of the Kings is a deep ravine in the limestone mountains of Thebes where 62 tombs were built. Many contain the remains of pharaohs, but others belonged to high dignitaries and some were simple burial shafts without inscriptions. The first pharaoh to be buried in the necropolis was probably Thutmosis I (1524–1518) at the start of the Eighteenth Dynasty and at the bottom of the valley. In this same spot, his grave is followed by that of Seti II and preceded by that of Siptah. In a small

side valley lie the tombs of Hatshepsut and Thutmosis IV, whereas those of a further 15 pharaohs are found in the heart of the necropolis.

The layout of the royal tombs is elaborate but generally includes a stairway, a descending corridor off which one or more rooms open, and at the end, a burial chamber holding the sarcophagus of the pharaoh. In this chamber, according to the Ancient Egyptian religion, the king was transformed into a divine entity. The walls were lined with multicolored bas-reliefs of the afterlife and the journey that the pharaoh had to make to get to the kingdom of Osiris.

At the time of its greatest splendor, Thebes represented the triumph of Egyptian power and was to the Greeks and Romans a place of wonder, but after the Arab conquest of the country, it fell into oblivion. It was only rediscovered at the start of the eighteenth century by the Jesuit Claude Picard, who came there in 1726. One of the first Europeans to draw pictures of Thebes was the Danish artist Frederik Ludwig Norden, followed by Richard Pococke, who drafted a detailed map of the Valley of the Kings. In the nineteenth century, as the Ancient-Egyptian "style" raged across Europe, the monuments of Thebes attracted archaeologists, scholars like Prosper Jollois and Edouard de Villiers, artists like David Roberts, not to mention many unscrupulous visitors seeking easy profit through the contraband of ancient objects.

Though many of the treasures in the Valley of the Kings were pilfered, European scholars contributed decisively to the deciphering of hieroglyphs and the excavation of the Egyptian capital throughout the nineteenth and twentieth centuries. Finally, in 1922, after a decade of hard work, Howard Carter discovered the last tomb, undeniably one of the most fascinating and mysterious, in the Valley of the Kings: the burial place of Tutankhamon, the boy pharaoh.

272-273 Various gods (with Hathor in the foreground) are present in the life of Amenhotep II, who wears the nemes *headdress in the paintings on the six pillars in the burial chamber of the Eighteenth Dynasty pharaoh's tomb.*

273 top The small dark smudges on the floor of the Valley of the Kings are the entrances to tombs. This new design was developed during the New Kingdom, and was based on long, downward-sloping corridors that led to the burial chamber. Tutankhamon's tomb lies in the light-colored area at the center of the photograph.

273 bottom The goddess Nephthys spreads her wings to protect a corner of the outermost sarcophagus of Tutankhamon, made from finely carved red quartzite. The fame of this tomb is due to the fact that it has been basically the only one to be found almost intact, but in fact it was small compared to those of other Egyptian kings.

Nemrut Dagi
TURKEY

EASTERN ANATOLIA
REGISTRATION: 1987
CRITERIA: C (I) (III) (IV)

In February 2003, Turkish archaeologist Mahmud Arslan announced the discovery of the burial chamber of Antiochus I, king of Commagene, inside the stone tumulus on the top of the 7,237-foot Mount Nemrut. Before the arrival of Arslan and his team of forty or so archaeologists and geologists, many scholars had attempted in vain to penetrate the mound of stones 165 feet high and 500 across, but only modern equipment made it possible to reach the four-sided chamber that had been cut out of the living rock and then sealed within it. Inside, three sarcophagi were found containing the remains of Antiochus I, his father Mithridates Callinicus, and another unidentified person.

Thanks to this discovery, a fundamental piece in understanding of one of the most mysterious places in Turkey has been added to the puzzle. In a spectacular position on a peak in the Taurus Mountains in eastern Anatolia, a geologist in the service of the Ottomans drew the megalomaniac personality of King Antiochus I out from the mists of history when he identified the site of Nemrut Dagi at the end of the nineteenth century.

Born in 80 BC out of the fragmentation of the Seleucid Empire, which had in turn come into being with the breakup of Alexander the Great's empire, the kingdom of Commagene acted as a buffer between the Roman and Persian empires. Its founder, Mithridates Callinicus, allied himself with Rome, but when his son Antiochus I came to the throne in 69 BC, the new king believed he could survive independently by implementing a policy in which he would provide information to the Persians though maintaining friendly relations with the Romans. Antiochus I also invented a genealogy that allowed him to claim

descent from Alexander the Great and, before him, from the gods of Olympus, but his boastful parentage brought him no benefit. After him, the kings of Commagene were no more than Roman puppets and, in AD 72, Emperor Vespasian put an end to the foolish situation by incorporating the kingdom into the province of Syria.

To judge by the wonderful temples and tumulus (Hierotheseion) that he had built for himself on Nemrut Dagi, Antiochus I

considered himself a great ruler. He left a long inscription on the site (the *Nomos*, composed of 217 lines of text) from which not only his pretentious claims to be descended from the gods can be deduced, but also those that his kingdom would last forever.

Three platforms were excavated in the rock next to the mound of stones. The one on the north side was used as accommodation for priests; its boundary stones still exist, but the bas-reliefs that

ANKARA

NEMRUT DAGI

274-275 *On the west terrace are the remains of five majestic statues. In the foreground, the head of Zeus sculpted from a single block weighing 8 tons can be seen. Zeus was associated with the Persian god Orosmasdes and is recognizable by his curly beard and stern gaze.*

275 top *Heracles (left) and Mithridates I greet one another in a bas-relief at Nemrut Dagi. Familiarity between heroes and kings was a common theme in these reliefs; in this case, the Commagene rulers wished to conceal in part their dependence on Rome.*

decorated them have been worn away by the wind and rain. However, the two to the east and west are monumental temple complexes, in each of which have been found the remains of five superb statues. Though they are now scattered on the ground, they once stood between 26 and 33 feet tall and were each formed of blocks of stone weighing over eight tons. They are interesting for their iconography in which the syncretism of Greek and Persian deities is evident. On both the platforms, Zeus is associated with the Persian god Ahura Mazda, then Apollo and Mithras, Heracles and Atagnes, Tyche (the Commagenean goddess of fertility), and Antiochus I. The tiaras worn on their heads, which now lie on the ground, are Persian, as are the clothes they wear in the platform's bas-reliefs illustrating Antiochus in the presence of the gods.

The most enigmatic figure in Nemrut Dagi is that of a lion carved on the west platform. On his mane, there are 19 stars, on his neck a crescent moon, and on his back the planets Mars, Jupiter, and Mercury. According to experts, the relief has a precise astronomic significance. Study of the various elements has led to the conclusion that they represent a particular date: July 7, 62 BC. Perhaps that was the day Antiochus I conceived the crazy idea of his immortality.

275 bottom left *A view of the west terrace. Like the east terrace, it was an open temple complex. The north side was used for the priests' housing and has no statues.*

275 bottom right *The east terrace in the clear morning light. On the left is the effigy of a lion; further away are the heads of five gods wearing Persian-style headdresses.*

Palmyra

SYRIA

Province of Homs
Registration: 1980
Criteria: C (I) (II) (IV)

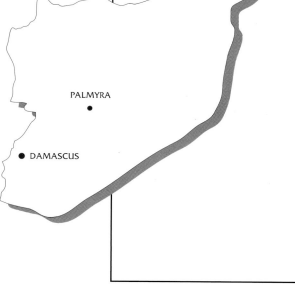

PALMYRA

● DAMASCUS

276-277 The fascinating ruins of Palmyra are surrounded by desert and overlooked by the hill on which the Qalaat ibn Maan stands, a fort built by the Arabs in the twelfth century.

276 bottom A view of the monumental arch and colonnaded street. Originally lined entirely with porticoes, it was divided into four sections and cut right through the city from east to west for 1,300 yards.

Asumptuous procession with elephants and gladiators parades through the streets of Rome. At its center, the triumphal chariot of the emperor Aurelian is preceded by a woman on foot dressed only in Eastern-style jewelry. Attached to her arms and legs are gold chains so heavy they have to be carried by a slave. This story is recounted in *Historia Augusta*, a monumental work celebrating the military triumphs of Rome. The year is AD 274 and the prisoner is Zenobia, the most beautiful woman in the East, and one who dared to challenge the power of Rome. The *Historia* continues, relating that Aurelian, who conquered her in battle, succumbed to her beauty, made her his lover, and gave her a villa in Tivoli.

Zenobia is one of the legendary women of antiquity. In addition to her beauty, it is known that she was the wife of Septimius Odenatus, ruler of Palmyra and faithful to Rome. We know that she learned from him the skills of government and military strategies, and that she learnt Greek, Latin, and Egyptian at court. She bore Septimius a son but had him assassinated so that she could take power. No one at the Palmyran court suspected Zenobia, with the result that she was able give the title of emperor to her son and that of *Augusta* for herself.

She allied herself to the Persians and began campaigns of conquest in the direction of Turkey and Egypt with the aim of creating an Eastern empire to counter the power of Rome. Nevertheless, her dreams of glory were smashed when Aurelian quickly abandoned his campaign against the Goths in order to send his troops to tame the rebels in Syria.

Zenobia deserved her punishment. Though Palmyra had always enjoyed a large degree of autonomy (it was part of the Roman province *Syria Phoenice*), it

had become the most important caravan city in the East thanks to Roman support. In AD 124, Hadrian honored it with the title *Civitas Libera*, and it was the Romans, as consumers of exotic goods, who had permitted the city to extend its commercial traffic as far as India and

China, with the result that it became fabulously wealthy.

The first evidence of the existence of a settlement called Tadmor is found in an Assyrian contract from the nineteenth century BC. The place name, now used again by the modern village found on the edge of the archaeological site of Palmyra, has been interpreted by experts as derived from the Semitic word *tamr*, meaning "date palms" in Arabic. This etymological root coincides with the

277 top The monumental arch was built by Septimius Severus (AD 193–211) when Palmyra enjoyed a period of great construction.

277 center The best-conserved section of the colonnaded street lies between the propylaea of the temple of Bel and the monumental arch. Note the brackets two-thirds of the way up the columns that originally held statues of prominent and wealthy Palmyran citizens.

277 bottom The remains of the temple of Baal-Shamin, lord of the Heavens in the Semitic pantheon believed to be responsible for the rain.

278 top The theater of Palmyra (second century AD) was one of the most magnificent in the Middle East. The stage is 157 feet wide and 34 deep; the backdrop imitated the façade of a palace of which only the ground floor has survived, with colonnades and doors crowned by niches.

278 bottom left Consecrated in 32 BC, the cella was the real temple of Bel, to which access was granted only to the priests. The statue of the god flanked by those of Yarhibol and Aglibol, the gods of the Sun and Moon were found here.

278 bottom right The imposing cella of the temple of Bel lies at the center of an immense court (230 by 224 yards) lined by high walls. Bel was the principal god of the Semitic pantheon and was associated with the Roman Jupiter.

279 top Standing at the opposite end of the long colonnaded street from the temple of Bel, the funerary temple (third century AD) was in fact a magnificent tomb preceded by a portico with six columns.

279 bottom Situated in the north section of the city on a transversal road that starts at the Tetrapylon, the temple of Baal-Shamin is in excellent condition considering that in the fifth century its cella was turned into a Christian church.

Latin name of the city, also derived from the word "palm." References to Tadmor are made in Babylonian tablets from the age of Hammurabi and, much later, in the accounts of Alexander the Great's war against the Persians.

From the first century BC on, during the Roman era, there is an increase in the number of material and literary references to the growth and development of Palmyra. The city of merchants seemed to enjoy a privileged position between the two major empires, the Roman and Persian. In AD 77, in his *Naturalis Historia*, Pliny the Elder wrote, "Palmyra is a noble city for the site it occupies, for the richness of its soil, and for the pleasantness of its waters. Expanses of sand surround its fields on every side, and it is as though it were isolated from the world by nature."

Despite its population being mostly Semitic, Palmyra gradually embraced the Roman political and social model, though it maintained an Eastern style in its art and customs. The ruins that can be seen today date mostly to the second and third centuries AD and reflect both a mix of styles and the increasing wealth of its citizens. Well-to-do merchants competed to embellish the city with ever more magnificent monuments.

The remains of the ancient city around the Efqa spring, which supplied abundant water for the crops of olives, dates, and pomegranates, cover an area of about four square miles. Though it had no particular city plan and its residential districts were typical of the cities of the East, the growth of Palmyra reflects the Greco-Roman principle of autonomy. Therefore, there was a large colonnaded street 1,300 yards long and 24 yards wide, a theater, a baths complex, and

278-279 The elegant Tetrapylon was formed by a platform on which four superb buildings once stood, each of which housed a statue. Only one of the original pink Aswan-marble columns remains, the others are faithful copies.

280-281 With those of Artaban and the "Three Brothers," the tomb of Bolha, son of Nabushuri (AD 89), is one of the most refined in Palmyra. Like the others, it is formed by a gallery topped by a barrel vault onto which the bays face. The bays contained the burial niches decorated with stucco friezes and sculptures.

280 bottom left These tower tombs are among the oldest and most original funerary constructions in Palmyra. They are mostly square, stand on a stepped platform, and are formed by various levels connected by a flight of steps.

281 top right This lady wearing a soft fabric headdress has been immortalized on a funerary effigy. The statues provide valuable information on the clothing and jewelry that were in style in Palmyra.

281 bottom A funerary stele decorated with bas-reliefsis held in the site's archaeological museum. As occurred in this case, stelae often show the dead during real events in their lives.

280 bottom right The tomb of Ehlabel (AD 103) is an elegant tower four stories high. The terrace gives a view over the Valley of the Tombs. The family buried here was one of the richest in the city and responsible for the construction of the temple of Nebo.

281 top left The details and unique facial features suggest that these funerary statues were realistic portraits of the dead. They were referred to as nafshâ, a word that in Semitic languages means "soul" or "person."

widespread use of Greek architectural orders, in particular Corinthian.

The colonnaded street is divided into four sections. The first runs from the monumental arch to the Temple of Bel. The second continues to the Tetrapylon – composed of four pedestals with four columns each – and was lined by the baths, the Temple of Nebo, the agora, and the Senate, whereas a cross street led to the Temple of Baal-Shamin. The third section cut through the residential quarters and led to the Funerary Temple, and the last section ended at the Gate of Diocletian that gave onto the Valley of the Tombs.

The most impressive temple is the one dedicated to Bel, the supreme Palmyran deity, construction of which began in AD 32. The enormous courtyard measures 230 yards by 224 and had a pool for ritual bathing, a sacrificial altar, a banquet room, and a *cella*. The cella was the most sacred section of the temple and was reserved for use by the priests. It contained a statue of Bel between Yarhibol and Aglibol, the Palmyran gods of the Sun and the Moon. The coffered geometric decorations and rosettes on the ceiling of the *cella* feature elements that later became typical of Byzantine and Arab art.

The Palmyrans were highly skilled and original in their sculptural art, especially in their carving of bas-reliefs. Those in the best state of conservation decorate the tombs – built in either hypogeum or tower form – of the rich families. Made from limestone, they feature detailed portrayals of the deceased with facial features, clothing, and jewelry. Of the few tombs open to the public, the most interesting are those of the Elahbel family, for the beauty of its sculptures, and of the Three Brothers, for its delicate frescoes.

Following Zenobia's downfall, the city began to languish, and though emperor Diocletian later gave Palmyra a new boost by stationing an immense military camp there, the city's fate was already marked out. It was just ruins when, in the twelfth century, the Arabs built a castle on the rocky spur overlooking the site, but this fort too was soon abandoned. What had once been the magnificent and ambitious Palmyra was soon covered over by the desert.

Baalbek

LEBANON

BEKAA VALLEY
REGISTRATION: 1984
CRITERIA: C (I) (IV)

In spite of its high-sounding name, Heliopolis, the "City of the Sun" founded by the Phoenicians, it was a city of modest wealth when Julius Caesar effortlessly conquered it in 15 BC. As was his custom, the emperor founded a colony there, which he named *Julia Augusta Felix Heliopolitana*, and stationed a legion on the site. At the same time, quite inexplicably, he decided to build there the most magnificent temple in the empire.

Considered one of the wonders of the world by historians of the fifth century, who were among the first to call it Baalbek, meaning "god *(Baal)* from the Bekaa Valley," the temple was dedicated to *Jupiter Heliopolitanus*. The building stands on a rectangular platform measuring 87 by 52 yards, made of stone blocks weighing at least 700 tons, and bordered by 54 columns seven feet three inches in diameter and 66 feet tall. Today only six columns still remain: eight were taken to Constantinople by Justinian to be used in construction of the Hagia Sophia, and the rest were either used to build another Byzantine basilica *in situ* (since destroyed) or were toppled by earthquakes. The temple held a gold statue of Jupiter, which was worshiped by pilgrims who visited from all corners of the Roman Empire.

Construction lasted about 150 years but was never completed, though the capitals and fragments of the architraves decorated with the heads of lions and bulls, acanthus leaves, and roses bear witness to the sophistication of the sculptural work, and many emperors committed themselves to

BAALBEK ●

● BEIRUT

282 left Caracalla (AD 211–217) was responsible for the construction of the elegant propylaea, considered an entrance worth of the religious complex of Baalbek. These consist of a portico with 12 columns flanked by two towers.

282 right A view of the temple of Jupiter. Triliths (blocks of three monoliths each weighing between 750 and 1,000 tons) were used to build the massive platform on which it stands.

283 A fragment of the architrave and the 6 superb columns that remain standing in the temple of Jupiter. Of the other 48, 8 were taken to Constantinople for the construction of the basilica of Hagia Sophia, and the others have been destroyed.

284 top and 285 right Built on the orders of Antoninus Pius (AD 138–161), the temple of Bacchus is still in magnificent condition. At 62 feet high, its 42 columns are still intact, and the narrative scenes carved in bas-relief on the portal of the cella are also well preserved.

making it as magnificent as Caesar had wished.

Around AD 60, Nero had a tower built in front of the temple that allowed pilgrims to view the statue of the god from a raised position. Trajan (AD 98–117) was responsible for the construction of an enormous entrance courtyard.

Measuring 123 yards per side, three of its sides were lined with 12 exedras, each of which was preceded by a portico with Egyptian pink-granite columns. Inscriptions inform us that the exedras provided shelter to the priests of the various communities and reception facilities to pilgrims of high birth.

In AD 145, Antoninus Pius ordered the construction of the Temple of Bacchus. Standing opposite the Temple of Jupiter, it covers an area measuring 75 by 39 yards. It is still in good condition and its elegant proportions, like the richness of its decorations, make it a masterpiece of Roman art. Inside, there were statues of the entire Roman pantheon that are still recognizable today, even though their faces have been smashed by iconoclastic Muslim invaders.

The third temple at Baalbek was built by Septimius Severus around AD 200, and its monumental propylaea by his successor Caracalla. Dedicated to Venus, the Severan temple is an elegant pentagonal building surrounded by columns and niches.

Eusebius of Caesarea, the first historian of the Christian Church, wrote horrified that here "men and women couple without shame, and fathers and husbands allow their daughters and wives to prostitute themselves to please the goddess."
In fact, the Romans had modified the practice of sacred prostitution taken from the local Semitic tradition, in the same way that the divine triad of Baalbek was the fruit of the syncretism of the Roman and Phoenician religions: Jupiter was identified with Baal, Venus with Astarte, and Bacchus, their son, with the spirit of nature.

Since 1955, Baalbek has come back to life and a "new syncretism," thanks to a music festival of renown. Now the majestic columns of the Temple of Jupiter provide a backdrop to artists of the caliber of Herbert von Karajan and Mstislav Rostropovich.

Masada
ISRAEL

REGION OF TAMAR
REGISTRATION: 2001
CRITERIA: C (III) (IV) (VI)

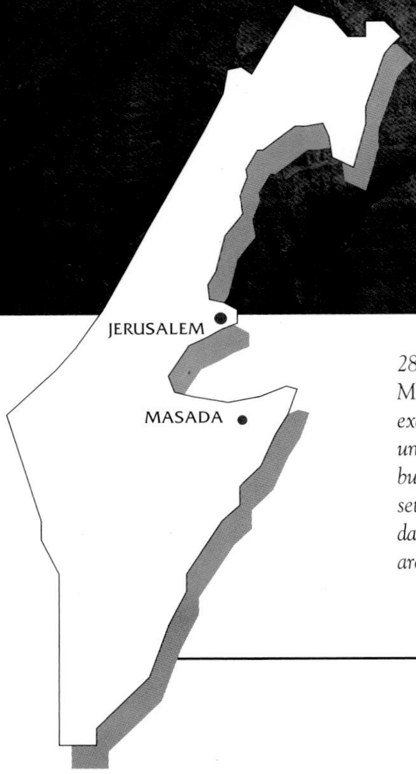

JERUSALEM

MASADA

286 top An aerial view of Masada. Begun in 1963, excavation has not only unearthed Herod's buildings but also vestiges of a settlement that seems to date to the Chalcolithic age, around 4000 BC.

286-287 The rock of Masada dominates the desert of Judaea close to the west bank of the Dead Sea and the oasis of Ein Gedi. The top of the mountain is flat and measures 330 by 660 yards in the shape of a diamond.

287 top left Covering 43,000 square feet, the west palace was where the Zealots barricaded themselves against the Roman siege in AD 73. Though they were not captured, they committed mass suicide and their skeletons were found in the fort.

287 top right When Masada was occupied by the Zealots, the furnishings in the west palace and Herod's luxury villa were removed to make space for the poor families of this Jewish sect.

In the most moving pages of the *History of the Jewish War*, the historian Flavius Josephus reports the words of Eleazar Ben Yair, head of the Zealots besieged by the Romans in the fort of Masada, "while our hands have a sword to grip, they will do us an act of kindness: we will die before our enemies can reduce us to slavery, and as free men we will bid farewell to life with our wives and children." He tells that on that dramatic night in AD 73, the Zealots embraced their nearest and dearest and then committed mass suicide.

The next morning, when the Romans reached the fort, they found 960 bodies and huge quantities of burned household goods. This was not the way in which they expected to tame the rebellion of the handful of Jews who fled Jerusalem following the destruction of the Temple, and who dared to challenge the power of Rome. Yet, this was a bitter victory for the Romans, despite Masada having been considered virtually unassailable.

Masada hill overlooks the desert of Judaea close to the west bank of the Dead Sea and the oasis of Ein Gedi. Like a rocky pedestal, it is topped by a diamond-shaped plateau measuring 325

by 650 yards. The presence of a *wadi* (seasonal torrent) allowed Herod, king of Judaea from 37 BC to AD 4, to construct a permanent military garrison there. He ordered his engineers to dig a network of canals and water tanks that would collect the water from the *wadi*, but then, taken by the beauty of the landscape, decided to use the place as a residence as well.

His ambitious plan is still evident today. In the northern section of the plateau, the palace was built on three terraces connected by steps cut in the rock, with porticoed courtyards, floors decorated with geometric mosaics, and frescoed walls. Next to the palace are the storerooms that could hold an amazing quantity of goods, and next to those are a synagogue and baths building for the use of guests and high officials at Masada.

The most elaborate room in the baths is the *calidarium*, featuring a floor supported by 200 columns and sprinkled with terracotta apertures that allowed hot air to enter from a furnace beneath. The most impressive building in the complex is the west palace, which covered 5,000 square yards and was used as an administrative center. The rest of

287

287 bottom left One of the store rooms to in the south of the baths' complex. Before excavation began, these were not visible as they were covered by earth and debris. They were destroyed by the besieged Zealots to prevent the Romans from plundering their goods.

287 bottom right The pool inside Herod's villa. Water was provided via a system of channels from the wadi to the west of the fort, which conveyed the water into 12 cisterns, that combined with a capacity of over 10,000,000 gallons.

288 top One of the medallions decorated with fruit and geometric patterns from the mosaic floor in the audience room of the west palace. Built by Herod, this was the enormous administrative center of Masada.

289 Laid out on three terraces connected by flights of steps, Herod's royal villa was built on the north tip of the plateau. The size of the building and its elegant interiors are evidence of the man's ambition (king of Judaea from 37 BC to AD 4).

the area was occupied by accommodation for the troops.

Although Masada was identified in the nineteenth century, systematic excavation only began in 1963. In addition to the majestic ruins of the buildings, a great quantity of goods, coins, and skeletons (probably those of the Zealots) have been found. The remains of the fortifications built by the Romans during the siege can be clearly seen at the base of the hill.

Masada is a symbol of the extreme sacrifice made by the Jews for their freedom. Yet, the resistance and suicide of the Zealots does not appear in the Jewish sacred text, the *Talmud*, and the only written record is that of Flavius Josephus, who learnt of it after meeting two women who survived the massacre by hiding in a water conduit. However, Flavius Josephus was a traitor: he was born a Jew but he sold himself to the Romans, and, over the centuries, he was erased from Jewish collective memory. With him, the episode of Masada was also forgotten, until 1920 when the writer Isaac Lamdan composed a poem entitled *Masada*. It was this tale that inspired the revolt of the Jews in the Warsaw ghetto against the Nazis in World War II.

288 center left This small Byzantine chapel was built in the fifth century by monks living in the grottoes near the fort. The mosaics that decorated the floor have been completely destroyed.

288 center right The lower terrace of Herod's villa overlooks the Dead Sea. To reach the fort, which in the past meant climbing a steep path, today visitors are transported by cable-car.

288 bottom The calidarium in the baths. Supported by the 200 columns in the photograph, the floor featured numerous terracotta holes, through which air heated in the furnace below entered the room.

Petra
JORDAN

Incense, saffron, myrrh, cardamom, pepper, ginger, and cinnamon to flavor foods and perfume ointments, balsams, and medicines; muslin and silk that, from the start of the first century AD, became the favorite fabric of the most refined Romans: all these goods – according to the *Periplo del Mare Eritreo*, a manual written by an anonymous Greek merchant – arrived from India by sea at the ports of Hadramauth in Yemen, the legendary kingdom of Sheba. From there, the Nabataeans transported them in caravans across the desert from the Arabian Peninsula to the fabulous city of Petra, where they were divided up for distribution throughout the Mediterranean, Persia, and Mesopotamia.

Little is known of the semi-nomadic merchants who won the respect of the Romans and Persians for their ability to supply such desirable goods. Some scholars identify them with the Edomites who stopped the exodus of the Jews led by Moses. The first written reference to the Nabataeans is much more recent and is found in Book XIX of the *Biblioteca Historica* by Diodorus Siculus (80–20 BC). The events to

which he refers date to 315 BC and regard the failed attempt by the Diadochs (Alexander the Great's successors) to overcome the Nabataeans living in Petra.

The next news we have of the tribe is from 63 BC when the Romans led by Pompey succeeded in extending their dominion over what are today Syria and Jordan, which were mostly inhabited by the Nabataeans. Nonetheless, they managed to hole themselves up in their capital and maintain their monopoly on goods coming from the Red Sea.

Rome only got the better of them in AD 106, when, upon the death of their king, Rabbele II, the Nabataeans gave their city up to Cornelius Palma,

governor of Syria under the emperor Trajan. That their surrender was probably the outcome of a diplomatic agreement is suggested by Roman coins minted after annexation, on which, to celebrate the event, the words *Arabia adquisita* were stamped rather than *Arabia capta*, in other words, an indication of a "passage of property" of an administrative nature.

In truth, despite the crushing superiority of their men and arms, the Romans would never have been able to take Petra by force. The Siq – the narrow passage formed over thousands of years by the Wadi Musa (Valley of Moses), one of the seasonal torrents in the zone – was the only means of entry to the city, and the mouth of the passage was practically invisible. From this point for 1,300 yards, there is a series of bends and right-angle turns along sandstone walls up to 330 feet high. It was the only means of taking the city but a suicidal one, even for an army like that of the Romans.

Now that it is no longer an unassailable military obstacle, the Siq is no more than a passage of great beauty on the way to reaching the Khazneh Fir'awn (Treasure of the Pharaoh), the immense building dug out of the rock that is one of the most extraordinary monuments of the ancient world. The

290 top Petra at sunset: the low, reddish light makes the buildings look even more extraordinary and brings out the wonderful gradations of color in the rock.

290 bottom left A horse-drawn carriage proceeds through the narrow, beautiful gorge called the Siq carved for 4,000 feet out of the sandstone. The Siq provides the only entry to the Nabataean city of Petra.

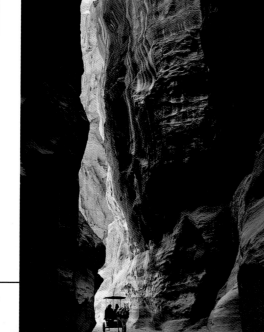

290 bottom right The façade of the Khazneh Fir'awn is two stories high and measures 131 feet tall by 92 wide. Its complex appearance was acheived by recessing the back wall, making it seem as though the building is set in a large frame.

291 The dramatic crevice of the Siq reveals the splendid architecture of the Khazneh Fir'awn (Treasure of the Pharaoh), which was very probably built in memory of Arete III, whose reign (84–56 BC) coincided with the Nabataean people's greatest period of prosperity.

HAMMAN

PETRA

English archaeologist Sir Leonard Woolley wrote, "the Nabataean architects dissected classical architecture and played with the various pieces, arranging them at pleasure with sublime disinterest in the function for which they were originally designed."

The Khazneh Fir'awn has a two-level façade (92 feet wide and 131 feet high) characterized by a very elaborate design. The lower level is formed by a portico with six columns, and the upper level is divided into a round *tholos* with a conical roof topped by an urn. At the sides there are two semi-gables framed by columns and kiosks. Everywhere there are ornamental motifs of very high quality: statues, capitals, and continuous friezes of garlands of flowers and berries reminiscent of Hellenistic models. Like most of the monuments at Petra, the building had a funerary function and was probably carved in memory of King Arete III (84–56 BC), whose rule coincided with the Nabataeans' period of greatest prosperity. The name Khazneh Fir'awn was given to it by the Arabs who were long convinced that the urn on the *tholos* contained a treasure. Their iconoclastic fury led them to destroy the statues on the façade, in the same way that that some Bedouin later destroyed the amphora in search of treasure.

From the Khazneh Fir'awn, the magnificent city opens into a hollow ringed by pink pinnacles where the only surviving building that has not been carved out of the rock has also been named mistakenly: the Qasr al Bint Fir'awn (Castle of the Pharaoh's Daughter). The structure of this vast, richly decorated temple is based on the

292 top left A colonnaded
street, monumentalized in
the late-first and early-
second centuries AD,
crosses the city from east to
west, from the temple of
Qasr el-Bint Fir'awn to the
royal temples.

292 top right Entirely
carved out of the sandstone,
the theater has a cavea that
could seat 8,500
spectators. Originally the
frons scenae was lined with
marble panels and brightly-
painted plaster.

292-293 A view of the
Corinthian Tomb with the
Palace Tomb on the left.
The name of the latter is
due to the belief that its
architectural style imitates
that of majestic Hellenistic
residences. Both structures
were collective tombs that
were probably used for
members of the royal
family.

293 top The Tomb of the
Obelisks owes its name to the
four full-relief obelisks that
symbolize the deceased buried
inside. It was excavated in a
position over the large
triclinium in the Bab el-Siq.
There probably was a
functional relationship between
the two buildings, the façades
of which are remarkable for
their refined architecture.

293 bottom As in many of
the other tombs at Petra,
the porticoed room in the
Garden Tomb, in the zone
of Wadi Farasa, was
supposed to host banquets
to commemorate the dead,
probably on the anniversary
of the death of the deceased.

architecture of the temples of the Nile
Valley. The origin of the name is derived
from the Egyptian influence on the local
culture that dated back to remote times,
owing to the commerce that took place
between Petra and Alexandria.
Moreover, the mercantile nature of the
Nabataeans ensured that they absorbed
the cultural and artistic characteristics of
the peoples with whom they came into
contact.

The majestic ad-Dayr (the
Monastery) is clearly Hellenistic in style.
It stands on the top of the mountain of
the same name and is reached by endless
steps cut in the rock, a sort of via sacra
lined by tombs and votive niches.

294 top This temple tomb from the end of the first century AD is called the Tomb of the Roman Soldier due to the sculpture of a man wearing armor in the central niche. This was an effigy of the high-ranking officer buried inside.

294 bottom The walls of the triclinium in the Tomb of the Roman Soldier are lined with half-columns and niches with large windows. In the middle of the chamber there are stone benches where guests would sit during funeral ceremonies.

294-295 Archaeologists believe that ad-Dayr (The Monastery) was a temple built in honor of a Nabataean sovereign (perhaps Oboda I) who was divinized after his death.

However, many of the tombs in Petra – like the Tomb of the Urn – and the stone triclinia where funeral banquets were held are adorned with stepped decorations typical of Assyrian art.

Nothing has remained of the Nabataean houses, which were probably built with perishable materials. Little is known of the people, who may have been absorbed by the Arabs. After the arrival of the Romans, the city gradually lost its importance, even though individuals like Strabo described it in enthusiastic terms. Then, in the third century AD, with the decline of the empire, the Romans lost interest in Petra. The memory of the city became a secret guarded by scattered groups of Bedouin tribesmen, until August 22, 1812 when it was rediscovered by the Swiss traveler Johann Ludwig Burckhardt.

His account, published in *Travels in Syria and the Holy Land*, found fertile terrain in romantic Europe of the nineteenth century. It persuaded a young Scot of humble origins to set out for the extraordinary city. His name was David Roberts and his roughly 100 sketches and paintings of Petra allowed him to crown his dream of glory. On his return to Britain, Roberts became famous as the greatest landscape painter of his time, and, after his views were published, Petra returned to life.

295 bottom left The tomb of Sextius Florentinus, the Roman governor of the province of Arabia in AD 127, has a female figure on the large central arch. This was probably a Gorgon, a symbol of Hellenistic derivation.

295 bottom right The façade of the Renaissance Tomb. This fanciful name reflects the details on the pediment resembling Italian buildings of that period. Another unusual decorative feature in the tombs of Petra is the bas-relief of a stairway.

Persepolis

IRAN

Province of Fârs
Registration: 1979
Criteria: C (i) (iii) (vi)

In the procession marking the start of the New Year celebrations, all the representatives of the immense Persian Empire paraded in great pomp. The colorful, festive celebration was a source of great pride for the ruler and entertainment for the spectators. It opened with the solemn march of the army of the Ten Thousand Immortals, then the Medians (who had the honor of opening the parade of Persian subjects), followed by the Elamites with lions on leashes, the Parthians, the Sogdians of central Asia who brought dromedaries and hides as gifts to the emperor, the Egyptians with their standards and a bull, the Sagartians with horses and magnificent clothing, the Bactrians on camels, the Armenians with vases filled with offerings, the Babylonians with cups and fabrics, the Cilicians with rams, the Scythians with their spiked hair, the Assyrians with lances, the Lydians with a chariot, the Ionians with plates, and finally, the peoples of India with dozens of great baskets.

The parade was held in Persepolis. It is recorded in great detail in the magnificent bas-relief a full 330 yards long, divided into various orders, on the walls of the steps of the *Apadana*. This monumental room – supported by 36 columns each 82 feet tall, decorated with capitals in the form of griffins, lions, and bulls – was dedicated to the receptions given by the King of Kings, the ruler of the dynasty of the Achaemenids, who was elected by the supreme god, Ahura Mazda. The superb construction was built on the orders of Darius (522–486 BC) who had made Persepolis his capital.

As soon as he mounted the throne, Darius launched a libertarian policy, instituting satrapies with extensive powers of government in each province. In fact, his "decentralized state" did not need a new seat of government, neither for administrative nor commercial purposes. Therefore, Persepolis was built as a center to hold official celebrations and the imperial coffers that stored the gifts sent to him and his successors from every corner of his empire.

296 top Construction of the city of Persepolis on an artificial platform 1,175 feet long, 984 wide, and 49 high was begun by Darius and continued by his successors with the use of thousands of slaves from every corner of the empire.

296 bottom Sculpted on a massive scale but with carefully executed details, this bull, now hornless, serves as the base for a pillar. Capitals and plinths in Persepolis were often in the form of animals.

296-297 As is documented, the magnificent Portal of the Nations was built by Xerxes I. It leads into the Apadana, the monumental room in which thousands of people could fit to attend official ceremonies.

297 top Persepolis was so rich that, as Herodotus recounted, when Alexander the Great destroyed the city in 330 BC, 10,000 mules and 5,000 camels were required to carry off its treasures.

297 bottom A symbol of Achaemenid power at the entrance to the Apadana, this mythological creature is a lamasu, a sphinx with the body of a bull, a human head, and a pointed beard.

298 top left When shown moving from place to place, as in this frieze on the Tripylon, Darius is always attended by slaves who carry a sunshade and a flyswater. In portraits, he always expresses a sense of power and almost supernatural beauty.

298 top right Enthroned and with his feet on a stool, Darius welcomes his subjects in a hieratic pose. In reliefs, the king is always shown larger than the other figures.

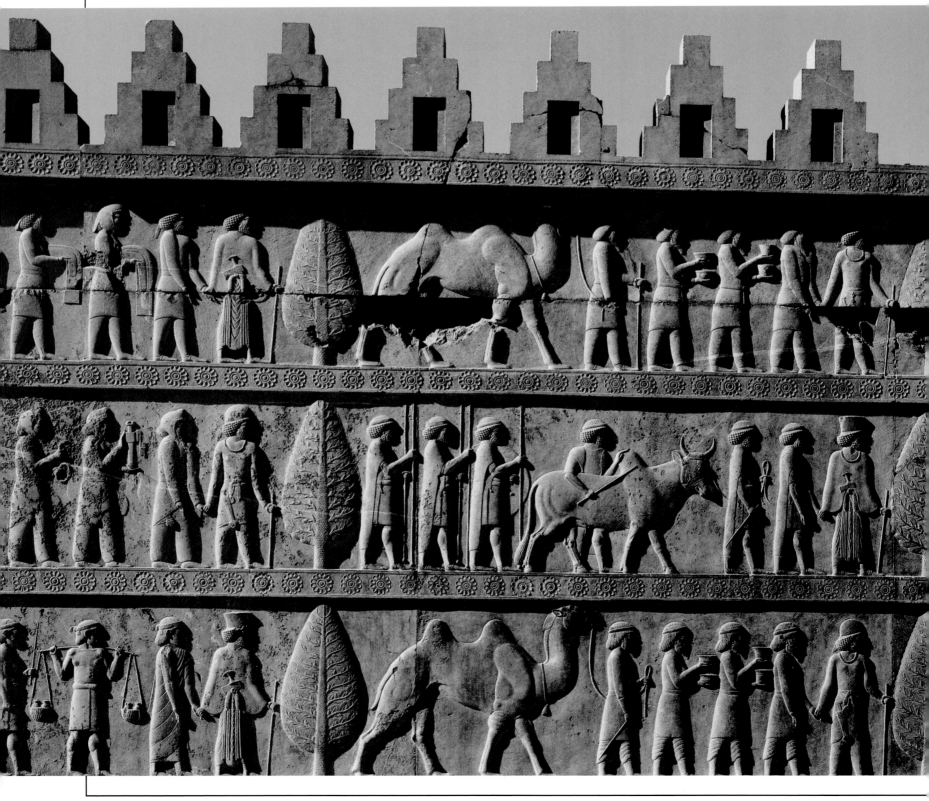

Built on a stone platform 492 yards long, 330 wide, and 50 feet high, the only entrance to Persepolis is a flight of steps ending in the Portal of the Nations, built by Darius's son Xerxes. This is a wide structure open on three sides and overlooked by 23-foot-tall stone bulls. A short distance from the *Apadana* are the two buildings built by Darius, the Tripylon (adorned with bas-reliefs) and the Tachana (Winter Palace), whose entrance is guarded by statues of bulls and *lamasu* (sphinxes with the body of a bull and head of a man with a pointed beard).

A little further on is the huge Throne Room, also called the Palace of a

Hundred Columns, and the unfinished Palace of Artaxerxes III (358–338 BC), the last ruler of the Achaemenid dynasty. The complex includes Xerxes' palace, an elegant square space onto which a variety of rooms faced. One of these is referred to as the *harem*, though no woman ever lived there, nor was the palace ever resided in, as it was simply a storeroom for the imperial treasury. In the court archives of 25,000 tablets inscribed with cuneiform characters, the treasurers minutely inventoried all the gifts brought to the ruler. In fact, 1,438 people were employed to guard and administer his wealth.

In 330 BC, Alexander the Great arrived at the city gates. His army was so large and well armed that the Persians surrendered without fighting. Nonetheless, and contrary to his custom, the Macedon destroyed Persepolis, reducing it to a pile of ruins. This was his revenge on the Achaemenids for having destroyed Athens in 480 BC. Then Alexander continued unstoppably on his way to the conquest of the East. However, it is said that on his return some years later, he wished to halt at Persepolis, by now nothing but a ghost. He climbed up on the platform, alone, as the sun was setting and cried tears of regret.

298-299 Darius's subjects are shown paying tribute to him in the frieze that decorates the base of the Apadana terrace. The rigidity of the official figuration is mitigated by the insertion of cypresses and palms, which were inspired by the gardens where the king and his court liked to relax.

299 top The motif of the lion and its prey, seen on the reliefs of the monumental stairway in Darius's palace, was a traditional one in Persian iconography. It was adopted by the Greeks and included in friezes on monuments in Athens.

299 center Darius's palace opens with a portico that looked onto what were once gardens where the king held banquets. Apart from the terrace and the stairway, what remains of the once magnificent building are the massive stone cornices of the doors.

299 bottom Fantastic animals decorate the capitals of the 36 columns that supported the cedar ceiling of the Apadana, which decomposed over the centuries.

300 top This is a detail from the frieze that shows the procession paying tribute to Persepolis. It symbolized the complete possession of the assets of subjected regions by the king, as well as the loyalty of his subjects.

300-301 Herodotus estimated that Darius's army numbered five million effective troops, not counting "the women that made the bread, the concubines, and the eunuchs." The figure was unrealistic: today it is thought that the Achaemenid military force did not exceed 50,000 men.

301 top The various peoples in the majestic procession can be identified by their clothing and the goods they bear as gifts. Here we see the Cilicians bringing Darius rams.

301 center top The representations of horses are particularly detailed and well-proportioned. As Xenophon wrote, the Persians were excellent horsemen and rode without the use of stirrups.

301 center bottom The Lydians carried their offerings to the king on a chariot. Each delegation was guided into the Achaemenid capital by a "gate officer."

301 bottom A royal guard in his parade uniform holds his lance with two hands and has his quiver slung over his back. This is a detail from a bas-relief on the east stairway of the Apadana.

The Tomb of the First Qin Emperor

CHINA

LINTONG PLAIN, PROVINCE OF SHAANXI
REGISTRATION: 1987
CRITERIA: C (I) (III) (IV) (VI)

BEIJNG

XI'AN

302 top *This model in Xi'an Museum was built according to the descriptions made in 249 BC by the court historian Sima Qian. It is a hypothetical reconstruction of the emperor's final dwelling place, though even today archaeologists have not discovered the burial chamber of Qin Shi Huangdi.*

302-303 *The roughly 8,000 statues that make up the Terracotta Army of the first emperor, Qin Shi Huangdi, are covered by a structure protecting them from the natural elements.*

303 top *Originally the soldiers bore weapons with wooden handles, but these have decomposed over the centuries. Other accessories, however, remain: bronze arrow heads, blades of daggers used in hand-to-hand combat, and signal bells.*

303 center *The significance of the statues is controversial. Some experts believe that they represent the real imperial guard, whereas others think they are mingqi ("surrogates") to avoid the sacrifice of human lives upon the death of the emperor.*

Aweek, journey time included: this was the duration estimated by the functionaries of Beijing for archaeologist Yuan Zhongyi's mission to Lutong, about 20 miles from the city of Xi'an. The young scholar had been given the task of confirming word that a terracotta statue had been found by a farmer while digging an irrigation canal on a shared farm in Yanzhai. It was 1974 and no one expected that the life-size statue of a warrior was but one tiny piece in the incredible mosaic that was the legendary tomb of Qin Shi Huangdi (259–210 BC), the first emperor of China.

Thirty years have passed and excavation of what is known across the world as the Tomb of the First Emperor is still ongoing. Yuan Zhongyi, now an archaeologist of world fame, is director of the site museum. His name will remain a part of the history of the People's Republic of China, linked to the most important archaeological discovery of the twentieth century in Asia.

The term "tomb" does not do justice to the monument. In 2002, an approximate map was finally drawn up of the underground city built in the form of a dragon covering about a hundred square miles of the plain, bordered to the north by the Lishan Mountains and to the south by the Wei River. For now, visitors can only enter three pits containing the roughly 8,000 statues of the terracotta army that were put in place to guard the emperor for eternity. Each of the statues is solid to the height of the belt and hollow in the trunk and head; they each weigh about 480 pounds and stand between five feet eight inches and six feet six inches

tall. There are foot-soldiers, cuirassiers, archers, crossbowmen, horsemen, senior officers of the imperial guard, horses, and war chariots, each armed with wooden and metal weapons, and each exceptionally realistic down to the smallest detail. Though many of the mineral colors with which they were painted have faded away, the facial features and individual characteristics of each and every statue that was forged are evident, down to their scars, harelips, and cut ears.

Though they are more than two thousand years old, they seem to be alive, in the same way that the emperor wanted

303 bottom *In addition to the statues, the mound was found to contain architectural fragments, tools, and a metal collar. The collar indicates that prisoners were used to build the mausoleum and confirms accounts from the third century BC. These refer to a total of some 700,000 slaves who worked for 36 years.*

his city – a replica of his empire – to exist in the afterlife.

The mound in which Qin Shi Huangdi was buried was entirely lined with bronze and lay over a water-bearing stratum. It lies near a miniature copy of his palace, which in turn is included in a perimeter wall seven and a half miles long. In a series of buildings arranged around courtyards, archaeologists have found a sequence of rooms in which gold, precious stones, sophisticated objects, food, and exotic birds were stored. In addition, they contained the bodies of concubines, servants, monks, and

304

304-305 top This covered chariot was part of the grave goods found in Pit 2, the one containing the officers of the imperial guard. Besides the terracotta horses, the remains of about 400 real horses were found southwest of the mound, which were probably buried alive during the funeral of Qin Shi Huangdi.

304-305 bottom A team of four horses is harnessed to the calash of a high dignitary. They are shown with their muscles tensed, nostrils flaring, and mane flying. The craftsmen of ancient China reached the height of their skills when modeling horses.

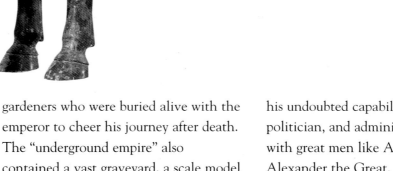

gardeners who were buried alive with the emperor to cheer his journey after death. The "underground empire" also contained a vast graveyard, a scale model of Chang'an (the ancient name of Xi'an, the capital of the Qin Empire), a planetarium in which the constellations were reproduced in pearls, and mechanically operated streams of mercury representing the most important rivers in China.

Completion of this immense project took 36 years and the labor of 700,000 slaves who, according to the legend, were walled up alive so that they could not reveal the secret of the treasures hidden underground. Qin Shi Huangdi himself ordered the construction in 246 BC. At the time, he was just 13 years old and had only just taken the throne of his clan, the Qin. Despite his tender years, he was already obsessed by the fear of death, and had he not been tormented by this nightmare – which turned into an illness leading him to surround himself with wizards, soothsayers, mystics, alchemists, and charlatans – he would be remembered for

his undoubted capabilities as a warrior, politician, and administrator, on a par with great men like Augustus and Alexander the Great.

It can be said that Qin Shi Huangdi was the man who brought China into being. In 221 BC, after freeing himself from the clutches of a difficult tutor, the greedy Lu Buwei, he conquered the lords of seven rival clans and found himself ruling a vast territory inhabited by many different sorts of people. To protect the empire, he began the construction of the extraordinary defensive system known as the Great Wall. He abolished feudalism, organized the territory using a complex bureaucratic system, encouraged the development of agriculture with the construction of large irrigation canals, and standardized weights, measures, and the distance between wheels on carts so that roads could be planned. He introduced a single currency based on round coins with a square hole at the center (a form that was to remain in use in China until the twentieth century) and created a single system of ideograms so that a standard written and spoken language existed in every corner of the empire.

306 left The statues display archaic traits and some errors of proportion (for instance, the arms are too short), but the realism of the details in the clothing, hairstyles, and, above all, the faces, which reveal the soldiers' regional origin, is quite astounding.

306 right The statues represent different types of both individuals and human. The individuality of the expression is accentuated by the multiplicity of the postures, like the one that characterizes the statue of the kneeling archer shown here (48 inches tall).

On the other hand, to build his fabulous tomb, which he did at the expense of the state, he needed a large and constant inflow of money, with the result that the people were subjected to increasingly heavy taxes. Moreover, Qin Shi Huangdi, who considered himself a god, wanted to cancel from the collective memory the teachings of Confucius, the sage that the emperor, in his megalomania, considered a rival. He therefore ordered the burning of all books of the Confucian school with the exception of those dealing with divination, medicine, pharmacology, agriculture, and gardening.

As he grew older, he became more and more of a

cruel despot, as his obsession with finding the magical formula of eternal life absorbed him completely. Affected by a physical as well as mental illness, he died in 210 BC as soon as he set foot on Chinese soil on his return from a journey to Japan where he had been told he would find the potion of immortality.

The funeral procession that crossed much of the empire was majestic. When his body reached the tomb, the first emperor was buried with at least 1,000 people, whom he had ordered to be sacrificed with him. The "underground empire" was then entirely covered with earth. Since then, the plain has been used to grow wheat.

307 left Traces of paint in certain points indicates the colors used, which in turn helps to identify the military rank of the soldiers. The kneeling archer, seen here from behind, wore a green uniform, while some red is still visible on the links between the plaques on his armor.

307 right Despite the abundance of detail, statues like this one of an armored foot-soldier cannot be considered portraits. It is known that they were stamped from one of eight possible molds, but the features of the faces were modeled by hand.

The Longmen Grottoes
CHINA

LUOYANG, PROVINCE OF HENAN
REGISTRATION: 2000
CRITERIA: C (I) (II) (III)

BEIJNG

LOMGMEN

Reading the number of grottoes at Longmen is like reading a list of Guinness world records. There are 2,345 of them; some just tiny niches, some large caves, which extend for almost a mile along the slopes of the mountains lining the Yi River. Together they contain more than 100,000 Buddhist images ranging in size from less than an inch to more than 55 feet, plus 43 pagodas and more than 3,600 stone tablets bearing inscriptions of priceless value relating to the history of ancient China.

Considered the richest collection of Chinese art from the period between the Northern Wei dynasty and the Tang dynasty, these images were sculpted over four centuries starting from AD 493 when the capital was moved from Datong to Luoyang. Lying on the Yi River, the city lies about seven miles from two mountains that face one another from either side of the river, creating a huge natural passage that the ancient Chinese called Yi Que, "the gate on the Yi River." When Luoyang became the capital, the name was changed to Longmen, "the gate of the dragon."

Among the thousands of Longmen grottoes, all of which have been dug out of the rock walls, the most impressive is probably the Feng Xian Si Temple, built between 672 and 675 during the Tang dynasty. When it was sculpted, it was closed over by a roof to protect from the elements the largest of the Longmen statues, a 56-foot-three-inch-high Buddha with two disciples and two *bodhisattvas* at its sides. According to tradition, the colossal statue demonstrates a perfect combination of moral integrity, elegance, and tranquility. In a more down-to-earth explanation, it is said that the features of the sculpture are those of the empress Wu Zetian, which is why it is also called by that name or the "Venus of the East."

No less interesting is the Gu Yang

308 *A view of the cliff, eroded by the Yi River, in which the 2,345 Longmen grottoes are located. They were created over a span of about 400 years starting in 493, at the time of the Northern Wei dynasty.*

308-309 *The king of the Heavens holds the Divine Pagoda in his hand and crushes a creature from the underworld. Next to him is Vajra, a demon with a ferocious appearance. These are two of the figures in the Feng Xian Si temple, decorated using iconography from the Tang era. The cave was built between 672 and 675.*

309 top left The most extraordinary statue at Longmen is the colossal figure of the Vairocana Buddha in the cave known as the Feng Xian Si temple. Here we see the face, which was modeled on the features of the empress Wu Zetian.

309 top right Wearing a precious diadem, this is one of the large statues that ring the Vairocana Buddha in the Feng Xian Si temple.

Grotto, dug out between 495 and 575 and the first to be excavated in the sides of these mountains. It contains the highest representations of the art of the Northern Wei: a Buddha meditating on an altar with two lions at his feet, as well as other sculptures, paintings, and 19 of the 20 Longmen scripts.

Wan Fo Grotto, built in 690, is distinguished by the number of representations of the Buddha it contains. Called the "Grotto of the 10,000 Buddhas," the actual number of statues sculpted out of its north and south walls is over 15,000, while on the back wall 54 lotus flowers have been carved, with a *bodhisattva* on each one. Lian Hua Grotto

310 top Thousands of images of the Buddha adorn the north wall of Wan Fo Grotto (the "Grotto of the Ten Thousand Buddhas"). In fact, there are at least 15,000, with the smallest less than an inch tall.

310-311 Commissioned in 690 by emperor Gaozong and his consort Wu Zetian to invoke the goodwill of the Buddha on their children, the Wan Fo Grotto centers on the statue of the Buddha seated on a lotus flower.

311 top left Protection and charity are the qualities expressed by the hand gestures of this Buddha, represented respectively by the open palm and the back of the hand facing downwards. Two bodhisattvas flank the Enlightened One.

311 top right Aside from the site's exceptional artistic value, the sculptures in the Longmen Grottoes have provided scholars with valuable information on civil architecture, the economy, and dress in China during the Northern Wei, Tang, Sui, and Song dynasties.

(Lotus Flower Grotto) has a single lotus flower on the ceiling, carved during the Northern Wei dynasty around 527.

Also of exceptional quality is the Ping Yang Grotto, a complex of three caves that required 25 years to dig out and, it is said, 800 people. Built between 500 and 523 by the emperor Yuan Lo in memory of the emperor Xiao Wen Di and his wife, the central cave measures 40 feet by 36 and is 30 feet high. Inside there are nine statues of the Buddha, the largest of which reaches 27 feet in height. On the ceiling, once again, there is a large lotus flower with ten servants. Unfortunately, the marvelous adoration scenes that decorated the walls were taken away in 1935 and are now displayed in an American museum.

Although they are generally in good condition, the Longmen Grottoes have suffered damage from natural causes like erosion as well as from vandalism, and the recent economic growth in the urban area of Luoyang has added the threat presented by acid rain and automobile fumes. However, the renewed awareness of the Chinese towards their artistic heritage has resulted in suggesting that the central and local governments consider taking radical measures such as moving all tourist facilities away from the area, transferring the nearby village of Longmen to another site, and rebuilding the access road to minimize vibrations and dust generated by motorized vehicles.

311 bottom The dimensions of the statues carved in the Longmen Grottoes vary substantially. The average, as in this case, is little larger than life size, but the tiniest are just an inch or so high and the largest over 50 feet tall.

The Buddhist Monuments at Sanchi

INDIA

State of Madhya Pradesh
Registration: 1989
Criteria: C (I) (II) (III) (IV) (VI)

312 top Sacred animals in the Buddhist cosmogony, these elegantly carved elephants protected by parasols are at the top of the west torana of the Great Stupa.

At first sight, it seems like just a small hill rising 300 or so feet out of the immense Indian plain, yet the place has an ascetic solemnity that makes one forget its modest size. Sanchi is the site of the subcontinent's most ancient religious monuments that uninterruptedly reflect the spiritual and iconographic progress of Buddhism from the third century BC to the thirteenth century AD, when the religion in India returned to Hinduism.

There is no evidence that Prince Siddhartha stopped at Sanchi on his path to nirvana. Credit for the sanctuary goes to Ashoka, the king of the Mauryan dynasty whose empire spread across most of the subcontinent from 273 to 236 BC. Converted to Buddhism with his wife, born at Vidisha near Sanchi, he ordered the construction of various stupas (hemispherical monuments made from bricks and mortar to symbolize the sacred mountain joining Earth to Heaven) to hold relics of the Buddha, such as his hair, teeth, and shoulder bones.

The most majestic of Sanchi's stupas is 121 feet in diameter, stands 56 feet high, and is crowned by a *chattra* (umbrella) symbolizing the Three Jewels of Buddhism: the Buddha himself, the Dharma (doctrine), and the Sangha (community of monks). It stands on a platform around which pilgrims continue to practice the rite of perambulation. The stone railing around the stupa is pierced by four *torana* (gateways) carved with exquisite bas-reliefs of the life of the Buddha, his previous incarnations, and chronicles of

the deeds of Ashoka in his spreading of Buddhism throughout his empire. Two of the most interesting reliefs feature the Buddha impassive to the temptations offered him by the evil demon Mara, and of the legend of Prince Makakapi Jataka, who saved 80,000 monkeys by extending himself like a bridge across the Ganges so that they could escape the enemies pursuing them.

Statues of the Buddha meditating welcome the faithful to the platform. These were added in the first century BC during Gupta rule when taboos prohibiting the human image of the

312 bottom left Detail from the second and third architrave on the northern torana of the Great Stupa. At the top there are sculptures of a lion and wood nymph.

312 bottom right This bas-relief of the Wheel of Law supported by bodhisattva is also from the north torana. The reliefs narrate episodes from the Vessantara Jataka, which tells the story of one of the incarnations of the Buddha before he achieved Enlightenment.

312-313 The northern torana is the most elaborate and best preserved of the four entrances to the Great Stupa (also called Stupa 1). They were added to complete the monument in the first century BC during the Satvahana dynasty.

313 top As it appears today, the Great Stupa dates back to the second century BC, but it incorporates an older section attributed to Ashoka, the emperor of the Mauryan dynasty that spread Buddhism throughout the subcontinent.

313 bottom Carved in sandstone and corresponding to the west torana, this effigy of the Buddha meditating is, like the other three in the Great Stupa, an addition made to the monument in AD 450 by the Gupta dynasty.

314 top The gana, the paunchy dwarves that are traditionally associated with Shiva in Hindu tradition, support the architrave of Stupa 3's only torana.

314 center left In 1851, two valuable relics were found in Stupa 3: they were fragments of bone set with pearls, crystals, amethysts, and lapis lazuli, and belonged to two of the Buddha's foremost disciples. Today these objects are in the British Museum.

314 center right With a single torana, Stupa 2 stands on a medhi (platform) and is enclosed by a balustrade decorated with bas-relief medallions. It was probably built in the second century BC.

314 bottom left Temple 17 is a splendid example of Gupta architecture and the precursor of the classical Hindu style that was later developed at Khajuraho and in Orissa. The temple has a flat roof supported by four columns decorated with lions.

divine became less stringent, whereas in the bas-reliefs of Ashoka, the Buddha is shown as a bo tree (under which he achieved enlightenment), as a wheel of the Law (which represents his sermons), as a horse (to symbolize his abandonment of earthly riches), and as a line (an emblem of his path towards nirvana).

Next to the south-facing *torana*, Ashoka placed a stone obelisk on which a sort of guide to the places of pilgrimage was carved in Pali, the most ancient language in India. Dozens of other stupas were built around the Great Stupa, all smaller and in various states of conservation, as are the remains of the temples and monasteries that belong to various stages of the Buddhist faith in Indian history. Temple 18, from the seventh century, is surprising for its unmistakablly Greek appearance, proof of the cultural legacy left by Alexander the Great during his expedition to India.

The merging of the asceticism of Buddhism with the more melodramatic and theatrical set of Hindu cults is demonstrated by monasteries 45 and 47 on the south side of the hill. Here the elaborate high reliefs portraying the Buddha surrounded by the divinities of the Ganges and Yamuna rivers, sensual dancers, and even erotic scenes inaugurated a new spiritual and artistic era that was to reach its apogee in the temples of Khajuraho.

314 bottom right Vihara 45 is Sanchi's most majestic and best-conserved monastery. Note the temple at the center; this was built between the ninth and tenth centuries when Buddhism was slowly being supplanted in India by Hinduism.

315 top The elephant is one of the animals depicted in the medallions carved on the balustrade of Stupa 2. Pilgrims practiced the deambulatory ritual called pradakshinapatha around it in a counter-clockwise direction.

315 bottom Crowned by a richly decorated halo of floral motifs, this statue of the Buddha meditating is found in Vihara 45. The monastic complex also has statues of the Hindu river gods Ganga and Yamuna.

The Caves at Ajanta

INDIA

State of Maharashtra
Registration: 1983
Criteria: C (i) (ii) (iii) (vi)

NEW DELHI

AJANTA

316-317 The monumental chaitya (a Buddhist sanctuary with naves) in Cave 26 has some of Ajanta's most refined architectural and decorative features. At the back of the room there is a stupa with an effigy of the seated Buddha that, curiously, faces west.

316 bottom The richly decorated exterior of Cave 26. This is part of a group of five caves, some of which were never completed, dug in the seventh century at the southwest end of Ajanta's horseshoe-shaped cliff.

I n the *Padmapani*, the Buddha is shown gracefully holding a blue lotus flower between the thumb and forefinger of his left hand. A heavy crown weighs down his head and his large almond-colored eyes are half-closed in an expression suggesting sublime peace. Around him, there is a festive group of musicians, lovers, monkeys, and peacocks. In the *Simhala*, though, the scene features cruel overtones, with a *bodhisattva* who saves a group of shipwrecked people from the cannibalism of a tribe of voluptuous and bloodthirsty she-devils.

These and many others are splendid illustrations of the *Jataka*, the sacred text recounting episodes from the life of the Buddha in the many incarnations he experienced on his path to enlightenment. Painted in the 30 caves at Ajanta, they are a series of works of extraordinary artistic and religious qualities. Moreover, they provide a vivid picture of the behavior and customs in India during the era of the Gupta dynasty.

Set in an attractive horse-shoe-shaped hill on a bend of the river Waghora in the Deccan Plain, the caves were home to a large community of monks from the second to sixth centuries, and provided shelter to travelers during the monsoon season. Some of the caves were temples (*chaitya*) and others monasteries (*vihara*). In the earliest of the caves, the iconography follows the dictates of the Hinayana school, in which the Buddha could only be represented through symbols, while in later caves the more libertarian Mahayana school is evident, in which each of the

Buddha's lives is described in figurative detail.

The scenes are very beautiful and feature large numbers of figures, and are at times cruel, serene, and sensual, and even have erotic undertones. They feature women, men, demons, creatures with human faces and birds' bodies (*yaksha*), musicians (*gandharva*), and heavenly dancers (*apsara*) in settings with flowers, trees, fruits, and animals. Many of the caves have architectural features and sculptures that merge perfectly with the paintings to create interiors of great beauty. Also remarkable is the iconographic

317 top right A colossal Parinirvana statue in Cave 26 represents the Buddha lying on one side at the moment he passes from terrestrial life to nirvana. As it filters through the cave entrance, the light increases the transcendent effect of the effigy.

317 center This is the façade of Cave 19; it was carved in the second half of the fifth century at a time when the Mahayana school of Buddhism had reached its zenith.

317 bottom The chaitya in Cave 19 is the most spectacular in Ajanta. The columns are decorated with delicate images of bodhisattva and Buddha.

317 top left Detail of a high-relief in Cave 26. To the right of the Buddha, who sits in the lotus position, stands the bodhisattva Vajrapani. He holds a scepter (vajra) from which the Varayana school of Buddhism took its name.

*318 top Carved in the sixth
century, Cave 2 is a
monastery (vihara). Note
the columns and ceiling,
which are adorned with
lotus flower medallions and
a patterned barrel-vault.
These were probably
vestiges of the Hellenistic
art brought to India by
Alexander the Great.*

*318-319 Detail of the
fresco in the portico of
Cave 17 where episodes of
the Buddha's previous
incarnations are narrated.
On the right, two
individuals of royal birth
embrace lovingly and share
a last cup of wine before
giving all their goods to the
poor.*

syncretism of the paintings, given that they were done largely by Hindu artists, particularly in the fourth and fifth centuries when Ajanta had a stable population of 200 monks.

The pictorial technique used was tempera *a secco*, in which the cave walls and ceilings were covered with a mixture of clay, cow dung, and vegetable fiber about three inches thick, and then with a thin coat of mud. Before the mud dried, the artist traced out the picture with a cinnabar stick. He then colored it in using natural pigments and lastly fixed it all with a layer of gluten.

Around 650, the caves at Ajanta were abandoned due to the decline in popularity of Buddhism relative to Hinduism and to the growing importance of the religious community at nearby Ellora. For centuries, the site remained forgotten, half-hidden by the vegetation. It was rediscovered by chance in 1819 by a group of British officers who had been led there by the traces of a tiger they were hunting. In contrast to this fortunate event, the

319 top On the left side of the Buddha's shrine in one of the niches in Cave 2, there are two magnificent statues of yaksha, Buddhist guardian deities.

319 bottom Portrayed in the portico of Cave 17, these two figures wear clothes cut in Central-asian style. The inclusion of "foreign" elements in frescoes is evidence of the frequency of commercial and cultural exchanges between peoples on the continent.

people who studied the masterpieces were struck by misfortune: in 1866, the English artist Robert Gill, who spent 26 years at Ajanta copying the paintings onto paper, saw his work go up in flames in a fire at Crystal Palace in London. Ten years later, another blaze in the Victoria and Albert Museum reduced the efforts of his assistant to ashes. In addition, the first, unrefined attempts at restoration in 1920, sponsored by the ruler of Ajanta, the *nizam* of Hyderabad, produced more harm than good.

Today the spell seems to have ended, and conservation work by the Archaeological Survey of India is producing excellent results.

Sigiriya

SRI LANKA

DISTRICT OF SIGIRIYA
REGISTRATION: 1982
CRITERIA: C (II) (III) (IV)

Their skin is amber-colored and their full breasts are barely covered by the thin fabric of their garments. They smile in a complicit manner and shoot glances filled with longing as they offer lotus flowers to the observer. Some of them dance, swaying their heads ringed by diadems and arms bound with bracelets.

Perhaps divine creatures – *apsara*, the celestial dancers of Buddhist and Hindu tradition – or perhaps handmaidens at court, the enchanting girls painted on the west wall of Sigiriya rock are an ode to love, and their astounding realism is a derivation of the long established artistic practice of the mimetic imitation of nature.

According to the *Sihigiri Vihara*, the ancient Singhalese book that contains a sort of "tourist guide" to Sigiriya, an artist (unfortunately anonymous) painted a magnificent procession of 500 girls on the rock. They were so beautiful that whoever looked upon them fell in love forever.

During the reign of King Kasyapa I, terracotta statuettes of the girls were made and donated to visitors as souvenirs. Today, more than 1,500 years later, only 22 girls remain from the procession, but they have not ceased to arouse admiration.

Sigiriya Fort, a magnificent princely city built on top of a sandstone monolith towering 660 feet above the dense tropical forest in the heart of Sri Lanka, looks like heaven on earth. However, the seat of the Singhalese kingdom between 477 and 495 was built as the result of a hideous crime: patricide. As recounted in the earliest text regarding Singhalese history, the *Mahavamsa*, Kasyapa I built it after killing his father, Dhatusena I, by hanging him upside down in a tomb while still alive, and then usurping the throne from his half-brother Mogallana.

320 left An aerial view of the fort 660 feet above the tropical plain. The palace on the top was the residence of the Singhalese king Kasyapa I from 477 to 495.

321 center The softness of the forms, the refinement of their gestures and expressions, and the profusion of detail in their clothing and jewelry make the girls of Sigiriya a masterpiece of Oriental art.

321 bottom According to the tradition, whoever looked upon the Sigiriya (originally 500) would fall madly in love with them.

garden, Kasyapa had an audience room built with a 16-foot-long throne, various cisterns to collect rainwater, and a small theater where the first performances of music and poetry in the history of the island of Ceylon were held.

Around 1,500 graffiti with short verses and romantic poetry covered the Kat Bitha (Mirror Wall), a stuccoed wall rendered as shiny as a mirror that led to the entrance to Kasyapa I's palace. Here, a monumental gate was built in the shape of a lion using brick and wood lined with stucco, of which all that remain are the two paws and claws carved out of the rock. Entering through the lion's mouth, the visitor was obliged to climb an almost vertical flight of steps up the face of the rock where the procession of girls was painted. Today, only the foundations can still be seen, as the ancient stairway has been replaced by a safer metal one, but the view is still worth the climb.

Kasyapa I lived in the palace at Sigiriya for almost 18 years, the time necessary for Mogallana to organize a powerful army and march on the fort. To avoid being taken prisoner by his half-brother, Kasyapa killed himself, his end marking the end for Sigiriya as well. The capital returned to Anuradhapura, whereas, until the end of the fourteenth century, an ascetic community of monks occupied what had once been a place of earthly pleasures.

Kasyapa then fled from Anuradhapura, the capital of the kingdom at the time, to Sigiriya. He had an orderly arrangement of gardens, low walls, and small dikes filled with water built at the base of the rock, which were in turn adorned with pools, fountains (some of which still work during the rainy season), and pavilions for his troops, court dignitaries, and a host of concubines. A little way up the rock, he had a rock garden made, the apparently wild appearance of which was, and still is, in perfect contrast to the symmetry of the gardens below. In a cave in the wild

Ayutthaya

THAILAND

The enemy was attacking from the north, hidden in the hills behind Sukhothai. There were many of them and they were well armed. To the king, U Thon, any attempt at resistance seemed pointless, so one day in the year 1350, he took the painful decision to abandon the capital of Siam, which had been founded little more than a century earlier. He called on his military planners and ascetics for advice on where to build a new city. The first counseled him to head south into the plain, where future enemies could not arrive without being seen a long distance off. The second consulted the sacred texts and suggested looking for the *nam*, the water at the root of the Thai people's symbolism, where it flowed in a spiral.

With these instructions, the king sent his emissaries to reconnoiter. They returned having found an ancient Khmer settlement at the center of a complex river system created by the confluence of the Mae Nam Lopburi, the Pasak, and the Chao Phraya. U Thon went to the chosen site and removed the first spadeful of earth, revealing, as he did so, a snail – the spiral predicted by the ascetics. This was the origin of Ayutthaya, whose name means "the Invincible." It is derived from a Sanskrit word referring to Ayodhya, the abode of the god Rama in the Indian epic poem *Ramayana*.

Although the new capital – which it was to last until 1767 when it was destroyed by the Burmese army – never

322 top left Wat Ratchaburana was destroyed in a fire in 1967, but restorations have ensured that its towers can still be admired. The crypt in the central tower, recently opened to the public, still has fragments of frescoes.

322 top right Adorned with a yellow silk drape, this effigy of the Buddha stands at the foot of the prang, the Khmer-style brick tower now in ruins that stands in the middle of the splendid Wat Phra Mahathat.

322 bottom left A series of Buddhas in the meditation pose, now headless, line the brick walls of Wat Phra Mahathat, built in 1374.

322 bottom right Roots of a Ficus religiosa wind around the face of the Buddha from a statue destroyed centuries ago.

323 Wat Ratchaburana was built in the fifteenth century by Borom Rachathirat II, the seventh king of Ayutthaya, to commemorate his two elder brothers. They were both killed during a duel on elephant-back to win the succession to the throne following the death of their father, Intharacha I, in 1424.

324 Two chedi, reliquaries similar to stupas in the Buddhist world, flank the prang (central tower) in Wat Ratchaburana. Inside the chedi, like in the crypt of the prang, various objects of great value have been found that now make up the nucleus of the collection in the Chao Sam Phraya National Museum in Ayutthaya.

325 top left The architecture of the mondop, a large rectangular building in front of Wat Ratchaburana's central tower, was strongly influenced by Burma. The mondop was a pavilion that provided access to the temple.

325 top right Elegant and well-proportioned, the prang of the Wat Phra Ram rests on a stepped platform marked by chedi. Founded in 1369, the temple owes its current appearance to a fifteenth-century restoration and still has fragments of stucco decorations.

equaled the beauty of Sukhothai in the eyes of its rulers, European and Chinese visitors who were admitted to the court of Ayutthaya left behind enthusiastic accounts of its fabulous treasures. The "Ayutthaya period," during which the city boasted as many as one million inhabitants, coincided with the greatest splendor of the kingdom of Siam, which slowly extended its territory into what are now Laos, Cambodia, and Myanmar.

During the monsoon season, Ayutthaya seemed to float on water. The houses and palace were built on stilts and were all made from wood, as stone was only allowed to be used for religious buildings. The temples were constructed on earthworks that symbolized the vessel of redemption of which Buddhist mythology spoke. Consequently, only the temples remain of that marvelous city. The largest, Wat Phra Si Sanpet, was used by members of the royal family and contained a statue of the Buddha 50 feet tall covered with 550 pounds of gold leaf, but the Burmese invaders melted it down. The temple complex centers on a lotus-filled rectangular pool and is dominated by three

large *chedi* (bell-shaped reliquary monuments). At a slight distance stands the Wat Phra Mahathat with a tower in Khmer style (called a *prang*) supported by statues of the sacred bird Garuda. The tower is ringed with brick and stucco statues of the Buddha, around some of which tree branches have grown. Opposite, there are the ruins of Wat Ratburana with some *chedi* still bearing fragments of frescoes.

The ruins of statues, *chedi*, and monastery foundations dot the valley, half-buried by the vegetation. Fortunately, this natural covering helped to prevent theft by treasure hunters over the centuries. Thanks to the recognition of UNESCO, Thai authorities have launched a program of restoration work and have provided the site with a small army of security staff. Today Ayutthaya exists once more as a religious symbol, monks have returned to the site, and the statues of the Buddha are draped with orange silk.

325 bottom left Once full of treasures, the majestic Wat Phra Si Sanpet (built in 1491) is part of the palace complex of the rulers of Ayutthaya. It was used as a prayer hall by the members of the royal family.

325 bottom right This effigy of the Buddha covered in gold-leaf is in the collection of Ayutthaya Museum. The site's most famous statue is held in Viharn Phra Mongkol Bopit, next to Wat Phra Si Sanpet, and is an object of profound devotion by the Thai people.

Angkor
CAMBODIA

PROVINCE OF SIEM REAP
REGISTRATION: 1992
INSCRIPTION ON THE WORLD HERITAGE IN DANGER LIST: 1992
CRITERIA: C (I) (III) (IV)

326

Zhou Ta-Quan arrived in Angkor in August 1296 as the legate of the Chinese emperor and remained for a year, noting down every secret of the Khmer Empire in his diary. "At the center of the kingdom stands a golden tower…," he wrote. "On the east side, there is a golden bridge guarded by two gold lions…[It is] an amazing sight…." The sovereign, who was treated like a demigod, lived surrounded by servants, wives, and concubines. The kingdom was governed by intricate ranks of ministers, generals, and priests under his command. The Khmer Empire had already begun its path of decline, but the account of Zhou

Ta-Quan – the only one to have survived of the civilization that dominated Southeast Asia from the ninth to fourteenth centuries – describes a world still flourishing, whose artistic sophistication had no equal in the Middle Ages.

The European discovery of Angkor is attributed to Henry Mouhot, who visited Indochina in the 1860s. "One of these temples" he claimed, in reference to Angkor Wat, "is more magnificent than any building left by the Greeks or Romans." Actually, Mouhot's *Voyage à Siam et dans le Cambodge* was published about ten years after the account written by the missionary Charles-Emile Bouillevaux, but that had gone unrecognized. Moreover, much earlier, Portuguese travelers had reached Angkor in the sixteenth century and described it as a city surrounded by walls. Even at the time of Mouhot's "discovery," Angkor Wat still accommodated a thousand or so monks.

Works of Khmer art were exhibited at the universal exhibition in Paris in 1878 with the result that Angkor soon became the destination of several French archaeological expeditions. These resulted in 1901 in the foundation of the Ecole Française d'Extrème Orient, the primary aim of which was to study the monuments of the Khmer Empire. Soon the first wealthy European tourists began to arrive, and the stones of Angkor became the highly sought-after prey of unscrupulous collectors. Among these treasure hunters was a young, enterprising French writer, André Malraux.

In 1924, Malraux sailed for the Far East in search of adventure. Given that he

326 top The central tower at Angkor Wat represents the most important of the five peaks on Mount Meru, the Hindu mountain of perfection, surrounded by continents and seas. At one time a gold statue of Vishnu, the god with whom the king identified, was held in the prang.

326 center Stretching more than 3,000 by 2,600 feet, the large perimeter wall at Angkor Wat has a gate on each side, but the main entrance, embellished by a portico 771 feet long and decorated with sculptures and carvings, stands on the west side.

326 bottom The third level of Angkor Wat has four courtyards surrounded by porticoes. Construction of the temple required laterite and sandstone from a quarry several miles away that was transported by raft down the Siem Reap river.

326-327 The temple is entered through the external wall down an avenue about 1,600 feet long flanked by balustrades in the form of naga, the sacred serpent of Indian mythology. Angkor Wat was built as the funerary temple of Suryavarman II, who ruled from 1112 to 1152.

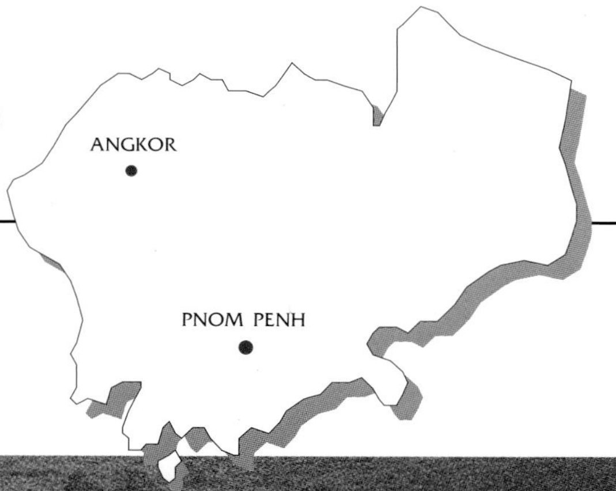

ANGKOR

PNOM PENH

328 top Apart from the remarkable bas-reliefs on the perimeter walls, Angkor Wat boasts abundant statues and carvings of rare harmonious proportions, like these two dancers. Note the detail in their hairstyles, closely-fitting clothes, and the jewelry on their arms and necks.

328 bottom and 328-329 Three details from the battle of Kurukshetra on the south section of the east gallery at Angkor Wat. The battle is described in the Hindu epic, the Mahabharata. The armies of the Kaurava and Pandava arrive respectively from north and south and meet furiously in the middle of the panel; the combatants strike, twist, and cling to one another with exceptional plasticity in a scene of great beauty.

was rather short of money, when he arrived in Angkor he stole several sculptural blocks from the Banteay Srei (Temple of the Women) in order to sell them back in Paris. However, all did not go as planned: he was arrested under the accusation of smuggling antiquities and was only saved by the diplomatic activity of his wife, who rushed back to France in search of influential friends. Based on this experience, Malraux wrote his autobiographical novel *La Voie royale* (*The Royal Way*, 1930), which became his first literary success.

Historically, the Khmer's settlement of the area began in 802 when King

on a small island in the middle of a large reservoir.

Although its architecture is Angkor's most interesting feature, the Khmer capital's vast and complex hydraulic system merits a description. At the heart of the 147-square-mile site, two large reservoirs, the *baray*, lie on either side of the Angkor Thom citadel walls. Measuring five miles long by a mile and a half wide, the *baray* were fed by floodwater from the nearby Tonle Sap Lake, and it is believed that their waters were used to irrigate the fertile alluvial plain on which the city stood.

The center of attraction in Angkor is

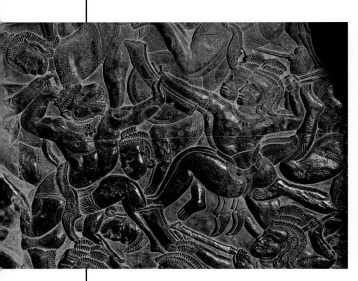

Jayavarman II established his capital on Phnom Kulen, a hill 18 miles northeast of Angkor. Towards the end of the ninth century, the Khmer started construction of the large, permanent temples in the Roluos group: the Preah Ko, with six brick towers decorated with sculpted sandstone and stucco reliefs, the Bakong dedicated to Shiva, consisting of a pyramid flanked by eight towers and secondary sanctuaries, and the Lolei, built

Angkor Wat, the magnificent temple built by King Suryavarman II, who ruled from 1112 to 1152. Surrounded by a dike in the shape of a giant rectangle measuring 207 yards across, 1600 yards long, and 1400 yards wide, Angkor Wat is an immense temple-mountain three stories high made from sandstone and laterite (the two types of stone used by the Khmer). At the corners of the second and third floors as well as at the center of

the latter, towers were built topped by pointed domes. The wat is a classical Hindu temple, as demonstrated by the almost 900 yards of wonderful bas-reliefs decorating the perimeter of the central temple. Wandering through the corridors, a depiction gradually unravels of the battle of Kurukshetra between the armies of the Kaurava and Pandava kingdoms, taken from the Hindu epic poem the *Mahabharata* and scenes from the *Ramayana*. One wall commemorates the

329 bottom Angkor Wat also has scenes of daily life, in particular on the corners of the portico. On the other hand, the large panels in the galleries are dedicated to war scenes, like the one between the army of Suryavarman II and the Cham, or represent mythological scenes from the Hindu tradition.

deeds of Suryavarman II, portrayed on an elephant majestically cutting through the ranks of his army, and another illustrates a metaphor of the Hindu hell and paradise. Finally, there is a rendering of the "churning of the great sea of milk," in which 88 devils (the *asura*) and 92 gods (the *deva*) turn the sea to butter in order to extract the elixir of immortality.

The triumph of Khmer architecture was achieved under Jayavarman VII, who reigned from 1181 to 1201. He was responsible for the construction of Angkor Thom (the citadel) and its 26-foot-high, seven-and-a-half-mile-long defensive wall. Within the walls there are many extraordinary buildings, such as the Bayon temple, in which Buddhism takes the place of Hinduism, with the spoils of the *bodhisattva* Alokitesvara featured above the 144 gigantic stone faces of the sovereign that gaze out in all directions. The walls of the Bayon are carved with fine bas-reliefs narrating the daily life at Angkor and the war conducted by Jayavarman against the Cham, the Khmer's traditional enemy.

The citadel contains many splendid temples, like the Baphuon, the Preah Palilay, the Tep Pranam, and above all, the Terrace of the Leprous King, a 23-foot-high platform decorated with five orders of superb sculptures that probably housed the crematorium of the Khmer sovereigns. Another outstanding construction is the Terrace of the Elephants, named after the pachyderm decorations on the walls, a long gallery that was used for reviewing the army.

Other temples worth mentioning out of the more than 100 in Angkor are the

330 bottom
Three-headed pachyderms on the Elephant Terrace stretch their trunks to the ground thus functioning as of a columns.

330-331 Built between 1181 and 1218 by Jayavarman VII, who was also responsible for many of Angkor's most memorable monuments, the Bayon was the first temple to mark the passage from Hinduism to Buddhism, and was, at the same time, one of the last mountain-temples at Angkor.

331 top Like Angkor Wat, the Bayon is decorated with superb bas-reliefs along all of its nearly 4,000 feet of perimeter walls, featuring more than 11,000 figures. Here we see the Cham army on the march.

331 bottom Until the 1920s, archaeologists studying Angkor believed that the Bayon was still a Hindu temple dedicated to Shiva. In 1928, Philippe Stern, curator at the Musée Guimet in Paris, and the epigraphist Georges Coedes revealed its Buddhist nature.

Ta Prohm, the walls of which are being crushed by the roots of enormous ceiba trees, the Preah Neak Pean, an unusual small temple on an islet in the middle of a large pool, and the Banteay Srei, the Temple of the Women that is considered the jewel of classical Khmer art for the delicacy of its sculptures and the sophistication of its engravings. Perhaps this was why it attracted the attention of an aesthete like Malraux.

Nevertheless, the times have not changed very much since the 1920s. In 1992, when Angkor was registered as a World Heritage site, UNESCO considered the Khmer capital to be one of the sites in danger. The United Nations had just intervened in the country after the war between Cambodia and Vietnam, and armed bandits were still active in the area despite much of it having been laid with mines by the Khmer Rouge under Pol Pot.

Today, with the political situation stablized, art thieves are the main worry. Impossible to guard because of its vast size, the site is exposed to frequent thefts of priceless sculptures and fragments. The impoverished condition in which the Cambodian people live does not help to protect the art treasures. Although more than 7,000 statues have been stored away from the public and substituted with modern copies, every year examples of the art of the greatest civilization of Southeast Asia head for the West.

332 left Situated 12 or so miles northeast of Angkor Thom (the "pink temple" or "temple of the women") is Banteay Srei, a jewel of Khmer traditional art.

332-333 Banteay Srei is probably the Khmer temple in the best state of preservation despite being more than 1,000 years old. In this bas-relief of incomparable beauty, we see Indra, god of the sky and dispenser of the rain, on his three-headed elephant Erawan.

333 top Built at the end of the tenth century and dedicated to Shiva, Banteay Srei features a square layout with entrances on the east and west sides. Until a few years ago, it was practically impossible to enter, as the area had been heavily mined during the war between the Khmer Rouge and the Vietnamese army.

333 center Unlike the rest of the complex, the three central sanctuary-towers, adorned with male and female gods and carvings of great artistic value, probably date back to the end of the thirteenth century.

333 bottom It was in the library of the Musée Guimet in Paris that the twenty-year-old André Malraux read Henri Parmentier's description of the devata – the gods sculpted at the corners of the Banteay Srei, which inspired him to set out on his calamitous journey to Cambodia.

334 top Seen from above it is clear that Borobudur was designed to imitate a mandala, the "sacred design" that Buddhists, Hindus, and Jainists consider a map of the Tantric course towards purification.

334-335 This spectacular view reveals the grandeur of the temple built in the eighth century by Samargunta, a ruler of the Sailendra dynasty that governed Java from the sixth to tenth centuries.

JAKARTA

BOROBUDUR

The Temple of Borobudur

INDONESIA

PROVINCE OF YOGJAKARTA, JAVA
REGISTRATION: 1991
CRITERIA: C (I) (II) (IV)

The name of Sir Thomas Stamford Raffles, the versatile and charismatic English colonial administrator, has always been linked to the natural world and history of Southeast Asia. In his honor, the largest flower in the world was named *Rafflesia*, which he discovered while exploring the forests of Malaysia. He was also responsible for the discovery of one of the most interesting and mysterious Buddhist monuments in the world.

The people of Java had always told fabulous tales about the temple of Borobudur – the name of which is an abbreviation of *Bhumisan Brabadura* (the Ineffable Mountain of Accumulated Virtues) – but when in 1814 Sir Thomas arrived in the valley that he had been told was the site of the fantastic monument, he found nothing but rocks scattered around the forest, half-buried by layers of volcanic ash. It took six weeks and the work of 200 men to clear away the debris and vegetation but, in the end, they found blocks of black granite, many of which were decorated with sophisticated bas-reliefs and sculptures. These were then numbered and catalogued, which left only for them to be reassembled in the correct order. The work begun by Raffles was completed successfully more than 150 years later thanks to UNESCO.

Today the temple of Borobudur stands majestically in the valley in all its ancient splendor. It is known that it was commissioned in the eighth century by Samargunta, the king of the Sailendra dynasty that governed the island of Java

from the sixth to tenth centuries. The Sailendra were a branch of the Indian Chandella dynasty (famous for having built the temples at Khajuraho) that had left the subcontinent after having converted to the Buddhist faith. It is therefore known that the construction techniques and iconography used were "Indian." What remains uncertain is the reason the temple was built, and what the meanings of the mass of symbols and esoteric messages inside the building were.

Borobudur is a sort of pyramid in the shape of the lotus, the flower that was sacred to the Buddha. It has six stepped, four-sided stories on which a further three circular levels stand, and these are crowned by a central stupa. The platform on which the monument stands is decorated with 160 bas-relief panels featuring scenes of the human world, which is governed by desires; the five successive stories bear 1,300 panels recounting the lives of the Buddha and 43 *bodhisattva*, with episodes narrated in the sacred text of the *Jataka*. The circular terraces above have no reliefs but are adorned with small stupas with square or diamond-shaped openings in which the statues of 92 Vajrasattva or Dhyani Buddhas are set. Each of these statues has its hands in a gesture (*mudra*) that indicates one of the five directions: the east, represented by the *mudra* that calls Earth to witness the Buddha's enlightenment; the south, denoted by the gesture of blessing; the west, with the *mudra* signifying meditation; the north, in which the hands indicate liberation

335 top and bottom Numerous statues of the Buddha stand on Borobudur's upper terrace (top); the last series of bas-reliefs (below) before reaching the terrace tells the story of the final phases of the Buddha's path to Enlightenment.

from all fear; and lastly, the center, in which the *mudra* represents the teaching of truth. The stupa that sits imposingly above symbolizes the Buddha, Enlightenment, and Infinity.

When looking at the overall layout of the Borobudur, it is clear that it was built as a *mandala*, or "sacred pattern," considered by the Buddhist, Hindu, and Jainist religions (three of the major faiths in India) a map of the Tantric path to purification. In consequence, beyond the magnificence of the monument and the refinement of its reliefs and sculptures, the temple is first and foremost a philosophical work, through which the rulers of the Sailendra dynasty wished to assert themselves, recognizing that it is only through rightful actions that man can aspire to eternal life.

336 bottom The detail refers to an episode in the Jataka, the sacred text that recounts the lives of the Buddha before he reached Enlightenment. The clockwise course followed by pilgrims towards the top of the Borobudur covers just over three miles. As the pilgrims study the bas-reliefs, they gradually obtain purification.

337 top Drummers follow a wedding procession in this detail of a relief from the middle terraces at Borobudur. It shows the world of humans still governed by the senses and the struggle between Good and Evil.

337 bottom Like the other bas-reliefs on the monument (which cover a total of 88,600 square feet), this panel of a group of musicians was originally painted in bright colors.

336 top The face of the Buddha in Borobudur is always portrayed with the characteristic traits that distinguish him from ordinary men: the bun on his head (ushinisha), half-closed eyes, a slight smile, long ears, and curls that spiral clockwise.

336-337 Extraordinary reliefs like the one shown, with graceful female figures among vegetation, have provided basic information on the architecture, daily life, art of war, moral values, clothing, dance, and commerce in Java in the eighth century.

Mesa Verde
UNITED STATES

COLORADO
REGISTRATION: 1978
CRITERIA: C (III)

Professor J. S. Newberry was the first to talk about the Mesa Verde. It was 1859 and the geologist was drafting his report on an expedition carried out for the United States. He described a vast plateau that reached an altitude of 8,500 feet in southeast Colorado. He was referring to the Mesa Verde, or "Green Table" in Spanish.

It took 15 years before a photographer from the U.S. Geological Survey, W. H. Jackson, discovered the first rock shelter hidden by the walls of the natural wonder. That particular zone of Colorado seemed to be of interest to the mining industry and a few prospecting engineers accompanied Jackson into Mancos Canyon, where he showed them what had unquestionably been a cliff dwelling, which, since then, has been called the Two-Story Cliff House. From this moment on, the area started to arouse much curiosity. A year later, another explorer sent by the government discovered the Sixteen Windows House, and shortly thereafter, the Balcony House.

On December 18th, 1888, while searching for cattle that had got separated from the herd, Richard Wetherill and his brother-in-law Charles Mason reached what today is called Sun Point, where they found a number of shelters, one of which was the Cliff Palace. A masterpiece of pre-Columbian architecture, Cliff Palace is built from rudimentary sandstone bricks and mud in the lee of the cliff and is one of more than 200 dwellings. There are also 23 religious constructions (called *kiva*), bedrooms, and storerooms for the harvest. According to specialists in the Mesa Verde Archaeological Project, who excavated the site from 1959 to 1972, Cliff Palace was built around the end of the twelfth century and could accommodate between 200 and 250 people.

The indigenous people, the Anasazi (Navajo for "the ancient ones'") settled here in the sixth century, living in the ravines or low shelters built on the plateau near the cliff face. They cultivated corn and beans on the flat top of the Mesa Verde (declared a national park in 1906) and hunted wild turkey. Their community numbered some thousands of inhabitants and was well protected from intruders because of the difficult approach to their territory. Only in the eleventh century did they begin to construct stone buildings with several floors, referred to as *pueblos*, a term also used to indicate the people to distinguish them from the native peoples who lived in teepees.

A little over a hundred years later, for reasons unknown, they abandoned the Mesa Verde to build new *pueblos* further south in the region of the Rio Grande.

338 top Characterized by elegant geometric designs, this terracotta vase was made by the indigenous people of the Acoma pueblo in New Mexico. They were one of the many tribes that considered the Anasazi their ancestors.

338 center A view from the top of Cliff Palace, the largest and most impressive of the Mesa Verde constructions. The people that lived in the area were the Anasazi, from which at least 23 indigenous tribes inhabiting Colorado, Arizona and New Mexico descended.

338 bottom In the photo the Spruce Tree House, takes its name from the huge Douglas fir that once stood in front of it. Built between 1200 and 1276, it has 140 rooms and nine kiwas, or ceremonial chambers.

338-339 Situated at the eastern end of Navajo Canyon, Square Tower House could accommodate 80 people. The focal element of this settlement is the three-story tower made of adobe, which has survived to the present day in excellent condition.

Around 3,900 sites of archaeological interest have been identified on the Mesa Verde, more than 600 of which are dwellings beneath overhanging rocks. Besides those mentioned, the most outstanding are the Long House (the second largest) and Spruce Tree House (the third largest), which was named by its discoverers in 1888 after the large Douglas fir cut down by another of the first explorers of the site. Step House is also remarkable because it is one of the few points in which evidence has been found of two successive occupations of the same site. A first basic shelter was built in the seventh century, whereas the grotto in which it was constructed was also occupied by a *pueblo* in the early thirteenth century. Recently, authorities have decided not to use the term Anasazi any longer to describe the peoples that inhabited the Mesa Verde and to refer to them instead with the more generic term "ancient peoples of the *pueblo*," the reason being that in addition to the Navajo, another 23 tribes claim to be descendants of the constructors of the Mesa Verde structures. These include the Ute, the Hopi of Arizona, and all the peoples whose ancestors lived in similar *pueblos* in New Mexico. None of these, though, reached the magnificent caliber of those built in the Mesa Verde.

Palenque
MEXICO

STATE OF CHIAPAS
REGISTRATION: 1987
CRITERIA: C (I) (II) (III) (IV)

340 left A steep flight of steps leads to the burial chamber in the Temple of the Inscriptions where the slab covering Pakal's sarcophagus was discovered.

340 right This extraordinary mosaic jade mask covered the face of Pakal (615–683), the lord of Palenque.

340-341 Thick tropical forest surrounds the lovely archaeological site of Palenque. The elegance of the architecture, the beauty of the landscape, the mist parted by shafts of sunlight, and the presence of water confer a mystical quality on this ancient Mayan city.

In the suffocating heat, with the torrential rain and clouds of insects, the effort of digging, at times just with hands protected by gloves, for hours each day, for months on end, is great. Then there are the snakes, the most dangerous of which was called *nawiaka* by the descendants of the Maya, whose bite would kill you within an hour. However, all this was forgotten, at least according to the accounts written by the Mexican archaeologist Alberto Ruz, when a triangular door was found at the end of a narrow stairway that opened into a chamber that had remained secret for centuries. It was shrouded by a thin mist and seemed like a cave lined with ice, with stalagmites and stalactites shining like crystals. Once his eyes had grown accustomed to the dark, Ruz found the finely-carved stone cover of a sarcophagus on the floor…

It may seem like a scene from the film *Raiders of the Lost Ark*, but this was really the way that, in 1952, after four years of digging, Ruz discovered the first pyramidal tomb in the Americas, the eternal abode of Pakal, the legendary ruler of Palenque. Today the exquisitely beautiful objects that made up his grave furnishings – including a priceless jade mask – can be seen in the Mexico City Museum, but the magnificent tombstone is still in the underground chamber at the heart of the Temple of the Inscriptions, the most spectacular pyramid in Palenque.

The name Palenque was given to the archaeological site long after the ancient

341 top Standing 82 feet tall, with eight sloping levels and a majestic flight of steps, the Temple of the Inscriptions is named for its ornate hieroglyphics telling the story of Palenque.

Maya had vanished, perhaps based on the name of a village at the edge of the ruins, Bahlam Kin. The Maya, however, called it *Lakam Ha*, or "Great Water," which perfectly describes its setting. Situated in the valley of the Río Usumacinta, the area with the highest rainfall in all of Mexico, Palenque lies in a dense forest featuring many waterfalls. It was this abundance of water and the fertility of the soil that allowed the city to develop and become rich. Although the history of the city covers the entire Classic Period from A.D. 300 to 900, the ruins seen today only date back to the period of the city's greatest splendor, which occurred in the seventh century during the reigns of Pakal and his son Chan-Bahlum.

Having ascended the throne at the age of 12 and died at almost 80, Pakal was a sort of Charlemagne of Mesoamerica. A man of great political and administrative skills, he encouraged the city's architectural and artistic development.

MEXICO CITY

PALENQUE

Besides the Temple of the Inscriptions – a steep pyramid 82 feet high divided into eight levels with a shrine on the top finely decorated with figures from Mayan mythology – the royal palace is in an excellent state of conservation. This is a set of residential and administrative buildings almost entirely covered with elaborate bas-reliefs. Also of great interest are the Temple of the Sun and Temple of the Cross, both of which are almost buried beneath liana vines. In pyramidal form, they have a sandstone shrine at the top adorned with reliefs of religious rituals and, on the inside, fragments of fine frescoes.

In Temple XIII, which stands a short distance from the Temple of the Inscriptions, a tomb similar to Pakal's was found a few years ago. It contained a series of jade and obsidian objects and trays that would have held food and drink for the journey to Xibalba, the Mayan world beyond the grave.

There were also the skeletons of a man and two women, one old and the other still an adolescent. The archaeologists tend to think that this is the tomb of Pakal's heir, Chan-Bahlum. Confirmation of the presumed family relationship between the two rulers awaits the publication of results of complicated laboratory tests that are currently attempting to reconstruct the DNA of the deceased.

342 top A general view of the Group of the Cross, which includes the Temple of the Cross and Temple of the Sun; the latter is set a little back from the Temple of the Cloverleaf Cross. These three pyramids have decorations linked to Mayan mythology: the symbol of the cross, for example, represents the encounter of the world of the living with the world of the dead.

342 bottom The North Group has five buildings used for ceremonial purposes built on a stepped terrace. One of these has a curious pagoda style of roof, and they all feature fragments of stucco decorations.

342-343 The sunset bathes the top of the Palacio with light. This set of administrative and residential buildings is the focus of Palenque. The purpose of the central tower is still debated: it was probably either a watchtower or an astronomical observatory.

343 bottom left The interior of the Temple of the Sun has panels of bas-reliefs that celebrate the power of Chan-Bahlum. The son and heir of Pakal, he took the throne in 684 and reigned for 18 years. He is credited with the construction of the temples in the Group of the Cross.

343 bottom right Superb reliefs of large figures, portraying elegantly dressed courtiers wearing feathered headdresses decorate the panels that line the base of the Palacio.

Chichén Itzá
MEXICO

STATE OF THE YUCATÁN
REGISTRATION: 1988
CRITERIA: C (I) (II) (III)

The Toltecs and Aztecs called it Quetzalcoatl, but to the Maya it was Kukulcán. The "serpent with the feathers of the quetzal bird" (the translation of the name) was the protector of the priests and sovereigns, and the master of knowledge and the winds. In the Mayan pantheon, populated by bloodthirsty divinities, Quetzalcoatl-Kukulcán only asked the faithful for sacrifices of snakes, birds, and butterflies, and it was thought that one day he would return to make the earth his paradise. It was on this understanding that the Aztec king, Montezuma II, welcomed Hernán Cortéz, believing him to be that god.

In the ninth century, long before the arrival of the Spanish, the divine Toltec king Quetzalcoatl conquered the wealthiest Mayan city in the Yucatán. This, at least, is what one of the legends referring to Chichén Itzá recounts. Founded in the fifth century, it flourished throughout the Classic Period, then, around 850, it was taken by the Toltecs – or according to some experts – by the Itzá, a people related to the Toltecs. This hypothesis is supported by the city's name, which means "rim of the well of the Itzá." Be that as it may, what is exceptional about Chichén Itzá is its perfect fusion between the cultures of the Maya and Toltecs seen in its architecture, sculpture, and painting, and also in what we know of its customs. This blend survived until 1400, when the city was mysteriously abandoned.

As it appears today, the site is divided into two parts. The more ancient, Chichén Viejo, consists of buildings

344 top The skulls on the platform of the Tzompantli served to intimidate anyone who dared attack the city. The place was dedicated to military glory, and it was here that the decapitated heads of enemies were displayed.

344-345 El Castillo (or the Pyramid of Kukulkán) seen from the platform of the Temple of the Warriors. Note the sculpture of the feathered serpent on the base of the temple's flight of steps.

mainly from the Classic Period. The other section, Chichén Nuevo, consists of monumental constructions. The 180-foot-high pyramid standing on the plain was dedicated to the god Quetzalcoatl-Kukulcán. Named El Castillo (The Castle) by the Spaniards, each side is composed of a steep flight of 91 steps. If added to the entrance platform, they total 365 and therefore represent a sort of calendar. El Caracol, a shell-shaped building that functioned as a sort of observatory, is also evidence of the astronomic knowledge of the inhabitants. Another indication is given by the snakeheads carved in the stone at

345 top The temple at the top of El Castillo, stands 180 feet tall. This monumental pyramid features many symbols from Mayan cosmogony. Its nine terraces represent the nine levels of the Underworld.

345 center The interior of the Temple of the Jaguars. In the foreground, there is the enigmatic effigy of Chaak Mool; in the background, a red ceremonial throne in the form of a jaguar, probably reserved for the sovereign.

345 bottom The columns of the so-called Market (even though there is no evidence of commercial activity) are part of the large Toltec plaza. Originally, the columns were covered by a straw roof.

346 top The Temple of the Warriors and the Group of the Thousand Columns were built between 900 and 1200 and together formed the heart of Toltec Chichén Itzá. Once lined with brightly painted stucco, the columns represent armed warriors.

346-347 The entrance to the upper shrine in the Temple of the Warriors, guarded by Chaak Mool. Offerings were placed on the idol's stomach as it was thought that it would relay the requests of the devotees to the gods.

347 top left A view of the Temple of the Jaguars and the ball-court. Although it is almost certain that the competition's cruel ceremony originated in Teotihuacan, it was at Chichén Itzá that the most highly decorated and impressive court was built.

347 top right The holy of holies on the top of the Temple of the Warriors. The entrance was flanked by superb carvings of the head of the feathered serpent.

the start of El Castillo's main flight of steps, which at sunset project their shadows as far as the top of the temple to create the sinuous pattern symbolizing the god.

The pyramid of Quetzalcoatl-Kukulcán encloses a temple that contains a stone throne, set with pieces of jade, in the form of a jaguar. This cat was the symbol of the Toltec warrior class, and its representations can also be seen in the Temple of the Warriors, the Temple of the Thousand Columns (both of which stand in the Great Toltec Plaza), and the Temple of the Jaguars. All these buildings are decorated with detailed bas-reliefs of warriors, priests, masks of the rain god Chac, eagles, feathered serpents, and sculptures of jaguars feeding on human hearts.

Chichén Itzá features the largest and most elaborate ball court in Mesoamerica. Just under 100 yards long, it is bounded by walls decorated with bas-reliefs that represent one of the most extraordinary examples of Mayan art. One shows the decapitation of a player in the presence of his fellow players. The stone rings in

the form of a serpent, through which the players had to pass the ball, are still found at either end of the court. Little is known of the game, and it is still debated whether it was the losers or the captain of the winning team to be beheaded at the end of the match. In any case, it is clear that the game was the most important moment in the religious rituals. In the *Popul Vuh*, the creation myth of the Maya, the divine heroes challenge the demons at the ball game. On that occasion, the future of an entire people was at stake.

347 center Curls perhaps representing fire or the invocation of the gods emerge from the mouth of a skull. This is one of the many bas-relief figures on the walls of the ball-court.

347 bottom A detail from the enormous bas relief around the ball-court. It shows moments from a game and the subsequent sacrifice. The horror of the players and the sacredness of the game are rendered with powerful expression.

348 top The upper part of the Observatory, also known as El Caracol due to its shell-like shape. The deep interest of the Mayans in astronomy resulted in their codification of a calendar that established the agricultural cycles and marked the social and economic events of the city.

348-349 The Nunnery lies in the southern and oldest section of Chichén Itzá. The architecture and decorations (including masks of the rain god Chac and other symbolic figures) make it a masterpiece of Puuc style.

349 top Erected between 1100 and 1300 in pure Toltec style, this platform was used to honor the god Kukulkán. It was named after Venus, an important planet in the astronomic knowledge and mysticism of the Mayans.

349 bottom Massive heads of the feathered serpent bound the Platform of the Eagles and Jaguars. This was probably built in homage to the warriors that formed the military elite in Chichén Itzá.

Tikal

GUATEMALA

PROVINCE OF EL PETEN
REGISTRATION: 1979
CRITERIA: C (I) (III) (IV); N (II) (IV)

D uring planning of the film *Star Wars*, the set designers had to use incredible amounts of imagination to create the spectacular locations for which the film was famous. Not many people know, though, that most of the landscapes of the galaxy on which the story took place were copied from real sites, and that the base of the rebels led by princess Leila was a reconstruction of Tikal.

This astonishing Mayan site deep in the forests of Guatemala is, it must be said, "a world apart." One of its monumental complexes has even been named *Mundo Perdido* (Lost World) for its structure, so labyrinthine and isolating that it competes with the surrounding jungle.

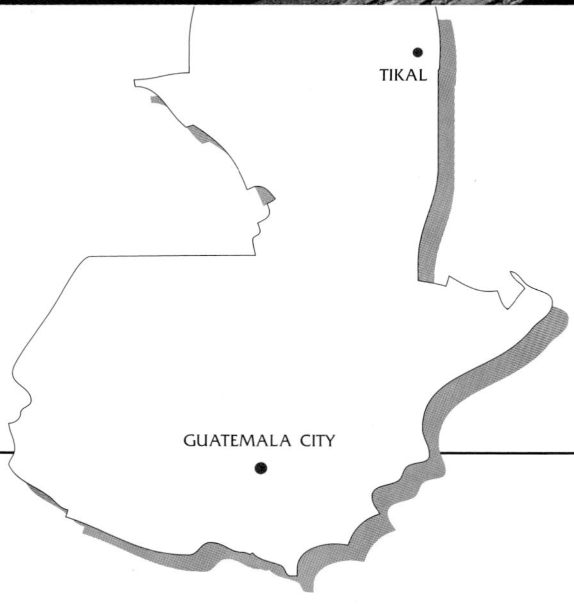

TIKAL

GUATEMALA CITY

350 left This magnificent burial mask made of jade, mother-of-pearl, obsidian, and serpentine has been dated at AD 527. When it was found inside Tomb 160, it lay in 174 separate pieces. Archaeologists were able to piece it back together with the help of similar images carved on the stelae at Tikal.

351 center Temple IV emerges from the Guatemalan vegetation. This pyramid (200 feet high) was the tallest building in the Americas until the construction of the first skyscrapers at the end of the nineteenth century.

351 bottom One of the pyramids in the Mundo Perdido group, which was erected in various phases over a long period. New buildings were actually constructed over existing ones. The earliest ones date back to 400 BC.

350-351 A view of the Great Plaza, Tikal's monumental heart. The building on the left is the Central Acropolis, a labyrinthine building that may have been the residence of the royal family. To the right stands the 125-foot high Temple II, or Temple of the Masks.

351 top The Tikal archaeological site is situated in the middle of the Maya Biosphere Reserve, an area of primary tropical forest with mahogany, ceiba, and sapodilla trees up to 165 feet tall. In the background, Temple I, rises behind and to the left of Temple V.

At one time, the many sandstone pyramids of the ancient city (which represent the mountains where corn, a food sacred to the Maya, originated) were covered with stucco painted in dazzling colors featuring scenes of religious rituals or even entirely red. For example, the stelae in the Great Plaza were red, the ones carved with the portraits of 26 of the kings that ruled Tikal. The colors, which have been washed away by centuries of rain, were identical to the plumage of the parrots, toucans, and hummingbirds that today nest in the cracks of the temples.

Now protected in a 3,900-acre national park, Tikal was one of the most important cities in Mesoamerica. It was founded in the sixth century B.C. on a high ground abundant in edible fruits, high quality wood like zapote, good for building, and flint, which ancient peoples used to make weapons and tools. Tikal was already an important city when, in A.D. 230, Yax-Moch-Xoc took the throne and founded a dynasty that was to reign on and off until the tenth century when the city was mysteriously abandoned. During its long period of glory, Tikal numbered up to 100,000 inhabitants, traded with cities as distant as Teotihuacan in Mexico, and extended its dominion as far as the present-day state of Belize. There are roughly 3,000 palaces, pyramids, ball courts, and even thermal baths providing evidence of the architectural and artistic skills and originality of its builders.

The most amazing of the religious buildings in the city dates back to the eighth century. It is known as Temple I, or the Temple of the Great Jaguar. It was built in honor of Ah Cacau (682–734), the twenty-sixth lord of Tikal. It is a pyramid 144 feet tall with a shrine at the top that once featured an architrave carved with a representation of the 13 kingdoms in the Mayan paradise. The grave of the sovereign was discovered inside the monument and, with it, grave furnishings made from jade, gold, pearls, bone engraved with patterns and

352 top Today held in the site museum, this remarkable terracotta idol is part of the set of grave goods found in what the inscriptions on the sarcophagus have identified as the tomb of Huh Chaan Mah K'ina (king Curved Nose), one of the sovereigns of the city.

352 center Scholars believe that Temple II (left) was probably built by king Ah Cacau in honor of his wife, even if no burial chamber was found inside to prove it.

352 bottom left The Group Q complex was built by Yax Ain II, the third lord of Tikal. Standing on the open area before it are several stelae adorned with bas-reliefs. They were once painted red, as in all the most important monuments in the city.

352 bottom right This finely painted terracotta incense-burner from the grave goods of Huh Chaan Mah K'ina dates back to the sixth century.

352-353 The burial place of Ah Cacau, Temple I, faces onto the Great Plaza. The Central Acropolis, in the background, is composed of a series of ceremonial terraces and rooms decorated with paintings portraying gods and the main events in the history of Tikal.

353 top left The North Acropolis was the burial place of the lords of Tikal for more than five centuries, until AD 550.

However, beneath the surface structures, there are traces of an earlier settlement dating back to 800 BC.

353 top right The various pyramids in the set of buildings referred to as the Mundo Perdido Complex were built in alignment with the position of the sun. The largest is called the Great Pyramid and stands around 100 feet high.

hieroglyphs, and parsnip thorns used for ritual blood-letting.

Also of great interest are the squares onto which the pyramid and chamber temples face, and the set of buildings known as the Acropolis. It is still uncertain whether this was a complex of royal residences or an administrative or ceremonial center. It is composed of a hundred or so rooms arranged in an apparently haphazard manner due to the Mayan custom of building over pre-existing structures. The most ancient parts of the Acropolis date to around 400 B.C., whereas the enormous terracing overlooking the complex, richly decorated with masks of jaguars, feathered serpents, and other animals sacred to the Maya, is from the era of Ah Cacau, the leader who was most influential in giving the city its monumental appearance.

The name of this sovereign in translation is, amusingly enough, "King Chocolate." However, it is also true that the Maya actually invented the world's favorite sweet. Furthermore, they were also the first to chew the extract of the *chicle* tree, the forerunner of today's chewing gum.

Machu Picchu

PERU

Province of Urubamba,
Cuzco Department
Registration: 1983
Criteria: C (i) (iii); N (ii) (iii)

A fire in the summer of 1988 raged through the forest surrounding Machu Picchu, destroying 10,000 acres of vegetation and risking the survival of many indigenous animal species as it licked at the edges of the ruins. Considered the worst ecological disaster in the history of Peru, it aggravated the already precarious situation of the eco-system in the magnificent Urubamba Valley, threatened by growing pressure from the development of tourism in the area and by the lack of funds and control from the Peruvian government.

It may seem an exaggeration to consider the archaeological site of Machu Picchu a fundamental element of the ecosystem, yet the beauty of the ruins rising above the rainforest are part and parcel of the landscape. Indeed, it was the presence of these mountains, the water of the Urubamba River, and the animals that determined the foundation of this fabulous city. The Inca people believed that the Pacha Mama (Earth Mother) was a creature with supernatural powers, and Machu Picchu was for them the sacred place where the world had originated.

Constructed between 1460 and 1470 under the leadership of the king, Pachacuti Inca Yupanqui, the ceremonial center of Machu Picchu was inhabited by about 1,200 people. Of these, the majority were women who had been chosen to be vestals of the Sun god (as demonstrated by the discovery of 175 mummies, 80 percent of which were female). The remaining 20 percent were priests and children.

The archaeological area consists of 200 buildings, most of which were either houses or warehouses, which were built on blocks of granite to "embrace" the rocks and exploit the morphology of the terrain. The doorways were trapezoid in shape and the roofs made from straw. The two-story houses were built in groups of ten around square courtyards and joined by narrow streets and raised passages. The areas set aside for domestic animals and the terraces on which the Incas grew corn and potatoes lay along the borders of the site.

The most important religious buildings were built around wide

354 View of one of the residential complexes at Machu Picchu. These comprised groups of ten two-story, straw-roofed stone houses set around courtyards and joined by narrow streets and raised passages.

354-355 A superb view of Machu Picchu, dominated to the north by the cone-shaped mountain called Huayna Picchu. Set in a natural cave on the side of this mountain the Temple of the Moon, and clinging to the mountain wall, is still a sacred place for the indios who live in the Urubamba Valley.

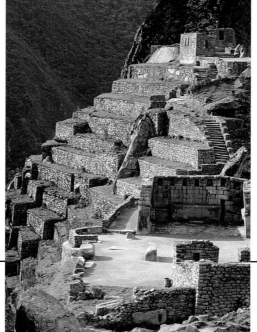

355 top left Built of perfectly squared and interlocked stones, the monumental trapezoid gates are a typical feature of Machu Picchu. This is what is referred to as a "double gate", which indicates the entrance to a sacred place.

355 top right With great skill, the Inca people dug the mountain into a series of terraces to be able to cultivate corn and potatoes to feed the community. The agricultural and residential areas of the ancient city cover 50 acres, double that of the ceremonial area.

356 top The ruins of the Temple of the Condor, so named its shape suggest the bird about to take flight. It was built in the lee of a rock in the niches of which the Incas placed their mummies. The condor was believed to transport the souls of the dead to the world beyond the grave.

356-357 The Temple of the Sun has a round tower that, according to archaeologists, was used as an astronomic observatory. On December 21, the winter solstice, the sun rises in line with the building's central window.

ceremonial plazas: these were the Temple of the Sun, a circular construction like a tower with fine bas-reliefs, the Temple of the Three Windows, the so-called Principal Temple, and the Royal Temple. Though this last building was really used for worship and no tombs have been found inside it, it takes its name from its sunken position, and it is thought that it represented the "spiritual" access to the heart of the mountain. The Intihuatana is a fascinating carved monolith in front of which the priests made sacrifices in honor of the sun on

with bas-reliefs and features a massive stone throne set in the middle. Even today, the local inhabitants bring offerings of corn, tobacco, and coca leaves to the temple for the god of the mountain.

When the Spaniards led by Pizarro arrived in Cuzco in 1532, they utterly destroyed the Inca Empire, but never learned of the existence of Machu Picchu. Five years earlier, an epidemic of bubonic plague had caused the death of 50 percent of the Inca population, and the sacred mountain had consequently been abandoned. For

357 Machu Picchu was constructed between 1460 and 1470 by king Pachacuti Inca Yupanqui and was inhabited by 1,200 people. Its agricultural terraces are seen to the right of the central building known as the "prison."

the day of the winter solstice (summer for those south of the equator). The Temple of the Moon stands on Huayna Picchu, the splendid cone-shaped mountain that looks down on the site. Set in a natural cave in which five niches were dug out, it is decorated

centuries, only the few inhabitants of the Urubamba Valley knew of the site's existence, until July 24t, 1911, when the American archaeologist Hiram Bingham rediscovered it. In the meantime, it had been completely absorbed into the forest.

The Lines and Geoglyphs of Nazca and the Pampas of Jumana

PERU

Province of Urubamba, Department of Cuzco

Registration: 1994

Criteria: C (i) (iii) (iv)

358-359 This curious human figure is known as "The Astronaut" and was often considered "proof" of the theory (always refuted outright by the entire scientific community) that the geoglyphs at Nazca were created by extraterrestrial beings.

358 bottom left This hummingbird one of the 18 different birds traced out on the pampas of Jumana. In addition, the Nazca people designed various animals in this desert area, including lizards, fish, a whale, a monkey, and a spider.

358 bottom right Two designs of hands and a tree. All the figures were created using a simple technique that involved removing the stones and boulders on the desert floor to reveal the pale colored soil beneath.

The ruins of irrigation systems built by local peoples in ancient history can be found along the coastal deserts of Peru. In 1941, Paul Kosok, an expert on pre-Columbian Latin America, was studying them in the Rio Nazca valley – one of the tributaries of the Rio Grande – when he came across what seemed to be a huge stylized bird on the ground, over 100 feet in length. It appeared that the design was deliberately traced out so that it would be visible from above.

Having enquired among his colleagues at Lima University, Kosok learned that there were several figures of that sort and that three years prior a Peruvian scholar had published an article in which he hypothesized that they were ceremonial images created by an unknown pre-Columbian civilization. Until that time, their presence had been pretty much ignored, with the exception of the occasional note made by Spanish chroniclers around 1600 and sketches drawn by archaeologist Julio Tello in 1926.

After an aerial reconnaissance mission in which he managed to identify a number of figures, Kosok left Peru with the idea that they were ancient viewing lines linked to astronomic observation, explaining his theory to the German astronomer and mathematician Maria Reiche who lived in Lima. Since that time, Reiche devoted forty years to the study of the Nazca lines, contributing to the discovery of their age and designers as well as a plausible explanation for their existence.

Half a century later, thirty or so images have been identified on the Colorada pampas, or the pampas of Jumana, the highlands covering more than 185 square miles that overlook the Rio Nazca valley. Some feature human or animal characteristics, whereas others are stylized plants. There are also famous images of birds, a monkey, a spider, and a killer whale, but there are also geometric patterns, in particular trapezoids and rectangles over a mile long, that apparently lack any immediate significance. The technique used to execute them is very simple: all that was done was remove the brownish stones covering the desert surface of the pampas, thus leaving the paler ones below to show through. Despite the simplicity of the method, the skill

used was masterful and the execution must have required enormous effort as there is no evidence that beasts of burden were used, and therefore one assumes that the work done was all manual.

A variety of hypotheses have been put forward over the years as to their meaning, including even outrageous ideas involving alien visitors, inspired by the vague similarity of the geoglyphs to airport runways and of the incredibly advanced technologies developed by ancient civilizations, but the Nazca figures are anything but a mystery. The lines on the Jumana pampas, and the many others along the Peruvian coast to the north, though less spectacular, had their origin in what is referred to as the "Nazca civilization," a pre-Columbian civilization that flourished between the second century B.C. and sixth century

A.D. This fact has been proven by pottery found in the more clement areas in the region where those responsible for the figures probably lived, and from fragments also found in the area of the Rio Nazca. Some of the finds are decorated with motifs bearing a remarkable similarity to some of the figures. The untiring work of Maria Reiche has confirmed that the geometric figures played a role in marking the important events in the calendar, such as the solstices and the cycle of the seasons. Owing to the unusually arid climate on the Jumana pampas and the absence of wind erosion of the soil, the Nazca lines have survived in perfect condition to the present day.

359 left The monkey with the enormous spiral tail is probably the best known figure at Nazca. Identical representations are seen on the pottery of the so-called "Nazca civilization", a culture that flourished on the Peruvian coast between the second century BC and fourth century AD.

359 right The spider geoglyph is roughly 150 feet long. Although many archaeologists refute the astronomic significance of the Nazca designs, Professor Gerald Hawkins has discovered that the position of the feet are aligned with the constellation of Orion.

Rapa Nui National Park

CHILE

RAPA NUI

SANTIAGO

EASTER ISLAND
REGISTRATION: 1995
CRITERIA: C (II) (III) (V)

Convinced that Polynesia was populated by adventurous navigators from South America who were able to reach the far-away islands in the Pacific Ocean by traveling in primitive boats, in 1947 the Norwegian explorer and archaeologist Thor Heyerdahl organized an daring expedition. Aboard the Kon Tiki, a balsawood craft identical to the ones used by Polynesians, he set out to cover the 5,000 miles separating the Peruvian coast from the atoll of Raroia in the Tuamotu Archipelago.

Encouraged by the success of the expedition, eight years later he wanted to show that the same thing had happened with Easter Island, the solitary volcanic formation that lies 2,400 miles from the nearest human habitation. Heyerdahl and his team set out on an archaeological exploration of the island, discovering that it was once covered by forests, which had been completely cut down by the island's inhabitants. Carbon dating of some of the island's famous statues showed that it had

been populated since roughly A.D. 380, at least a thousand years before anyone had thought. The tradition of the inhabitants, however, claimed that their ancestors had arrived from the Far East. Over time, detailed analysis of the archaeology, physical anthropology, and genetics of the people confirmed that Heyerdahl had been wrong. The island was given its name by the sailor Jacob Roggeveen, because he had first seen it on Easter Day 1722. Only many years later, in 1863, it was called Rapa Nui by a group of Tahitian sailors who thought it looked like Rapa Iti, a small island in French Polynesia. To the local population, the island was Te Pito O Te Henua, meaning the Vessel of the World.

Polynesians were also the colonizers of Easter Island. In the fifth century, a complex and enigmatic culture began to develop there, producing Rongorongo, the only written language in Oceania. A number of rock inscriptions and the remains of houses, places of worship, wooden sculptures, clothes made from tree bark (tapa), and handicrafts have been found on the island. However, Rapa Nui is most famous for the Moai, the gigantic heads carved out of rock. At least 288 once stood upright on bases called ahu, which have counterparts in Polynesian culture. About 250 Moai encircle the edges of the island, while another 600, in different stages of production, are scattered around the coast and near Rano Raraku Volcano, where the quarries in which they were carved are located. Mostly executed between 1000 and 1650, they stand a maximum of 33 feet high with a weight of 80 or so tons. One of these, however, carved partially from its rock bed, is double the size and would have weighed, if completed, about

360 top The moai of Ahu To Ko Te Riku, with the characteristic block of lava (called a pukao) on the head.

360 center and bottom Groups of moai in the southeast part of the island. The statues vary in height from six to 33 feet and can weigh up to 80 tons each.

361 These moai stand in Anakena, the place where, according to tradition, the first ruler of Rapa Nui landed on the island.

160 tons. The most accredited theory is that they had a religious value as they impersonated the mana, the spirits of the ancestors, in accordance with Polynesian tradition. To some experts, though, they are symbols of both religious and political authority. The society of Rapa Nui prospered for centuries, but with the growth of the population decline inexorably set in. At its peak, the island must have had around 10,000 inhabitants, but this number was too high for its 44 square miles of land. By the fifteenth century, the fragile eco-system was compromised to the point where there were no more trees to build canoes, as the last had been cut down to make space for crops. Rivalry broke out between clans that led to a breakdown in the social fabric, full-scale battles, and ultimately, cannibalism. The arrival of Europeans only worsened the situation. They brought disease, and many inhabitants of Rapa Nui were deported to be sold into slavery. In 1877, the population was reduced to 111 people (today it has once more grown to 2,000 inhabitants, many of whom are continental in origin). Though the worst was past, the violent and irreversible events in the island's history have led to Rapa Nui being considered a symbol of ecological catastrophe.

Nature Sanctuaries
introduction

President Ulysses S. Grant signed the deed founding the world's first national park on 1 March 1872 to protect the incredible natural spectacle of fumaroles, geysers and hot springs of Yellowstone, an area on the borders of Wyoming, Montana and Idaho. Industrial growth and the frenetic process of modernization have since distorted the geography of many regions of the world, but at the same time humankind has gradually become aware of the need to protect the delicate balances of the environment and nature, creating increasingly extensive and numerous protected areas.

Ever since its establishment in 1972, the objectives of the UNESCO World Heritage Convention have included the grouping together under its aegis of the most precious and unspoiled natural areas of the Earth in every continent. Almost 200 incredibly varied sites are inscribed in the World Heritage List for their outstanding natural importance. They range from the great parks, such as the Serengeti and Ngorongoro in Tanzania or the Virunga Mountains in the Congo, which conserve the marvelous habitat of the large African mammals, to the icy expanses of the Alaskan-Canadian border region, and from the most important areas of paleontological excavation, where the fossils of prehistoric animals allow for the reconstruction of the history and evolution of life on Earth, to the huge expanses of ocean and its natural structures, such as the Great Barrier Reef, which stretches along Australia's northeastern coast, or the Aldabra Atoll in the Seychelles, one of the richest marine reserves in the world. They also include the Galápagos Islands, where Charles Darwin drew up his theory of evolution, and rugged lands dominated by spectacular and highly active volcanoes, such as Hawaii and the Russia's Kamchatka Peninsula.

This marvelous natural atlas features 73 countries in all continents, albeit with substantial differences. Although Africa, Australia and the Americas account for the lion's share, due to the sheer size of their territories combined with a relatively limited human impact, Asia has protected areas in the huge uninhabited plains of eastern Russia and among the imposing peaks of the Himalayas, but also in countries such as China, India and Japan, where the pressure exerted on the environment by humans is becoming increasingly unsustainable. Europe brings up the rear, although it too boasts 30 or so sites in this section of the World Heritage List. However, most of these cover small areas, in a continent that has by far the highest population density in the world, with an average of 337 inhabitants per square mile.

Today conservation of the natural and environmental heritage is considered a priority by a large part of the population, also in many developing countries, where national parks and other protected areas often represent an important economic resource, due to ever-increasing flows of tourists. Nonetheless, a large number of natural World Heritage Sites find themselves facing serious threats for their conservation, despite the commitment of international institutions and environmental associations. There are several reasons for this: wars and poaching, the exploitation of mineral resources, the illegal use of protected zones or the expansion of urban areas and pollution, as witnessed in the Everglades in Florida – in a country where awareness of environmental problems is nonetheless very high.

The natural heritage protected by UNESCO is thus all that remains of our planet before humankind dominated every latitude, and is the best legacy that we can leave to those who will follow us.

363 Kingdom of the African elephant, the Mana Pools National Park is home to one of southern Africa's densest concentrations of wildlife. Instituted in 1963, it was added to the UNESCO list in 1984.

The Giant's Causeway

UNITED KINGDOM

NORTHERN IRELAND, MOYLE DISTRICT
REGISTRATION: 1986
CRITERIA: N (I) (III)

In 1693 Sir Richard Bulkeley, an eminent scholar at Trinity College, Dublin, caused a stir among the members of the Royal Society when he presented a paper in which he described the discovery, made a year previous by the Count-Bishop of Derry, of a singular stretch of coast on the northeastern tip of Ireland. On the coastline of County Antrim stood some rocks that were too regular in shape to have been molded by nature. Four years later, the London institution sent an artist to the spot to illustrate the 'natural curiosity'.

For all of the eighteenth century the Giant's Causeway was visited by artists and scientists who wondered at the origin of the 40,000 basalt columns that are aligned so that they seem to form a paved road leading out to sea. For the ancient inhabitants of the area, the columns were the work of the giant Finn McCool, the commander for the king of Ireland's army. At this point versions of the legend differ. In the most common version, McCool built the stretch of rock to go to win his consort on Staffa in the Hebride Islands (where there is a similar formation); in another version, the giant made use of them so that he could fight his enemy in Scotland.

It was only at the end of the eighteenth century that one group of geologists offered the theory that the formation of rocks was of volcanic origin; while another, led by Richard Kirwan, believed that they were the result of the precipitation of minerals in the sea water. From 1830, when the first road alongside the Giant's Causeway was built, the cliffs began to become part of the Grand Tour made by the well-to-do of the period and was referred to in the works of Romantic poets.

At this time the official explanation of the origin of the Giant's Causeway was about to crumble. In the Tertiary period, between 60 and 50 million years ago, the area of Antrim was subject to intense volcanic activity. Masses of extremely fluid, molten rock were pushed upwards through cracks in the limestone surface to form a lava plateau. Rapid cooling caused the solidifying lava to contract and the different speeds at which the material cooled (which were the result of the different depths) created vertical cracks similar to those seen in mud when it dries.

With time the softest rock was eroded away by the action of the sea to leave the spectacular and perfectly adjacent columns that line the coast for 300 yards and that stretch 160 yards out to sea. Most of the columns are hexagonal (but there are also four-,

364 bottom right The Auks razorbill (Alca torda) is one of about 80 species of birds, resident and migratory, that stop around the Giant's Causeway. For this reason the Royal Society for the Protection of Birds considers the area an important regional zone for birdlife.

364 top The Atlantic puffin (Fratercula arctica) is a member of the charadriiform family that lives in large groups on the coasts of all northern seas. The species is characterized by unmistakable colored stripes on the beak.

364 bottom left First described in 1693, the Giant's Causeway was embroiled in legend and scientific disputes until the mid-nineteenth century, when knowledge of earth sciences became extensive enough to explain its formation.

365 With the passing of
the millennia, erosion
caused by tidal action
where the sea is most
powerful has slowly worn
away the geometrical
shapes of the basalt.

BELFAST

DUBLIN

LONDON

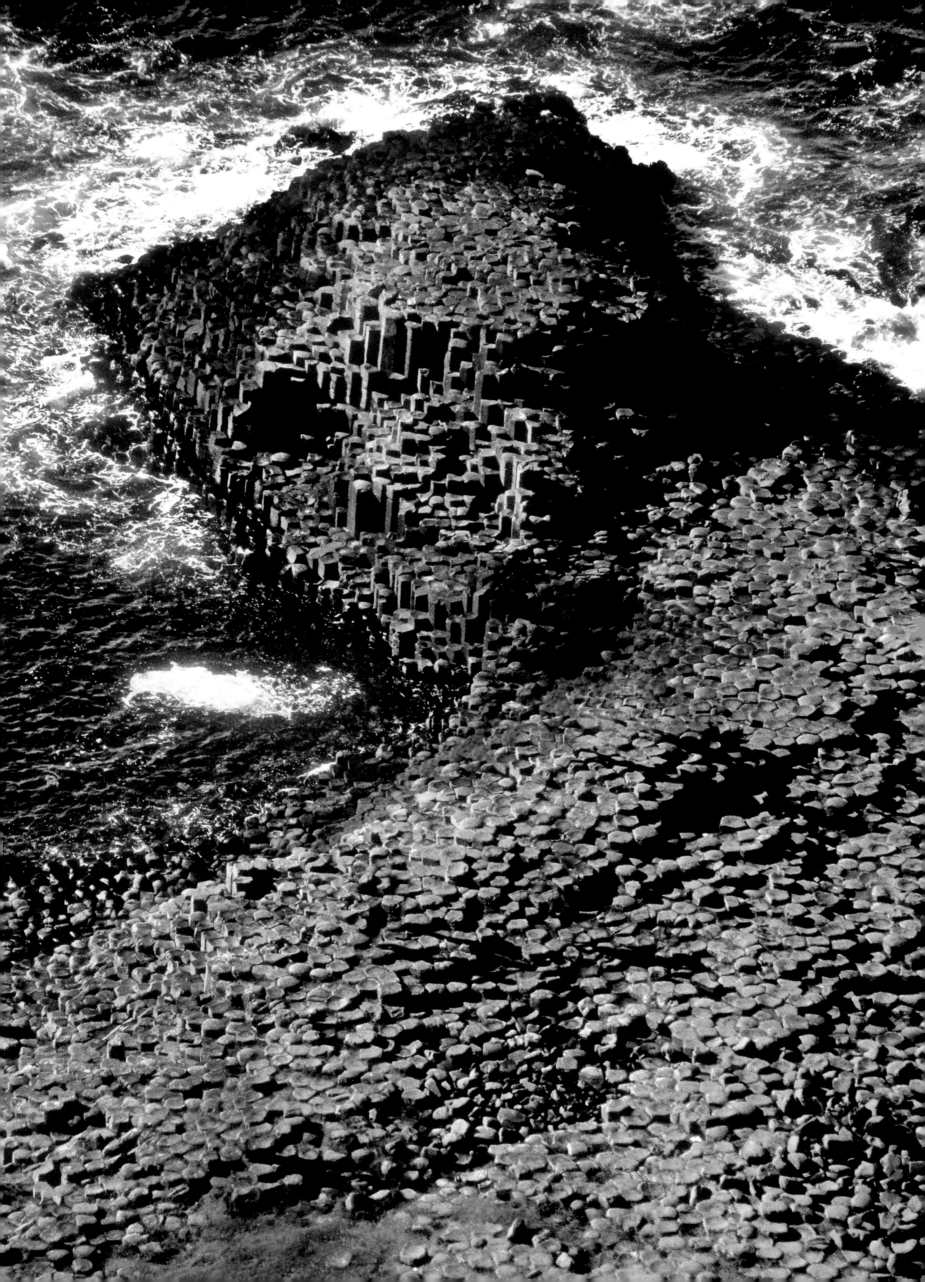

five-, eight- and ten-sided columns) and do not exceed 20 feet in height. Exceptions to these are those in the Giant's Organ, which reach a height of 40 feet. Erosion by atmospheric agents has also created circular formations around basalt cores known as the Giant's Eyes.

Although the geological aspects of the Giant's Causeway are its major attraction, the coastline is also a habitat for many species of sea birds, including the Arctic petrel, double-crested cormorant and razorbill. And The National Trust has drawn up an inventory of the many botanical species found on the top of the cliffs, which have survived three centuries of visitors.

366 Formed after intense volcanic activity 60-50 million years ago, the Giant's Causeway numbers roughly 40,000 basalt columns along a stretch of coast around 320 yards long and extending under the sea for about 160 yards.

367 top left The columns in the Giant's Organ – some of the tallest in the Causeway – reach 40 feet in height.

367 top right Normally the shape of the basalt columns is hexagonal, but there are some with four, five, eight and 10 sides.

367 center right Along with the Arctic ptarmigan, the Arctic petrel (Fulmarus glacialis) is one of the birds that nests in the far north, even in the Arctic Circle.

367 bottom The Causeway Coast is a striking set of basalt cliffs about 330 feet high formed by lava during the Tertiary period on the Antrim Plateau and covering about 1,500 square miles.

Parque Nacional de Coto Doñana
SPAIN

GUADALQUIVÍR DELTA, ANDALUSIA
REGISTRATION: 1994
CRITERIA: N (II) (III) (IV)

It was, it is said, a disappointment in love that prompted Ana de Silva y Mendoza, the Duchess of Medina Sidonia, to isolate herself in the Spartan residence that stands in the Guadalquivír Delta where the monarchs of Castille had established a hunting reserve. From that time on, the inhabitants of the nearby fishing villages referred to the area as the forest of Doña Ana or, more simply, Doñana.

Many centuries later, in 1969, the Spanish government set up the Parque Nacional de Coto Doñana that extends over 135 square miles of the delta of what the Moors named the Wada-al-Kebir ('big river') and that is now known as the Guadalquivír. The delta is a very unusual one, to the extent that some prefer to call it an estuary, as only

one branch of the river enters the Atlantic, which it does to the north of Sanlúcar de Barramela. The other branches have been progressively blocked by the barrier of sandbar that stretches from the mouth of the Rio Tinto near Palos to the opposite bank to Sanlúcar. This barrier has gradually been modeled into a complex formation of tall dunes by the winds. On the other side of the dunes lie the *marismas*, or marshes, that make Doñana a unique area in Europe.

Currently the Arenas Gordas ('fat sands') that mark the edge of the Doñana marshes extend for roughly 45 miles north to south but are cut at the southernmost point by the mouth of the river. The *marismas* themselves cover an area of 444 square miles. The complex ecosystem of coastal dunes, marshes and freshwater pools forms an environment for typical Mediterranean vegetation such as heather, lentisc, rosemary and lavender, beyond which extend the remains of forests of cork oak.

For 12 months a year, the Parque Nacional de Coto Doña is a refuge to over 300 species of birds, some of which are non-migratory. Some migrate from northern Europe during winter and others arrive from Africa to spend summer there. The winter rains

368 The marismas of the Parque Nacionál de Coto Doñana is the meeting place for over 300 species of birds, only a few of which are permanent residents. Some migrate from northern Europe during the winter and others arrive from Africa to spend the summer.

368-369 Established in 1969, the park covers an area of 135 square miles across, more or less, the Guadalquivír Delta, and includes a complex ecosystem of coastal dunes, marshes and freshwater pools with Mediterranean flora.

369 top A group of female fallow deer (Dama dama) explores the marsh called Madre de las Marismas del Rocio in search of food. Originally from Asia Minor, fallow deer were introduced to Europe by the Phoenicians.

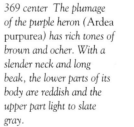

369 center The plumage of the purple heron (Ardea purpurea) has rich tones of brown and ocher. With a slender neck and long beak, the lower parts of its body are reddish and the upper part light to slate gray.

369 bottom Found right around the world, the cattle egret (Bubulcus ibis) frequents wetlands in colonies. It nests in trees, reed beds or bushes.

MADRID

370 top The common tern (Sterna hirundo) is a migratory bird about 17 inches long. Those that nest in Doñana leave Europe between August and October to pass the winter in west Africa.

370-371 The coastal dunes of the Cerro de los Ansares ('hill of the ducks') create a constantly changing barrier that stretches inland. It changes the morphology of the land each day.

371 top left Seen from above, the coastal vegetation in north Coto Doñana stretches out of sight near Matalascañas beach.

contribute to the formation of a vast marsh from 12-24 inches in depth in which *vetas* (islands) are used as nesting grounds by waders, terns and other aquatic birds. The presence too in winter of ducks and geese make Doñana a crossroads where at least a million birds find shelter.

In February the white spoonbills (*Platalea leucorodia*) arrive from North Africa to nest in the cork oaks. A month later the water level begins to drop and this is the period in which the Spanish imperial eagle (*Aquila heliaca*) lays its eggs. Researchers then have the opportunity to count this fearsome bird of prey, which is on the way to extinction.

The park is home to about fifteen pairs, which represent a third of all those in existence. For survival, each pair needs 1 square mile of hunting ground in the summer months and even more in winter, and this requirement makes its survival all the more difficult.

At the time of the duchess, Doñana was unmarked on maps but, over recent decades, the boundaries of the area have been built up. However, it is the proximity of agriculture that is the most serious threat as it washes quantities of pesticides into the water; in addition, the sulfur mines in Aznalcóliar, near Seville, contribute to the pollution of the waters with their waste products.

371 top right Doñana is home to large hoofed animals, like the deer (Cervo elaphus), of which about 90 live in the park.

371 bottom The huge expanse of Pinar de la Algaida – one of the few European forests still in good condition – is populated by communities of common pine (Pinus pinea) and lentisk.

The delta of the Danube
RUMANIA

PROVINCE OF TULCEA
REGISTRATION: 1991
CRITERIA: N (III) (IV)

372 top In June the whiskered tern (Chlidonias hybridus) builds a nest from a raft of aquatic vegetation that it anchors to plants growing above the water surface. Sometimes it nests on a lily leaf.

The word 'delta' is used in several languages to mean the terminal section of a river – where arms branch off from the main course before the river flows into the sea – and was coined by the Greeks owing to the similarity in shape between the triangular letter 'delta' in the Greek alphabet and the river and its arms. The first river delta they saw, explored and described was that of the Danube, the great river that the historian Herodotus of Halicarnassus recognized in 450 BC as playing a fundamental role in European civilization.

With a length of 1,800 miles and navigable for almost its entire length, the basin of the Danube measures half a million square miles and contains roughly 80 million people in eight different countries. Its delta, of which 1,600 square miles lies in Rumania and the remaining 295 in Ukraine, is geologically the youngest zone in Europe. Declared a Biosphere Reserve in 1990 and inscribed as a UNESCO World Heritage site and on the Ramsar Convention a year later, the delta of the Danube is an area in continual evolution, being forged by the 180,000-325,000 cubic foot per second flow of the river itself and by the 55 million tons of alluvial detritus that are swept towards the sea each year.

There are four main branches in the Danube Delta, the Chilia, Tulcea, Sulina and Sfantu Gheorghe, to which can be added many freshwater lakes connected by canals. In the southern section there are vast brackish marshes separated from the Black Sea by sand banks, which are continually modeled by the combined action of the river and sea tides.

Only 10% of the delta territory is permanently above water level but, in recompense, the marshlands are the largest in Europe and home to what is probably the largest expanse of rushes on the planet. The rushes are mostly from the species *Phragmites australis* and form numerous small islands (called *plaur*) that stand above the water ferns and yellow and white lilies that cover the marshes.

Where the Danube meets the sea is where the scenery is most surprising: here, there are islands that exist by day but are submerged by night tides, grass-covered sand dunes that enclose wet

372 center The huge marshes of the Danube are often covered by white and yellow water lilies.

372 bottom Near the mouth of the Danube, oak trees have adapted to live with the trunk exposed to the action of the tides.

BUCHAREST

372-373 The terrain of the Danube Delta is constantly altered by the large river, which has a flow of 180,000-325,000 cubic feet per second and carries 50 million tons of alluvial detritus downstream every year.

373 top An example of a glossy ibis (Plegadis falcinellus) in its speckled winter plumage. In summer its colors are brighter: the body and neck are rust colored, while the wings and head are metallic green.

373 bottom A skilful diver, swimmer and fisher, the common pelican (Pelecanus onocrotalus) has no rivals for elegance in flight. They fly in flocks and exploit thermals to give them height.

valleys and long barriers of alluvial land on which tall trees grow. The most interesting example of the land barriers is called Letea and lies at the mouth of the Sulina. It is about 13 miles long and no more than 10 miles wide and is characterized by oaks (*Quercus robur* and *Quercus pedunculiflora*) up to 115 feet tall and by pines and ash trees, which in turn are besieged by various climbing plants – *Periploca graeca, Clematis vitalba, Vitis sylvestris* and *Humulus lupulus* – giving the scene a curiously 'tropical' appearance.

The water meadows, lakes, dunes and other 'high' zones in the Danube Delta provide the largest ornithological reserve in Europe in terms of both quantity and

do not nest in the delta, in the winter months there are roughly 45,000 red-breasted geese (*Branta ruficollis*).

It has not yet been quantified precisely but the number of small mammals like the otter, coypu, hare, wild cat, viper and muskrat is important on a European level. And Letea Barrier is home to a moth, the *Rhyparioides metelkana*, which is unique in Europe.

Of the 70 or so species of freshwater fish (30 of which are typical of the delta), mention should be made of the Danube herring, the carp and, above all, the sturgeon, a favorite catch of fishermen for its caviar.

The inhabitants in the delta number about 15,000, are distributed in small

374 top Islets of rushes, which are mostly from the species Phragmites australis, *are known as plaur. Overall, they cover an area of 368 square miles.*

*374 bottom left Unlike other herons, the shy purple heron (*Ardea purpurea*) spends its life among the rush beds in the huge marshes where it is best camouflaged.*

*374 bottom right Included in the IUCN's Red List, the pygmy cormorant (*Phalacrocorax pygmaeus*) is the smallest and rarest cormorant. Over half the world's population lives in the protected area.*

variety of bird species. Of the over 300 species that visit the reserve from around the Mediterranean, continental Europe and even remote areas of Asia, 176 nest here. These include the pygmy cormorant (*Phalacrocorax pygmaeus*), whose population of 2,500 pairs represents 61% of the world total, and the largest European colony of the two pelicans, *Pelecanus onocrotalus* and *Pelecanus crispus*. There are also many ibis, purple herons, storks, egrets and white swans, of which there are at least 1,000 in each species. And, though they

villages and are mainly Orthodox Ukrainians. However, the delta is being depopulated as a result of the increasingly strict restrictions imposed by the Rumanian government following pressure from international organizations. Checks are being placed on activities related to systematic fishing and agriculture, both of which are considered unsustainable. This goes in complete contrast to the 1980s when, under the Ceausescu regime and aegis of the Soviet Union, a massive plan was introduced to exploit the zone. Numerous low-lying areas were dug for

experimentation with crops such as rice and maize, while vast areas were deforested to make space for poppy plantations in sight of paper mills. Meanwhile, heavy industries dumped tons of poisons into the Danube upstream.

Though the collapse of the Soviet Union and its satellite countries brought dramatic political, economic and social consequences, it was a cure-all for the delta's delicate ecosystem. According to experts, it is in good health, at least for the moment.

374-375 A group of
common pelicans gather in
a marshy area. It has been
estimated that the delta is
home to 2,500 pairs, i.e.,
half of the Palearctic
population.

375 bottom With its
unmistakable green and
blue plumage and hooked
beak, the long common
roller (Coracias garrulus)
lives in pairs or small
groups.

Aïr and Ténéré Natural Reserves

NIGER

DEPARTMENT OF AGADÈS
REGISTRATION: 1991
INSCRIPTION ON THE WORLD HERITAGE IN
DANGER LIST: 1992
CRITERIA: N (II) (III) (IV)

After becoming famous for being the decisive stretch of the exhausting Paris-Dakar car and motorcycle race, during the 1990s the Ténéré Desert hit the headlines for political reasons.

The revolt by the Tuareg, who were at one time the unchallenged masters of the Sahara, was putting the stability of Niger and Mali at risk and interrupting the already few north-south routes across the huge African desert.

The kidnapping in February 1992 of six members of the staff of the Aïr and Ténéré Natural Reserves produced the request by the government of Niger to include the area in the World Heritage in Danger list.

The kidnapping ended without victims and on 20 April 1995 the parties signed an agreement that opened the way for the World Wildlife Fund to examine the area. Fortunately, the delicate local environment had suffered less damage than expected, even though some species, like the ostrich, continue to be at grave risk owing to poaching.

With an area of just under 30,000 square miles, the Aïr and Ténéré Natural Reserves form the largest protected area in Africa. Approximately rectangular in shape, approximately 35-40% of its surface is occupied by the Aïr Mountains. These are nine granite massifs with igneous elements that rise out of the desert sands.

The rest of the area is the Ténéré Desert, one of the largest sand seas in the Sahara, whose platform is composed of Cambrian metamorphic rocks subjected to continual and intense erosion. Out of this emerge the ergs – huge fields of sand dunes whose height can reach 1,000 feet where they have a rocky base to rest on.

Amply described in the scientific literature, the vegetation runs to more than 350 species that are particularly widespread in the Sahelian environment of Aïr. The main communities are of Balanites

376 top The paleolithic paintings of Anakom are one of the most important examples of early human existence in the Sahara. 0

376 bottom Much of Ténéré is covered by ergs, the immense sand dunes that are created by the constant erosion of the Cambrian substrate.

377 top left The fennec (Fennecus zerda) is also known as the desert fox. It is a small nocturnal predator weighing less than 5 pounds that is particularly suited to hot, dry climates.

377 top right The desert owl (Bubo ascalaphus) is the smallest nocturnal bird of prey in the owl family. It can be recognized by its incredibly yellow eyes and light-colored plumage. It preys mostly on reptiles and small mammals.

NIAMEY

376-377 Measuring 30,000 odd square miles, the Aïr and Ténéré reserves together form the largest protected area in Africa. This aerial view shows the outreaches of the mountains of Aïr rising beyond the enormous expanse of sand sea.

aegyptiaca, which contains a steroid that cures schistosomiasis, Salvadora persica, which is the green shrub used in the Sahel to clean teeth, Ziziphus mauritiana and Acacia laeta.

In the Ténéré, the acacias are Acacia tortilis raddiana and Acacia ehrenbergiana.

The wild varieties of some food plants such as olives, millet and sorghum are particularly important and have recently been subjected to genetic study by the International Board for Plant Genetic Resources.

Despite the harshness of the climate, with recorded temperatures at an annual average of 28 degrees and rainfall scarce or non-existent, there are 165 species of birds, 18 reptiles and 40 mammals, many of which are in danger of extinction, for example, the 12,000 dorcade gazelles (Gazella dorcas), the 170 Dama gazelles (Gazella dama), and the 3,500 Barbary sheep or aoudad (Ammotragus lervia).

Even the Addax antelope (Addax nasomaculatus), which to the Tuareg is the 'queen of the desert', is in continual decline from indiscriminate hunting. It is estimated there are only 15 left.

The climatic conditions make Aïr and Ténéré difficult for man to inhabit and the villages of Iférouane and Tin Telloust have only 2,500 fixed inhabitants plus 1,500-4,500 Tuareg nomads. Yet this region has traces of settlements dating to 30,000 years ago when the glacial age had made the Sahara a land able to support the livestock-grazing lifestyle of its inhabitants. Their passing is documented in many rock paintings.

378-379 With about 12,000 remaining, the dorcas gazelle (Gazella dorcas) is one of the ungulates in danger of extinction that finds refuge in the protected area. Others are the Dama gazelle, barbary sheep and Addaz antelope.

379 top Ruthlessly hunted during the Tuareg rebellion, the ostrich (Struthio camelus) has become quite rare in the Aïr and Ténéré reserves.

379 right Bee-eater is the common name for various species of birds belonging to the Meropidae family (Merops spp.), whose diet is almost exclusively composed of bees and wasps.

Lake Turkana National Parks

KENYA

MARSABIT DISTRICT, EASTERN PROVINCE
REGISTRATION: 1997, 2001
CRITERIA: N (I) (IV)

NAIROBI

When Richard Leakey first flew over the east shore of Lake Turkana in 1967, he noticed a tangle of blackened sandstone that looked like the waste from a coal mine and began to wonder about the past of the place. Months later, when he had been appointed director of the Kenya National Museum, the young scholar (the son of the world's most famous pair of 'hominid hunters') began exploring Koobi Fora, where he discovered the richest fossil beds on the African continent. They are especially valuable for the period from 3 to 1 million years ago.

First, he found a fragment of a skull 2 million years old, which was classified as *Homo habilis*, but over the course of a decade, Leakey uncovered more than 160 remains of hominid fossils and their stone tools. In addition there are more than 4,000 parts of mammals and fish, including giant tortoises (*Petusios broadleyi*), crocodiles up to 50 feet in length (*Euthecodon brumpti*), prehistoric elephants (*Elephas recki*), giant baboons, pigs the size of rhinoceroses and the ancestors of the modern horse, cat and antelope families.

Called Lake Rudolf by the first Europeans to reach it in 1888, Lake Turkana is not just important for the extraordinary collection of fossils found in Koobi Fora. Lying in a position with a semi-desert climate, Lake Turkana is the most saline of the great African lakes and the northernmost of those in the Great Rift Valley. The area was classified a World Heritage site in 1997 and includes Sibiloi National Park (there is a petrified forest 7 million years old on the slopes of Mount Sibiloi) and Central Island National Park, a small volcanic island. To these was added South Island National Park in 2001, creating an overall site of more than 620 square miles.

The aridity of the region restricts the growth of vegetation, with what little there is being dominated by acacias and savannah. Nonetheless, Lake Turkana is an exceptional location for studying the wildlife on its banks.

The mammals to be observed there are Burchell's and Grevy's zebras (*Equus burchelli* and *Equus grevyi*), Grant's gazelles (*Gazella granti*), oryx (*Oryx gazella beisa*), antelopes like the red hartebeest (*Alcelaphus buselaphus*), the sassaby (*Damaliscus korrigum*) and the lesser kudu (*Tragelaphus imberbis*) and predators like lions (*Panthera leo*) and cheetahs (*Acinonyx jubatus*).

The lake is also an important stopping-off point for migrating birds, of which 350 species have been recorded, including a population of African skimmers (*Rynchops flavirostris*), which nests on Central Island, flamingos, nightingales, yellow wagtails and sandpipers (*Calidris minuta*). Above all, it is home to the largest community in existence of Nile crocodiles (*Crocodylus niloticus*), of which 12,000 inhabit these waters.

The future of what used to be one of the largest tributaries to the White Nile,

380 bottom right Called the 'Jade Sea' for its greenish blue water, Lake Turkana is surrounded by spectacular desert scenery.

381 top Similar to rocks, the petrified forest trees on Mount Sibiloi date to roughly 7 million years ago and suggest the area used to be rainy and densely populated.

and which today is a lake without an emissary, is under threat. Not so much from man – who has restricted his activities to a subsistence economy practiced by small groups of nomadic herders from the Turkana, Gabbra and Rendille peoples – as from global warming. And the state of the lake has been further jeopardized by the disastrous drought that has affected East Africa in recent years.

380-381 Nyabuyatom Volcano lies on the south shore of Lake Turkana. Its name means 'elephant stomach' in the Turkana language.

380 bottom left Lake Turkana is the most saline lake in Africa. It covers an area of 2,606 square miles.

381 center A colony of flamingos (Phoenicopterus ruber) crowds the water in Lake Turkana. It is an important refuge for over 350 species of birds, most of which are migratory.

381 bottom Grant's gazelle (Gazella granti) is the most common of the 13 species of this genus and one of the most tolerant of drought.

Virunga National Park
DEM. REP. OF CONGO

DEMOCRATIC REPUBLIC OF THE CONGO REGIONS OF KIVU AND UPPER ZAIRE
REGISTRATION: 1979
INSCRIPTION IN THE WORLD HERITAGE IN DANGER LIST: 1994
CRITERIA: N (II) (III) (IV)

The cover of the January 1970 *National Geographic* had a photograph of a young veterinary doctor from Louisville who, for three years, with the help of the National Geographic Society and the Wilkie Foundation, had settled in Zaire and, later, the Karisoke Research Center in Rwanda to study the most fascinating of the large primates: the mountain gorilla.

After poachers had shot Digit, the silverback male to which she had come to care about, Dian Fossey launched a campaign to raise awareness of the future of a community that was being thinned down year after year.

It was in the Karisoke Research Center that her strenuous defense of the gorilla came to a sudden end when, on 27 December 1985, Dian Fossey became the victim of a raid on her camp.

Her cry for help, however, was heard by Hollywood and the autobiography she had published just two years previous – *Gorillas in the Mist* – was turned into a highly successful film.

More than 30 years after the magazine cover appeared, the future of

KINSHASA

the mountain gorillas in Virunga National Park, where Dian Fossey did her research, is still uncertain.

In memory of Dian Fossey, the foundation continues to look after the gorillas, and its work is less troubled. Since 1994, the 3,050 square mile park, which borders the Ugandan Rwenzori Mountains National Park, has been inscribed in the World Heritage in Danger list as a result of the massive influx of refugees caused by the civil war in Rwanda.

According to the UN High Committee for Refugees, there are roughly 2 million people camping mainly in the province of Kivu, thereby increasing the population in the area of Virunga out of all proportion.

The war between Rwanda and the Democratic Republic of the Congo – which came to an end when peace was signed on 30 July 2002 – resulted in the occupation of the eastern Congo by the Rwandan army with disastrous consequences for the park. It is estimated that at least 1,900 square miles were transformed into agricultural land or their trees were cut down for firewood, with an average consumption of 600 tons per day. But poaching is just as insidious a risk. The population of the hippopotamus has collapsed from 30,000 to 3,000 and of the elephant from 3,000 to less than 500. And although they live in the most remote areas of the mountains, not even the gorillas escaped the destruction. Poachers shot 12, not

382 bottom The dense rainforest on the slopes of the Rwenzori mountain range is mainly constituted of bamboo and Hagenia abyssinica.

383 top Standing over 5 feet tall and weighing as much as 350 pounds, male silverbacks are the dominant individuals in the extended families of gorillas that number up to 30 members.

383 bottom Mountain gorillas in Virunga were made famous in the 1970s by the awareness campaign carried out by Dian Fossey whose autobiography, Gorillas in the Mist, became a very successful film.

382 left Sabinyo Volcano is one of the numerous cones in the Virunga volcanic region. Two others are Nyiragongo and Nyamuragira, both of which have recently recorded violent activity.

382-383 Estimated to have a population of 280 in 1986, the mountain gorillas of Virunga have suffered from the recent crisis in the Great Lakes region and have been reduced in number by at least a dozen from poaching and killing.

to mention several of the park's guards.

Despite these setbacks, Virunga remains one of the world's most extraordinary protected areas, above all for the diversity of its habitats.

There are spectacular environments between the lowest valleys at 2,600 feet above sea level and the 16,795 feet of the summits of the Rwenzori Mountains.

The territory covers a part of Lake Edward (part of the Nile Basin), the Semliki River Valley and Lake Kivu, from which a branch of the Congo River departs. There are inland deltas, savannahs, lavic plateaus, glaciers, snowfields and low-level equatorial forests.

Owing to its position at the boundaries of several different biogeographic zones, the park includes both tropical rainforests and steppes.

The mountain slopes are dominated by forests of bamboo and *Hagenia abyssinica*, whilst along the Semliki Valley there are species typical of equatorial forests. Trees and grasslands predominate in the Rwindi Plains, and there are steppes featuring the genera *Carissa, Capparis, Maerua* and *Euphorbia*.

The lavic plateaus are suitable terrain for species like Neobutonia *macrocalyx*, while the marshes feature various types of reeds. At higher altitudes, the alpine forest includes giant lobelias.

Up until 10 or more years ago, there used to be one of the greatest concentrations of wild animals in Africa along the rivers of Virunga National Park. In addition to those already mentioned, the most important populations were of buffalo (*Syncerus caffer*), waterhog (*Phacochoerus aethiopicus*), lion (*Panthera leo*) and antelopes like the kob (*Kobus kob*), waterbuck (*Kobus ellipsiprymnus*) and topi (*Damaliscus lunatus*).

Unlike that of other animals, the number of lions seems to be on the increase.

A census carried out in 1986 estimated that there were roughly 280 mountain gorillas (*Gorilla gorilla berengei*), but no one has any idea of the current situation.

The danger imposed by man is added to by various volcanoes, which were formed during the Pleistocene epoch along the Rift Valley.

The highest, at 14,786 feet, is Karisimbi, in Ruandan territory.

The most active is Nyiragongo, which, in January 2002, erupted spectacularly and devastatingly, forcing half a million people to flee and destroying various villages near Goma. The explosion was the worst volcanic eruption in the last decade.

Less damaging but still violent was the successive eruption of Nyamuragira, whose rivers of lava destroyed dozens of square miles of cultivated land and polluted many water sources in July 2002.

384 An amphibian mammal more active at night, the hippo (Hippopotamus amphibius) weighs up to 3 tons. This bulk requires a diet of 90 to 130 pounds of grass a day.

385 top The flatter parts of Virunga are threaded by many watercourses that make the region one of the most important hydrological basins in central Africa.

385 center left The lion (Panthera leo) is one of the few species in Virunga National Park that does not seem to have been affected by the many years of war. Its population appears to be on the increase.

385 center right A jackal (Canis aureus) has just caught a Thomson's gazelle (Gazella thomsonii) in the grasslands of Rwanda.

385 bottom The largest community of hippos in all Africa lives in the rivers of Virunga National Park. With the war in Rwanda, their number dropped from 30,000 to just 3,000 in ten years.

Kilimanjaro National Park

TANZANIA

REGION OF MOSHI
REGISTRATION: 1987
CRITERIA: N (III)

It must certainly have been a surprise to Johannes Rebmann when, in 1848, he reached the foot of a gigantic mountain covered with snow that stood just 186 miles south of the equator in the African highlands. The Chagga, the people who lived on its slopes, called it Kilimanjaro and worshipped it as a sacred mountain, but the geologist Hans Meyer, the first to climb it, in October 1889, renamed it Kaiser Wilhelm Spitze in honor of the German emperor.

Many years later, the independent Tanzanian government imposed the name Uhuru Peak after the Swahili word meaning 'freedom', but nonetheless, to everyone else, the solitary mountain has returned to being Kilimanjaro though the origins of this name remain uncertain. Rebmann believed it meant 'mountain of greatness' but others interpret it as 'shining mountain', 'white mountain' or 'mountain of water'.

Whatever it may be, Kilimanjaro remains as fascinating today as it was when seen by the first European visitors. Often its summit is covered by thick cloud that prevents the sight of its permanent snowcap. Kilimanjaro is 19,317 feet high, of volcanic origin and has three craters: Shira (12,999 feet), Mawenzi (16,893 feet) and Kibo, the highest. In all it is spread over an area measuring 1,500 square miles, making it one of the largest volcanoes in the world, and, though its last eruptions were 1 million years ago, it still shows traces of activity in a fumarole at the center of Kibo crater.

386 top Kilimanjaro is Africa's highest mountain. Although its last eruptions date to the Pleistocene, the center of the main crater still shows signs of modest activity.

386-387 Kilimanjaro covers an area of 1,500 square miles and has three craters: Shira, 12,999 feet, Mawenzi, 16,893 feet and Kibo, the highest at 19,317 feet.

Declared a nature reserve by the colonial German government in 1921, the current Kilimanjaro National Park covers an area of 291 square miles and is surrounded by a further forestry reserve of 358 square miles. Between the 6,000-foot high Marangu Gate, where the protected area begins, and the summit, there are four different botanical ecosystems that might be termed mountain forest, high-altitude heath, alpine marshes and alpine desert.

From 15,100 feet upwards only moss and lichen grow, whereas down at the level of the high-altitude heath the vegetation is mainly heather and shrubs. Apart from the two species of genus Senecio and an endemic giant lobelia (*Lobelia deckenii*), which are common at this height, the most interesting species grow in the forest band that lies between 6,000 and 8,900 feet, for example, camphor (*Ocotea usambarensis*) and various species of *Podocarpus*. Plants that are absent are bamboo and hagenia, which are common in other regions of central Africa.

Kilimanjaro provides shelter to many mammals, including eland, bushbuck, two types of duiker, buffalo (*Syncerus caffer*), leopards, an estimated population of 220 elephants and various primates (cercopithecids, galagos and colobus monkeys). There are no black rhinos, however.

Although the protection inside the park is absolute and the government has blocked all concessions for tree cutting, the resources available to the park personnel are insufficient.

A recent aerial reconnaissance of the entire area, promoted by the United Nations Environment Programme and local authorities, has shown that intense anthropic activities are continuing, for example, the cutting down of valuable species like camphor and cedar, agriculture, animal breeding and wood burning to make charcoal.

There are no longer any stretches of untouched mountain below the height of 8,200 feet.

387 top Kibo Crater is surrounded by perennial snow and glaciers at up to 14,760 feet but near Mawenzi, the snows are semi-permanent. Remains of past glaciations can be seen on all three peaks, with morainic detritus visible at up to 11,800 feet.

387 bottom A herd of elephants heads towards a waterhole at the foot of Kilimanjaro. Covering 291 square miles, Kilimanjaro National Park has five different botanical ecozones that support a rich and diverse fauna.

DAR-ES-SALAAM

Ngorongoro Conservation Area
TANZANIA

REGION OF ARUSHA
REGISTRATION: 1979
CRITERIA: N (II) (III) (IV)

Ngorongoro is almost a perfect circle just under 12 miles in diameter and, as such, is one of the largest craters in the world, though it has not turned into a lake over the millennia. Its rim now has walls that vary in height between 1,300 and 2,000 feet but it has not always been like that. When it formed at the end of the Mesozoic and start of the Cenozoic eras, Ngorongoro was a powerful volcano larger, according to scientists, than its neighbors (Loolmalasin, 11,768 feet; Oldeani, 10,394 feet; and even Kilimanjaro, Africa's highest mountain at 19,317 feet), however, it erupted with such force that it fell in on itself.

With the passage of time, its concave shape meant that it became a safe haven, unmatched in Africa, for wildlife, a sort of 'circus' that contains an extraordinary spectacle of nature at its wildest.

Considered a protected area since 1959, the crater is the culmination of the enormous ecosystem represented by the Serengeti Plain.

Besides being the point of arrival of large migrations of gnu, Burchell's zebra and many species of gazelle, it is also home to elephants, hippopotami, giraffes and buffaloes, a large number of baboons and birds (including 30 or so birds of prey) and all the large predators. In addition, it is one of the last refuges of the black rhinoceros.

The animal, however, that deserves a separate mention is the cheetah (*Acinoryx jubatus*), which here, unlike the rest of the continent where it is diminishing in numbers, still flourishes.

The cheetah has been identified as the forefather of all the large cats and is the fastest animal in the world, being able to accelerate to 68 mph in just 3 seconds, but scientists so fear for its survival that they are considering an extreme measure: cloning.

The reason for the abundant wildlife in the crater lies in the variety of vegetal habitats it contains, which provide excellent sources of food and shelter. The bottom of the crater has many pools of water that, during the rainy season, are turned into lakes, and the presence of water has produced a thick carpet of grass.

As one moves towards the edges of the crater, there are two springs that nourish the forests of Lerai (mostly *Acacia xanthopholea* and *Rauwfolia*

388-389 Ngorongoro Crater is almost a perfect circle enclosing 102 square miles of land and has walls varying in height between 1,300 and 2,000 feet.

388 bottom The most prevalent trees in the forest of Leraií are Acacia xanthopholea and Rauwfolia caffra. The forest is one of the few areas in the crater where trees predominate and thus is a favorite area for elephants to feed.

DAR-ES-SALAAM

389 top and bottom
During long droughts, the
crater is turned into a
desert but during normal
conditions of rainfall it is
covered by nutritious
herbaceous plants that
support the large
populations of gnu, zebra
and antelope.

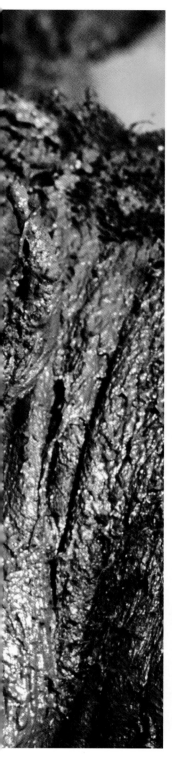

caffra) and Laiyani (*Acacia lahai, Albizzia gummifera* and *Cassipourea malosana*).

The crater's highly fertile soil provides excellent support to the flora. The volcano Ol Doniyo Lengai lies at the edge of Ngorongoro and, as it is still active, periodically covers the crater with ashes that are rich with nutritious substances.

The crater has been important to man too. Around the edge, fossils have been found of *Homo erectus, Australopitecus boisei* and *Homo habilis*, which have contributed to the theory that Africa was where our species originated. And, more recently, for the Maasai people, who have been the dominant ethnic group in this region for centuries, Ngorongoro has been crucial to their subsistence based on livestock grazing and, to a lesser extent, agriculture. For this reason, notable

390-391 Close-up of a buffalo (Syncerus caffer) covered with mud from a pool. Recent estimates suggest that there are about 4,000 buffaloe in Ngorongoro.

390 bottom left Gazelles do not need to drink much as they absorb the liquid in grass, leaves and succulent fruit.

390 bottom right A group of hippos passes a river bank packed with egrets (Ardeola ibis).

391 top The crater is the destination of the gnus' migration. Both males and females have horns but the male is taller (on average 4.5 feet at the withers) and weighs 550 pounds against the female's 350.

391 center Ostriches are the largest birds on the planet. Though they cannot fly, they run extremely fast. If threatened by predators they can maintain a speed of 31 mph for 30 minutes, a demonstration of endurance that is very rare in the animal world.

391 bottom Thousands of flamingos (Phoeiconaias minor) crowd a pool. Few species of large birds are as gregarious as these. Flamingos gather in large numbers in pools and lakes that are too saline or alkaline for fish, with which they would otherwise have to compete for food.

efforts have been made by the government of Tanzania and international organizations to create an experimental project for multiple use of the territory that will allow the needs of the Maasai to be met as well as those of the wildlife, and that will also conserve the environment.

392 top The black rhino (Diceros bicornis) is increasingly rare. The population in the crater has declined over the last 40 years from several hundred to just 15 or so.

392 center left During daytime, lions generally laze in the shade. They hunt at night, usually led by the lionesses.

392 center right The behavior of the spotted hyena (Crocuta crocuta) is unusual. The female is dominant: she weighs at least 22 pounds more than the male and is much more aggressive.

392 bottom Thompson's gazelle is the most common antelope in central-eastern Africa. There are about 3,000 in Ngorongoro.

393 A lioness has between one and five cubs at a time and is very protective towards them. However, females in a group live in a sort of gynaecium and wean each others' cubs.

Mosi-oa-Tunya/ Victoria Falls

ZAMBIA/ZIMBABWE

LIVINGSTONE (ZAMBIA),
VICTORIA FALLS (ZIMBABWE)
REGISTRATION: 1989
CRITERIA: N (II) (III)

In early November 1855 a group of Kololo indigenes led Dr. Livingstone to the place they called Mosi-oa-Tunya, 'the smoke that thunders'. After a short trip along the Zambezi River, the British explorer saw for the first time what 'at a distance of 6 miles or so seemed the smoke that rises, in Africa, when vast tracts of savannah are burned'. Instead, he was looking at the vaporized water produced by the river as it leaps from Makgadikgadi Pan into the basalt gorges below.

Livingstone dedicated this spectacle of nature to Queen Victoria but he only made the discovery known in Europe when he returned to London four years later. On 3 August 1860 William Baldwin was the second traveler to reach Victoria Falls, which, from that time, became one of Africa's most popular tourist destinations. Visitors arrived on foot, horseback or ox-drawn carts following the route that ran from the Transvaal into the 'hunters' way' along the modern Botswana-Zimbabwe border. Later, it all became much easier thanks to Cecil Rhodes who, in 1900, organized a railway line to the falls, despite never having visited the place himself, and also the construction of a bridge near enough to the bottom of the waterfall for the carts to be reached by the spray.

The Victoria Falls Reserve was created by the colonial government in 1934 but was substituted in 1972 by two national parks (Mosi-oa-Tunya and Victoria Falls), which cover 34 square miles and protect the falls on both the Zambian and Zimbabwean sides of the river.

Formed roughly 2 million years ago

following the rise of the left bank of the river, Victoria Falls is the widest fluvial waterfall in the world: it stretches more than 5,500 feet across and has a maximum drop of 355 feet. During the flood season of the Zambezi (February and March) the river has a flow rate of over 140 million gallons per minute and the sound of the impact can be heard 13 miles away. Placid until that point, at the bottom of the falls the river becomes turbulent and runs violently between the basalt walls of seven successive gorges that correspond to the positions of the falls in remote epochs.

Although the area has no particular wildlife attractions of its own, its contiguity to the Zambezi National Park means that it is frequented by elephants, giraffes, zebras, warthogs and lions, whilst in the calm bends of the river colonies of hippos and crocodiles idle. In contrast, the fluvial fauna is noteworthy as the falls form an evolutional barrier between different sets of species. Equally interesting is the narrow strip of rainforest that grows on the Zimbabwean bank where the land is bathed by the water vapor. The forest is home to many species typical of latitudes closer to the equator

394 top Below the Victoria Falls, the Zambesi River threads its way through a series of basalt gorges creating violent rapids. These clefts mark the position of the falls in ancient times.

394 bottom Indifferent to the majesty of the falls, a Thomson's gazelle (Gazella thomsonii) stands on the Zimbabwean bank of the Zambesi River.

such as ebony (*Diospyros mespiliformis*), date palms (*Phoenix reclinata*) and various species of *Ficus*.

A century and a half after its discovery, Victoria Falls continues to exert an irresistible fascination on its thousands of visitors. And the ancient legend of Yami-Yami, the god of the waterfalls that a chosen few are lucky enough to espy in the churning waters, has developed into a business: the symbol of the pagan god is carved on fragments of basalt and sold as a souvenir, aiding the local economy that has become the most prosperous in all Zimbabwe.

394-395 *Marking the border between Zimbabwe and Zambia, the Victoria Falls form the longest curtain of water in the world in February and March (during the flood season of the Zambesi River) with a flow of 140 million gallons per minute.*

395 right *Mosi-oa-Tunya ('the smoke that roars') is the Kololo name for the Victoria Falls. The nebulized water is similar to a curtain of smoke and the crash can be heard 13 miles away.*

395 bottom *The extraordinary morphology of the territory that has created the Victoria Falls has encouraged the differentiation of fluvial fauna to which the enormous drop represents an uncrossable evolutional boundary.*

ZAMBIA

LUSAKA

HARARE

ZIMBABWE

396

SWAZILAND

PRETORIA

LESOTHO

396 top left With about 300 species of birds, the ecoregion of the Drakensberg is the last refuge of the lammergeier (Gypaetus barbatus) in southern Africa. About 85% of this bird's diet is formed by the bones of dead animals.

396 top right The Drakensberg massif is one of the richest hydrological basins in South Africa, mostly as a result of the abundant rainfall it receives, especially in the summer months from November to March.

Ukhahlamba/Drakensberg Park

SOUTH AFRICA

KwaZulu-Natal
REGISTRATION: 2000
CRITERIA: N (III) (IV); C (I) (III)

Around 8,000 years ago, when Europe and the Middle East were living through the early phases of the Neolithic period, southern Africa was still inhabited by groups of semi-nomadic hunter-gatherers who lived in caves or beneath rock spurs in the bare valleys of the Drakensberg Mountains. One of these peoples, the San, began to decorate the walls and roofs of their caves with paintings of idols, hunting scenes and life in an inhospitable environment where the struggle for survival was daily. Although the vestiges of human settlements suggest that the region has been inhabited for a million years, the rock 'chronicles' of the San are the most concrete evidence of the Paleolithic period in South Africa, and they cover a span of time that reaches right up to the nineteenth century. This was when the country's European colonists, coming up from the Cape, and African peoples like the Zulu and Zhosa, pushed the San out of the mountains towards the stony edges of the Kalahari.

The beauty of the Drakensberg Mountains and their wildness inspired the colonial government of Natal to set up a faunal park in 1903, which developed into the Natal National Park in 1916. In 1947 its boundaries were expanded and the park was renamed the Royal Natal National Park. And, in 1998, officially reverting to African idioms, the government of South Africa again renamed the park, this time the uKhahlamba-Drakensberg Park. Lying between altitudes of 4,200 and 11,480 feet, the 937 square miles of the Drakensberg park are characterized by an extraordinary variety of topography, including plateaus, mountain peaks, rock faces of basalt and sandstone, deep wide valleys and harsh rock formations. A rich hydrological basin favored by a subtropical climate, the park has a lush vegetation that differs strongly between the valleys, mountainsides and plateaus. Overall, there are 2,153 vegetal species, almost 2,000 of which belong to the angiosperm family. More than 200 are endemic to the park and region and 109 of these are considered to be in danger.

The fauna has 48 species of mammals, almost 300 birds, 48 reptiles, 26 amphibians and eight fish, but the invertebrates too – of which no precise census has been taken – contribute fundamentally to the ecological balance. They include 74 species of butterfly (equal to 7% of all those in South Africa), 32 millipedes and 44 dragonflies. The amphibians include three species of especially interesting frogs (*Rana vertebralis*, *R. dracomontana* and *Strongylopus hymenopus*) as they only live at high altitudes and in low temperatures, while the birds include many endemics. The mammals number 16 species of rodents, the largest population of otter in South Africa, 15 carnivores and 11 artiodactyls, of which there are 1,500 antelope (*Pelea capriolus*) and 2,000 eland (*Taurotragus oryx*), the world's largest antelope. The park is not home to mammals threatened by extinction and, surprisingly, has none of Africa's large predators. These can now only be seen in the hunting scenes painted by the San.

396-397 The natural amphitheater in the Drakensberg is a hemicircle of volcanic rock over 3 miles in diameter. The 937 square miles of the park enclose an extraordinary topographical variety.

397 bottom An expanse of red-hot poker plants (Kniphofia uvaria) covers the valley bottom overlooked by the massive Drakensberg amphitheater. The protected area lies at an altitude between 4,200 and 11,500 feet.

Tsingy de Bemaraha Strict Nature Reserve

MADAGASCAR

NORTHERN PART OF THE REGION
OF ANTSINGY
REGISTRATION: 1990
CRITERIA: N (III) (IV)

The sifaka (*Propithecus verraux deckeni*) is the largest and mainly a daytime creature, whereas the tilitilivaha (*Microcebus murinus*) is no larger than a rat and only comes out at night, but there are nine other species of lemur in the Tsingy de Bemaraha reserve that range between these two extremes.

There are golden-crowned Sifaka *Propithecus tattersalli* and the mongoose lemur (*Eulemur mongoz*), Perrier's sifaka (*Propithecus diadema perrieri*) and the Milne-Edwards lemur (*Lepilemur edwardsi*). And recently observed is one of the most rare species of lemur, the aye-aye (*Daubentonia madagascariensis*), which loves the depths of the forest.

The 587 square miles of the Tsingy de Bemaraha Nature Reserve, in the west of Madagascar, were placed under protection for the first time in 1927 to safeguard an environment of extraordinary beauty that was once almost inaccessible to man. Bounded to the east by a 1,000-1,300-foot precipice that drops down to the Manabolo River, the Bemaraha Plateau is formed by a karstic limestone mass that the erosive action of the river and rain waters has sculpted into a network of ravines and fissures separated by sharp pinnacles and spires: the Tsingy.

The climate is tropical with a dry season that lasts six to eight months and a wet one from November to March. The relatively high rainfall has fostered the proliferation of a dense deciduous forest that alternates, in the less hostile areas, with anthropogenic savannah. The few studies made on the vegetation have recorded roughly 430 species of which 85% are endemic, owing to the different evolution of island species. For example, the east coast ebony (*Diospyros perrieri*), the only wild banana tree in Madagascar (*Musa perrieri*) and various species of *Delonix* are unique. There are also baobabs, Orchidaceae, Euphorbiaceae,

Bombaceae and leguminous plants and many xerophytic plants like the aloe.

Equally scarce have been studies on the park's fauna, for which the number of species is very uncertain and the sources are in disagreement. Besides the lemurs, the more interesting species are a small endemic rodent (*Nesomys rufus lambertoni*) and the chameleon (*Brookesia perarmata*) of which only a few have been seen. In total, there are 13 species of amphibians and some dozens of reptiles, including the Nile crocodile (*Crocodylus niloticus*) and species of the *Uroplatus* and *Brookesia* genera. The zone is also frequented by numerous birds, both terrestrial and aquatic: 30 of the 100 pairs of ospreys in Madagascar – one of the rarest birds of prey in the world – nest at the entrances to the ravines or by the Tsingy Lakes.

A curious fact is that though Tsingy de Bemaraha is the largest protected area in west Madagascar in size and biodiversity, it suffers from lack of maintenance. In fact the World Wildlife Fund emphasized the need for greater attention to be paid to its conservation. Whereas the park was impenetrable by man until a few years ago, now several families have settled inside it where they graze animals and cultivate crops, as do the inhabitants of nearby villages. This means fires in the open areas and on the edges of the forests; and the primary deciduous forests that used to cover Madagascar before human settlement have already been reduced by 3%.

398-399 The chaotic deciduous forest in Tsingy grows in ravines, fissures and gorges and has a very high percentage of endemic species.

399 top Extraordinary canyons exist in Tsingy. The difficulty of moving around in this zone has prevented accurate classification of the flora and fauna, which still remain largely unknown.

399 bottom Having remained impenetrable to man until the mid-twentieth century, today Tsingy de Bemaraha Natural Reserve has been invaded by local peoples, with the consequent risk of compromising the exceptional biodiversity with their agriculture and livestock grazing.

398 Bemaraha highland is an immense mass of limestone with karstic phenomena. Erosion by rainwater and surface water has created the pinnacles ('tsingi') that has given the park its name.

ANTANANARIVO

Aldabra Atoll

SEYCHELLES

REGISTRATION: 1982
CRITERIA: N (II) (III) (IV)

400 top Aldabra is the only place in the Indian Ocean where the red-footed booby nests.

400 bottom The atoll is home to 150,000 giant tortoises, the last on the planet.

Aldabra is the largest atoll in the world and lies to the south of the main island in the Seychelles, Mahé, towards Madagascar. The first documentation of the atoll was made in 1511 by the Portuguese when one of their maps mentioned Ilha Dara (Aldabra), a name with an Arab origin: *al Khadra* ('the Green One'). It seems that the Portuguese navigators were facing in such a direction that they saw the green reflection of the waters inside the atoll.

The first to place a flag on one of the 13 islands that compose the atoll were the French in 1742 when the expedition led by Lazare Picault and Jean Grossin discovered the Seychelles Archipelago. At the start of the nineteenth century the islands were conquered by the British navy and, later, began to be appreciated by British naturalists, first and foremost Charles Darwin.

The first to make extensive studies of the atoll's ecosystem was Jacques-Yves Cousteau when he sailed there in 1954 on the Calypso. The distance of the atoll from the other islands in the archipelago and its lack of fresh water have prevented permanent human settlement but that did not stop the British navy from proposing it as a naval base at the start of the 1960s.

The intervention of the Royal Society and the Smithsonian Institution brought an end to the project and so Aldabra Atoll has remained one of the most remote and unspoiled environments in the world.

Like all formations of this type, the atoll is volcanic in origin, created roughly 125,000 years ago.

The islands that surround it are set on two separate tables, at 13 and 26 feet above sea level. The lagoon is nearly 22 miles across and covers a surface area of roughly 40 square miles. It communicates with the ocean through four main outlets. The maximum depth of the lagoon is little more than 10 feet at high tide and 80% of the bed is exposed at low tide.

The flora on the atoll consists of 198 vegetal species, 19 of which are endemic, but what makes Aldabra so special is the variety of its fauna.

Its most outstanding inhabitant is the giant tortoise (*Geochelone gigantea*), which was one of the first species to be protected in the world thanks to the efforts of Darwin who made entreaties on its behalf to the Governor of Mauritius. Once common throughout the Indian Ocean, this animal now remains only on Aldabra, where there are approximately 150,000, three times the population of the famous tortoises in the Galápagos Islands. As a male adult can reach a length of nearly 4 feet, weigh 550 pounds and live for 100 years, the impact of the species on the atoll's fragile environment is comparable to that of the elephants in the African savannah. Aldabra is also an egg-laying area for the green turtle (*Chelonia mydas*).

There are many species of birds, some of which are very rare, like the white-throated rail (*Dryolimnas cuvieri aldabranus, the last flightless bird in the Indian Ocean*), a species of egret

401 top Seen from above,
Aldabra Atoll is a
patchwork of crystalline
colors, with all shades of
turquoise, aquamarine,
lapis lazuli and cobalt. The
lagoon has a diameter of 21
miles and has a surface area
of 37 square miles.

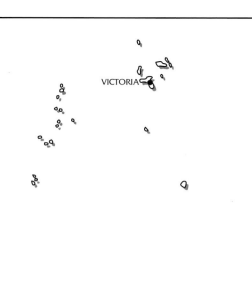

400-401 Aldabra has four
outlets to the ocean, one of
which can be seen like a
branched river in the upper
right of the picture. The
maximum depth is roughly
10 feet at high tide, but
80% of the bed remains
exposed at low tide.

401 bottom In the western
channel of Aldabra atoll there
are spectacular rock
'mushrooms' shaped by the
erosion of the sea. The local
currents are considered by
some to be one of the
strongest natural forces on
the planet.

402 top A tangle of mangrove roots in the shallow waters of the atoll. Aldabra has 198 species of vegetation, 19 of which are endemic.

402 center A nurse shark (Nebrus ferrugineus) moves cautiously over the lagoon bed. About 10 feet long, like other sharks of this type it is generally harmless to man.

402 bottom Aldabra is the kingdom of turtles and tortoises. Besides the Geochelone gigantica, here there are green turtles (Chelonia mydas), the loggerhead turtle (Caretta caretta), and the hawksbill turtle (Eretmochelys imbricate). These long-living reptiles rival the sharks for being the most ancient creatures on the planet.

(*Egretta gularis dimorpha*) and the sacred ibis of Aldabra (*Threskiornis aethiopica abbottii*).

Particular mention should be made of the marine fauna that lives along the coral reef. The many varieties of coral and sponges favor the proliferation of microorganisms that provide nourishment to approximately 200 species of highly colored tropical fish. These include angel fish, butterfly fish, scorpion fish, needlefish and puffer fish; then there are many species of crab, large bivalves, anemones and mollusks, which make Aldabra a paradise for the few and fortunate divers allowed here.

402-403 A shoal of snappers (Lutjanus monostigma and Lutjanus eherembergi) explore the submerged mangrove roots. Snappers get their name from their aggressive behavior towards other members of the same species.

403 bottom Of Aldabra's 13 land birds, there are the Aldabran drongo (Dicrurus aldabranus), which nests in the mangroves, and the white-throated rail (Dryolimnas cuvieri aldabranus), which is the only flightless bird in the Indian Ocean.

404

404 top right Gorgonias
(sea fans) are so called for
their similarity to the hair of
the ancient Greek gorgon.
They form colonies with an
appearance like trees. They
belong to the Class
Anthozoa and have a horny
skeleton but, unlike
calcareous corals, they are
flexible.

404 center A long-nose
hawkfish (Oxycirrhites
typus) rests on a soft coral
or alcyonaria.

404 bottom The sea
cucumber is a member of
the echinoderm family. It
has a soft, flexible and
warty skin and it moves
slowly, contracting its
longitudinal and circular
muscles.

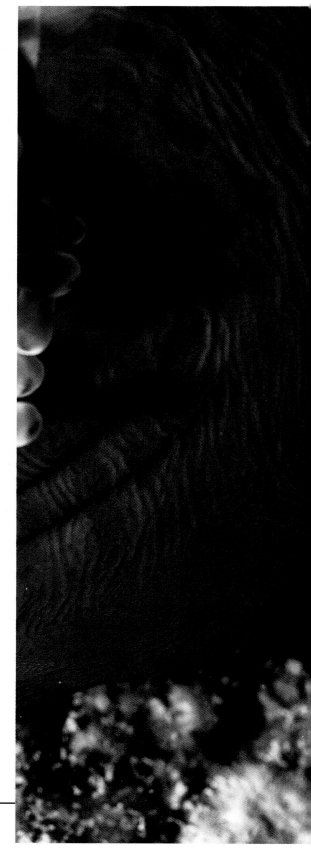

404-405 *The porcelain crab is found throughout the Indian Ocean. It lives in association with large anemones (seen here with a Hetaractis magnifica), and it camouflages itself in their tentacles.*

405 top *A school of snubnose pompano (Trachinotus blochii) dazzles the reef waters with silvery glints. These fish are generally mid-sea dwellers but towards sundown they move close to rocks or coral where they feed mainly on bivalve mollusks.*

Pamukkale

TURKEY

406 top Pamukkale ('cotton castle') is the modern Turkish name of the ancient spa town of Hierapolis. The name emphasizes the site's unusual limestone formations.

The long colonnaded avenue, the Plateia, was a wide road paved with enormous blocks of travertine by the Romans in the second century AD and was the hub around which the daily life of Hierapolis revolved. Hierapolis was an important spa city, situated 14 or so miles north of Denizle in southwest Turkey, that was founded in the second century BC by Eumenes II, the king of Pergamum, on a site where a community had flourished many centuries earlier.

Hierapolis ('Sacred City') owed this

406 bottom The spring water that flows down the Cal Dag'i Plateau halts in large pools where it cools, freeing calcium carbonate that it has collected from the subsoil. The carbonate then flows over the edges of the pools to create columns of travertine.

attention to an unusual property found in its subsoil: water rich with the mineral salt calcium bicarbonate. The water collects the salt as it passes through a limestone stratum on its passage to the surface. This water provides the thermal baths that, according to the ancients, are of exceptional curative powers as well as

being of dramatic appearance. Their white rocky formations have given rise to their modern Turkish name, *Pamukkale*, which means 'cotton castle'. And this is their principal aspect of interest.

Descending the gentle slope of Cal Dag'i Plateau, the mineral rich spring water, which has a temperature of 95°F, collects in pools and ravines where it cools, thus liberating the dissolved calcium carbonate. As the water cools first on the edges of the pools, the travertine precipitates more quickly there and columns of increasingly thicker layers are formed. On average, Pamukkale's springs deposit over 140,000 cubic feet of travertine each year. Over their estimated life of 14,000 years, the accumulation of deposits has created an unreal landscape of mineral forests, petrified cascades, spires and terraces that has always attracted the curiosity of the local people.

The therapeutic powers of Pamukkale's waters have been legendary since before the Roman era. The geographer Strabo reported that Hierapolis was famous for its thermal waters and the Plutonium, a paved room that collected fumes that are poisonous to both men and animals. For the local population, the spring waters have the necessary chemical properties to clean the cotton produced in the area (another reason for Pamukkale's name) and to fix the colors of the materials when they are dyed. The therapeutic value of the thermal springs is derived from their mineral content, in particular, calcium carbonate and sulfate, and iron, sulfur and magnesium salts.

Pamukkale springs and the ruins of the cultural site of Roman Hierapolis continue to be a very popular tourist attraction. It is to preserve the naturalistic and archeological value of this site that the Turkish authorities have launched a series of conservation projects since 1976 as part of an agreement between the countries that ring the Mediterranean.

406-407 It is thought that 14,000 years were required for the water rich in mineral salts to form the 330-foot tall forest of petrified waterfalls, spires and terraces seen today.

407 bottom Spread across a mile and a half, the spring-water waterfalls of Pamukkale deposit a volume of 140,000 cubic feet of travertine each year. The mineral salt content is prevalently calcium carbonate and calcium sulphate and is responsible for the legendary curative properties of the water.

ANKARA

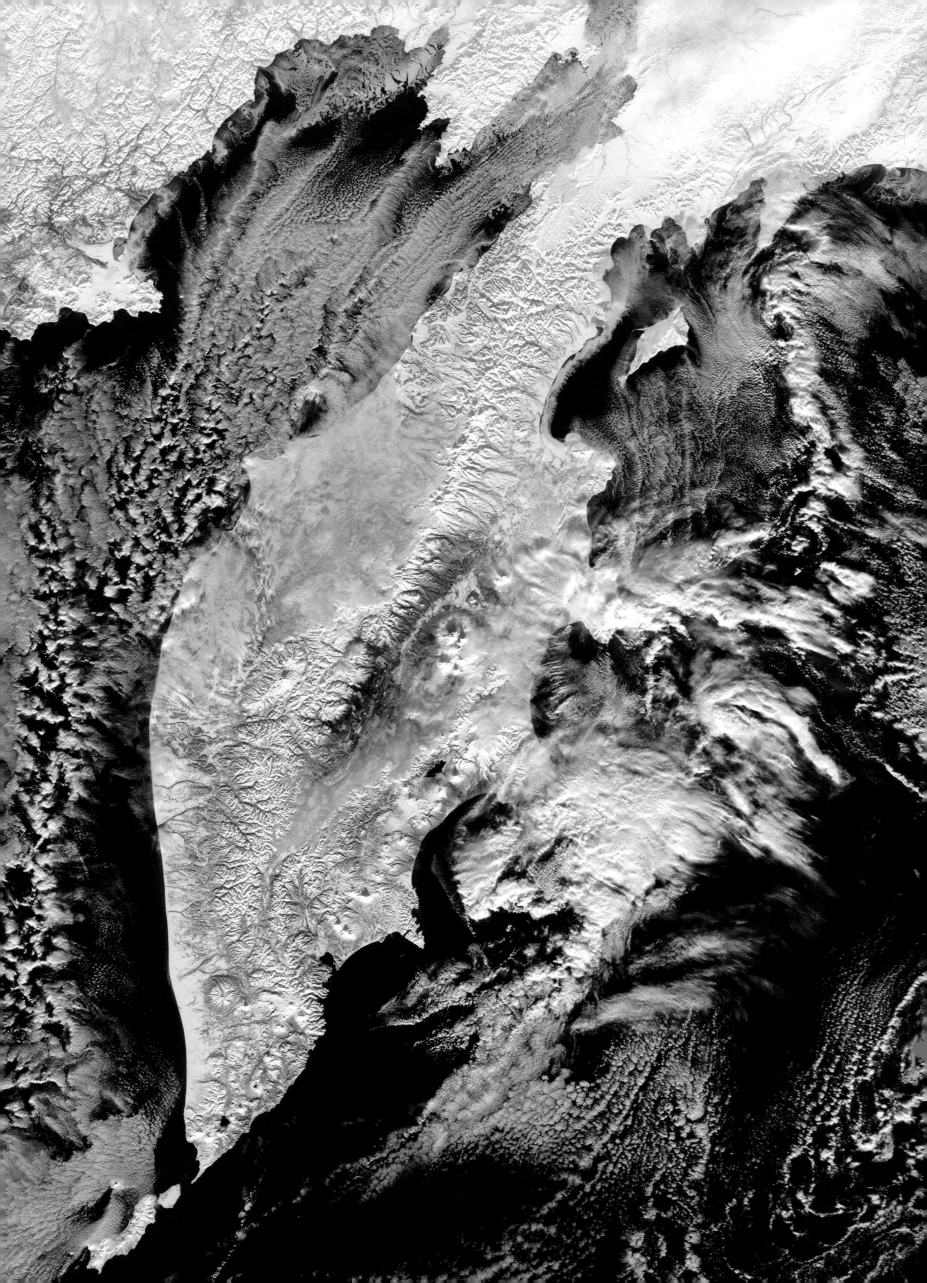

The Kamchatka Volcanoes
RUSSIAN FEDERATION

KAMCHATKA PENINSULA
REGISTRATION: 1996, 2001
CRITERIA: N (I) (II) (III) (IV)

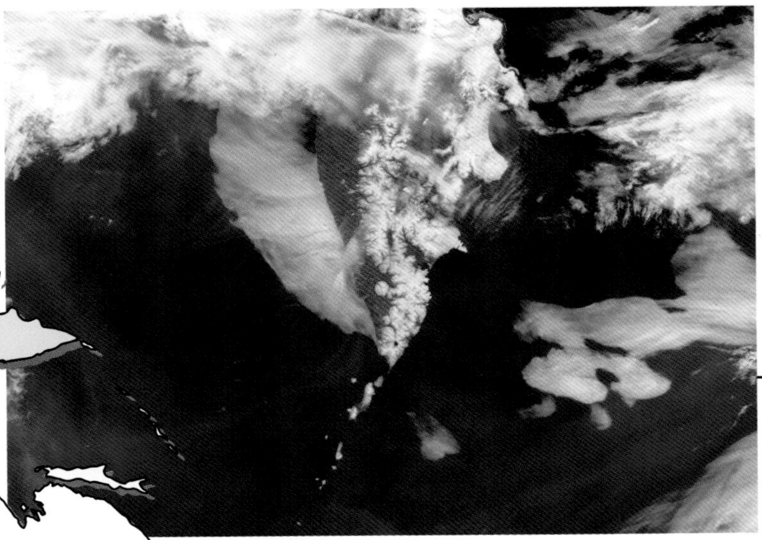

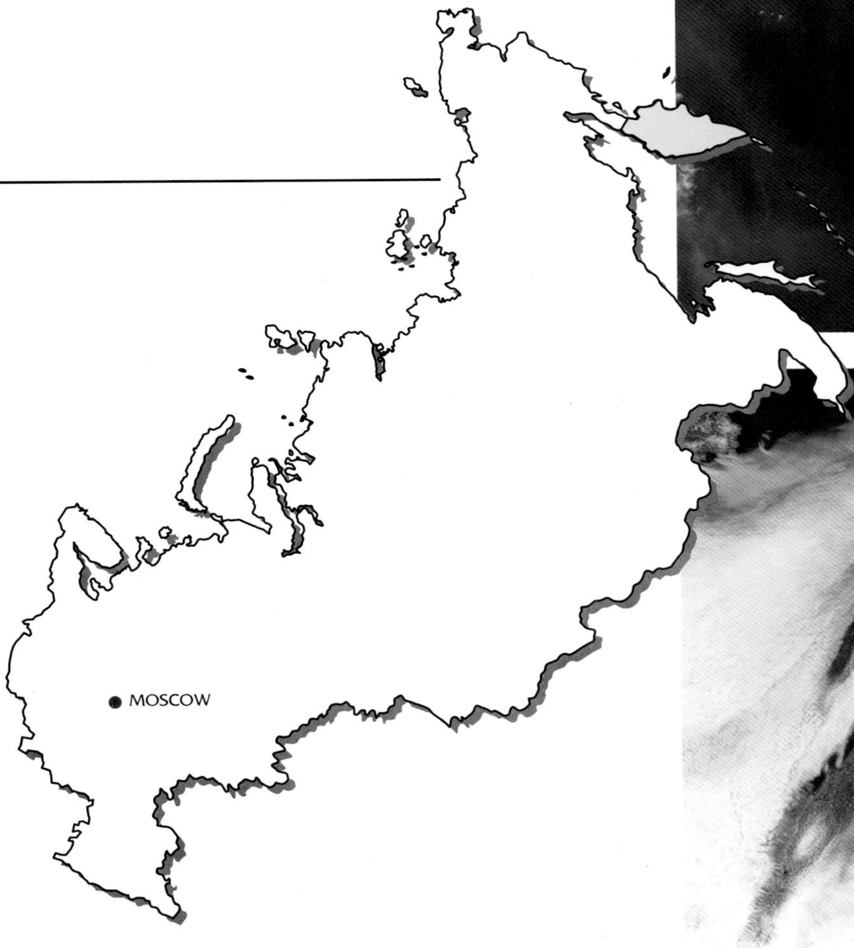

• MOSCOW

408 *During winter Kamchatka is completely covered by ice, as is seen in this photograph taken from a NASA satellite of the valleys that slope down into Sredinnyyi Khrebet, the volcanic chain in the center of the peninsula.*

409 top *Photographed from space in 2001, we see a long plume of smoke streak the skies of Siberia.*

409 bottom *The 14,270 square miles of the Kamchatka Volcano Reserve covers 29 active volcanoes, 300 extinct volcanoes and 150 thermal springs.*

At a height of 15,600 feet above sea level, the perfectly conical Mount Kluchevskoy is the highest active volcano in Eurasia; it and its sister mountains Kamen, Bezymyanny and Plosky Tolbackik, together form the volcanic complex of Kluchevskaya. Its first eruption to be recorded by man occurred in 1697 when the Russian explorer Vladimir Atlasov found himself before it for the first time. Since then, vulcanologists have noted at least one eruption every five years, but Kluchevskoy, like Kamchatka's other volcanoes, has never been a danger to the local people.

This is not the only attraction on the peninsula that stretches between the Sea of Okhotsk and the Bering Sea. The 11,575-foot high Mount Kronotsky is also a perfect cone though it is not so high. The Uzon Volcano, formed 40,000 years ago, is one of the most interesting geological phenomena in the area; it covers an area of 36 square miles and has a crater like an enormous bowl with walls between 650 and 2,600 feet high. A vast hydrothermal system has been formed inside in which minerals are in processes of constant production.

Included in the World Heritage list in 1996, the vast Kamchatka Volcano Reserve covers 14,270 square miles.

It is divided into six sections that offer a complete overview of the many volcanic activities that occur in the region. The peninsula lies on the meeting point of different circumpacific tectonic plates in an area subject to intense volcanic activity.

The reserve covers many of the 29 volcanoes still active in the peninsula, roughly 300 extinct volcanoes and over 150 thermal and mineral sources. Dozens of geysers, fumaroles and waterfalls line the sharply peaked mountains, on whose flanks turquoise lakes and fields of colored seaweed make the Geyser Valley a fairytale landscape.

The great variety of climates in the volcanic region has encouraged the development of an extremely rich and diverse vegetation, including vast expanses of tundra and taiga, and 1,168 species of giant grasses and wild berries, 10% of which are endemic to Kamchatka.

The fauna numbers 145 species of birds such as eagles, cormorants, puffins, geese, ducks, gulls and swans. The 33 mammals include brown bears, elk, gray wolves, caribou, mountain sheep and foxes. An endangered species is Steller's sea eagle (*Haliaetus pelagicus*), half of whose world population lives here in Kamchatka. Another animal under threat is the Kamchatka bear (*Ursus arctos*), which is a subspecies of the brown bear. It is also related to the 10,000 grizzly bears that make the peninsula their home.

The most extraordinary sight on Kamchatka occurs between the start of summer and winter when millions of salmon – belonging to the five species

410 top Taken from the Endeavor space shuttle on 30 September 1994, this photograph shows one of the most recent eruptions of Kluchevskoy, which, at 15,584 feet, is the highest active volcano in Asia.

410 center Lying on the meeting point of various tectonic plates, Kamchatka is one of the most intense volcanic areas on the ring that circles the Pacific Ocean.

410 bottom Inside the reserve there is a glacial lake that formed in the crater of an extinct volcano.

410-411 The perfect cone of most of the volcanoes in Kamchatka is a characteristic of their nature as stratovolcanoes, which means they have been formed over tens or hundreds of thousands of years by the accumulation of eruptive materials.

411 This aerial view of the Kliuchi group is dominated in the background by the cone of Kluchevskoy. The group includes the volcanoes Udina, Zimina, Bezymianny, Kaman and Tolbachik, which ring the highest peak.

412 top Geysers, fumaroles, turquoise lakes and fields of polychrome algae make Geyser Valley a unique sight. The remote Kamchatka was explored by Russians at the end of the seventeenth century.

412-413 A close relation of the American grizzly, the Kamchatka bear is a subspecies of Ursus arctos. During hibernation – which ends in May – it loses about 30% of its body weight.

of Pacific salmonids – tackle the currents of the many rivers to reach their place of birth and reproduction. In that period of the year, Kamchatka has the most crowded salmon population in the world.

The peninsula's recent opening up to tourism and mineral exploitation has created a serious risk to the delicate environmental balances.

A plan for gold mining a few miles from the Bystinsky Nature Park has not yet been approved by the government, simply because of a lack of sufficient funding. If the project does go ahead, it would inevitably affect one of the unspoilt ecosystems of the region.

413 top Around 10,000 Kamchatka bears live on the peninsula. After the mating season, these plantigrades spend most of their time solitarily.

413 center At the start of summer, millions of fish from the five species of Pacific salmon begin their journeys up the rivers, where the bears lie in wait for them.

413 bottom The fox (Alopex lagopus) is white in winter and tawny in summer. It does not hibernate and, during winter, feeds on carcasses or prey killed by other animals.

Huanglong
and Jiuzhaigou
CHINA

PROVINCE OF SICHUAN
REGISTRATION: 1992
CRITERIA: N (III)

It cannot be said that the Chinese are not trying everything possible to save the giant panda (*Ailuropoda melanoleuca*), which, for more than 40 years, has been the emblem of the World Wildlife Fund and the symbol of all species threatened by extinction, for, in addition to protecting the fragile habitat in which this mammal lives (though in a rather disjointed and reluctant manner), they have tried to stimulate the apparent reduction in sexual desire of the pandas, using pornographic films and Viagra, and have even made a weak attempt at cloning.

The situation is not rosy but artificial insemination has produced some results. In Wulong, for example, the population of the pandas has risen to 55 compared to 20 in 1998. Fewer in number are the pandas in the Jiuzhaigou Valley, which were estimated to be just 17 in 1996, while in the adjacent reserve of Huanglong four communities have been recorded in the five areas able to provide them with a habitat. They are not many and

their proximity to Wanglang Reserve heightens their chances of survival.

Situated in northern Sichuan – China's gateway to inland Asia – the histories of the Huanglong and Jiuzhaigou Valleys run in parallel. Created at the end of the 1970s, they have respective areas of 270 and 278 square miles. They lie in a mountainous area of complicated tectonic development where the peaks reach 16,400 feet. Both sites are crossed by fault lines that produce intense and frequent seismic activity. From a geological standpoint, both are characterized by Paleozoic carbonate rock covered by recent deposits of alluvial gravel and glacial moraines. On these lie deposits of calcite that form huge areas of travertine and limestone, which give rise to karstic phenomena. There are many glacial lakes at high levels and the landscape is strongly characterized by ravines and precipices; in fact, the name Jiuzhaigou means 'the valley of the nine ravines'.

The contiguity of the two areas is also reflected in their fairly uniform vegetation. At low levels, between 5,500 and 7,500 feet, there is a strip of forest dominated by Chinese fir (*Picea asperata*) and maples (*Acer yiu, Acer*

414 top The protected area of Huanglong lies in the climatic transition zone between the Himalayan, sub-tropical and tropical regions in the Northern Hemisphere. The temperatures range from -11 to +86°F.

414 bottom Huanglong's surface is 65.8% covered by forest. At low levels (between 5,600 and 7,500 feet) the predominant species are Chinese fir (Picea asperata) and three species of maple.

414-415 The area of Huanglong is renowned for the number of water sources with high mineral levels that appear to have curative properties. The water that gushes from Zhuzhuhu hydrothermal has a temperature of 70°F and forms a series of natural swimming pools.

415 top Chosen by the World Wildlife Fund as the symbol of nature conservation, the giant panda (Ailuropoda melanoleuca) now only lives in the mountains of Sichuan. Despite attempts by scientists, its population is dropping rapidly and attempts to encourage reproduction in captivity have produced very poor results.

BEIJING

416 top left Jiuzhaigou is a complex hydrological system: its main rivers all flow into the Jiailing which, in turn, feeds into the immense river system of the Yangtze.

416 top right The bottom of Lake Wolonghai has a curious limestone formation that the locals consider to be a dragon. Traditional legends – and recent belief – has it that monsters live in the lakes of Jiuzhaigou, a claim that some scientists are taking seriously.

416 bottom The 19 lakes in Shuzeng and 18 in Nuorilang all lie in the protected area of Jiuzhaigou. They are like water terraces separated by formations of travertine that resemble small dikes.

erianthum and Acer davidii). Higher up there are conifers with various species of fir, larch and birch, while at heights of 12,000-13,800 feet the land develops into large alpine meadows of grass and shrubs. The many botanical species in both sites (101 in Huanglong and 92 in Jiuzhaigou) are considered to be of extreme interest for the rate of endemics, their ornamental value and for their use in traditional Chinese medicine.

Besides the giant panda, the fauna includes 59 mammals in Huanglong but only 10 or so in Jiuzhaigou, though these figures are the result of unsystematic research. The most interesting mammals are the snub-nosed langur (*Pygatrix roxellanae*), which is also under threat owing to reduction of its natural habitat, the lesser panda (*Ailurus fulgens*), the Asiatic black bear (*Selenarctos*

thibetanus) and the takin (*Budorcas taxicolor thibetana*).

Although wrapped in legend for the role they have played in Tibetan religion and tradition, the inaccessibility of these mountains has made them unsuitable for human settlement and the two valleys of Huanglong and Jiuzhaigou are only inhabited by small villages with a total population of just 1,500. Yet that does not mean that no threat from man exists to the areas; indeed their conservation is a worrying task. A massive government campaign to encourage tourism in internal China has increased the number of visitors to the zone enormously, which have now reached 300,000 a year. In addition, large sections of the forest have been cut down for agricultural use by the surrounding populations and fires and pollution have also added to the threats to the pandas.

416-417 *Zhengshutan Waterfall is the one that attracts most attention of the many in Jiuzhaigou. Its is 1,017 feet wide and has an average drop of 92 feet over a travertine hill. Formations of this nature, in continual evolution, are as common in this area as in Huanglong.*

417 top 2.2 miles long, *the spectacular Huanglonggou ('Throat of the Yellow Dragon') is a series of travertine pools in which algae tint the water with extraordinary purity, giving hues of yellow, green and blue.*

Shirakami-Sanchi

JAPAN

PREFECTURE OF AOMORI AND AKIRA,
REGION OF HONSHU
REGISTRATION: 1993
CRITERIA: N (II)

Respect for the past, for ancestors and tradition is a characteristic of the Japanese and this is why the last beech forest to have survived in the country is looked after with such care and strict conservation regulations. These beech trees, of the species *Fagus crenata*, grow in the Shirakami Mountains in northern Honshu.

The forest is called Shirakami-Sanchi and has been protected since 1992. It is 65 square miles in size and lies in a remote area at between 3,280-3,940 feet in altitude. It suffers cold, snowy winters owing to its proximity to the Sea of Japan and the masses of cold air that arrive from Siberia. From a geomorphological viewpoint, the Shirakami Mountains are formed by sedimentary rocks over a base of granite and were created following strong telluric movements during the Quarternary period. The landscape is a dizzying sequence of ravines and slopes, most of which are steeper than 30 degrees. The rare paths often disappear between the rocks, as there is almost no trace of human presence despite ancient documents alluding to mining during the Daido period at the start of the ninth century. It even seems that the famous statue of the Giant Buddha of Nara was fused using copper mined at Shirakami. The villagers at the foot of the mountains occasionally climb up to the forest to collect mushrooms and medicinal plants, and each year roughly 3,000 sportsmen and hunters climb Mount Huatsamori on the edge of the protected area to perpetuate an ancient bear-hunting ceremony called *Matagi*.

In addition to the beech trees, Shirakami-Sanchi forest has 500 vegetal species. This number is not particularly high if compared to other Japanese mountain areas, but the flora is of great interest for its endemic species, for several plants considered to be in global danger, such as *Hylotelephim tsugaruense* and *Poa ogamontana*, and for unusual varieties of orchids such as *Calanthe discolor*, *Cypripedium yatabeanum* and *Tipularia japonica*.

The trees and rocky spurs are the favorite nesting places of the birds. Of the 87 species that have made the forest their home, some – like the black woodpecker (*Dryocopus martius*), golden eagle (*Aquila chrysaetos*) and hawk eagle (*Spizaetus nipalensis*) – are on the International Union for the Conservation of Nature's Red List and have been awarded the status of National Monument in Japan. This title has also been conferred upon two mammals that live in Shirakami: the serow (*Capricornis crispus*), a large primitive looking herbivore, and the Japanese dormouse (*Glirulus japonicus*), which is a nocturnal rodent that hibernates in the hollows of trees, rolled up into a ball.

Considering animals and plants as National Monuments (on a level with the pagodas of Kyoto) is an attitude explained by the philosophies of the Far East. Their protection is, for the Japanese, imperative and is instilled in the conscience of each individual. So much so that in 1981, well before the protected area was set up, a battle was won by the local population against the authorities that had approved the construction of a road to join the prefectures of Aomori and Akira, but which would most certainly have endangered the environmental balance.

TOKYO

418 left The beech trees of the Fagus crenata species dominate typical Japanese temperate forests. Unfortunately, the 65 square miles of Shirakami-Sanchi are the last remaining shred of primary forest in the country.

418 top right A recent discovery is that the Harlequin duck (Histrionicus histrionicus), a multicolored sea duck, nests on the Akaishi River in the Shirakami Mountains.

419 Having adapted to living in cold climates, the population of the Japanese macaque (Macaca fuscata) has been decimated over the last few decades by deforestation and illegal hunting and the creature is now on the IUCN's Red List.

Sagarmatha National Park

NEPAL

KHUMBU

REGISTRATION: 1979

CRITERIA: N (III)

They walk barefoot in the snow and are amazingly strong and adapted to the inclement climate. They enjoy long lives and are a peaceful, pragmatic people who follow the philosophy of Tibetan Buddhism to the letter. They are the Sherpa, the 'people who came from the east', who live in the Nepalese region of Khumbu on the slopes of the world's highest mountain, Everest. They arrived here from Kham in eastern Tibet at the end of the sixteenth century, having crossed Nangpa La pass at a height of 19,350 feet.

To the Sherpa, mountains are sacred and in ancient times they considered climbing them a blasphemous act. Everest – at 29,029 feet high – in their language was called *Chomolangma*, the 'mother-goddess', to whom was attributed the role of supreme deity in the Himalayas. The region of Khumbu, most of which lies in Sagarmatha National Park (the Nepalese name for Everest), encloses three mountains over the magic figure of 26,246 feet: they are Lhotse (27,940 feet), Cho Oyu (29,906 feet) and of course Everest itself.

About 3,500 Sherpa live within the boundaries of the world's highest park and their livelihood has been increasingly dependent on mountain tourism since 1953, when Everest was first climbed by the New Zealander Edmund Hillary and Tenzing Norgay, the first Sherpa to violate the sacred mountain. Forty years later, the first woman to reach the summit was Pasang Lhamu.

Sagarmatha National Park covers an area of 443 square miles. It contains glaciers, ravines, wide valleys and the sources of two rivers (the Dudh Kosi and the Bhote Kosi). The lowest point in the park is at a height of 9,343 feet and traveling from there up to the peaks one passes through four different climatic zones. In the first grow juniper, birch, fir, bamboo and rhododendrons that grow up to 30 feet in height. The blooming of the rhododendrons in March and April is one of the most spectacular sights in the region. The second climatic zone is dominated by dwarf trees and bushes, then higher up plant life is restricted to mosses and lichen before disappearing altogether around 18,700 feet where lies the permanent snowline.

The lowest section of Sagarmatha offers an ideal habitat to 118 species of birds and many mammals. Common are the musk deer (*Moschus moschiferus*) and the tahr (*Hemitragus jemlahicus*), which is a beardless mountain goat with short horns that curve backwards. But

KATHMANDU

Sagarmatha is not really a park for observation purposes. Many of its most interesting inhabitants are both rare and shy, like the snow leopard (*Felis uncia*), the Himalayan black bear (*Selenarctos tibetanus*) and a species of panda with tawny fur (*Ailurus fulgens*). With the arrival of the monsoon season, the park is populated by 26 species of butterfly.

In recent years, even the paradise that surrounds the roof of the world has suffered from environmental problems. Although the Sherpa are very respectful of their land, the many climbing expeditions have left behind them tons of waste that have attracted the attention and protests of ecological groups. Various clean-up campaigns have been conducted and an annual limit on the number of expeditions is being considered, but there is another threat lying in wait: the shrinking of the glaciers caused by global climate change will not spare even the sacred mountains of the Himalayas.

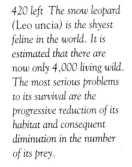

420 left The snow leopard (Leo uncia) is the shyest feline in the world. It is estimated that there are now only 4,000 living wild. The most serious problems to its survival are the progressive reduction of its habitat and consequent diminution in the number of its prey.

420-421 The sacredness of the highest points on the planet is represented by chorten, which are the Tibetan and Nepalese equivalents of the Indian stupa. Prayer flags are tied to the chorten so that the wind can spread their invocations across the world.

421 top A little to the south of Mount Everest, Mount Lhotse is a worthy neighbor of the giant. At a height of 27,939 feet, it is the third tallest mountain in the world and one of the most difficult to climb.

421 bottom Seen here from Kala Pattar (18,448 feet), the unmistakable, pyramidal summit of Everest is seen blazing in the dawn light.

Keoladeo National Park

INDIA

BHARATPUR, RAJASTHAN
REGISTRATION: 1985
CRITERIA: N (IV)

Unsurprisingly, it was the ancient temple of Keoladeo dedicated to Shiva, the Hindu god that creates and destroys, after which one of the most extraordinary protected areas in the subcontinent was named, as it was brought back to life following destructive modifications made to the landscape by man. Now its 11 square miles are a favorite stopping area for migrating birds.

Keoladeo National Park lies close to the edge of the Rajasthan city of Bharatpur and is not a 'natural environment' in the strict sense. Man has molded the countryside in an attempt to save Bharatpur from flooding caused by the monsoons. As early as 1760, the local maharajah had a dam built at Ajan on the edge of a depression in the land to create a lake. Then, at the start of the twentieth century a system of dikes and locks was added to allow the level of the water in the different sections of the lake to be controlled.

These building projects transformed the area into a series of bogs, marshes and meadowland that became a refuge for many species of birds. In consequence, the maharajahs of Bharatpur decreed the zone a duck shooting reserve that attracted famous foreign guests, for example, the British viceroy Lord Curzon. When India gained independence in 1948, Keoladeo became a bird sanctuary but the maharajahs retained shooting rights until 1972. In 1981 Keoladeo was finally awarded the status of a national park.

From September to February the reserve is home to approximately 1 million birds of over 360 migrating

422 top left The axis deer (Cervus axix) with its white-spotted fawn coat, is one of the world's loveliest deer.

422 bottom left Keoladeo is a mosaic of marshes created by man in the eighteenth century.

422 top right The rhesus monkey (Macaca mulatta) is one of the two primate species found in the park.

422 bottom right The trees in Keoladeo are always crowded with birds such as ibis, cormorants and cranes.

423 The water meadows in the park are inhabited by babul trees (Acacia nilotica) and many aquatic plants that form the basis of the diet of many birds.

species, from the gigantic Dalmatian pelican (*Pelecanus crispus*) – which has a wingspan of over 6 feet – to the minuscule Siberian chiffchaff (*Phylloscopus collybita tristis*), which is no longer than a small finger.

Cormorants, egrets, ibises, ducks and cranes arrive from Russia, Europe, China, Mongolia and the plains of Siberia.

A special attraction in the Park is the Siberian crane (*Grus leucogeranus*) – one of the rarest birds on the planet – of

which there are now just a few hundred in existence. To spend the winter here, it flies 425 miles over Afghanistan and Pakistan from the basin of the Ob River.

The park's wealth of microfauna, fish and aquatic flora (such as lotus plants and water lilies) also attracts numerous species of non-migratory birds, like the kingfisher, woodpecker, golden oriole and several species of pigeon.

With the arrival of the summer monsoons, another great spectacle begins in Keoladeo: the nesting of 17 species of heron, which collect in a very restricted area where the *babul* tree (*Acacia nilotica*) is prevalent. Up to 100 nests belonging
to several different species will be built in each tree; the pairs choose to live so close together to unite their forces to defend their young against predators like the peregrine falcon and imperial eagle.

Life in the park is not limited to its birds. Keoladeo is also home to mammals of naturalistic interest like the Bengal fox (*Vulpes bengalensis*), the golden jackal (*Canis aureus*), the boar (*Sus scrofa*) and the black buck (*Antilope cervicapra*). Among the reptiles, there is also an abundant population of pythons.

Being such a superb birdwatching site, Keoladeo receives hundreds of thousands of visitors each year, who represent an important source of income to the local inhabitants.

Of the many varied services offered, visitors can enjoy birdwatching excursions in a traditional rickshaw.

424 top The sarus crane (Grus antigone) is featherless on the upper part of its neck and red head, and is renowned for its complicated courting ritual.

424 bottom The painted stork (Mycteria leucocephala) is one of the many species of waders that live in the park. Another is the Siberian crane, one of the most rare birds on the planet.

424-425 Seen on top of a tree with their wings spread are two painted storks in all their beauty.

425 bottom A visitor to Keoladeo in the winter months, the bar-headed goose (Anser indicus) spends the rest of the year in the Himalayas where it has been seen flying even over Mount Everest.

Ha Long Bay

VIETNAM

GULF OF TONGKING
REGISTRATION: 1994, 2000
CRITERIA: N (I) (III)

The literal translation of Ha Long is 'the place the Dragon entered the sea'. The legend, which was handed down orally until the nineteenth century, says that Ha Long Bay was created during a naval battle between the Viet people and their enemies who sailed down the coast from the north. The Viet were about to lose the battle when the Jade Emperor sent the Mother of all Dragons and one of her young sons to their aid. A huge number of pearls flowed from the dragons' mouths that, on contact with the water, were transformed into beautiful islands that the boats of the enemy ran into and broke upon. And, as the bay was so beautiful, the dragons remained there

to live. This story is so rooted in local tradition that fishermen still talk about a giant sea creature that occasionally appears on the surface of the sea.

Human history in this superb bay is given by archeological studies in the caves that have revealed evidence of the first settlements, dating from 25,000 years ago, in what is today Vietnam.

Ha Long is often described as a natural work of art and has inspired verses by many poets. An area of 580 square miles is dotted with 1,969 islands that range in height from 160 to 640 feet, 989 of these islands have been given names that refer to their picturesque morphology, for example, fighting cocks, pairs of swans, human heads and so forth. And many of the islands have underground caves and hollows that provide the habitat for extremely rare species.

Leaving aside the legend, the geological history of Ha Long Bay began around 500 million years ago with orogenetic processes and tectonic shifts. It continued through the Carboniferous and Permian periods (350-240 million years ago) when the zone was occupied by a sea, the bottom of which was formed by a layer of sandstone up to 1,100 yards thick. Over a period of 20 million years from the Miocene to Pleistocene epochs, strong erosion of the sandstone table (which by then had become a coastal plain) gave origin to the formations of schist and sandstone that today emerge in the bay. The return of the water occurred at the end of the last Ice Age around 10,000 years ago.

Ha Long's biodiversity can be divided into three main ecosystems: the tropical

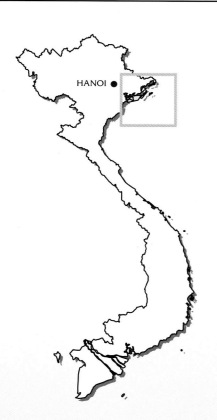

forest and the coastal and marine habitats. The first is typified by an extraordinary variety of botanical species; seven of have been identified by the International Union for the Conservation of Nature as unique in this environment. The forest has 477 species of magnoliophytes, four species of amphibians, eight reptiles, 40 birds and 14 small mammals. The coastal habitat is characterized by 20 varieties of mangrove, whose branches provide shelter to 200 species of birds. And the marine habitat is also very fertile: it contains 170 species of coral (mostly of the genus *Scleractinia*) and 91 algae. The animals include 81 species of gastropods, 130 bivalves, nine crustaceans and 313 fish that feed principally on phytoplankton and zooplankton.

Ha Long's natural ecosystems have recently been joined by an artificial one – fish-breeding – which has caused the destruction of huge areas of mangrove swamp and threatens to alter the biological balance of the bay. And the headlong economic development of Vietnam is exploiting its tourist potential: plans have been made for the construction of a 100 million dollar hotel complex on the island of Tuan Chau.

426-427 There are almost 2,000 islands that range between 160 and 650 feet in height in spectacular Ha Long Bay. Their unusual shapes – with caves hollowed out by sea and rain water – have resulted in their being given traditional picturesque Eastern names.

Kinabalu National Park
MALAYSIA

428 top Weighing 20 pounds and 4.5 feet in diameter, Rafflesia arnoldii is the largest flower on the planet.

'A Hollywood creation' is the term most commonly associated with *Rafflesia arnoldii*, the largest flower in nature. It has a bright red fleshy mass , reaches 3 feet in diameter, can weigh 20 pounds and does not have a pleasant smell. To see it in all its splendor is not an easy task as *Rafflesia arnoldii* is a parasite, without roots or leaves, and can only germinate at the base of Tetrasigma, a woody stem of the vine family. It grows for an entire year and then blooms during a single rainy night, lasting just one week before withering.

The flower was named as a tribute to Sir Thomas Stanford Raffles (1781-1826), the enterprising Englishman who founded the city of Singapore. It was, however, discovered by the botanist Joseph Arnold, who accompanied Raffles on many expeditions to the island of Borneo.

It is easy to imagine his amazement on finding this extraordinary plant in the jungle on the slopes of Mount Kinabalu, and time has not diminished its interest to scientists. Today 16 species of *Rafflesia* have been identified, the last of which was in 1988. Apart from the occasional example found on Sumatra, *Rafflesia* is considered native to Borneo.

This is the location of Mount Kinabalu, the highest mountain in Southeast Asia at 13,435 feet.

Its morphology is the result of volcanic and tectonic activity that took place about 1.5 million years ago, sedimentary processes during the Tertiary period and erosion from glaciation. If that were not enough, scientists have recently recorded a growth in the mountain of a fifth of an inch a year.

The national park that encloses Mounts Kinabalu, Tambuyukon (8,461 feet) and Templer (3,719 feet) and their surrounding countryside contains one of the most profuse ranges of flora on earth. In addition to giants like *Rafflesia arnoldii*

428 bottom left At 13,345 feet, Kinabalu is the highest mountain in Southeast Asia. Its slopes are lined with rainforests that are differentiated biologically depending on altitude.

428 bottom right The many botanical species on Kinabalu include nine carnivorous plants of the Nepenthes genus, 4 of which are endemic to the park.

429 top Langanan Waterfall in the center of the park makes seven leaps, the last of which is a spectacular 490 feet.

429 bottom The wrinkled summit of Kinabalu is deeply furrowed by erosion from ancient glaciers that created moraines, U-shaped valleys and cirques. According to geological estimates, the mountain is growing at a speed of four-tenths of an inch per year.

KUALA
LUMPUR

430 *A colony of 120 orangutans (Simia satyrus) lives on Kinabalu. This number is all that remains after drastic reduction caused by fires (which devastated Borneo) and poaching.*

431 *top left A tree-dwelling primate that lives mainly on fleshy fruits, during periods of scarcity the orangutan gets by on tree bark.*

431 *top right Generally described as solitary primates, orangutans tend to socialize during the mating season and where there are large food resources.*

431 *bottom Territorial animals, orangutans occupy large areas (from 100 acres to 2.5 square miles) and the territory of each overlaps with that of others.*

and the largest insect-eating plant in the world (*Nepenthes rajah*), roughly 6,000 species belonging to 200 families and 1,000 genera have been cataloged, with a high number of endemic plants. There are 1,000 types of orchid, 24 rhododendrons, 52 palms, 135 *Ficus* and 608 ferns. Botanists consider it a point of convergence of the genera of China and the Himalayas with those of Australia and New Zealand and even find affinities there with plants from the American continent.

Inside the park, six zones at levels between 500 feet and the top of Kinabalu contain a large variety of fauna. There are 90 species of mammal that live at low levels and 22 mountain species, including colonies of orangutan and other primates. The birds and butterflies are particularly profuse with 326 and 200 species respectively.

Kinabalu is also a sacred mountain to the Dusun and Kazadan peoples. Its name is derived from the Kazadan words *Aki* and *Nabalu*, which together mean 'the Sacred Place of the Dead'. This sanctuary was the theater of what was sadly known as the Sandakan-Ranu march of death. In September 1944 the Japanese army made 2,400 British and Australian prisoners-of-war walk 150 miles through the jungle. Only six survived. On his return home, one of the survivors, Major Carter of the British army, founded the Kinabalu Memorial Committee. In the United Kingdom, interest for the area led to the organization of many naturalistic expeditions financed by the Royal Society, which, in 1964, resulted in the creation of the National Park.

Komodo National Park

INDONESIA

ISLANDS OF KOMODO, RINCA, PADAR, GILI
DASAM, GILI MOTONG, FLORES
REGISTRATION: 1991
CRITERIA: N (III) (IV)

Due to its size, the inhabitants of the islands called it buaja darat ('land crocodile'), as an adult can measure ten feet in length and weigh around 150 pounds; but the Komodo dragon (*Varanus komodoensis*) is not a crocodile, it belongs to the family of *Varanidae*, of which lizards are members. The *buaja darat* is in fact the largest representative of the order of scaly reptiles and offers researchers an exceptional chance to study evolution. Walter Auffenberg, a pioneer of the study of these descendants of the dinosaurs, said, 'When this animal decides to attack, nothing can stop it.'

This is perhaps the reason why innumerable legends have flourished about the capabilities of this fearsome predator, despite it only being able to move at most at 12 mph. What is certain is that it was to protect this extraordinary example of evolution that the islands of Padar and Rinca were declared a Nature Reserve as far back as 1938, to which the island of Komodo was added in 1965. In 1980 the Komodo National Park was set up over an area of 290 square miles. Four years later a part of Flores was added and some of the waters that encircle these islands in the Sonda Archipelago, so that the park now covers almost 850 square miles.

The morphology of the islands reflects their position in the middle of the Sonda volcanic platform. The land is marked by a continuous series of steep ridges that continue out to sea and enclose inaccessible inlets.

Komodo, the largest island, is dominated by a chain of hills aligned north to south that do not exceed 1,850 feet in height. This is a structure also seen on other islands.

The vegetation is typical of a tropical though not particularly rainy climate (31-39 inches during the monsoon season from November to April), and is predominated by grasslands of anthropic origin that cover roughly 70% of the land surface of the National Park. Some of the most widespread grasses are *Eulalia leschenaultiana*, *Setaria adhaerens* and *Chloris Barbata*, while the most common of the forest trees is the species of palm *Borassus flabellifer*.

The wildlife on Komodo includes many species of birds, reptiles and

432 top Situated in the southeast section of the Sonda Archipelago, between Sumbawa and Flores, Komodo has an area of 130 square miles and is dominated by a chain of hills that do not exceed 1,970 feet in height.

432 bottom left The Komodo dragon (Varanus komodoensis) measures up to 10 feet in length, weighs 300 pounds and is the largest scaly reptile on earth. In the past it was erroneously believed to be poisonous like other reptiles, but its bite is so strong that it can cause serious infections and even be lethal to man. Eating mainly carcasses, the creature is a carrier of dangerous bacteria that breed in its jaws.

432 bottom right A group of 'dragons' drinks from a freshwater pool. Used to living alone or in small groups, this reptile's favorite habitat is deciduous tropical forest or, to a lesser extent, open grassland.

433

433 Measuring 7.8 square miles in area, the island of Padar is the only one on which the Komodo dragon is now extinct (since the 1970s), probably because its prey was exterminated by hunters.

JAKARTA

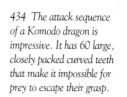

434 *The attack sequence of a Komodo dragon is impressive. It has 60 large, closely packed curved teeth that make it impossible for prey to escape their grasp.*

amphibians; there are also seven species of terrestrial mammals, including the endemic rat *Rattus rintjanus*. Others of interest are the macaque (*Macaca fascicularis*) and the Timor deer (*Cervus timorensis*). Komodo National Park can also boast a large coral reef that is home to one of the most abundant fish fauna in the world but whose ecosystem has been seriously threatened by poaching over the last few decades; it has not been unknown for dynamite to be used. The seas contain mammals such as the blue whale (*Balaenoptera musculus*), which is in danger of extinction, the sperm whale (*Physeter catodon*) and 10 species of dolphin, including the highly threatened dugong (*Dugong dugon*).

Equally vulnerable is the attraction of the National Park, the Komodo dragon. A recent count suggests that roughly 5,700 remain though the species seems to have disappeared from the island of Padar as no signs have been seen for several years. The reason for the danger is extensive hunting of the Timor deer, the dragon's favorite food. It is obvious that even the most terrible hunting machine in the world will have a hard time when it has no prey.

434-435 *Estimated to be around 5,700 in number, the Komodo dragon population is divided between 2,900 on Komodo, 900 on Rinca, 100 or so on Gili Motong and the rest in the coastal areas of the island of Flores.*

435 bottom left The genus Varanus to which the Komodo dragon belongs, is a latinization of the Egyptian word waran meaning 'alarm'. It is derived from the legend in which the lizards of this family in the Nile warned the people of the presence of crocodiles.

435 bottom right Some of the preferred prey of the dragon are goats, boar and the Timor deer but it is quite happy to eat birds, snakes, fish, crabs, water buffalo and even the young of its own species.

Canadian Rocky Mountains parks

CANADA

ALBERTA AND BRITISH COLUMBIA
REGISTRATION: 1984*
CRITERIA: N (I) (II) (III)

*THE BURGESS SHALE SITE, INSCRIBED ON THE WORLD HERITAGE LIST IN 1980, HAS NOW BEEN SUBSUMED INTO THIS SITE

In 1886, when the geologist R. G. McConnell of the Geological Survey of Canada discovered the Burgess Shale fossil deposits, the workers on the Canadian Pacific Railway had already made their personal collections of trilobites. Thanks to the pioneering work of the construction of the railway, the Canadian government had created a nature reserve of 10 square miles around the mineral springs of Cave and Basin, thinking, as the directors of the railway did, that one day they would become a tourist attraction.

That act marked the beginning of the string of national parks in Canada and the place formed the nucleus around which the Rocky Mountains Park was constituted two years later.

Basin National Historic Site.

Today the area includes four national parks – Banff National Park, Jasper National Park, Kootenay National Park and Yoho National Park – and three provincial parks –Hamber Provincial Park, Mount Assiniboine Provincial Park and Mount Robson Provincial Park – making a total of 8,907 square miles of protected land along the border of Alberta and British Columbia.

Geologically, the Canadian Rocky Mountains are formed by schist, dolomite, sandstone and limestone, and were created between the Precambrian era and the Cretaceous period. They range in height from 3,280 feet to Mount Robson's 12,972 feet and have several large glaciers, the biggest of

which is the Columbia Icefield that covers 125 square miles.

The continental climate has fostered the development of three ecoregions – montane, subalpine and alpine – that alternate depending on altitude and exposure to atmospheric agents. The classified species include 996 vascular plants, 243 mosses, 407 lichens and 53 bryophytes. The mountain region is covered with forests of Douglas fir (*Pseudotsuga menziesii*), white spruce (*Picea glauca*) and poplars (*Populus tremuloides* and *Populus balsamifera*). At a height between 5,905 and 6,900 feet, the subalpine region (which is the most extensive with over 445 square miles of forest) is dominated by firs (*Picea engelmannii* and *Abies lasiocarpa*) and pines (*Pinus flexilis* and *Pinus contorta*).

The name of the park was changed to the Banff National Park in 1930. As the years passed, the Rocky Mountains became the symbol of environmental conservation in Canada, and to commemorate that first protected area, the hot, emerald-green springs in Banff have been renamed the Cave and

436 top left After a drop of 75 feet, the Maligne River dives into a spectacular gorge that the violence of the river has dug out of the limestone rock.

436 bottom left The elk (Cervus elaphus) is the largest of the deer family. Unlike the others, evolution has given it an upper canine tooth, which, in the nineteenth century, became a fashionable item of jewelry.

436 bottom right At an altitude of 4,921 feet, Moraine Lake is one of the pearls of Banff National Park. This was the first park instituted in Canada and was opened in 1885 with the name Rocky Mountains Park.

437 left In the heart of Jasper National Park, Medicine Lake has the Maligne River as a tributary but it does not seem to have an emissary. In fact, the lake is drained by one of the largest underground water systems in North America.

437 right The redness of the antlers is given by the presence of surface blood vessels and indicates the sex and youth of this moose. Only males have antlers, which usually start to grow at around one year of age.

OTTAWA

438-439 Peyto Lake is one of the most spectacular in the Canadian Rocky Mountains. The local lakes are fed by glaciers, the largest of which, the Columbia Icefield, has an area of 125 square miles.

438 bottom At 11,870 feet, Mount Assiniboine is a dramatic, isolated pyramid of limestone in the heart of Assiniboine Provincial Park. It dominates Lake Magog, around which a rich wild fauna abounds. Overall, the protected area of the Canadian Rocky Mountains encloses four national parks and three provincial parks, making a total of 8,880 square miles.

Higher up, the alpine flora includes low species such as *Salix arctica* and *Betula glandulosa*, heathers, like *Cassiope tetragona*, and rosales (*Dryas integrifolia* and *Dryas hookeriania*).

The most representative mammals are the herbivores that have their habitat in the alpine meadows. They include the mountain goat and mountain sheep (*Oreamos americanus* and *Ovis canadensis*), the pika (*Ochotona princeps*), which is a sort of hare and the hoary marmot (*Marmota caligata*); there are forest mammals like the moose (*Alces alces*), the elk (*Cervus canadensis*) and the caribou (*Rangifer tarandus*); and carnivores such as the gray wolf (*Canis lupus*), the grizzly bear (*Ursos arctos horribilis*), the American black bear (*Ursus americanus*), the lynx (*Lynx canadensis*) and the puma (*Puma concolor*).

Of the 280 species of birds, mention should be made of the northern three-toed woodpecker, the partridge (*Lagopus*

439 top At one time distributed right across Canada, the puma (Felis concolor) now only lives in the Rocky Mountains. Male adults can reach a length of 9 feet and weigh close to 200 pounds.

439 center The gray wolf (Canis lupus) has only recently returned to the Rocky Mountains. A long study in Banff National Park estimates there are about 40 living there.

439 bottom During their migration across North America, each autumn thousands of golden eagles (Aquila chrysaetos) take refuge along the eastern slopes of the Rocky Mountains.

leucurus), the gray jay (*Perisoreus canadensis*), Clark's nutcracker (*Nucifraga columbiana*) and, of course, the golden eagle (*Aquila chrysaetos*).

With the exception of a plan for an open-pit coal mine just outside Jasper National Park – which would seriously compromise the health of the area – the Rocky Mountains do not seem subjected to grave environmental risk, despite the fact that every year they receive almost 10 million visitors.

440 top It is unknown what the function of the bony crest of the Parasaurolophus was, but perhaps the animal required a horn for communication purposes.

440-441 The rocks in the provincial park were deeply furrowed by the movement of the water during the melting of the icefields.

441 top Hoodoos are unusual sandstone mushroom-like formations a few miles from Drumheller and one of the park's attractions.

Formed by the wind and water, they dissolve very quickly when the stone that covers and protects them is eroded by the atmosphere.

441 center The progressive emersion of ancient layers of sediment has unearthed more than 300 complete dinosaur skeletons and thousands of fossil fragments.

OTTAWA

Dinosaur Provincial Park

CANADA

SOUTHERN ALBERTA
REGISTRATION: 1979
CRITERIA: N (I) (III)

The year 2000 was a good one for the team of paleontologists of the Royal Tyrrell Museum in Drumheller, a former mining town in the Canadian province of Alberta. As usual, they were busy with their yearly excavations on the banks of the Red Deer River. According to the statement written up by Don Brinkman, the coordinator of the Dinosaur Research Program, the scientists–supported by eight students and 25 volunteers who wanted to experience a paleontological excavation–fully recovered the skeleton of a *Dasplaetosaurus* begun the year before and discovered a new fossil of a large carnivore, of which part of the skull was uncovered. But the most curious discovery was that of a pair of tortoises of the genus *Basilemys*, from the late Cretaceous period, whose shells seem to have been crushed by a passing sauropod. The area of the Dinosaur Provincial Park has been one of the most remarkable fossil beds of the Cretaceous period since its discovery at the end of the nineteenth century. And the Royal Tyrrell Museum of Paleontology, which is famous as one of the best museums in North America, has 50 or so complete skeletons and over 80,000 fragments of various natures, which make it the largest collection of dinosaurs in the world.

Around 75 million years ago, southern Alberta – where the Dinosaur Provincial Park lies – was a coastal plain on the edge of the Bearpaw Sea. The climate was then subtropical, which allowed an extensive fauna to develop, including the first mammals as well as fish, amphibians, birds and the large reptiles that dominated the world, the dinosaurs. Over the geological eras, an intricate river system built up a bed of sediments nearly 2,000 feet thick that covered the carcasses of many animals. About 15,000 years later, the erosive action of the glaciers cut gashes in the sediments, like the twisting beds of the Red Deer River and Judith River, revealing the fossil remains of these creatures.

From a botanical viewpoint, Dinosaur Provincial Park is of no particular interest, but the layers of sandstone and schist exposed by glaciation have revealed an extraordinary cross section of the world of the dinosaurs. Between 1979 and 1991, 23,347 finds were made, including 300 skeletons of dinosaurs belonging to 35 different species. These numbered creatures from the *Hadrosauridae*, *Ornithomimidae*, and *Nodosauridae families*, and even some of the most feared predators of the Cretacean period, Tyrannosaurus Rex.

The relative mildness of the modern climate permits hoofed animals to survive the winters, like pronghorn (*Antilocapra americana*) and mule and white-tailed deer (*Odocoileus hemionus* and *Odocoileus virginianus*). The local fauna includes 150 species of birds, such as the golden eagle (*Aquila chrysaetos*), the prairie falcon (*Falco mexicanus*), the ferruginous hawk (*Buteo regalis*) and the pigeon hawk or merlin (*Falco columbarius*).

The number of visitors to the Dinosaur Provincial Park is on the increase but it remains a quiet place for the species that inhabit it, as the tourists are more interested in searching for fossils. Large discoveries are fairly rare event as the excavations only last a few weeks during the summer but disappointed visitors are always able to console themselves with the treasures of the Royal Tyrrell Museum.

441 bottom Large dinosaur bones in the foreground stick up out of the sediment in Dinosaur National Park. Those found on the site (one of the richest fossil beds from the Cretaceous period) belong to 35 different species.

Yellowstone National Park

UNITED STATES

WYOMING, MONTANA AND IDAHO
REGISTRATION: 1978
CRITERIA: N (I) (II) (III) (IV)
INSCRIBED ON THE WORLD HERITAGE
IN DANGER LIST IN 1995

When William Hanna and Joseph Barbera created the willful bears Yogi and Boo boo, and the patient red-jacketed ranger whose duty it was to protect the picnic baskets of the visitors to Jellystone Park, it was clear they had based their ideas on the astounding Yellowstone Park in North America. The creation of this, the first national park in the world, by President Ulysses Grant on 1 March 1872, opened the era of environmental conservation.

In 1870, when the United States was still suffering the wounds of the Civil War, the son of the senator for Montana, Walter Trumball, organized an expedition to Yellowstone led by General Henry D. Washburn to check tales brought back by the region's earliest explorers. In 1807, John Colter had returned from a mission to the frontier territories, telling of valleys that ended in lakes of boiling mud, fumaroles, jets of steam and hot springs, which together formed a Dantesque vision of hell. The stories circulated enough for the phrase 'Colter's Hell' to be coined.

Armed only with these tales, Washburn and his companions soon discovered a steam vent that rose 100 feet into the air in a fountain of boiling water. This was what was later to become Yellowstone's most famous geyser, Old Faithful, which was so named for the regularity of its eruption (every 74 minutes).

442 Unique in the world, the incredible plays of color in the Giant Prismatic Spring (Yellowstone's largest thermal spring) are created by algae and microorganisms in the water and by mineral deposits on the banks.

443 top left An area rich in geothermal phenomena, the Porcelain Basin is named after the whiteness of its limestone deposits. It has several geysers; this is Africa Geyser, which gives off continuous puffs of steam.

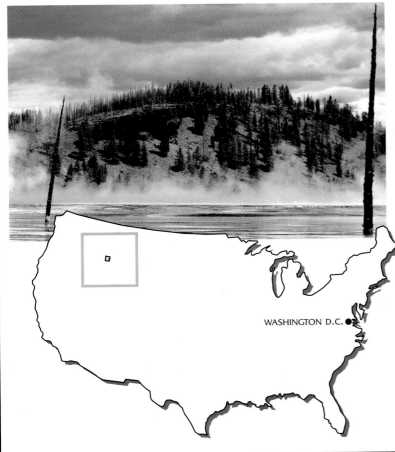

WASHINGTON D.C.

443 top right Lower Yellowstone Falls run into a bright yellow gully, though the color here is nothing to do with the name of the river or Park. 'Yellowstone' refers to the color of the rock where the Yellowstone river meets the Missouri 620 miles to the east.

443 bottom left In the pale winter atmosphere, the steam from the Giant Prismatic Spring creates an interesting color effect against the background of conifers.

443 bottom right Mammoth Hot Springs form spectacular travertine terraces created by the resurfacing of water rich in carbonic acid. They are the clearest surface indication of the volcanic forces at work in Yellowstone's subsoil.

This was only the first of the many surprising natural phenomena the expedition discovered during that glorious expedition. In the park's 3,468 square miles, there are more than 10,000 geothermal phenomena and more than 300 geysers – two thirds of the world's total. Formed by an accumulation of rhyolites dating to 65,000 years ago, Yellowstone Plateau has the peculiarity of lying above the crater of an ancient volcano in a zone where – following vulcanist phenomena – the earth's crust is often just a few miles thick.

Consequently, the heat from the

dramatic and colorful effect. There are also fumaroles, craters and lunar landscapes like Firehole River, where the water flows over a bed of boiling springs, creating a ribbon of steam for a long stretch of its course. The comparatively ordinary Yellowstone River flows into a spectacular canyon with striking waterfalls that drop into Yellowstone Lake. The lake has a drainage area of 137 square miles, a perimeter of 110 miles and is one of the largest alpine lakes in the world.

Almost 80% of the park is covered by forest, most of which is pine (*Pinus contorta*). The large range over which

444 top A young elk, or wapiti, rests near one of Yellowstone's many watercourses. Despite the huge influx of tourists, the wildlife in the park has been successfully conserved.

444 center left According to historical sources, moose (Alces alces) were rare in Wyoming around 1872, the year in which Yellowstone was declared a national park. However, the protection measures taken have led to a large increase in its numbers.

earth's interior warms the water that circulates through the intricate underground drainage system and sends it violently up through the subsoil in the form of vapor when the pressure becomes excessive.

However, Yellowstone contains much more than geysers. There are phenomena like the Grand Prismatic Spring, whose sulfurous crystalline water deposits salts on the banks, creating a

444 center right Bison (Bison bison) *are the largest mammals in Yellowstone and the only ones completely free in the United States.*

444 bottom Eradicated in the area in the 1930s, the gray wolf (Canis lupus) was reintroduced in 1995 to help control the burgeoning number of ungulates. In 2002, 10 groups were counted.

444-445 Although it is becoming rather rare in other areas of the country, the elk (Cervus elaphus), or wapiti, has its last stronghold in Yellowstone. The population in 1998 was estimated to be 25,000.

445 top A Yellowstone wapiti snorts in the cold autumn air. Cool in summer, the local winter temperature dives to an average 10°F.

446 top Bison often fall victim to the cold Wyoming winters. In 1996 more than 1,000 died, but fortunately in 1998 there were still roughly 2,200 left.

446 bottom The almost 3,500 square miles of Yellowstone Park contains the largest number of geysers (around 300, 66% of the world total) and geothermal phenomena in the world.

the forests stretch, from 5,600-11,360 feet, has encouraged the establishment of various botanical communities (including 1,100 species of vascular plants), semi-arid steppe and alpine tundra.

Apart from the roughly 200 grizzlies (*Ursus arctos horribilis*) and many black bears (*Ursus americanus*) on which Yogi and Boo boo were based, Yellowstone has eight indigenous species of ungulates such as elk (*Cervus elaphus*), mule deer (*Odocoileus hemionus*), American bison (*Bison bison*), moose (*Alces alces*), bighorn sheep (*Ovis canadensis*), pronghorn (*Antilocapra americana*), Rocky Mountain goat (*Oreamnos*

reintroduce the animal, and the project has been successful.

1995 was the unhappy year that UNESCO placed Yellowstone National Park on the World Heritage in Danger list. The reason was the plan by a Canadian company to construct a mine to extract gold, silver and copper just a few miles from the park's north-east boundary.

As the mine would have lain

upstream of three torrents that flowed into Yellowstone, it would have threatened to pollute the water and cause damage to the ecosystem. The Clinton Administration placed a moratorium on the project before reaching an agreement with the company involved. The park was saved by a payment of 65 million dollars; nonetheless, the Administration was accused by certain pressure groups of having ceded jurisdiction of American territory to the United Nations. Yet Yellowstone was and remains the worldwide symbol of the history of conservation.

americanus) and white-tailed deer (*Odocoileus virginianus*).

Species under threat include the bald eagle (*Haliaeetus leucocephalus*), peregrine falcon (*Falco peregrinus*) and the largest example of its genus, the trumpeter swan (*Cygnus buccinator*).

Some years ago wolves (*Canis lupus*) were reintroduced to the Canyon and Lamar Valley, having been exterminated in the 1930s with the approval of the local authorities as they threatened local herds.

It was only some decades later it was realized that, being the largest predator of the ungulates in the area, wolves were irreplaceable in maintaining the dynamic balances of the Yellowstone ecosystem intact.

In 1995, therefore, it was decided to

447 top Yellowstone Park is 80% covered by coniferous forest. Most of these are tall pines from the species Pinus contorta.

447 center left Formidable predators, the bald eagles (Haliaeetus leucocephalus) in Yellowstone share the position at the top of the food chain with peregrine falcons, wolves and coyotes.

447 center right With the return of the wolves, the coyotes (Canis latrans) have had to modify their hunting territories and, to deal with the new threat, cohesion within the packs has notably increased.

447 bottom The Rocky Mountain bighorn sheep (Ovis canadensis) is easily recognized by the long curved horns of the male. The resident population in Yellowstone is considered to be little more than 200 individuals.

Redwood National Park

UNITED STATES

CALIFORNIA

REGISTRATION: 1980

CRITERIA: N (II) (III)

448 top Mountain lions (Felis concolor) avoid flat, open land, preferring higher terrain and forests, which are better suited to their tactic of ambushing prey and for protecting their young.

448-449 The giant sequoia (Sequoia sempervirens) in Redwood National Park are often associated with the indigenous species Douglas fir (Pseudotsuga menziesii).

WASHINGTON D.C.

The English and Spanish ignored northern California until the mid-nineteenth century, when the discovery of gold in the region led to the Gold Rush. This, in turn, led to the exploitation of the immense forest resources of the state, beginning with the sequoia (*Sequoia sempervirens*) that grew along the whole of the coastline to the north of San Francisco. In the past, local natives used these trees to build canoes and houses.

The sequoia is an extraordinary legacy of the gigantic evergreen conifer forests that used to dominate the temperate areas of the planet during the Jurassic period, but today it is limited to California and Oregon. It takes a sequoia 400 years to reach maturity and it lives to an age of 2,000 years. Its dry, thick bark is rich in tannin, which protects it from fire and parasites. The tallest tree in the world grows in the Redwood National Park and has reached a height of 367 feet; in 1933 in the same area, an older sequoia was cut

down whose rings showed it to be over 2200 years old.

The National Register of Historic Places estimates that 96% of the original sequoia forests have been irredeemably lost and that 42% of what remains lies within the Redwood National Park. Created in 1968 with the aim of preserving the last sequoia forests, the park covers 172 square miles, to which can be added the 10 square miles of Del Norte Redwoods State Park, the 15 square miles of Jedediah Smith Redwoods State Park and the 22 square miles of the Prairie Creek Redwoods State Park.

Redwood stretches along 34 miles of rocky coast and overlooks dizzying drops into the Pacific Ocean and the occasional sandy beach. The vegetation is very rich, with 856 species of which 699 are

indigenous. These latter include the Douglas fir (*Pseudotsuga menziesii*), the western hemlock (*Tsuga heterophylla*), the tanbark oak (*Lithocarpus densiflorus*), the grand fir (*Abies grandis*), the Sitka spruce (*Picea sitchensis*) and the Oregon maple (*Acer macrophyllum*). The fauna boasts large communities of 75 types of mammal (with lynx, elk, silver fox, black bear, otter and puma), 400 species of birds, many fish, and invertebrates, which generally inhabit the tidal area. However, the unquestioned attraction of the Redwood National Park is the sequoia, partly because its safeguarding marked a crucial step in the history of conservation. At the end of the nineteenth century, when exploitation of the sequoias reached its peak, almost all the forest area was owned privately, so logging continued without obstacle until 1918 when the paleontologists Henry Fairfield Osborn, Madison Grant and John C. Merriam instituted the Save-the-Redwoods League, an *ante litteram* environmental association

through which it was proposed that large tracts of forest should be purchased for conservation reasons. Between 1920 and 1960, the organization placed 170 square miles of forest under protection – then entrusted this land to the California Department of Parks and Recreation before it was turned into the Redwoods National Park – a part of which, already exploited by logging companies, was reforested.

Logging of sequoias continues in unprotected areas, despite the protests of environmental groups, but these trees have shown that they are strong survivors, thanks to a very unusual capability: besides their normal sexual means of reproduction, a sequoia can regenerate by rooting from a large branch or from the roots of a fallen tree, thereby creating a clone of itself.

449 top The sequoia is the tallest and largest organism in the vegetal world and is also very special: it is said, for example, that no human has ever seen one caused to topple by natural causes.

449 bottom left Sequoia are very long living owing to the large quantity of tannin in their trunks. Tannin inhibits attack by insects and makes these trees very resistant in the event of fire.

449 bottom right A young mule deer (Odocoileus hemionus) watches carefully from the edge of a clearing. Areas of transition between woodland and grassland are the preferred grazing land of this defenseless animal; and they are hunted ruthlessly outside of the protected areas.

448 bottom Situated in the counties of Humboldt and Del Norte in northeast California, the park is about 50 miles long and varies in width between 300 yards and 9 miles.

Yosemite National Park

UNITED STATES

CALIFORNIA
REGISTRATION: 1984
CRITERIA: N (I) (II) (III)

450

450 top left Covering an area of more than 1,160 square miles, Yosemite obtained the status of national park on 1 October 1890. Currently the protected area is visited by over 4 million visitors a year.

450 bottom left The 'incomparable valley', as Yosemite Valley is nicknamed, is a perfect example of glacial erosion. The perfectly vertical sides of the mountains on either side were created by the advance of the glaciers in the gorge formed by the Merced River.

One of the most famous photographs taken by the master Ansel Adams was titled 'Monolith, the face of Half Dome' and showed the granite wall that looks down on Yosemite Valley. In order to get the receding view of this immense block, Adams was obliged to carry his heavy equipment up onto a shoulder of the Half Dome. It was that day in Winter 1927 that Adams decided to dedicate his life to photography, with the result that he spent the next 30 years of his life in Yosemite Valley. Probably discovered by the first colonists in 1833, this astounding canyon was dug out by the Merced River in the granite of the Sierra Nevada, and it rivals the equally famous Yellowstone for being the first protected area in history. Though Yellowstone became the first national park in 1872, Yosemite Valley and the Mariposa sequoia forest were recognized as an inalienable part of the public heritage by a document of 30 June 1864, which was signed by President Lincoln. Later, worried by the exploitation of the Sierra Nevada by gold hunters, the insistence of naturalist, poet and mountain climber John Muir convinced President Theodore 'Teddy' Roosevelt to accord Yosemite the status of a national park too. On 1 October 1890, the first tourists arrived to admire the region that was to inspire generations of artists and writers. Today Yosemite National Park, whose boundaries were repeatedly enlarged up to 1984, has an area of 1,190 square miles and receives over 4 million visitors a year. All the protected area (from a height of 2,200 to 13,116 feet), is dominated by the mountains

450 right This view of the valley is taken from Glacier Point, one of the most spectacular in Yosemite. Sited on the edge of a sheer drop, it offers an extraordinary view over the most fascinating rock formations in the park.

451 Partially hidden by the winter mist, the granite block known as El Capitan rises over 3,000 feet from the valley floor. A delight for rock climbers, it was first scaled in 1958.

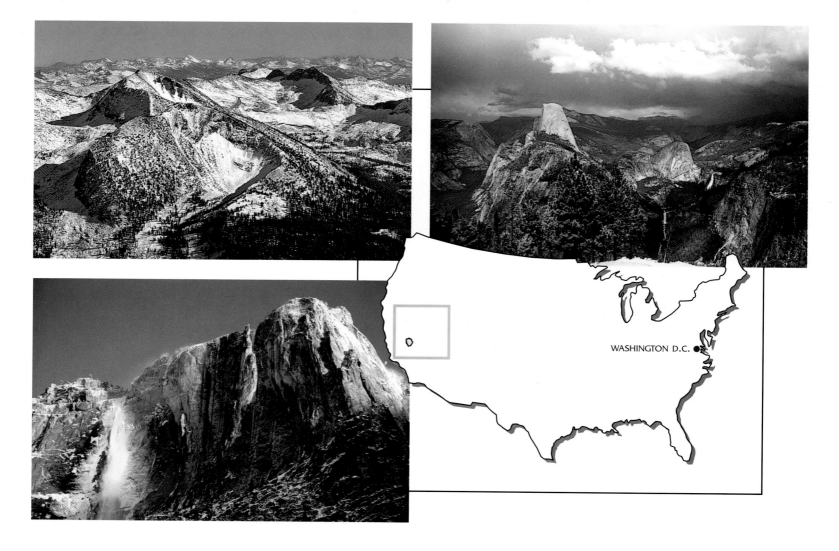

WASHINGTON D.C.

452 top Also called cougar and mountain lion, the puma (Felis concolor) is not uncommon in Yosemite despite being included on the list of endangered animals by the U.S. Wildlife Service.

452-453 Sunset over El Capitan (left) and Half Dome, another of the geological marvels in the park. Half Dome gets its name from the dome-shaped cut in the rock by the passage of the glaciers.

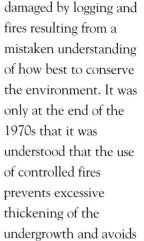

453 top With a leap of nearly 1,000 feet from a saddle on El Capitan, Horsetail Falls is the most famous of the many waterfalls in the park.

453 bottom left Three woods of sequoia (*Sequoiadendron giganteum*), covering 417 acres, survive in the park. The most famous individual tree is the Grizzly Giant, which stands 213 feet tall.

453 bottom right Fed by five streams that run down from the Sierra Nevada, Mono Lake's huge basin of volcanic tufa provides a habitat for a large variety and number of birds.

of the Sierra Nevada. This mountain chain was formed around 100 million years ago when a huge mass of magma filtered up from the bowels of the earth, through the crust, and generated a string of volcanoes above a granite base. Later, erosion wore and pushed away the volcanic rock leaving the granite below exposed. Yosemite Valley is a narrow canyon tens of miles long with rock walls up to 3,100 feet high and is the result of fluvial and glacial erosion over the last tens of thousands of years. This action has created not only Half Dome but also the El Capitan monolith – a block of granite that rises over 3,000 feet from the valley floor and from which the 1,000-foot Horsetail Falls cascades from the top. The glaciation has also left

damaged by logging and fires resulting from a mistaken understanding of how best to conserve the environment. It was only at the end of the 1970s that it was understood that the use of controlled fires prevents excessive thickening of the undergrowth and avoids the risk of much more serious damage if uncontrolled fires get started. The park provides a habitat to more than 230 species of birds, including the American bald eagle (*Haliaeetus leucocephalus*), the peregrine falcon (*Falco peregrinus*) and the great gray owl (*Strix nebulosa*). Of the 74 recorded mammals, there are the yellow-bellied marmot (*Marmota flaviventris*), the coyote (*Canis latrans*) and the mule deer (*Odocoileus*

U- and V-shaped valleys, moraines and glacial circles. This is the setting for 27 botanical communities and 16 types of forest. The forests are composed of silver fir (*Abies alba*), pine (*Pinus contorta*) and Norway spruce (*Picea abies*), but also noteworthy are species like the Californian black oak (*Quercus kelloggi*), Douglas fir (*Abies douglasii*), various other pines (*Pinus sabiniana, Pinus lambertiana* and *Pinus monticola*) and juniper (*Juniperus occidentalis*). In Mariposa, Merced and Tuolumne there are three sequoia woods (*Sequoiadendron gigantum*) that together cover 420 acres; they have been repeatedly

hemionus). Even more rare are the martens (*Martes americana* and *Martes pennati*), the wolverine (*Gulo luscus*) and the puma (*Puma concolor*).

Yosemite is also home to a community of 300-500 black bears (*Ursus americanus*). Over recent decades, the pressure created by tourism has introduced human food to them, which has affected their behavior. Some bears, which have become too aggressive, have had to be shot by rangers. Thus there is also the risk that they too will end up being restricted to certain areas or even disappear from Yosemite.

WASHINGTON D.C.

454 Considered one of
the wonders of the world,
the Grand Canyon is 278
miles long and nearly
5,000 feet deep, and has a
width that varies between
600 yards and 19 miles.

455 top Also known as
the bobcat, the American
red lynx (Lynx rufus) is
an elegant creature of
medium size that is
frequently seen on the
South Rim.

Grand Canyon National Park

UNITED STATES

ARIZONA
REGISTRATION: 1979
CRITERIA: N (I) (II) (III) (IV)

Looking down for the first time on the chasm of the Grand Canyon, the naturalist Donald Culross Peattie said he was aware of the 'will of God', and the writer J. B. Priestley described the spectacle of the Colorado River winding through the immense rock walls as 'the Last Judgment of nature'. Both these remarks – which make recourse to the ultramundane to explain the magnificence of the Grand Canyon – date to the end of the nineteenth century, when America was discovering the aesthetics of nature. Until then, the huge landscapes of the Wild West were seen rather as lands to be conquered and exploited.

The Grand Canyon has been known to the white man for centuries, since 1540, when it was discovered by the Spanish army captain, García Lopez de Cardenas, who was sent north by the viceroy of Mexico in search of the seven legendary golden cities of Cibola; but with such an ambitious commission, his arrival at the Grand Canyon only caused him disappointment. In consequence, the only subsequent visitors to the area were missionaries whose goal was more to save the souls of the Navajo and Hopi natives than to record geological phenomena or botanical oddities. Even Major John Wesley Powell, the veteran of the Civil War, who, leading an expedition of nine, was the first to descend the rapids of the Colorado, was less interested in geographic or naturalistic wonders than ethnological aspects. The expedition lasted three months, during which three members of the team lost their lives, but at the end of the study on the languages spoken by the natives, the Bureau for American Ethnology was set up in the Smithsonian Institution. However, the extraordinary beauty of the Grand Canyon affected Major Powell and his descriptions stirred the curiosity of his geological colleagues in the prestigious scientific institute.

The magnificence of the Grand Canyon's scenery defies any definition. This spectacular gorge is 4,900 feet deep, 277 miles long and between 1,800 feet and 20 miles wide. The Colorado River has an average flow of 850 cubic yards per second and at least 100 rapids. The horizontal rock layers in the Grand Canyon were formed over a period of 2 billion years and provide samples from the four main geological eras: the Precambrian, Paleozoic, Mesozoic and Cenozoic. It is therefore a field site of scientific interest only matched in degree by its physical beauty; no one can

455 bottom left In the area of the Grand Canyon the prairie hawk (Falco mexicanus) shares the territory with the rarer peregrine falcon (Falco peregrinus anatum).

455 bottom right The number of coyotes (Canis latrans) in the park is on the increase to the extent that measures have been taken to control its population.

456 top left The conifers on the edge of the South Rim – like the Utah juniper and Pinon pine – are species able to hold water in their roots for long periods.

456 top right Snow is not unusual at higher levels. The North Rim has a damper climate than the South Rim, therefore its vegetation is more varied and abundant.

456-457 The colorful stratification of the Grand Canyon is caused by ferrous minerals that take on red, orange, yellow and green hues when oxidized.

457 top Formed over a period of 2 billion years, the horizontal layers of the Grand Canyon bear witness to the four main geological eras: Precambrian, Paleozoic, Mesozoic and Cenozoic.

remain untouched by the splendor of the rocks smoothed by the ceaseless action of the water and by the incredible colors created by the different compositions and age of the rocks. And up on the Kaibab Plateau at the top of the canyon, it is easy to find the remains of fossilized coral, shells, seaweed and even fish.

There are innumerable lookout points along the canyon carved by the Colorado, and 'natural sculptures' the

names of which once more refer to deities; for example, the Diana Temple and the Shiva Temple, though the presence of this latter god is highly improbable in this part of the world. These 'sculptures' have always been sacred to the Hopi natives who believe them to enclose the spirits of their ancestors.

The two sides of the Grand Canyon – the South and North Rims – are different worlds. The former is mostly a desert with various species of cactus, agave and yucca as well as species of conifer, like the Utah juniper and the Pinon pine, able to retain water for a long time in their roots.

The North Rim has a damper, cooler climate, and therefore more abundant vegetation, with conifer forests of Douglas and Ponderosa pines, and, in the more protected valleys, communities of aspen and birch. The result of this diversity is a difference in the fauna of the two sides of the canyon, though some species, like the coyote, puma and American goat are present on both. An example of a species living on one side only is, on the South Rim, a rare indigenous subspecies of rattlesnake (*Crotalus viridis abyssus*). Another interesting case is the Kaibab squirrel that inhabits the North Rim, and the Albert squirrel that is on the South Rim. Despite being descended from a single ancestor, the different conditions on either side of the river have led to two distinct species evolving.

Those able to travel freely between the two sides are the more than 300 species of birds recorded in the area, of which there are at least 60 pairs of peregrine falcons, making this the largest population of this species in the southern United States.

The discovery of the natural beauties of the Grand Canyon at the end of the nineteenth century coincided with the dawn of mass tourism. In 1901 a railway was built to the South Rim and, a year later, the luxurious El Tovar Hotel was opened, with Theodore Roosevelt being one of its first guests. Like many of the early visitors, the President came for 'sport' as

hunting was allowed even though a forest reserve was instituted in the Grand Canyon way back in 1893. It is estimated that between 1900 and 1905 alone at least 600 pumas were shot. The institution in 1919 of the Grand Canyon National Park under Woodrow Wilson finally put an end to that disaster for the wildlife of the area. Now, the animals and birds have only to deal with the 5 million visitors to the canyon, all armed with cameras.

457 bottom The first white man to see the Grand Canyon was the Spanish army captain García Lopezde Cardenas in 1540.

Everglades National Park

UNITED STATES

FLORIDA
REGISTRATION: 1979
INSCRIPTION ON THE WORLD HERITAGE
SITES IN DANGER LIST: 1993
CRITERIA: N (I) (II) (IV)

Americans rightly claim a founding role in the conservation policies of the world's natural heritage but still the national conscience is not completely clear. Whereas America created the myth of the wilderness with the creation of the Grand Canyon and Yellowstone National Parks, an area that was of equal interest in southern Florida did not arouse the slightest interest.

The Everglades is an inhospitable area, it is true. The hot, damp climate of what seems no more than a swamp infested by mosquitoes and alligators is not particularly inviting, but the Pa-Hay-Okee ('Grass River' as the Seminole Indians call it), which flows at an imperceptible rate for 130 miles from Lake Okeechobee to the Bay of Florida and reaches a width of 50 miles, is the only tropical ecosystem in North America. And, paradoxically, recognition of its value coincided with its inexorable decline.

When President Harry Truman instituted the Everglades National Park in 1947, there were only 500,000 inhabitants in southern Florida. In 1985, the year the state authorities raised the alarm, the population had reached 6 million and industrialization had produced a catastrophic environmental disaster. The Everglades habitat had been reduced by 20%, 14 species of animal were in serious danger of extinction and

458 top Communities of mangroves of the species Rizophora mangle, Avicennia germinans and Laguncularia racemosa grow alongside the canals and river estuaries, offering a perfect habitat to many birds, fish and crustaceans.

458 center The undisputed master of the park is the American alligator (Alligator mississippiensis). This ferocious predator feeds on birds, fish, turtles, crabs, otters, frogs and, occasionally, members of its own species.

458 bottom There are 16 species of waders in the park, including Egretta caerulea (illustrated here) whose numbers are diminishing worryingly. It is estimated that its numbers have declined by 93% over the last 50 years.

WASHINGTON D.C.

all the aquatic fauna were contaminated by mercury. Furthermore, the flora was threatened by 221 species of exotic infestant plants. In 1993, inscription of the site on the list of World Heritage sites in danger caused tens of millions of dollars to be set aside for what is one of the largest environmental cleaning programs in the world. Nonetheless, today, the situation seems even more serious.

Spread over 2,300 square miles, the

458-459 Covering 2,317 square miles, the Everglades National Park is the only tropical ecosystem in North America. Botanists are drawn by the huge quantity of vegetal species – 60-70% – found in the Caribbean area and the high proportion of endemic species.

459 top The 'River of Grass' flows at an imperceptible speed for 125 miles between Lake Okeechobee and Florida Bay.

459 right Although less rare in the Everglades than the white pelican, the brown pelican (Pelecanus occidentalis) is suffering from mercury poisoning of the fish that form the basis of its diet.

461 right A skilful fisher, the common egret (Casmerodius alba) winters among the mangroves in the constantly warm and humid climate of the Everglades. In summer it moves to the northern United States.

461 left A roseate spoonbill (Ajaia ajaja) is reflected in the waters of Mud Lake. It is estimated that over 200 pairs of this bird nest in Florida Bay between November and March, spread between Sandy Kay, Tern Key and Joe Key.

460-461 An osprey (Pandion haliaetus) seizes its prey. This splendid bird has a wingspan of up to 5.5 feet. The curvature of its wings in flight make it easily distinguishable from other birds of prey.

460 bottom left An American darter (Anhinga anhinga) has just captured a catfish. This species swims with

only its neck and head out of the water, which has earned it the nickname of the 'snakebird'.

460 bottom right An extremely non-aggressive and vulnerable creature, the manatee (Trichecus manatus) can weigh over 1,000 pounds. In the Everglades its population has declined to roughly 1,000.

park contains many different habitats, from the marine environment of the Bay of Florida to the drier environment near Lake Okeechobee, where 200 tropical plant species live close to pines characteristic of temperate climes. Between these two extremes there are several communities of mangroves, which live where the salt and fresh waters meet. Further inland there are mudflats covered by herbaceous plants, water meadows and communities of cypress that have developed the ability to survive in stagnant water. Above all, there is the 'Grass River' that advances just 100 feet a day and has a depth of 10 feet in the center and less than 3 feet at the sides; the river is punctuated by islands on which oaks and red maples grow.

Though the population is falling, there are 800 aquatic and terrestrial animal species in the Everglades. The one that causes most worry is the

manatee (Trichecus manatus), of which only 1,000 or so remain. The manatee is closely followed by the Florida panther (Felis concolor coryi); of the 30 remaining, more than half now wear a radio-collar so that their movements can be monitored. With regard to the bird population, the many species of waders are of concern as their numbers have fallen 93% in the past 50 years.

Enjoying good health, however, are most of the 60 species of reptiles and amphibians. The undisputed king of the Everglades is the American alligator (Alligator mississippiensis), which is the most ferocious predator in the park. Visitors, nevertheless, are more afraid of the 43 different species of mosquito that proliferate exponentially in the swamps: between them they lay 10,000 eggs for every square foot of land. They too are protected, as they are a fundamental link in the food chain, though that does not bring peace of mind to the tourists.

462 top A river of
incandescent lava flows
over a pahoehoe field. This
Hawaiian word has
entered the international
geological vocabulary
to define a very smooth
basalt lava surface with
a fibrous crust like
bread.

462-463 The lava that
has been exuded for
20 years uninterruptedly
from Kilauea – 4,100
feet high and considered
the most active volcano on
the planet – flows into
the Pacific Ocean
producing large clouds
of vapor.

463 The ceaseless
eruption of Kilauea has
been a tourist attraction
since 1840. In 1866
the volcano was visited
by Mark Twain who
praised its beauty.
In 1912 the U.S.
Geological Survey
observatory was built.

HONOLULU

Hawaii Volcanoes National Park

UNITED STATES

HAWAII
REGISTRATION: 1987
CRITERIA: N (II)

Lieutenant James King, on board James Cook's 1779 expedition, estimated the height of Mauna Loa to be 16,020 feet. A few years later, the barometric measurements taken by botanist Archibald Menzies (the first to reach its peak) were the first to record it fairly accurately, with a reading of 13,563 feet. In fact, according to the U.S. Geological Survey Hawaiian Volcano Observatory, founded in 1912, Mauna Loa in the southwest of Hawaii is 13,678 feet high.

When, however, the roughly 16,400 feet from the bottom of the ocean are added, and the 26,250 feet of the depression that has been formed by the upward thrust of the volcano, at a total height of over 55,000 feet (10.5 miles), Mauna Loa is the tallest mountain in the world, almost double the height of Everest. It is certainly the most voluminous as it contains approximately 20,000 cubic miles of volcanic rock and covers an area above sea level of 2,035 square miles.

It is one of the most active volcanoes on earth, with 33 eruptions recorded in the historical period, but even this figure is easily beaten by its neighbor Kilauea, which was in continuous eruption for over 20 years up until 1907 and then began again in fits and starts in 1952 before another continuous eruption started in 1983 and which has so far shown no signs of abating. This type of eruption is referred to as 'Hawaiian'; it is rarely explosive and features a continuous flow of lava that often spills from the side of the volcano.

Over millennia, these flows of fluid magma have deposited layer over layer of lava that have produced the spectacular volcanic panorama of the island of Hawaii.

Both volcanoes are part of the Hawaiian National Park created in 1916 and later extended to cover its current area of 359 square miles.

Instituted to preserve the landscape modeled by 70 million years of geological evolution, the park has

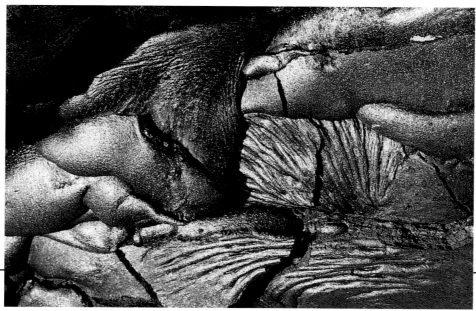

464 top A small triangular tongue of lava creeps into the already cooled deposits of magma, cracking them with its pressure and creating the typical woven appearance of the pahoehoe.

464-465 The lava from Kilauea slides into the sea from the top of a cliff. The uninterrupted accumulation of large quantities of magma has given the island of Hawaii a lunar landscape.

become the refuge of autochthonous plant and animal species.

The isolation of the Hawaiian Archipelago and the peculiar nature of the soil have encouraged the growth of botanical communities with a high percentage of endemic species even though, as is typical of islands in general, the biodiversity is relatively less than that of continental areas.

The ferns are of particular importance, as they represent a substantial percentage of the indigenous flora that still prevails at altitudes above 4,900 feet, whereas imported plants have contaminated the environment below 2,000 feet.

The only original mammal to inhabit Hawaii is the *Lasiurus cinereus*, the most common bat in the Americas.

The birds are of great interest with several exemplifying adaptive radiation.

465 top Kilauea is the most active volcano in the world and Mauna Loa is the largest, formed by 20,000 cubic miles of volcanic rock. The mountain's overall height from its base on the bottom of the ocean 5 miles down exceeds 55,000 feet.

465 bottom Kilauea originated between 600,000 and 300,000 years ago. The incessant eruptions of the last two centuries are probably a reliable indicator of the behavior of this volcano over the last 100,000 years.

466 Akaka Falls is one of the loveliest waterfalls in Hawaii. It falls 440 feet down a face covered completely in mosses. The surrounding forest, in which giant ferns dominate, was declared a territorial park in 1923.

467 top Kilauea's crater seems quiet in this picture but the volcano only appears to be sleeping. The eruptions from the cone exit from the cracks low down on the sides of the mountain.

Many endemic species are rare or endangered; these include the *akepa* (*Loxops coccineus*), the *akiapola'au* (*Hemignathus wilsoni*), the Hawaiian petrel (*Pterodroma sandwichensis*), the omao (*Phaeornis obscurus*), the *apapane* (*Himatione sanguinea*), the *elepaio* (*Chasiempis sandwichensis*), the *amakihi* (*Hemignathus virens*) and the *iiwi* (*Vestiaria coccinea*).

The entire park, unfortunately, is seriously compromised by the invasiveness of the species introduced by man. Wild goats and pigs have destroyed entire areas of indigenous plants and the mongoose has decimated the reptile population.

The *nene* (*Branta sandvicensis*), the last survivor of nine species of endemic wild goose, recently elevated to being the symbol of Hawaiian conservation, has suffered from hunting and from alteration of its natural habitat. Estimates say there were around 25,000 when James Cook arrived but no more than 50 were left in the mid 1940s.

A program of reintroduction begun in the 1970s has had some success but the survival of the *nene* is still dependent on man's care.

467 bottom left The ohelo (Vaccinium reticulatum) is an endemic berry that only grows on the islands of Hawaii and Maui. Its rare fruits are one of the favorite foods of the nene (Branta sanvicensis), the last species of wild goose on Hawaii.

467 bottom right The unusual haleakala (Argyroxiphium sandwicense) is perhaps the plant that best typifies Hawaii. Thanks to the island's isolation, 90% of the flowering plants on Hawaii are endemic but this heritage is greatly threatened by imported species.

The Galápagos Islands

ECUADOR

REGISTRATION: 1978, 2001
CRITERIA: N (I) (II) (III) (IV)

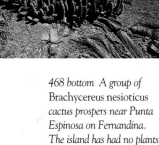

468 top The incandescent magma flowing from the sides of the volcano near Punta Espinosa on the island of Fernandina is a magnificent sight. Fernandina is the westernmost island in the archipelago and lies a few miles south of the equator.

468 bottom A group of Brachycereus nesioticus cactus prospers near Punta Espinosa on Fernandina. The island has had no plants or wildlife introduced by man and is one of the very rare natural environments left on the planet.

It was in 1835 that the young naturalist Charles Darwin reached the Galápagos Islands on H.M.S. Beagle and recognised: 'a highly unusual group of finches, similar to one another in the structure of their beak, their short tail and the form of their body and plumage [...]. Observing this gradation and diversity of structure in a small and very homogeneous group of birds, one can truly imagine [...] that a species has been altered so as to perform different purposes.' A further 24 years were to pass before his theory took shape in his book *On the Origin of Species*.

In this book Darwin proposed different postulates, amongst which was a gradual and continual evolution of living species, the descent of all organisms from a common ancestor and the selection of the next generation through the 'survival of the fittest' in the struggle for existence. And those brownish birds that belonged to 13 species, together known as Darwin's finches, played a decisive role in the development of the theory of evolution.

In truth the Galápagos Islands, discovered exactly 300 years earlier by the Bishop of Panama, Tomás de Berlanga, have experienced every sort of vicissitude. Originally uninhabited, in the seventeenth and eighteenth centuries they became the refuge of pirates and buccaneers who stopped off there to fill up with fresh water and the famous giant tortoises, which they loaded on board live so they could eat fresh meat. Fascinated by these exceptional creatures – after which the islands are named, *galápago* is Spanish for tortoise – Darwin too found the taste delicious, underlining in his notes how good the meat tasted when roasted in its shell as well as the soup made with younger tortoises.

Owing to the almost complete isolation of the islands, like Darwin's finches, the giant tortoise (*Geochelone elephantopus*) are an extraordinary example of evolution, growing to weigh 550 pounds and able to live for more than 100 years. Although they have been classified as a single species descended from a few individual tortoises that reached the Galápagos in remote history, there are in fact 14 subspecies, three of which are now extinct, while of another there is only one remaining. It is unknown whether the adaptations that have occurred over the millennia would allow a cross

QUITO

468-469 With a dark, bare landscape often marked by eruptive phenomena, and home to many marine iguanas, Fernandina is an inhospitable island yet contemporaneously the most interesting on the archipelago.

469 top The landscape of Bartolomé, the youngest and most spectacular island in the archipelago, is decidedly lunar. It is formed by a series of half-moon beaches and picturesque lava formations, the best known of which is Pinnacle Rock.

469 bottom left Punta Suarez on Hood Island is famous for this blowhole that spurts water between 50 and 100 feet into the air depending on the force of the waves.

469 bottom right A small crater lies in Santiago, the east coast of which has a huge pahoehoe lava field resulting from a violent eruption in 1897.

470-471 The majestic great frigate (Fregata minor) reproduces only once every two years because it takes more than one year to wean the chicks. This photo shows a female with her young.

470 bottom The waved albatross (Diomedea irrorata) is able to spend a full year without touching land. At Gardener Bay on Hood Island there are 10,000 pairs, almost the entire world population.

471 top A falcon attacks a giant tortoise (Geochelone elephantopus), of which there are roughly 150,000 on the archipelago.

between different populations. With the arrival of whale hunters – including Hermann Melville who found inspiration for his novel *Moby Dick* here – the fate of the tortoises seemed at hand. It is estimated that over 100,000 have been hunted, leaving a population of roughly 15,000.

Lying just south of the equator and 500 miles from the coast of South America, the archipelago is composed of 13 major islands, seven smaller ones and 100 or so tiny islets and reefs over a total of 3,100 square miles. It is formed by volcanic lava and magma and still has several active volcanoes.

When the islands were annexed by Ecuador in 1832, the Quito government began a project of colonization that led

islands. Both were registered as World Heritage sites in 1978 and 2001 respectively.

Finches and tortoises apart, the Galápagos Islands are an extraordinary open-air laboratory to study the fauna and flora, which has evolved independently, resulting in the highest percentage of endemism in the world. In total the endemic species include over 300 fish, 1,600 insects, 80 spiders, 300 coleopteras and 650 mollusks. There are also endemic species of sea birds like the flightless cormorant, an albatross, three gannets and two gulls. In addition the archipelago is home to the only penguin to live in tropical waters, sea lions and the Galápagos seal, which was highly prized by

471 bottom left The blue-footed booby (Sula nebouxii) is not endemic to the Galápagos but is also found in the Gulf of California and other areas of the Pacific.

471 bottom right The only non-flying cormorant, the Phalacrocorax harrisi is one of the species most at risk on the archipelago.

to the settling of various communities. The current population of roughly 18,000 is concentrated in the capital, Puerto Baquerizo Moreno, and the two towns of Puerto Ayora and Santa Cruz. In 1959, 97% of the archipelago's surface area was designated a national park and in 1986 a marine reserve was instituted to protect the waters that surround the

nineteenth-century fur hunters.

The reptiles merit a separate description as they have evolved freely in an environment void of predators. There are geckos, snakes, lava lizards and land iguanas, but special mention must be made of a marine iguana, the only species of aquatic lizard in the world. Practically every rock in the

Galápagos is inhabited by these reptiles, which live on the land but feed in the water on algae. Their population, estimated to be 200,000-300,000, is under serious threat from the oil that leaked in 2001 from the tanker *Jessica*. The June 2002 edition of *Nature* magazine reported that the mortality rate of the marine iguanas on the island of Santa Fe had increased exceptionally since the accident.

The Galápagos have an extremely fragile ecosystem that human presence has already profoundly altered. In 1976 a group of wild dogs attacked a colony of 500 land iguanas, killing them all, and in the 1990s poachers killed at least 120 giant tortoises. If this were not enough, the work of the Charles Darwin Foundation, which looks after the archipelago, is hard pushed by the Ecuadorian government, which, since the 1980s, has established incentives for the islands to be populated and the number of inhabitants is growing at around 8% a year.

472 top left A prevalently terrestrial animal, the marine iguana (Amblyrhynchus cristatus) is also able to swim and feeds exclusively on seaweed. Other iguanas do not share this custom and so the marine iguana has an almost unlimited source of food but is vulnerable to marine predators.

472 top right Almost every rock in the Galápagos is a home to marine iguanas. The total population of this species is estimated at 200,000-300,000. The concentration along the coast reaches roughly 3,000 every 1,000 yards.

472 center An endemic subspecies of the Californian sea lion, the Galápagos sea lion (Zalophus californianus wollebaeki) probably swam to the island, settled and began to differentiate from its nearest relatives.

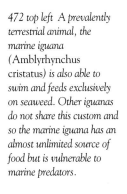

472 bottom Genetically close to Magellan penguins, the Galápagos penguins (Spheniscus mendiculus) can survive in the archipelago's equatorial waters thanks to the cold Humboldt Current that reaches Fernandina and Isabela Islands.

472-473 A group of sea lions lazes on the beach of Mosquera Island. Like the penguins and cormorants, the numerous population of this marine mammal has suffered from el Niño. During the event of 1997-98, the population of the main colonies was reduced by 48 percent.

473 top A green turtle (Chelonia mydas) takes pains to lay her eggs safely on a beach of Bartolomé but, just a few yards away, a Galápagos buteo (Buteo galapagoensis) awaits its moment.

Pantanal Conservation Area

BRAZIL

STATES OF MATO GROSSO AND
MATO GROSSO DO SUL
REGISTRATION: 2000
CRITERIA: N (II) (III) (IV)

The hyacinthine macaw (*Anodorhynchus hyacinthinus*) has a wingspan of 3 feet and cobalt blue plumage. It can live to an age of 80 and, in the wild, eats prevalently the fruit of the *acurí*, a palm endemic to Brazil. Besides its beauty and longevity, the largest parrot in the world has other gifts; it is a perfect companion, becomes fond of its owner and is able to repeat phrases in human language and do exercises of ability. The result of these qualities means that on the illegal animal market (which is estimated to be worth 5 billion dollars a year), a single macaw costs between 8,000 and 10,000 dollars.

474 Pantanal lies in an area of ecological tension between the Cerrado (i.e., the dry savannah in central Brazil) and the semideciduous forests of the southeast. The interaction between the vegetative habitats has created an extraordinary biodiversity.

474-475 Covering 89,000 square miles, the Pantanal is the largest freshwater marsh ecosystem in the world. UNESCO has placed a representative section that lies entirely in Brazil under protection.

Roughly 2,500 hyacinthine macaws live in captivity but there are only about 3,000 still living free in the Pantanal, an area of 920,000 square miles (almost as big as Great Britain), of which 560,000 square miles lie in Brazil and the rest is distributed between Bolivia and Paraguay. Poachers who capture the birds live for resale, or who kill caimans for the equally profitable skin market, consider the Pantanal a 'nature supermarket'. For scientists, on the other hand, it is one of the largest and most interesting ecosystems in the world. For this reason UNESCO registered a representative section of the Pantanal in its list of World Heritage sites in 2000. This section is the 725 square mile Pantanal Matogrossense National Park, which lies entirely in Brazil, is also considered of international importance by the Ramsar Convention.

The territory has a variety of ecological subregions: river channels, intricate gallery forests, permanent marshes and islands, floating islands of fluvial vegetation, called *camalotes*, and grassy plains subject to seasonal flooding. The principal source of water in the Pantanal is the Cuiaba, a river 560 miles long that flows into the Río Paraguay. During the rainy season between October and March, roughly two thirds of the Pantanal is submerged to create a huge sheet of water about 10 times the size of the

475 top During the rainy season between October and March, up to two thirds of the Pantanal is submerged. The extremely complex hydrological system includes surface river basins and underground watercourses.

475 bottom left The main water source in the Pantanal is the Rio Cuiaba, which flows roughly 620 miles southwest inside the protected area before joining the Rio Paraguay.

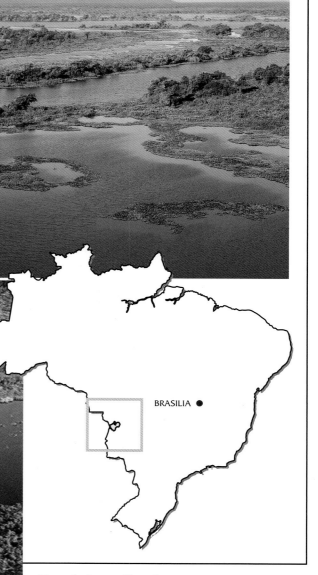

Everglades in Florida.

The diversity and interaction of the different habitats is reflected in an immense variety of plant species, though to date they have not been widely studied. They grow in an area of ecological tension between the dry savannah of central Brazil and the semi-deciduous forests of the south. Besides its dense fluvial vegetation and many herbaceous plants in the alluvial plains, the Pantanal is famous for its immense expanses of palms and lilies and for a curious, softwood fig-tree called *figueira mata-pau* ('tree-killer fig') as, in order to

475 bottom right A giant anteater (Myrmecophaga tridactyla) explores a baía, a plain subject to seasonal flooding. It features semideciduous vegetation of small trees and shrubs.

476 top The capybara (Hydrachaeris hydrachaeris) is at home in the water. The world's largest rodent is an able swimmer and diver thanks to the membrane between its toes, similar to fins.

476 bottom left A green anaconda (Eunectes murinus) waits for a meal in the aquatic vegetation. These reptiles are very prolific: at least 40 are born in a single clutch. At birth they are already 18 inches long.

476 center Despite their harmless appearance, the giant otter (Pteronura brasiliensis) is one of the region's greatest predators. They feed on fish, crabs, snakes and even caimans and eat 10 pounds of food a day.

476 bottom right A magnificent example of a banded tiger heron (Tigrisoma lineatum) has successfully made a catch.

survive, it has to wrap itself around the palms in a spiral.

Zoologists deem the Pantanal to be one of the wet zones with the largest variety of species, which, including the cursorily studied category of invertebrates, roughly totals the amazing figure of 150,000. There are 80 or so mammals, including the jaguar, ocelot, giant anteater, armadillo, tapir and capuchin monkey. The largest mammals are the elegant swamp deer (*Blastocerus dichotomus*) and the capybara

476-477 With a population of caimans (Crocodylus jacare) estimated at around 10 millions, the Pantanal is the area with the highest concentration of crocodiles in the world. It is said that there are 22 'visible' in every square mile.

477 bottom Although just in the 1980s around 130,000 yellow anaconda (Eunectes notaeus) skins were put on the black market, having been hunted in the Pantanal, this reptile is still very common in the area.

(*Hydrochoerus hydrochaeris*), which, at a weight of 66 pounds, is the largest rodent in the world. The birdlife numbers 656 species belonging to 66 families; in addition to the hyacinthine macaw and 26 other sorts of parrot, there is a large number of herons, egrets and other aquatic birds. The symbol of the Brazilian park is the jabiru (*Jabiru mycteria*), a crane, whose white plumage has a red ring on the lower part of its neck. With a wingspan of 9 feet, it is one of the most majestic fliers in the world. The 400 or more species of fish make the Pantanal the largest freshwater fish reserve in the continent, and the roughly 10 million caimans (*Crocodilus*

yacare) give the area the largest concentration of crocodiles on the planet. Their reputation as being dangerous to man is unmerited, given that caimans are not very aggressive, but the same is not true of the anaconda (*Eunectes murinus*), the most common reptile in the Pantanal.

Aside from poaching, the Pantanal's ecosystem is threatened by two massive engineering projects that would affect a vast part of its territory. The first is the construction of a 2 billion dollar gas pipe between Río Grande in Bolivia and Rio de Janeiro. The second, which according to scientists would literally change the characteristics of the

478 top The Pantanal is an excellent habitat for the jaguar judging by the size of those that live there. However, it is estimated that only one adult remains for every 25 square miles of territory.

478 bottom The roseate spoonbill (Ajaja ajaja) gets its coloring from the level of carotene in the crustaceans it feeds on.

environment, is the creation of the Idrovia, a network of navigable canals 2,140 miles in length, as part of a joint project between Argentina, Bolivia, Brazil, Uruguay and Paraguay. Put on paper at the end of the 1980s, this network would halve the cost of goods' transport, which are currently all carried by road. So far the work has not been begun owing to the massive costs involved, which would be difficult to support by the countries suffering serious

economic difficulty – or perhaps because of the campaign being waged across all of Brazil to save the Pantanal. Although most Brazilians did not even know of its existence until 1990, they suddenly became impassioned about its fate that year. Thanks to a television soap opera called 'Pantanal', which narrated the lives and loves of a family of animal breeders who lived in a *fazenda* on the edges of the protected area, the country was glued to the set for months.

479 bottom During the mating season, two male egrets (Casmerodius albus) fight bitterly while in flight.

Iguazú Falls
ARGENTINA/BRAZIL

BUENOS AIRES

PROVINCE OF MISIONES (ARGENTINA),
STATE OF PARANÁ (BRAZIL)
REGISTRATION: 1986
INSCRIPTION IN THE WORLD HERITAGE LIST
IN DANGER IN 1999-2001
CRITERIA: N (III) (IV)

It rises in the Serra do Mar, not far from the Atlantic Ocean and runs 800 miles along the Paraná plateau receiving the waters of 30 tributaries and widening to almost a mile across. But it is only after this docile jaunt that it earns itself the name that it has been given by the indigenous peoples: Iguazú. In the Guaraní language, the name Iguazú (or *Iguaçú* in the Brazilian transliteration) means 'great water'. Even more impressive is the spectacle of the river as it launches itself from a semicircular amphitheater of basalt lava 2.5 miles wide and 260 feet high in a curtain of 275 separate falls. Accompanied by crashing thunder and the immense mass of vapor shot through by rainbows, this extraordinary place has been described as 'the most beautiful border in the world'.

Iguazú Falls are shared between Argentina and Brazil. 'Only' 2,700 feet of the falls lie on Brazilian territory but, in recompense, it is from a natural Brazilian observation point that visitors have the best view of the Garganta del Diablo (Devil's Throat), the falls' most famous cataract. After its drop, the river rushes into a canyon just 260 feet wide (over which the Puente Tancredo Neves has been built to unite the two countries) and runs for 20 or so miles before flowing into the Río Paraná.

To protect the falls and subtropical forest that, thanks to a constant humidity level of 80-90%, covers almost all the area adjacent to the falls and the many islands in the river, the Argentine and Brazilian governments long ago set up two national parks. In both territories the wet subtropical forest is rich with species of ferns, including the gigantic *Dicksonia selowiana*, bamboo, lianas and other climbing plants, bromeliaceae and epiphytes, of which there are 80 different types of orchid. The banks of the river are typified by the association of the tree *Aspidosperma polynerum* that can reach a height of 100 feet, with numerous species of palms, such as *Euterpe edulis*.

The fauna is also varied and interesting, including many mammals in danger of extinction. There is the giant otter (*Pteronura brasilensis*), jaguar (*Panthera oncha*), giant anteater (*Myrmecophaga tridactyla*) and puma (*Felis concolor*). There is also an enormous variety of birds, including five species of toucan and many parrots.

In recent years, pressure from humans has raised worries for the protection of the ecosystem. Three sizeable urban centers lie at the edge of the parks: Foz do Iguaçu in Brazil, Puerto Iguazú in Argentina and Rio de la Plata in nearby Paraguay. In Foz do Iguaçu alone (which had 30,000 inhabitants in 1960 and now has 200,000) there are 160 hotels and it is estimated that the Brazilian section of the park receives 1 million visitors a year. The guards in both parks have reported illegal fishing and indiscriminate cutting down of palms as their hearts are considered a food delicacy. But perhaps the greatest danger to the falls lies with the gigantic Itaipu dam opened in 1991 a little downstream of the falls. Though, on the one hand, the 12.5 million kilowatts produced by the hydroelectric plant provide 40% of the needs of Argentina and Brazil, on the other hand, it has caused notable morphological and climatic imbalances.

480-481 The 'great water' – this is the meaning of the word iguazú in the Guaraní language – leaps into a semi-circular basalt amphitheater 236 feet deep and nearly 3,000 yards across.

480 bottom left With constant humidity of 80-90%, the area around Iguazú Falls is covered by an intricate subtropical forest with many species of ferns, bamboos, bromeliads, lianas and orchids.

480 bottom right The Ramphastos toco, with its striking bill, is one of five species of toucan in the park. In the area next to the falls 422 species of birds have been recorded.

481 top The rainbow created by the spray that rises from the base of the waterfall makes the sight of the Garganta del Diablo even more spectacular. This is the most famous of the 274 cataracts in Iguazú.

Parque Nacionál Los Glaciares

ARGENTINA

PROVINCE OF SANTA CRUZ
REGISTRATION: 1981
CRITERIA: N (II) (III)

BUENOS AIRES

482-483 Covering an area of 96 square miles, the Perito Moreno Glacier is an arm of the immense Campo de Hielo Patagónico. In complete contrast to other glaciers in the region and most of the planet, its mass is constantly on the increase.

482 bottom An iceberg opens a passage along the Canál de los Tímpanos, which is a narrow stretch that connects the Perito Moreno Glacier with the main basin of Lake Argentino. Situated on the 50th parallel, the lake is the southernmost of the great Andean lakes in Argentina.

Although he was only 25 years old, Francisco Pascasio Moreno was already on his fifth voyage to the inhospitable land of Argentinian Patagonia when, on 15 February 1877, he found himself standing before one of the most spectacular sights in that region: an immense glacial lake stretched out at the feet of the southern Andes into which large glaciers slid slowly down the mountain sides.

In fact he was not the first to discover the lake; that honor belonged to second lieutenant Valentin Feilberg, who had visited the region four years previous but thought he had arrived on the shores of Lake Viedma some tens of miles further north. It was Moreno, therefore, who named the lake, which he baptized Lake Argentino, using the rather rhetorical speech sometimes heard from great explorers.

Many years later the most fascinating natural feature of the zone was named in his honor; the glacier Perito Moreno in which the word 'perito' is the title he was given at the end of the nineteenth century when the government asked him to deal with the delicate question of the border between Argentina and Chile. Spread over an area of about 96 square miles, the Perito Moreno is a strip of the Campo de Hielo Patagónico, the largest iced area in the world outside of the polar caps. A legacy of the ice that covered the Southern Hemisphere during the last Ice Age, the Campo de Hielo covers 5,400 square miles and its many arms stretch into the wide valleys eroded by the movement of ice over the millennia.

The Perito Moreno is one of these arms, and its mass is in continuous increase as it is fed by the Campo de Hielo. The glacier

overlooks Canàl de los Tímpanos, a narrow passage that connects the Brazo Rico and the Brazo Sur to the main section of Lake Argentino. At regular intervals the front of Perito Moreno – 3 miles wide and 200 feet high – reaches the opposite bank, thereby blocking the channel and preventing the exchange of the two bodies of water. That causes a rise in the waters of Brazo Rico of up to 80 feet. With the increase in pressure the glacier begins to fracture and water enters the ice, whereupon it collapses in a thunderous crash. During the twentieth century, this spectacular phenomenon was repeated every 30 years or so, the last in 1988.

Though extraordinary, the Perito Moreno is only one of the 47 main glaciers to be found in the 1,722 square miles of the Parque Nacional Los Glaciares instituted in 1937. Nor is it even the largest, as it is exceeded in size by the Upsala (230 square

484 top Though all less than 13,000 feet high, the three peaks of Cerro Torre, Torre Egger and Cerro Stanhardt have few rivals in the history of extreme mountaineering. The major difficulties are posed by the weather – often prohibitive – and the isolation of the region.

484-485 The majestic Cerro Fitz Roy is reflected in the cold water of Desierto Lake. The lakes in the park have an overall area of 367 square miles. The largest are Lake Viedma, in the north, and Lake Argentino.

miles) and the Viedma (222 square miles). The park also contains more than 200 secondary glaciers, each less than 1 square mile in size and not connected to the Campo de Hielo Patagonico. The size of the Campo occupies 1,000 square miles inside the park, i.e., more than 50% of its overall surface.

The glacial activity is concentrated around Lake Argentino and Lake Viedma, whose waters flow into the Rio Cruz before being carried to the Atlantic Ocean. The erosion caused by glaciation during the Quaternary epoch also created many steep, pointed Andean peaks in the area, for example, the Cerro Fitz Roy (or Cerro Chalten, which, at 11,070 feet, is the highest mountain in the park) and mounts Peineta, Heim and Agassiz. The Cerro Torre, on the other hand – at 10,262 feet, the second highest mountain in the region – is rounded.

Being mostly covered by glaciers and lakes, the Parque Nacionál Los Glaciares has little fauna or flora, but there are two well defined phytogeographic formations: these are the sub-Antarctic forest and the Patagonian forest. The former is spread over the mountain slopes and characterized by the ñire and *guindo* (*Cohiue magallanico*) trees, as well as by various species of beech, one of which is the *lenga* (*Nothofagus*

pumilio). A recent observation has been the return of the Guaitecas cypress (*Pilgerodendron uviferum*).

The Patagonian steppe is composed of grasslands featuring the extremely widespread *calafate*, the notro, *saúco del diablo* and the *topa-topa*. The *calafate* is a bush that produces bittersweet berries and the *notro* is recognizable by its lovely red leaves.

A full survey has not yet been completed of the park's fauna, mostly because there is very little information on the vertebrates that inhabit the region with the exception of the birds. There are a hundred or so species of birds, including the Andean condor (*Vultur gryphus*), which nests at high altitude in colonies called condoreras. The most notable mammals are the puma (*Felis concolor*), the gray fox (*Duscicyon griseus*), the piche, which is a small armadillo, the guanaco (*Lama guanacoe*) and the huemul (*Hippocamelus bisulcus*).

During recent years, Patagonia has experienced growing tourism but no danger has been registered to the local flora and fauna. Experts are instead worried by the contraction of the glaciers caused by global warming. Recent satellite photography has shown that all the glaciers in the Campo de Hielo are shrinking – except for one, the Perito Moreno.

485 top left In the clear air of a Patagonian autumn, the terrain at the foot of Fitz Roy is tinted with the bright hues of a sub-Antarctic beech forest of Nothofagus pumilio.

485 center left Cerro Torre is the sharp peak on the left, and Fitz Roy the tall one on the right. They flank a wide glacial valley in one of the loveliest mountain scenes in the world. Generally, the Andes are almost completely isolated from human activity.

485 top right The north face of Cerro Torre is swept by a storm. This formidable granite tower – considered one of the most difficult to climb in the world – was first conquered in 1959 by climbers Cesare Maestri and Toni Egger.

485 bottom From the top of Loma del Peque Umbado, dawn reveals the glorious scenery of Fitz Roy (also known as Cerro Chaltén at 11,073 feet) and Cerro Torre (at 10,262 feet).

Kakadu National Park

AUSTRALIA

NORTHERN TERRITORY

REGISTRATION: 1981; EXTENSIONS 1987, 1992

CRITERIA: C (I) (VI); N (II) (III) (IV)

With his feet planted solidly on the ground, and body covered with ritual paintings, the evil spirit with the unpronounceable name of Nabulwinjubulwinj triumphs on Nourlangie Rock, which towers over the alluvial plains to the west of the Australian continental scarp. The cosmogony of the Gagudju aboriginals is not limited to evil spirits: there is also Warramurrungundji, 'the mother of the earth', who, having arrived from the islands to the northeast, created child spirits and taught them how to speak and hunt. She also created the rivers, plants and animals of the world before turning herself into a rock.

The spirits of the ancestors are one of the favorite subjects in the rock paintings of the aboriginals that have inhabited north Australia for at least the last 25,000 years, but their art also illustrates hunting, the nature that surrounded them and even their first contact with white men. The 1,000 archeological sites and 7,000 examples of aboriginal rock art are the reason why the Kakadu National Park is one of the few sites registered in the UNESCO World Heritage sites both for its cultural and natural values.

Created originally in 1964 as the Woolwonga Aboriginal Reserve to protect the 300 or so people who lived there, Kakadu National Park has gradually been expanded from its initial 195 square miles to cover 7,700. It lies in a zone that is tectonically relatively stable, having been formed 2.5 billion years ago, but has been remodeled over time to display geomorphological features that illustrate much of this planet's history.

Although six geological formations can be recognized, the main element is the system created by the plateau in Arnhem Land and the continental scarp, which rises rapidly to 1,000 feet and runs 320 miles down the eastern edge. It is thought that 140 million years ago much of Kakadu was covered by a shallow sea. Once the water level dropped, the rock formation that at the time were cliffs, formed the continental scarp, and the vast plain known as Koolpniyah Surface originated at its foot. In antiquity, crags like Nourlangie Rock used to be islands near the coast of this shallow sea.

Other features are drainage basins, alluvial plains formed by torrents that dragged sediments downstream during the rainy season, the southern hills of volcanic origin, and the estuarine flatlands that were affected by tides that used to arrive 60 miles inland.

486 left The saltwater crocodile (Crocodylus porosus) inhabits the Alligator Rivers area. Of the 128 species of reptiles in Kakadu, the crocodiles represent three and the snakes 39.

486 right The jabiru or black-necked stork (Xenorhynchus asiaticus) is also known as the 'policeman bird' for the color of its plumage. Unlike other species of waders, it is a solitary bird.

486-487 The alluvial plain of Magela Creek was once a sea bed. It stretches out of sight, dotted with the occasional tree.

487 top A large community of common egrets (Egretta alba) populates a coastal lagoon. These ecosystems stretch up to 60 miles inland and are inhabited by animal and vegetable species that have adapted to living on saline mud.

487 right This very young nankeen (Nycticorax caledonicus) or nocturnal heron belongs to one of the 274 species of birds classified in Kakadu National Park; these represent 33% of all those in Australia.

487 bottom Some magpie geese (Anseranas semipalmata) wander in search of food in a lagoon in flower. This aquatic bird is hunted by aboriginals for its meat.

CANBERRA

The biodiversity of the park has no equal anywhere in Australia. More than 1,600 plants have been recorded, 58 of which are considered of maximum importance for reasons of conservation, and a further 97 are rare or threatened. The flora of Arnhem Land is important, with many endemic species. The area features 13 floral communities, three of which are rainforests, seven are dominated by different species of eucalyptus and the others by salicornias, marshes of *melaleuca* and mangroves swamps along the coast.

Most of the 64 mammals in Kakadu inhabit the forests; 26 are bats, 15 rodents, eight kangaroos and possums, bandicoots and quolls. Endangered at a global level are the dugong *(Dugong dugon)* and the bat *Macroderma gigas*. Of the 128 reptiles, those declared vulnerable or threatened with extinction are the saltwater crocodile *(Crocodylus porosus)* and three species of turtle *(Caretta caretta, Chelonia mydas* and *Eretmochelys imbricata)*.

The monsoon climate brings rain from November to April, and this, with the huge variety of ecosystems, has created ideal conditions for a wide assortment of birdlife. The area is home to 274 species, which is one third of all the species that inhabit Australia. Important birds are the red goshawk *(Accipiter radiatus)*, Gouldian finch *(Chloebia gouldiae)* and the hooded parrot *(Psephotus dissimilis)*.

Being unaffected by the presence of man, the primary threats to the environmental balance in Kakadu have historically been created by the buffalo *(Bubalus bubalis)*, which damages the indigenous vegetation, thereby accelerating erosion. Once the population of the buffalo had been cut down, the worst threat to the biodiversity passed to two infestant grasses: *Mimosa pigra* and *Salvinia molesta*. Since 1984, significant efforts have been made to eradicate the mimosa from river estuaries, but the threat remains. As for Salvinia molesta, the infestation has reached such a point that plans have been made to control it biologically with an insect *(Cryptobagus salviniae)*, which is its natural enemy. The entire area of the Magela Torrent in the northeast of the park has been put in quarantine. For the moment, the battle against *Salvinia molesta* seems to have been won, and therefore a dangerous situation of eutrophication of the waters has been avoided, and Kakadu has returned to being one of the parks with the lowest percentage of infestant grasses in the world.

488 *These red rock walls near Blomfield springs in Arnhem Land stand in a section of the park that is both aesthetically and geologically spectacular.*

489 *top left Similar to a cathedral, this gigantic termite mound is the work of* Nasutitermus triodia.

489 *top right The blue-winged kookaburra* (Dachelo leachii) *has a very distinctive sound like a human laugh.*

489 *bottom There are about 1,000 archeological sites and 7,000 examples of rock art in the park, all dating to a period ranging from 25,000 years ago to the first meetings with European colonists in the seventeenth century.*

The Great Barrier Reef

AUSTRALIA

REGISTRATION: 1981
CRITERIA: N (I) (II) (III) (IV)

The Great Barrier Reef Marine Park Act is the name of the official document with which, in 1975, the Australian government instituted what is the largest protected area in the world. With an area of 127,900 square miles, (though the zone that forms the UNESCO World Heritage site is even lager), it is 48 times the size than Texas, but the UNESCO World Heritage site is even larger, extending into the Pacific Ocean for more than 1,240 miles from Australia's east coast and from the Tropic of Capricorn to the coastal waters of Papua New Guinea.

This sweep of the Pacific contains the largest expanse of coral reef in the world. Overall there are 3,400 single reefs measuring between 2 acres and 380 square miles, roughly 300 coral islands of which 213 lack any vegetation and 618 islands that were once part of the Australian continent. The form and structure of each reef vary extremely but fall within two main types: platform reefs that are the result of radial growth and wall reefs that are usually found in areas where there are strong underwater currents.

The surface flora is poor, and prevalently *Pisonia grandis* on Heron and Musgrave Islands, whilst on Hoskin Island there is an unusual forest of pandans, *Pisonia* and *Ficus apposita*. Elsewhere there are casuarinas, which are sturdy trees named after the cassowary owing to the similarity of the branches to the plumage of the large flightless bird, and grasses of various genera. The underwater flora, however, is spectacular, with many small but very

490-491 Hardy Reef is a typical platform formation of roughly 11 square miles. It is an underwater mountain of organic origin and rises 250 feet from the bottom of the ocean.

490 bottom Hardy Reef and Hook Reef together form one of the most spectacular complexes in the Great Barrier Reef. The thin dark band that separates them is a narrow passage called 'the River'.

productive algae that provide an important source of nutrition for turtles, fish, echinoderms and mollusks, besides being an important component in the formation of the reefs.

The incredible fauna of the Great Barrier Reef is indicated by statistics: there are more than 1,500 species of fish, 400 corals, 4,000 mollusks, 242 birds and an extraordinary variety of sponges, anemones, sea worms and crustaceans. There are many cetaceans, including humpback whales (*Megaptera novaengliae*), blue whales (*Balaenoptera acutorostrata*) and the killer whale (*Orcinus orca*); other mammals are the bottle-nosed dolphin (*Tursiops truncatus*), the Irrawaddy dolphin (*Orcaella brevirostris*), spinner dolphin (*Stenella longirostris*) and the Indo-Pacific humpback dolphin (*Sousa chinensis*). The islands are nesting places of worldwide importance to the green turtle (*Chelonia mydas*) and the common sea turtle (*Caretta caretta*).

Finally, the Great Barrier Reef is also the most important refuge for the dugong (*Dugong dugon*), which is a marine mammal (whose closest relative above sea level is the elephant) in the same family as the manatees, which Christopher Columbus believed were mermaids on his trip towards the Americas. A placid herbivore that grazes on underwater meadows and

491 top Stretching from southern Australia to Papua New Guinea and with a surface area as large as Italy, the Great Barrier Reef is easily the largest protected area in UNESCO's World Heritage sites.

491 center Heaven for divers, Heron Island lies across the Tropic of Capricorn 331 miles north of Brisbane in the Capricorn-Bunker Group. This is a section of the Great Barrier Reef measuring 4,720 square miles in area.

491 bottom With the coral reef lying a short distance from the beach, Heron Island is one of the unspoilt paradises of the Great Barrier Reef. Approximately 850 species of fish have been recorded in its lagoon.

CANBERRA

492 top During their winter migration, humpback whales pass by Heron Island; sea turtles use the island to lay their eggs.

492-493 A view of the clear waters of Tongue Bay on Whitsunday Island. This is the largest of the 74 islets and islands in the Whitsunday Group.

The archipelago represents the remains of a coastal mountain range that was submerged by the rise in sea level following the end of the last Ice Age.

492 bottom left Completely uninhabited, Whitsunday Island is covered by mangrove forests, as is shown by the photograph taken from Hill Inlet.

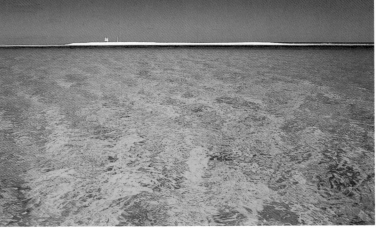

492 bottom right Most of the 300 cays (coral islets that poke several feet above sea level) were recently formed and are still devoid of vegetation.

493 top Whitehaven Beach is on Whitsunday Island. James Cook discovered the island on Pentecost Sunday (Whitsunday) in 1779.

The 4 miles of this narrow white sandy beach are one of the favorite destinations of the 3 million tourists that visit the Great Barrier Reef every year.

493

lives in coastal waters, the dugong can reach 10 feet in length and 450 pounds in weight. Recently the James Cook University in Townsville raised the alarm over the survival of this rare mammal, which has already disappeared from the seas around the Philippines, Japan, Cambodia and Vietnam. A very limited number survives, perhaps 80, in the seagrass meadows in the Andaman Sea near the southwest coast of Thailand. Even the colonies that live near Dunk Island in the Barrier Reef have been reduced in number by half recently.

During the last couple of decades, the astounding scenery of the coral reefs has become an important source of income for the aboriginal peoples that live on the islands of the Great Barrier Reef. Three million visitors a year contribute to the transition from a subsistence economy based on fishing to a more prosperous one based on tourism.

493 bottom Five hours by steamer from Brisbane, Lady Musgrave Island is a typical coral atoll. Its 35 acres of land are covered by a forest of Pisonia grandis that provides a home to many birds, and the 4.6 square miles of lagoons were declared a national park in 1938.

494 top left and right Pale sunlight illuminates the delicate ramifications of the colonies of gorgonias, which can take the shape of a fan (left) or bunch together to form conglomerates resembling a bush (right).

494-495 Made up of 3,400 individual reefs, the Great Barrier Reef comprises roughly 400 species of coral, which provide an extraordinary habitat for thousands of types of marine animals.

495 top Around 130 feet down the currents favor the growth of many types of gorgonias, including the flexible colonies like the one illustrated. Their ramifications spread out from a short central stem.

495 bottom There is an enormous variety in the form and structure of the reefs, though they are generally divided into two classes: platform reefs, the result of radial growth, and reefs produced by vertical growth.

Uluru-Kata Tjuta National Park

AUSTRALIA

NORTHERN TERRITORY
REGISTRATION: 1987, 1994
CRITERIA: C (V) (VI), N (II) (III)

The mythology of the Anangu aboriginals tells that in the beginning there was the *Tjukurpa*, the Dreamtime. The earth was flat and empty, without either light or darkness, and nature awaited the arrival of the divine heroes to bring form and life. It was the heroes that created Uluru – the Red Center – the sacred mountain that would witness all following events. Uluru was the location of the intersection of the *Iwara*, the Songlines, which is a maze of invisible paths that runs across all of Australia. The *Mara* (wallaby), *Liru* (poisonous snake) and *Kunija* (python) – totemic ancestors of the aboriginals – came out from a pool of water on the summit of the red mountain to sing everything that they saw, thereby creating the world through song.

During his wanderings, the British writer, Bruce Chatwin, learned of the Songlines, handed down from generation to generation orally, and decided to cross the bare terrain that they spoke of. He was astounded by the vision the aboriginals had of the world. As he wrote, 'they moved across the Earth with a light step. The less they

took from the Earth, the less they had to restore to it.'

The spectacular scenery of Uluru is one of the supreme manifestations on the planet of the interaction of man and the natural environment. Nor does the creation myth of the Anangu differ much from the scientific explanation that geologists give of its origin. This enormous sandstone monolith – whose reddish color is the result of oxidation of its ferrous components – rises in the oldest region in the world. If there ever were a Dreamtime, it could have been the Precambrian era, which possibly began as much as 3,800,000,000 years ago, when primordial oceans and continents were being bombarded by the ultraviolet rays of the sun, the atmosphere was composed of gases issued by volcanoes, and the surface of the land was a sort of chemical laboratory ready to welcome the miracle of life. Geologists do not know precisely when the monolith emerged from the submarine depths, but it is certain that it occurred long before Pangea (the supercontinent that included Australia, Africa, South America, India and the Antarctic) began to break up into a

*496 bottom left
A semispherical mass of sandstone that emerged from the endless expanses of the Australian desert, Uluru has a circumference of 5.8 miles and rises almost 1,150 feet above the arid land.*

496 bottom right Uluru was first climbed by William Gosse in 1873, who named it Ayers Rock in honor of Sir Henry Ayers, Prime Minister of Australia and the sponsor of Gosse's expedition; climbing Uluru was, and still is, considered sacrilegious by the aboriginals.

496-497 In aboriginal mythology, the term Ulura can be translated as 'the Red Center'. It is the sacred mountain where the Songlines intersect, a crisscross of invisible paths that envelop the entire Australian continent.

497 top Uluru's unmistakable red color is the result of oxidation of the ferrous minerals in the rock. It is thought to be the largest monolith in the world.

CANBERRA

mosaic of drifting continental masses.

Uluru is therefore one of the most mysterious and interesting geological phenomena on earth and fully merits the respect it is paid by the aboriginals; to them, even today, to climb this amazing hemispheric mountain constitutes a sacrilegious act. The first man to reach the top – 1,140 feet above the desert below – was the English

497 bottom The lack of precipitation does not encourage a rich flora but it is possible to distinguish five concentric vegetative bands that encircle Uluru. The dominant species include herbaceous plants and perennial shrubs.

498-499 Also called 'the Olgas', Kata Tjuta ('Many Heads') rise almost 2,000 feet above the plain. The arid-desert climate means that surface water is limited to small seasonal pools.

498 bottom Covering an area of 13.5 square miles, Kata Tjuta are a series of 36 rock domes with almost perfectly vertical walls and rounded tops. They have been subjected to the same erosive processes as Uluru.

499 top Perfectly adapted to the region's climate, dromedaries introduced by Europeans compete with indigenous species and threaten their survival.

499 bottom The 19 miles that separate Ulura from Kata Tjuta is a desolate landscape of mobile dunes continuously fashioned by the wind.

explorer William Gosse in 1873. Taking advantage of the adherence offered by the smooth sandstone sides, which have a gradient of up to 80%, and, above all, aided by Kamran, his Afghan camel-driver, Gosse got to the top by opening a route on the south wall. In his notes, Gosse compared the experience to 'scaling the body of a giant whale'; when he returned to civilization, he very prosaically dedicated the sacred mountain to Sir Henry Ayer, the Australian Prime Minister who had financed the expedition.

The two names – Ulura and Ayer's Rock – represent the sacred and profane natures of the same mountain. It took years of struggle with the Australian government, which had instituted the national park in 1977 (although the rock was officially protected since 1958), for the aboriginals to have the right to part manage the territory and to place certain limitations on access to the sacred places in their ancestral myths. Today, climbing Uluru is discouraged but is not prohibited to tourists, but many waterfalls, ravines and caves containing ancient graffiti, confirming man's stable presence in the area for the past 20,000 years, are off limits. Included in the protected area are the Kata Tjuta ('Many Heads'), which is a chain of 36

mountains with near vertical walls and hemispheric summits that rise up to 1,970 feet from the plateau and lie 19 or so miles east of Uluru. Between the two rock formations stretches a landscape of red sand dunes that are constantly shifting due to the action of the wind.

The presence of water across the whole of the park territory is limited to short stretches and seasonal pools. In summer – from November to March – the climate is very dry and the temperature reaches 113°F. In consequence, the vegetation is very limited and is divided into five categories, which lie in concentric circles around Uluru. Closest to the rock there are perennial bushes from the *Cymbopogon* and *Tripogon* species. As one moves out into the desert, one finds isolated clumps of eucalyptus and acacia trees. The fauna includes 22 indigenous mammals, like the dingo and species of marsupials and rodents, and 150 types of birds, 66 of which are resident. But the symbols of Uluru are the reptiles, such as the clamidosaurus and the *Moloch horridus*, animals of prehistoric appearance. These creatures are the principal subjects in traditional aboriginal paintings, which are an artistic transposition of the *Inma*, the songs from the Dreamtime.

List of the Sites

The sites in bold also belong to the *List of World Heritage in Danger*

AFGHANISTAN
Minaret and Archaeological Remains of Jam (2002)
Cultural Landscape and Archaeological Remains of the Bamiyan Valley (2003)

ALBANIA
Butrint (1992, 1999)

ALGERIA
Al Qal'a of Beni Hammad (1980)
Tassili n'Ajjer (1982)
M'Zab Valley (1982)
Djémila (1982)
Tipasa (1982)
Timgad (1982)
Kasbah of Algiers (1992)

ANDORRA
Madriu-Perafita-Claror Valley (2004)

ARGENTINA
Los Glaciares (1981)
Jesuit Missions of the Guaranis: San Ignacio Mini, Santa Ana, Nuestra Señora de Loreto and Santa Maria Mayor (Argentina), Ruins of Sao Miguel das Missoes (Brazil) (1983, 1984)
Iguazu National Park (1984)
Cueva de las Manos, Río Pinturas (1999)
Península Valdés (1999)
Ischigualasto / Talampaya Natural Parks (2000)
Jesuit Block and Estancias of Córdoba (2000)
Quebrada de Humahuaca (2003)

ARMENIA
Monasteries of Haghpat and Sanahin (1996, 2000)
Cathedral and Churches of Echmiatsin and the Archaeological Site of Zvartnots (2000)
Monastery of Geghard and the Upper Azat Valley (2000)

AUSTRALIA
Kakadu National Park (1981, 1987, 1992)
Great Barrier Reef (1981)
Willandra Lakes Region (1981)
Tasmanian Wilderness (1982, 1989)
Lord Howe Island Group (1982)
Central Eastern Rainforest Reserves (Australia) (1986, 1994)
Uluru-Kata Tjuta National Park (1987, 1994)
Wet Tropics of Queensland (1988)
Shark Bay, Western Australia (1991)
Fraser Island (1992)
Australian Fossil Mammal Sites (Riversleigh/ Naracote) (1994)
Heard and McDonald Islands (1997)
Macquarie Island (1997)
Greater Blue Mountains Area (2000)
Purnululu National Park (2003)
Royal Exhibition Building and Carlton Gardens (2004)

AUSTRIA
Historic Centre of the City of Salzburg (1996)
Palace and Gardens of Schönbrunn (1996)
Hallstatt-Dachstein Salzkammergut Cultural Landscape (1997)
Semmering Railway (1998)
City of Graz - Historic Centre (1999)
Wachau Cultural Landscape (2000)
Historic Centre of Vienna (2001)
Fertö/Neusiedlersee Cultural Landscape (2001)

AZERBAIJAN
Walled City of Baku with the Shirvanshah's Palace and Maiden Tower (2000)

BANGLADESH
Historic Mosque City of Bagerhat (1985)
Ruins of the Buddhist Vihara at Paharpur (1985)
The Sundarbans (1997)

BELARUS
Belovezhskaya Pushcha / Biaowieza Forest (1979, 1992)
Mir Castle Complex (2000)

BELGIUM
Flemish Béguinages (1998)
The Four Lifts on the Canal du Centre and their Environs, La Louvière and Le Roeulx (Hainault) (1998)
Grand-Place, Brussels (1998)
Belfries of Flanders and Wallonia (1999)
Major Town Houses of the Architect Victor Horta (Brussels) (2000)
Neolithic Flint Mines at Spiennes (Mons) (2000)
Notre-Dame Cathedral in Tournai (2000)
Historic Centre of Brugge (2000)

BELIZE
Belize Barrier-Reef Reserve System (1996)

BENIN
Royal Palaces of Abomey (1985)

BOLIVIA
City of Potosi (1987)
Jesuit Missions of the Chiquitos (1990)
Historic City of Sucre (1991)
Fuerte de Samaipata (1998)
Tiwanaku: Spiritual and Political Centre of the Tiwanaku Culture (2000)
Noel Kempff Mercado National Park (2000)

BOTSWANA
Tsodilo (2001)

BRAZIL
Historic Town of Ouro Preto (1980)
Historic Centre of the Town of Olinda (1982)
Jesuit Missions of the Guaranis: San Ignacio Mini, Santa Ana, Nuestra Señora de Loreto and Santa Maria Mayor (Argentina), Ruins of Sao Miguel das Missoes (Brazil) (1983, 1984)
Historic Centre of Salvador de Bahia (1985)
Sanctuary of Bom Jesus do Congonhas (1985)
Iguaçu National Park (1986)
Brasilia (1987)
Serra da Capivara National Park (1991)
Historic Centre of São Luis (1997)
Historic Centre of the Town of Diamantina (1999)
Discovery Coast Atlantic Forest Reserves (1999)
Atlantic Forest Southeast Reserves (1999)
Central Amazon Conservation Complex (2000, 2003)
Pantanal Conservation Area (2000)
Brazilian Atlantic Islands: Fernando de Noronha and Atol das Rocas Reserves (2001)
Cerrado Protected Areas: Chapada dos Veadeiros and Emas National Parks (2001)
Historic Centre of the Town of Goiás (2001)

BULGARIA
Boyana Church (1979)
Madara Rider (1979)
Thracian Tomb of Kazanlak (1979)
Rock-hewn Churches of Ivanovo (1979)
Rila Monastery (1983)
Ancient City of Nessebar (1983)
Srebarna Nature Reserve (1983)
Pirin National Park (1983)
Thracian Tomb of Sveshtari (1985)

CAMBODIA
Angkor (1992)

CAMEROON
Dja Faunal Reserve (1987)

CANADA
Nahanni National Park (1978)
L'Anse aux Meadows National Historic Site (1978)
Dinosaur Provincial Park (1979)
Kluane/Wrangell-St. Elias/Glacier Bay/Tatshenshini-Alsek (1979, 1992, 1994)
SGaang Gwaii (Anthony Island) (1981)
Head-Smashed-In Buffalo Jump (1981)
Wood Buffalo National Park (1983)
Canadian Rocky Mountain Parks (1984, 1990)
Historic District of Québec (1985)
Gros Morne National Park (1987)
Waterton Glacier International Peace Park (1995)
Old Town Lunenburg (1995)
Miguasha National Park (1999)

CENTRAL AFRICAN REPUBLIC
Manovo-Gounda St Floris National Park (1988)

CHILE
Rapa Nui National Park (1995)
Churches of Chiloé (2000)
Historic Quarter of the Seaport City of Valparaíso (2003)

CHINA
Mount Taishan (1987) The Great Wall (1987)
Imperial Palaces of the Ming and Qing Dynasties in Beijing and Shenyang (1987, 2004)
Mogao Caves (1987)
Mausoleum of the First Qin Emperor (1987)
Peking Man Site at Zhoukoudian (1987)
Mount Huangshan (1990)
Jiuzhaigou Valley Scenic and Historic Interest Area (1992)
Huanglong Scenic and Historic Interest Area (1992)
Wulingyuan Scenic and Historic Interest Area (1992)
Mountain Resort and its Outlying Temples, Chengde (1994)

Temple and Cemetery of Confucius and the Kong Family Mansion in Qufu (1994)
Ancient Building Complex in the Wudang Mountains (1994)
Historic Ensemble of the Potala Palace, Lhasa (1994, 2000, 2001)
Lushan National Park (1996)
Mount Emei Scenic Area, including Leshan Giant Buddha Scenic Area (1996)
Old Town of Lijiang (1997)
Ancient City of Ping Yao (1997)
Classical Gardens of Suzhou (1997, 2000)
Summer Palace, an Imperial Garden in Beijing (1998)
Temple of Heaven: an Imperial Sacrificial Altar in Beijing (1998)
Mount Wuyi (1999)
Dazu Rock Carvings (1999)
Mount Qingcheng and the Dujiangyan Irrigation System (2000)
Ancient Villages in Southern Anhui - Xidi and Hongcun (2000)
Longmen Grottoes (2000)
Imperial Tombs of the Ming and Qing Dynasties (2000, 2003,2004)
Yungang Grottoes (2001)
Three Parallel Rivers of Yunnan Protected Areas (2003)
Capital Cities and Tombs of the Ancient Koguryo Kingdom (2004)

COLOMBIA
Port, Fortresses and Group of Monuments, Cartagena (1984)
Los Katios National Park (1994)
Historic Centre of Santa Cruz de Mompox (1995)
National Archeological Park of Tierradentro (1995)
San Agustín Archeological Park (1995)

COSTA RICA
Talamanca Range-La Amistad Reserves / La Amistad National Park (1983, 1990)
Cocos Island National Park (1997, 2002)
Area de Conservación Guanacaste (1999, 2004)

CÔTE D'IVOIRE
Mount Nimba Strict Nature Reserve (1981, 1982)
Taï National Park (1982)
Comoé National Park (1983)

CROATIA
Old City of Dubrovnik (1979, 1994)
Historical Complex of Split with the Palace of Diocletian (1979)
Plitvice Lakes National Park (1979, 2000)
Episcopal Complex of the Euphrasian Basilica in the Historic Centre of Porec (1997)
Historic City of Trogir (1997)
The Cathedral of St. James in Sibenik (2000)

CUBA
Old Havana and its Fortifications (1982)
Trinidad and the Valley de los Ingenios (1988)
San Pedro de la Roca Castle, Santiago de Cuba (1997)
Viñales Valley (1999)
Desembarco del Granma National Park (1999)
Archaeological Landscape of the First Coffee Plantations in the Southeast of Cuba (2000)
Alejandro de Humboldt National Park (2001)

CYPRUS
Paphos (1980)
Painted Churches in the Troodos Region (1985, 2001)
Choirokoitia (1998)

CZECH REPUBLIC
Historic Centre of Prague (1992)
Historic Centre of Cesk Krumlov (1992)
Historic Centre of Telc (1992)
Pilgrimage Church of St John of Nepomuk at Zelená Hora (1994)
Kutná Hora: Historical Town Centre with the Church of St Barbara and the Cathedral of Our Lady at Sedlec (1995)
Lednice-Valtice Cultural Landscape (1996)
Gardens and Castle at Kromeríz (1998)
Holasovice Historical Village Reservation (1998)
Litomysl Castle (1999)
Holy Trinity Column in Olomouc (2000)
Tugendhat Villa in Brno (2001)
Jewish Quarter and St Procopius' Basilica in Trebíc (2003)

DEMOCRATIC PEOPLE'S REPUBLIC OF KOREA
Complex of Koguryo Tombs (2004)

DEMOCRATIC REPUBLIC OF THE CONGO
Virunga National Park (1979)
Garamba National Park (1980)

Kahuzi-Biega National Park (1980)
Salonga National Park (1984)
Okapi Wildlife Reserve (1996)

DENMARK
Jelling Mounds, Runic Stones and Church (1994)
Roskilde Cathedral (1995)
Kronborg Castle (2000)
Ilulissat Icefjord (2004)

DOMINICA
Morne Trois Pitons National Park (1997)

DOMINICAN REPUBLIC
Colonial City of Santo Domingo (1990)

ECUADOR
Galapagos Islands (1978, 2001)
City of Quito (1978)
Sangay National Park (1983)
Historic Centre of Santa Ana de los Ríos de Cuenca (1999)

EGYPT
Memphis and its Necropolis - the Pyramid Fields from Giza to Dahshur (1979)
Ancient Thebes with its Necropolis (1979)
Nubian Monuments from Abu Simbel to Philae (1979)
Islamic Cairo (1979)
Abu Mena (1979)
Saint Catherine Area (2002)

EL SALVADOR
Joya de Ceren Archaeoloical Site (1993)

ESTONIA
Historic Centre (Old Town) of Tallinn (1997)

ETHIOPIA
Rock-hewn Churches, Lalibela (1978)
Simien National Park (1978)
Fasil Ghebbi, Gondar Region (1979)
Lower Valley of the Awash (1980)
Tiya (1980)
Aksum (1980)
Lower Valley of the Omo (1980)

FINLAND
Old Rauma (1991)
Fortress of Suomenlinna (1991)
Petäjävesi Old Church (1994)
Verla Groundwood and Board Mill (1996)
Bronze Age Burial Site of Sammallahdenmäki (1999)
High Coast (2000)

FRANCE
Mont-Saint-Michel and its Bay (1979)
Chartres Cathedral (1979)
Palace and Park of Versailles (1979)
Vézelay, Church and Hill (1979)
Decorated Grottoes of the Vézère Valley (1979)
Palace and Park of Fontainebleau (1981)
Amiens Cathedral (1981)
Roman Theatre and its Surroundings and the "Triumphal Arch" of Orange (1981)
Roman and Romanesque Monuments of Arles (1981)
Cistercian Abbey of Fontenay (1981)
Royal Saltworks of Arc-et-Senans (1982)
Place Stanislas, Place de la Carrière and Place d'Alliance in Nancy (1983)
Church of Saint-Savin sur Gartempe (1983)
Cape Girolata, Cape Porto, Scandola Nature Reserve and the Piana Calanches in Corsica (1983)
Pont du Gard (Roman Aqueduct) (1985)
Strasbourg - Grande île (1988)
Paris, Banks of the Seine (1991)
Cathedral of Notre-Dame, Former Abbey of Saint-Remi and Palace of Tau, Reims (1991)
Bourges Cathedral (1992)
Historic Centre of Avignon (1995)
Canal du Midi (1996)
Historic Fortified City of Carcassonne (1997)
Pyrénées - Mont Perdu (1997, 1999)
Routes of Santiago de Compostela in France (1998)
Historic Site of Lyons (1998)
Jurisdiction of Saint-Emilion (1999)
Belfries of Flanders and Wallonia (1999)
The Loire Valley between Sully-sur-Loire and Chalonnes (2000)
Provins, Town of Medieval Fairs (2001)

GAMBIA
James Island and Related Sites (2003)

GEORGIA
City-Museum Reserve of Mtskheta (1994)
Bagrati Cathedral and Gelati Monastery (1994)
Upper Svaneti (1996)

GERMANY
Aachen Cathedral (1978)
Speyer Cathedral (1981)

Würzburg Residence with the Court Gardens and Residence Square (1981)
Pilgrimage Church of Wies (1983)
Castles of Augustusburg and Falkenlust at Brühl (1984)
St. Mary's Cathedral and St. Michael's Church at Hildesheim (1985)
Roman Monuments, Cathedral of St. Peter and Church of Our Lady in Trier (1986)
Hanseatic City of Lübeck (1987)
Palaces and Parks of Potsdam and Berlin (1990, 1992, 1999)
Abbey and Altenmünster of Lorsch (1991)
Mines of Rammelsberg and Historic Town of Goslar (1992)
Maulbronn Monastery Complex (1993)
Town of Bamberg (1993)
Collegiate Church, Castle, and Old Town of Quedlinburg (1994)
Völklingen Ironworks (1994)
Messel Pit Fossil Site (1995)
Cologne Cathedral (1996)
Bauhaus and its Sites in Weimar and Dessau (1996)
Luther Memorials in Eisleben and Wittenberg (1996)
Classical Weimar (1998)
Museumsinsel (Museum Island), Berlin (1999)
Wartburg Castle (1999)
Garden Kingdom of Dessau-Wörlitz (2000)
Monastic Island of Reichenau (2000)
Zollverein Coal Mine Industrial Complex in Essen (2001)
Upper Middle Rhine Valley (2002)
Historic Centres of Stralsund and Wismar (2002)
Town Hall and Roland on the Marketplace of Bremen (2004)
Muskauer Park / Park Muzakowski (2004)
Dresden Elbe Valley (2004)

GHANA
Forts and Castles, Volta Greater Accra, Central and Western Regions (1979)
Asante Traditional Buildings (1980)

GREECE
Temple of Apollo Epicurius at Bassae (1986)
Archaeological Site of Delphi (1987)
Acropolis, Athens (1987)
Mount Athos (1988)
Meteora (1988)
Paleochristian and Byzantine Monuments of Thessalonika (1988)
Archaeological Site of Epidaurus (1988)
Medieval City of Rhodes (1988)
Mystras (1989)
Archaeological Site of Olympia (1989)
Delos (1990)
Monasteries of Daphni, Hossios Luckas and Nea Moni of Chios (1990)
Pythagoreion and Heraion of Samos (1992)
Archaeological Site of Vergina (1996)
Archaeological Sites of Mycenae and Tiryns (1999)
Historic Centre (Chorá) with the Monastery of Saint John "the Theologian" and the Cave of the Apocalypse on the Island of Pátmos (1999)

GUATEMALA
Tikal National Park (1979)
Antigua Guatemala (1979)
Archaeological Park and Ruins of Quirigua (1981)

GUINEA
Mount Nimba Strict Nature Reserve (1981, 1982)

HAITI
National History Park - Citadel, Sans Souci, Ramiers (1982)

HOLY SEE
Historic Centre of Rome, the Properties of the Holy See in that City Enjoying Extraterritorial Rights and San Paolo Fuori le Mura (1980, 1990)
Vatican City (1984)

HONDURAS
Maya Site of Copan (1980)
Río Plátano Biosphere Reserve (1982)

HUNGARY
Budapest, including the Banks of the Danube, the Buda Castle Quarter and Andrássy Avenue (1987, 2002)
Old Village of Hollókö and its Surroundings (1987)
Caves of Aggtelek Karst and Slovak Karst (1995, 2000)
Millenary Benedictine Abbey of Pannonhalma and its Natural Environment (1996)
Hortobágy National Park - the Puszta (1999)
Early Christian Necropolis of Pécs (Sopianae) (2000)
Fertö/Neusiedlersee Cultural Landscape (2001)
Tokaj Wine Region Historic Cultural Landscape (2002)

ICELAND
flingvellir National Park (2004)

INDIA
Ajanta Caves (1983)
Ellora Caves (1983)

Agra Fort (1983)
Taj Mahal (1983)
Sun Temple, Konarak (1984)
Group of Monuments at Mahabalipuram (1984)
Kaziranga National Park (1985)
Manas Wildlife Sanctuary (1985)
Keoladeo National Park (1985)
Churches and Convents of Goa (1986)
Khajuraho Group of Monuments (1986)
Group of Monuments at Hampi (1986)
Fatehpur Sikri (1986)
Group of Monuments at Pattadakal (1987)
Elephanta Caves (1987)
Great Living Chola Temples (1987, 2004)
Sundarbans National Park (1987)
Nanda Devi National Park (1988)
Buddhist Monuments at Sanchi (1989)
Humayun's Tomb, Delhi (1993)
Qutb Minar and its Monuments, Delhi (1993)
Darjeeling Himalayan Railway (DHR) (1999)
Mahabodhi Temple Complex at Bodh Gaya (2002)
Rock Shelters of Bhimbetka (2003)
Champaner-Pavagadh Archaeological Park (2004)
Chhatrapati Shivaji Terminus (formerly Victoria Terminus) (2004)

INDONESIA
Borobudur Temple Compounds (1991)
Ujung Kulon National Park (1991)
Komodo National Park (1991)
Prambanan Temple Compounds (1991)
Sangiran Early Man Site (1996)
Lorentz National Park (1999)
Tropical Rainforest Heritage of Sumatra (2004)

IRAN (ISLAMIC REPUBLIC OF)
Tchogha Zanbil (1979)
Persepolis (1979)
Meidan Emam, Esfahan (1979)
Takht-e Soleyman (2003)
Pasargadae (2004)
Bam and its Cultural Landscape (2004)

IRAQ
Hatra (1985)
Ashur (Qal'at Sherqat) (2003)

IRELAND
Archaeological Ensemble of the Bend of the Boyne (1993)
Skellig Michael (1996)

ISRAEL
Masada (2001)
Old City of Acre (2001)
White City of Tel-Aviv -- the Modern Movement (2003)

ITALY
Rock Drawings in Valcamonica (1979)
Historic Centre of Rome, the Properties of the Holy See in that City Enjoying Extraterritorial Rights and San Paolo Fuori le Mura (1980, 1990)
Church and Dominican Convent of Santa Maria delle Grazie with "The Last Supper" by Leonardo da Vinci (1980)
Historic Centre of Florence (1982)
Venice and its Lagoon (1987)
Piazza del Duomo, Pisa (1987)
Historic Centre of San Gimignano (1990)
I Sassi di Matera (1993)
City of Vicenza and the Palladian Villas of the Veneto (1994, 1996)
Historic Centre of Siena (1995)
Historic Centre of Naples (1995)
Crespi d'Adda (1995)
Ferrara, City of the Renaissance, and its Po Delta (1995, 1999)
Castel del Monte (1996)
The Trulli of Alberobello (1996)
Early Christian Monuments of Ravenna (1996)
Historic Centre of the City of Pienza (1996)
18th-Century Royal Palace at Caserta, with the Park, the Aqueduct of Vanvitelli, and the San Leucio Complex (1997)
Residences of the Royal House of Savoy (1997)
Botanical Garden (Orto Botanico), Padua (1997)
Portovenere, Cinque Terre, and the Islands (Palmaria, Tino and Tinetto) (1997)
Cathedral, Torre Civica and Piazza Grande, Modena (1997)
Archaeological Areas of Pompei, Herculaneum and Torre Annunziata (1997)
Costiera Amalfitana (1997)
Archaeological Area of Agrigento (1997)
Villa Romana del Casale (1997)
Su Nuraxi di Barumini (1997)
Archaeological Area and the Patriarchal Basilica of Aquileia (1998)
Historic Centre of Urbino (1998)
Cilento and Vallo di Diano National Park with the Archeological sites of Paestum and Velia, and the Certosa di Padula (1998)
Villa Adriana (Tivoli) (1999)

City of Verona (2000)
Isole Eolie (Aeolian Islands) (2000)
Assisi, the Basilica of San Francesco and Other Franciscan Sites (2000)
Villa d'Este, Tivoli (2001)
Late Baroque Towns of the Val di Noto (South-eastern Sicily) (2002)
Sacri Monti of Piedmont and Lombardy (2003)
Val d'Orcia (2004)
Etruscan Necropolises of Cerveteri and Tarquinia (2004)

JAPAN
Buddhist Monuments in the Horyu-ji Area (1993)
Himeji-jo (1993)
Yakushima (1993)
Shirakami-Sanchi (1993)
Historic Monuments of Ancient Kyoto (Kyoto, Uji and Otsu Cities) (1994)
Historic Villages of Shirakawa-go and Gokayama (1995)
Hiroshima Peace Memorial (Genbaku Dome) (1996)
Itsukushima Shinto Shrine (1996)
Historic Monuments of Ancient Nara (1998)
Shrines and Temples of Nikko (1999)
Gusuku Sites and Related Properties of the Kingdom of Ryukyu (2000)
Sacred Sites and Pilgrimage Routes in the Kii Mountain Range (2004)

JERUSALEM (Site proposed by Jordan)
Old City of Jerusalem and its Walls (1981)

JORDAN
Petra (1985)
Quseir Amra (1985)
Um er-Rasas (Kastrom Mefa'a) (2004)

KAZAKHSTAN
Mausoleum of Khoja Ahmed Yasawi (2003)
Petroglyphs within the Archaeological Landscape of Tamgaly (2004)

KENYA
Mount Kenya National Park / Natural Forest (1997)
Lake Turkana National Parks (1997, 2001)
Lamu Old Town (2001)

LAO PEOPLE'S DEMOCRATIC REPUBLIC
Town of Luang Prabang (1995)
Vat Phou and Associated Ancient Settlements within the Champasak Cultural Landscape (2001)

LATVIA
Historic Centre of Riga (1997)

LEBANON
Anjar (1984)
Baalbek (1984)
Byblos (1984)
Tyre (1984)
Ouadi Qadisha (the Holy Valley) and the Forest of the Cedars of God (Horsh Arz el-Rab) (1998)

LIBYAN ARAB JAMAHIRIYA
Archaeological Site of Leptis Magna (1982)
Archaeological Site of Sabratha (1982)
Archaeological Site of Cyrene (1982)
Rock-Art Sites of Tadrart Acacus (1985)
Old Town of Ghadames (1986)

LITHUANIA
Vilnius Historic Centre (1994)
Curonian Spit (2000)
Kernave˙ Archaeological Site (Cultural Reserve of Kernave˙) (2004)

LUXEMBOURG
City of Luxembourg: its Old Quarters and Fortifications (1994)

MADAGASCAR
Tsingy de Bemaraha Strict Nature Reserve (1990)
Royal Hill of Ambohimanga (2001)

MALAWI
Lake Malawi National Park (1984)

MALAYSIA
Kinabalu Park (2000)
Gunung Mulu National Park (2000)

MALI
Old Towns of Djenné (1988)
Timbuktu (1988)
Cliff of Bandiagara (Land of the Dogons) (1989)
Tomb of Askia (2004)

MALTA
Hal Saflieni Hypogeum (1980)
City of Valletta (1980)
Megalithic Temples of Malta (1980, 1992)

MAURITANIA
Banc d'Arguin National Park (1989)
Ancient Ksour of Ouadane, Chinguetti, Tichitt and Oualata (1996)

MEXICO
Sian Ka'an (1987)
Pre-Hispanic City and National Park of Palenque (1987)
Historic Centre of Mexico City and Xochimilco (1987)
Pre-Hispanic City of Teotihuacan (1987)
Historic Centre of Oaxaca and Archaeological Site of Monte Albán (1987)
Historic Centre of Puebla (1987)
Historic Town of Guanajuato and Adjacent Mines (1988)
Pre-Hispanic City of Chichen-Itza (1988)
Historic Centre of Morelia (1991)
El Tajin, Pre-Hispanic City (1992)
Whale Sanctuary of El Vizcaino (1993)
Historic Centre of Zacatecas (1993)
Rock Paintings of the Sierra de San Francisco (1993)
Earliest 16th-Century Monasteries on the Slopes of Popocatepetl (1994)
Pre-Hispanic Town of Uxmal (1996)
Historic Monuments Zone of Querétaro (1996)
Hospicio Cabañas, Guadalajara (1997)
Archeological Zone of Paquimé, Casas Grandes (1998)
Historic Monuments Zone of Tlacotalpan (1998)
Historic Fortified Town of Campeche (1999)
Archaeological Monuments Zone of Xochicalco (1999)
Ancient Maya City of Calakmul, Campeche (2002)
Franciscan Missions in the Sierra Gorda of Querétaro (2003)
Luis Barragán House and Studio (2004)

MONGOLIA
Uvs Nuur Basin (2003)
Orkhon Valley Cultural Landscape (2004)

MOROCCO
Medina of Fez (1981)
Medina of Marrakesh (1985)
Ksar of Ait-Ben-Haddou (1987)
Historic City of Meknes (1996)
Archaeological Site of Volubilis (1997)
Medina of Tétouan (formerly known as Titawin) (1997)
Medina of Essaouira (formerly Mogador) (2001)
Portuguese City of Mazagan (El Jadida) (2004)

MOZAMBIQUE
Island of Mozambique (1991)

NEPAL
Sagarmatha National Park (1979)
Kathmandu Valley (1979)
Royal Chitwan National Park (1984)
Lumbini, the Birthplace of the Lord Buddha (1997)

NETHERLANDS
Schokland and Surroundings (1995)
Defence Line of Amsterdam (1996)
Mill Network at Kinderdijk-Elshout (1997)
Historic Area of Willemstad, Inner City and Harbour, Netherlands Antilles (1997)
Ir.D.F. Woudagemaal (D.F. Wouda Steam Pumping Station) (1998)
Droogmakerij de Beemster (Beemster Polder) (1999)
Rietveld Schröderhuis (Rietveld Schröder House) (2000)

NEW ZEALAND
Tongariro National Park (1990, 1993)
Te Wahipounamu - South West New Zealand (1990)
New Zealand Sub-Antarctic Islands (1998)

NICARAGUA
Ruins of León Viejo (2000)

NIGER
Air and Ténéré Natural Reserves (1991)
W National Park of Niger (1996)

NIGERIA
Sukur Cultural Landscape (1999)

NORWAY
Urnes Stave Church (1979)
Bryggen (1979)
Røros (1980)
Rock Drawings of Alta (1985)
Vegaøyan -- The Vega Archipelago (2004)

OMAN
Bahla Fort (1987)
Archaeological Sites of Bat, Al-Khutm and Al-Ayn (1988)
Arabian Oryx Sanctuary (1994)
The Frankincense Trail (2000)

PAKISTAN
Archaeological Ruins at Moenjodaro (1980)
Taxila (1980)
Buddhist Ruins of Takht-i-Bahi and Neighbouring City Remains at Sahr-i-Bahlol (1980)

Historical Monuments of Thatta (1981)
Fort and Shalamar Gardens in Lahore (1981)
Rohtas Fort (1997)

PANAMA
Fortifications on the Caribbean Side of Panama: Portobelo-San Lorenzo (1980)
Darien National Park (1981)
Talamanca Range-La Amistad Reserves / La Amistad National Park (1983, 1990)
Archaeological Site of Panamá Viejo and Historic District of Panamá (1997, 2003)

PARAGUAY
Jesuit Missions of La Santisima Trinidad de Parana and Jesus de Tavarangue (1993)

PERU
City of Cuzco (1983)
Historic Sanctuary of Machu Picchu (1983)
Chavin (Archaeological Site) (1985)
Huascaran National Park (1985)
Chan Chan Archaelogical Zone (1986)
Manu National Park (1987)
Historic Centre of Lima (1988, 1991)
Rio Abiseo National Park (1990, 1992)
Lines and Geoglyphs of Nasca and Pampas de Jumana (1994)
Historical Centre of the City of Arequipa (2000)

PHILIPPINES
Tubbataha Reef Marine Park (1993)
Baroque Churches of the Philippines (1993)
Rice Terraces of the Philippine Cordilleras (1995)
Historic Town of Vigan (1999)
Puerto-Princesa Subterranean River National Park (1999)

POLAND
Cracow's Historic Centre (1978)
Wieliczka Salt Mine (1978)
Auschwitz Concentration Camp (1979)
Belovezhskaya Pushcha / Biaowieza Forest (1979, 1992)
Historic Centre of Warsaw (1980)
Old City of Zamosc (1992)
Medieval Town of Torun (1997)
Castle of the Teutonic Order in Malbork (1997)
Kalwaria Zebrzydowska: the Mannerist Architectural and Park Landscape Complex and Pilgrimage Park (1999)
Churches of Peace in Jawor and Swidnica (2001)
Wooden Churches of Southern Little Poland (2003)
Muskauer Park / Park Muzakowski (2004)

PORTUGAL
Central Zone of the Town of Angra do Heroismo in the Azores (1983)
Monastery of the Hieronymites and Tower of Belem in Lisbon (1983)
Monastery of Batalha (1983)
Convent of Christ in Tomar (1983)
Historic Centre of Evora (1986)
Monastery of Alcobaça (1989)
Cultural Landscape of Sintra (1995)
Historic Centre of Oporto (1996)
Prehistoric Rock-Art Sites in the Côa Valley (1998)
Laurisilva of Madeira (1999)
Historic Centre of Guimarães (2001)
Alto Douro Wine Region (2001)
Landscape of the Pico Island Vineyard Culture (2004)

REPUBLIC OF KOREA
Seokguram Grotto and Bulguksa Temple (1995)
Haeinsa Temple Janggyeong Panjeon, the Depositories for the Tripitaka Koreana Woodblocks (1995)
Jongmyo Shrine (1995)
Changdeokgung Palace Complex (1997)
Hwaseong Fortress (1997)
Gyeongju Historic Areas (2000)
Gochang, Hwasun, and Ganghwa Dolmen Sites (2000)

ROMANIA
Danube Delta (1991)
Villages with Fortified Churches in Transylvania (1993, 1999)
Monastery of Horezu (1993)
Churches of Moldavia (1993)
Historic Centre of Sighisoara (1999)
Wooden Churches of Maramures̗ (1999)
Dacian Fortresses of the Orastie Mountains (1999)

RUSSIAN FEDERATION
Historic Centre of Saint Petersburg and Related Groups of Monuments (1990)
Kizhi Pogost (1990)
Kremlin and Red Square, Moscow (1990)
Historic Monuments of Novgorod and Surroundings (1992)
Cultural and Historic Ensemble of the Solovetsky Islands (1992)
White Monuments of Vladimir and Suzdal (1992)
Architectural Ensemble of the Trinity Sergius Lavra in Sergiev Posad (1993)
Church of the Ascension, Kolomenskoye (1994)

502

Virgin Komi Forests (1995)
Lake Baikal (1996)
Volcanoes of Kamchatka (1996, 2001)
Golden Mountains of Altai (1998)
Western Caucasus (1999)
Historic and Architectural Complex of the Kazan Kremlin (2000)
The Ensemble of Ferrapontov Monastery (2000)
Curonian Spit (2000)
Central Sikhote-Alin (2001)
Citadel, Ancient City and Fortress Buildings of Derbent (2003)
Uvs Nuur Basin (2003)
Natural System of Wrangel Island Reserve (2004)
Ensemble of the Novodevichy Convent (2004)

SAINT KITTS AND NEVIS
Brimstone Hill Fortress National Park (1999)

SAINT LUCIA
Pitons Management Area (2004)

SENEGAL
Island of Gorée (1978)
Niokolo-Koba National Park (1981)
Djoudj National Bird Sanctuary (1981)
Island of Saint-Louis (2000)

SERBIA AND MONTENEGRO
Natural and Culturo-Historical Region of Kotor (1979)
Stari Ras and Sopocani (1979)
Durmitor National Park (1980)
Studenica Monastery (1986)
Decani Monastery (2004)

SEYCHELLES
Aldabra Atoll (1982)
Vallée de Mai Nature Reserve (1983)

SLOVAKIA
Banská Stiavnica (1993)
Spissk Hrad and its Associated Cultural Monuments (1993)
Vlkolínec (1993)
Caves of Aggtelek Karst and Slovak Karst (1995, 2000)
Bardejov Town Conservation Reserve (2000)

SLOVENIA
Skocjan Caves (1986)

SOLOMON ISLANDS
East Rennell (1998)

SOUTH AFRICA
Greater St. Lucia Wetland Park (1999)
Fossil Hominid Sites of Sterkfontein, Swartkrans, Kromdraai, and Environs (1999)
Robben Island (1999)
UKhahlamba / Drakensberg Park (2000)
Mapungubwe Cultural Landscape (2003)
Cape Floral Region Protected Areas (2004)

SPAIN
Historic Centre of Cordoba (1984, 1994)
Alhambra, Generalife and Albayzin, Granada (1984, 1994)
Burgos Cathedral (1984)
Monastery and Site of the Escurial, Madrid (1984)
Parque Güell, Palacio Güell and Casa Mila in Barcelona (1984)
Altamira Cave (1985)
Old Town of Segovia and its Aqueduct (1985)
Monuments of Oviedo and the Kingdom of the Asturias (1985, 1998)
Santiago de Compostela (Old Town) (1985)
Old Town of Avila with its Extra-Muros Churches (1985)
Mudejar Architecture of Aragon (1986, 2001)
Historic City of Toledo (1986)
Garajonay National Park (1986)
Old Town of Cáceres (1986)
Cathedral, Alcazar and Archivo de Indias in Seville (1987)
Old City of Salamanca (1988)
Poblet Monastery (1991)
Archaeological Ensemble of Mérida (1993)
Royal Monastery of Santa Maria de Guadalupe (1993)
Route of Santiago de Compostela (1993)
Doñana National Park (1994)
Historic Walled Town of Cuenca (1996)
La Lonja de la Seda de Valencia (1996)
Pyrénées - Mont Perdu (1997, 1999)
Las Médulas (1997)
The Palau de la Música Catalana and the Hospital de Sant Pau, Barcelona (1997)
San Millán Yuso and Suso Monasteries (1997)
Rock-Art of the Mediterranean Basin on the Iberian Peninsula (1998)
University and Historic Precinct of Alcalá de Henares (1998)
Ibiza, biodiversity and culture (1999)
San Cristóbal de La Laguna (1999)
Archaeological Ensemble of Tárraco (2000)
Palmeral of Elche (2000)
Roman Walls of Lugo (2000)
Catalan Romanesque Churches of the Vall de Boí (2000)

Archaeological Site of Atapuerca (2000)
Aranjuez Cultural Landscape (2001)
Renaissance Monumental Ensembles of Úbeda and Baeza (2003)

SRI LANKA
Sacred City of Anuradhapura (1982)
Ancient City of Polonnaruwa (1982)
Ancient City of Sigiriya (1982)
Sinharaja Forest Reserve (1988)
Sacred City of Kandy (1988)
Old Town of Galle and its Fortifications (1988)
Golden Temple of Dambulla (1991)

SUDAN
Gebel Barkal and the Sites of the Napatan Region (2003)

SURINAME
Central Suriname Nature Reserve (2000)
Historic Inner City of Paramaribo (2002)

SWEDEN
Royal Domain of Drottningholm (1991)
Birka and Hovgården (1993)
Engelsberg Ironworks (1993)
Rock Carvings in Tanum (1994)
Skogskyrkogården (1994)
Hanseatic Town of Visby (1995)
Church Village of Gammelstad, Luleå (1996)
Laponian Area (1996)
Naval Port of Karlskrona (1998)
High Coast (2000)
Agricultural Landscape of Southern Öland (2000)
Mining Area of the Great Copper Mountain in Falun (2001)
Varberg Radio Station (2004)

SWITZERLAND
Old City of Berne (1983)
Convent of St Gall (1983)
Benedictine Convent of St John at Müstair (1983)
Three Castles, Defensive Wall and Ramparts of the Market-town of Bellinzone (2000)
Jungfrau-Aletsch-Bietschhorn (2001)
Monte San Giorgio (2003)

SYRIAN ARAB REPUBLIC
Ancient City of Damascus (1979)
Ancient City of Bosra (1980)
Site of Palmyra (1980)
Ancient City of Aleppo (1986)

THAILAND
Historic Town of Sukhotai and Associated Historic Towns (1991)
Historic City of Ayutthaya and Associated Historic Towns (1991)
Thungyai - Huai Kha Khaeng Wildlife Sanctuaries (1991)
Ban Chiang Archaeological Site (1992)

THE FORMER YUGOSLAV REPUBLIC OF MACEDONIA
Ohrid Region with its Cultural and Historical Aspect and its Natural Environment (1979, 1980)

TOGO
Koutammakou, the Land of the Batammariba (2004)

TUNISIA
Medina of Tunis (1979)
Site of Carthage (1979)
Amphitheatre of El Jem (1979)
Ichkeul National Park (1980)
Punic Town of Kerkuane and its Necropolis (1985, 1986)
Medina of Sousse (1988)
Kairouan (1988)
Dougga / Thugga (1997)

TURKEY
Historic Areas of Istanbul (1985)
Göreme National Park and the Rock Sites of Cappadocia (1985)
Great Mosque and Hospital of Divrigi (1985)
Hattusha (1986)
Nemrut Dag (1987)
Xanthos-Letoon (1988)
Hierapolis-Pamukkale (1988)
City of Safranbolu (1994)
Archaeological Site of Troy (1998)

TURKMENISTAN
State Historical and Cultural Park (1999)

UGANDA
Bwindi Impenetrable National Park (1994)
Rwenzori Mountains National Park (1994)
Tombs of Buganda Kings at Kasubi (2001)

UKRAINE
Kiev: Saint-Sophia Cathedral and Related Monastic Buildings, Kiev-Pechersk Lavra (1990)
L'viv - the Ensemble of the Historic Centre (1998)

UNITED KINGDOM OF GREAT BRITAIN AND NORTHERN IRELAND
Giant's Causeway and Causeway Coast (1986)
Durham Castle and Cathedral (1986)
Ironbridge Gorge (1986)
Studley Royal Park including the Ruins of Fountains Abbey (1986)
Stonehenge, Avebury and Associated Sites (1986)
Castles and Town Walls of King Edward in Gwynedd (1986)
St. Kilda (1986, 2004)
Blenheim Palace (1987)
Westminster Palace, Westminster Abbey and Saint Margaret's Church (1987)
City of Bath (1987)
Hadrian's Wall (1987)
Henderson Island (1988)
Tower of London (1988)
Canterbury Cathedral, St Augustine's Abbey, and St Martin's Church (1988)
Old and New Towns of Edinburgh (1995)
Gough and Inaccessible Islands (1995, 2004)
Maritime Greenwich (1997)
Heart of Neolithic Orkney (1999)
Historic Town of St George and Related Fortifications, Bermuda (2000)
Blaenavon Industrial Landscape (2000)
Saltaire (2001)
Dorset and East Devon Coast (2001)
Derwent Valley Mills (2001)
New Lanark (2001)
Royal Botanic Gardens, Kew (2003)
Liverpool - Maritime Mercantile City (2004)

UNITED REPUBLIC OF TANZANIA
Ngorongoro Conservation Area (1979)
Ruins of Kilwa Kisiwani and Ruins of Songo Mnara (1981)
Serengeti National Park (1981)
Selous Game Reserve (1982)
Kilimanjaro National Park (1987)
Stone Town of Zanzibar (2000)

UNITED STATES OF AMERICA
Mesa Verde (1978)
Yellowstone (1978)
Kluane/Wrangell-St. Elias/Glacier Bay/Tatshenshini-Alsek (1979, 1992, 1994)
Grand Canyon National Park (1979)
Everglades National Park (1979)
Independence Hall (1979)
Redwood National Park (1980)
Mammoth Cave National Park (1981)
Olympic National Park (1981)
Cahokia Mounds State Historic Site (1982)
Great Smoky Mountains National Park (1983)
La Fortaleza and San Juan Historic Site in Puerto Rico (1983)
Statue of Liberty (1984)
Yosemite National Park (1984)
Chaco Culture National Historical Park (1987)
Hawaii Volcanoes National Park (1987)
Monticello and the University of Virginia in Charlottesville (1987)
Pueblo de Taos (1992)
Waterton Glacier International Peace Park (1995)
Carlsbad Caverns National Park (1995)

URUGUAY
Historic Quarter of the City of Colonia del Sacramento (1995)

UZBEKISTAN
Itchan Kala (1990)
Historic Centre of Bukhara (1993)
Historic Centre of Shakhrisyabz (2000)
Samarkand - Crossroads of Cultures (2001)

VENEZUELA
Coro and its Port (1993)
Canaima National Park (1994)
Ciudad Universitaria de Caracas (2000)

VIET NAM
Complex of Hué Monuments (1993)
Ha Long Bay (1994, 2000)
Hoi An Ancient Town (1999)
My Son Sanctuary (1999)
Phong Nha-Ke Bang National Park (2003)

YEMEN
Old Walled City of Shibam (1982)
Old City of Sana'a (1986)
Historic Town of Zabid (1993)

ZAMBIA
Mosi-oa-Tunya / Victoria Falls (1989)

ZIMBABWE
Mana Pools National Park, Sapi and Chewore Safari Areas (1984)
Great Zimbabwe National Monument (1986)
Khami Ruins National Monument (1986)
Mosi-oa-Tunya / Victoria Falls (1989)
Matobo Hills (2003)

The 1972 Convention

Convention Concerning the Protection of the World Cultural and Natural Heritage

THE GENERAL CONFERENCE of the United Nations Educational, Scientific and Cultural Organization meeting in Paris from 17 October to 21 November 1972, at its seventeenth session,

Noting that the cultural heritage and the natural heritage are increasingly threatened with destruction not only by the traditional causes of decay, but also by changing social and economic conditions which aggravate the situation with even more formidable phenomena of damage or destruction,

Considering that deterioration or disappearance of any item of the cultural or natural heritage constitutes a harmful impoverishment of the heritage of all the nations of the world,

Considering that protection of this heritage at the national level often remains incomplete because of the scale of the resources which it requires and of the insufficient economic, scientific, and technological resources of the country where the property to be protected is situated,

Recalling that the Constitution of the Organization provides that it will maintain, increase, and diffuse knowledge, by assuring the conservation and protection of the world's heritage, and recommending to the nations concerned the necessary international conventions,

Considering that the existing international conventions, recommendations and resolutions concerning cultural and natural property demonstrate the importance, for all the peoples of the world, of safeguarding this unique and irreplaceable property, to whatever people it may belong,

Considering that parts of the cultural or natural heritage are of outstanding interest and therefore need to be preserved as part of the world heritage of mankind as a whole,

Considering that, in view of the magnitude and gravity of the new dangers threatening them, it is incumbent on the international community as a whole to participate in the protection of the cultural and natural heritage of outstanding universal value, by the granting of collective assistance which, although not taking the place of action by the State concerned, will serve as an efficient complement thereto,

Considering that it is essential for this purpose to adopt new provisions in the form of a convention establishing an effective system of collective protection of the cultural and natural heritage of outstanding universal value, organized on a permanent basis and in accordance with modern scientific methods,

Having decided, at its sixteenth session, that this question should be made the subject of an international convention,

Adopts this sixteenth day of November 1972 this Convention.

I. DEFINITION OF THE CULTURAL AND NATURAL HERITAGE
Article 1
For the purposes of this Convention, the following shall be considered as "cultural heritage":
- monuments: architectural works, works of monumental sculpture and painting, elements or structures of an archaeological nature, inscriptions, cave dwellings and combinations of features, which are of outstanding universal value from the point of view of history, art or science;
- groups of buildings: groups of separate or connected buildings which, because of their architecture, their homogeneity or their place in the landscape, are of outstanding universal value from the point of view of history, art or science;
- sites: works of man or the combined works of nature and man, and areas including archaeological sites which are of outstanding universal value from the historical, aesthetic, ethnological or anthropological point of view.

Article 2
For the purposes of this Convention, the following shall be considered as "natural heritage":
- natural features consisting of physical and biological formations or groups of such formations, which are of outstanding universal value from the aesthetic or scientific point of view;
- geological and physiographical formations and precisely delineated areas which constitute the habitat of threatened species of animals and plants of outstanding universal value from the point of view of science or conservation;
- natural sites or precisely delineated natural areas of outstanding universal value from the point of view of science, conservation or natural beauty.

Article 3
It is for each State Party to this Convention to identify and delineate the different properties situated on its territory mentioned in Articles 1 and 2 above.

II. NATIONAL PROTECTION AND INTERNATIONAL PROTECTION OF THE CULTURAL AND NATURAL HERITAGE
Article 4
Each State Party to this Convention recognizes that the duty of ensuring the identification, protection, conservation, presentation and transmission to future generations of the cultural and natural heritage referred to in Articles 1 and 2 and situated on its territory, belongs primarily to that State. It will do all it can to this end, to the utmost of its own resources and, where appropriate, with any international assistance and co-operation, in particular, financial, artistic, scientific and technical, which it may be able to obtain.

Article 5
To ensure that effective and active measures are taken for the protection, conservation and presentation of the cultural and natural heritage situated on its territory, each State Party to this Convention shall endeavor, in so far as possible, and as appropriate for each country:
1. to adopt a general policy which aims to give the cultural and natural heritage a function in the life of the community and to integrate the protection of that heritage into comprehensive planning programmes;
2. to set up within its territories, where such services do not exist, one or more services for the protection, conservation and presentation of the cultural and natural heritage with an appropriate staff and possessing the means to discharge their functions;
3. to develop scientific and technical studies and research and to work out such operating methods as will make the State capable of counteracting the dangers that threaten its cultural or natural heritage;
4. to take the appropriate legal, scientific, technical, administrative and financial measures necessary for the identification, protection, conservation, presentation and rehabilitation of this heritage; and
5. to foster the establishment or development of national or regional centres for training in the protection, conservation and presentation of the cultural and natural heritage and to encourage scientific research in this field.

Article 6
1. Whilst fully respecting the sovereignty of the States on whose territory the cultural and natural heritage mentioned in Articles 1 and 2 is situated, and without prejudice to property right provided by national legislation, the States Parties to this Convention recognize that such heritage constitutes a world heritage for whose protection it is the duty of the international community as a whole to co-operate.
2. The States Parties undertake, in accordance with the provisions of this Convention, to give their help in the identification, protection, conservation and presentation of the cultural and natural heritage referred to in paragraphs 2 and 4 of Article 11 if the States on whose territory it is situated so request.
3. Each State Party to this Convention undertakes not to take any deliberate measures which might damage directly or indirectly the cultural and natural heritage referred to in Articles 1 and 2 situated on the territory of other States Parties to this Convention.

Article 7
For the purpose of this Convention, international protection of the world cultural and natural heritage shall be understood to mean the establishment of a system of international co-operation and assistance designed to support States Parties to the Convention in their efforts to conserve and identify that heritage.

III. INTERGOVERNMENTAL COMMITTEE FOR THE PROTECTION OF THE WORLD CULTURAL AND NATURAL HERITAGE
Article 8
1. An Intergovernmental Committee for the Protection of the Cultural and Natural Heritage of Outstanding Universal Value, called "the World Heritage Committee", is hereby established within the United Nations Educational, Scientific and Cultural Organization. It shall be composed of 15 States Parties to the Convention, elected by States Parties to the Convention meeting in general assembly during the ordinary session of the General Conference of the United Nations Educational, Scientific and Cultural Organization. The number of States members of the Committee shall be increased to 21 as from the date of the ordinary session of the General Conference following the entry into force of this Convention for at least 40 States.
2. Election of members of the Committee shall ensure an equitable representation of the different regions and cultures of the world.
3. A representative of the International Centre for the Study of the Preservation and Restoration of Cultural Property (Rome Centre), a representative of the International Council of Monuments and Sites (ICOMOS) and a representative of the International Union for Conservation of Nature and Natural Resources (IUCN), to whom may be added, at the request of States Parties to the Convention meeting in general assembly during the ordinary sessions of the General Conference of the United Nations Educational, Scientific and Cultural Organization, representatives of other intergovernmental or non-governmental organizations, with similar objectives, may attend the meetings of the Committee in an advisory capacity.

Article 9
1. The term of office of States members of the World Heritage Committee shall extend from the end of the ordinary session of the General Conference during which they are elected until the end of its third subsequent ordinary session.
2. The term of office of one-third of the members designated at the time of the first election shall, however, cease at the end of the first ordinary session of the General Conference following that at which they were elected; and the term of office of a further third of the members designated at the same time shall cease at the end of the second ordinary session of the General Conference following that at which they were elected. The names of these members shall be chosen by lot by the President of the General Conference of the United Nations Educational, Scientific and Cultural Organization after the first election.
3. States members of the Committee shall choose as their representatives persons qualified in the field of the cultural or natural heritage.

Article 10
1. The World Heritage Committee shall adopt its Rules of Procedure.
2. The Committee may at any time invite public or private organizations or individuals to participate in its meetings for consultation on particular problems.
3. The Committee may create such consultative bodies as it deems necessary for the performance of its functions.

Article 11
1. Every State Party to this Convention shall, in so far as possible, submit to the World Heritage Committee an inventory of property forming part of the cultural and natural heritage, situated in its territory and suitable for inclusion in the list provided for in paragraph 2 of this Article. This inventory, which shall not be considered exhaustive, shall include documentation about the location of the property in question and its significance.
2. On the basis of the inventories submitted by States in accordance with paragraph 1, the Committee shall establish, keep up to date and publish, under the title of "World Heritage List," a list of properties forming part of the cultural heritage and natural heritage, as defined in Articles 1 and 2 of this Convention, which it considers as having outstanding universal value in terms of such criteria as it shall have established. An updated list shall be distributed at least every two years.
3. The inclusion of a property in the World Heritage List requires the consent of the State concerned. The inclusion of a property situated in a territory, sovereignty or jurisdiction over which is claimed by more than one State shall in no way prejudice the rights of the parties to the dispute.
4. The Committee shall establish, keep up to date and publish, whenever circumstances shall so require, under the title of "List of World Heritage in Danger", a list of the property appearing in the World Heritage List for the conservation of which major operations are necessary and for which assistance has been requested under this Convention. This list shall contain an estimate of the cost of such operations. The list may include only such property forming part of the cultural and natural heritage as is threatened by serious and specific dangers, such as the threat of disappearance caused by accelerated deterioration, large- scale public or private projects or rapid urban or tourist development projects; destruction caused by changes in the use or ownership of the land; major alterations due to unknown causes; abandonment for any reason whatsoever; the outbreak or the threat of an armed conflict; calamities and cataclysms; serious fires, earthquakes, landslides; volcanic eruptions; changes in water level, floods and tidal waves. The Committee may at any time, in case of urgent need, make a new entry in the List of World Heritage in Danger and publicize such entry immediately.
5. The Committee shall define the criteria on the basis of which a property belonging to the cultural or natural heritage may be included in either of the lists mentioned in paragraphs 2 and 4 of this article.
6. Before refusing a request for inclusion in one of the two lists mentioned in paragraphs 2 and 4 of this article, the

Committee shall consult the State Party in whose territory the cultural or natural property in question is situated.

7. The Committee shall, with the agreement of the States concerned, co-ordinate and encourage the studies and research needed for the drawing up of the lists referred to in paragraphs 2 and 4 of this article.

Article 12
The fact that a property belonging to the cultural or natural heritage has not been included in either of the two lists mentioned in paragraphs 2 and 4 of Article 11 shall in no way be construed to mean that it does not have an outstanding universal value for purposes other than those resulting from inclusion in these lists.

Article 13
1. The World Heritage Committee shall receive and study requests for international assistance formulated by States Parties to this Convention with respect to property forming part of the cultural or natural heritage, situated in their territories, and included or potentially suitable for inclusion in the lists mentioned referred to in paragraphs 2 and 4 of Article 11. The purpose of such requests may be to secure the protection, conservation, presentation or rehabilitation of such property.
2. Requests for international assistance under paragraph 1 of this article may also be concerned with identification of cultural or natural property defined in Articles 1 and 2, when preliminary investigations have shown that further inquiries would be justified.
3. The Committee shall decide on the action to be taken with regard to these requests, determine where appropriate, the nature and extent of its assistance, and authorize the conclusion, on its behalf, of the necessary arrangements with the government concerned.
4. The Committee shall determine an order of priorities for its operations. It shall in so doing bear in mind the respective importance for the world cultural and natural heritage of the property requiring protection, the need to give international assistance to the property most representative of a natural environment or of the genius and the history of the peoples of the world, the urgency of the work to be done, the resources available to the States on whose territory the threatened property is situated and in particular the extent to which they are able to safeguard such property by their own means.
5. The Committee shall draw up, keep up to date and publicize a list of property for which international assistance has been granted.
6. The Committee shall decide on the use of the resources of the Fund established under Article 15 of this Convention. It shall seek ways of increasing these resources and shall take all useful steps to this end.
7. The Committee shall co-operate with international and national governmental and non-governmental organizations having objectives similar to those of this Convention. For the implementation of its programmes and projects, the Committee may call on such organizations, particularly the International Centre for the Study of the Preservation and Restoration of cultural Property (the Rome Centre), the International Council of Monuments and Sites (ICOMOS) and the International Union for Conservation of Nature and Natural Resources (IUCN), as well as on public and private bodies and individuals.
8. Decisions of the Committee shall be taken by a majority of two-thirds of its members present and voting. A majority of the members of the Committee shall constitute a quorum.

Article 14
1. The World Heritage Committee shall be assisted by a Secretariat appointed by the Director-General of the United Nations Educational, Scientific and Cultural Organization.
2. The Director-General of the United Nations Educational, Scientific and Cultural Organization, utilizing to the fullest extent possible the services of the International Centre for the Study of the Preservation and the Restoration of Cultural Property (the Rome Centre), the International Council of Monuments and Sites (ICOMOS) and the International Union for Conservation of Nature and Natural Resources (IUCN) in their respective areas of competence and capability, shall prepare the Committee's documentation and the agenda of its meetings and shall have the responsibility for the implementation of its decisions.

IV. FUND FOR THE PROTECTION OF THE WORLD CULTURAL AND NATURAL HERITAGE
Article 15
1. A Fund for the Protection of the World Cultural and Natural Heritage of Outstanding Universal Value, called "the World Heritage Fund", is hereby established.
2. The Fund shall constitute a trust fund, in conformity with the provisions of the Financial Regulations of the United Nations Educational, Scientific and Cultural Organization.
3. The resources of the Fund shall consist of:
  1. compulsory and voluntary contributions made by States Parties to this Convention,
  2. Contributions, gifts or bequests which may be made by:
    1. other States;
    2. the United Nations Educational, Scientific and Cultural Organization, other organizations of the United Nations system, particularly the United Nations Development Programme or other intergovernmental organizations;
    3. public or private bodies or individuals;

3. any interest due on the resources of the Fund;
4. funds raised by collections and receipts from events organized for the benefit of the fund; and
5. all other resources authorized by the Fund's regulations, as drawn up by the World Heritage Committee.
4. Contributions to the Fund and other forms of assistance made available to the Committee may be used only for such purposes as the Committee shall define. The Committee may accept contributions to be used only for a certain programme or project, provided that the Committee shall have decided on the implementation of such programme or project. No political conditions may be attached to contributions made to the Fund.

Article 16
1. Without prejudice to any supplementary voluntary contribution, the States Parties to this Convention undertake to pay regularly, every two years, to the World Heritage Fund, contributions, the amount of which, in the form of a uniform percentage applicable to all States, shall be determined by the General Assembly of States Parties to the Convention, meeting during the sessions of the General Conference of the United Nations Educational, Scientific and Cultural Organization. This decision of the General Assembly requires the majority of the States Parties present and voting, which have not made the declaration referred to in paragraph 2 of this Article. In no case shall the compulsory contribution of States Parties to the Convention exceed 1% of the contribution to the regular budget of the United Nations Educational, Scientific and Cultural Organization.
2. However, each State referred to in Article 31 or in Article 32 of this Convention may declare, at the time of the deposit of its instrument of ratification, acceptance or accession, that it shall not be bound by the provisions of paragraph 1 of this Article.
3. A State Party to the Convention which has made the declaration referred to in paragraph 2 of this Article may at any time withdraw the said declaration by notifying the Director-General of the United Nations Educational, Scientific and Cultural Organization. However, the withdrawal of the declaration shall not take effect in regard to the compulsory contribution due by the State until the date of the subsequent General Assembly of States parties to the Convention.
4. In order that the Committee may be able to plan its operations effectively, the contributions of States Parties to this Convention which have made the declaration referred to in paragraph 2 of this Article, shall be paid on a regular basis, at least every two years, and should not be less than the contributions which they should have paid if they had been bound by the provisions of paragraph 1 of this Article.
5. Any State Party to the Convention which is in arrears with the payment of its compulsory or voluntary contribution for the current year and the calendar year immediately preceding it shall not be eligible as a Member of the World Heritage Committee, although this provision shall not apply to the first election.

The terms of office of any such State which is already a member of the Committee shall terminate at the time of the elections provided for in Article 8, paragraph 1 of this Convention.

Article 17
The States Parties to this Convention shall consider or encourage the establishment of national public and private foundations or associations whose purpose is to invite donations for the protection of the cultural and natural heritage as defined in Articles 1 and 2 of this Convention.

Article 18
The States Parties to this Convention shall give their assistance to international fund-raising campaigns organized for the World Heritage Fund under the auspices of the United Nations Educational, Scientific and Cultural Organization. They shall facilitate collections made by the bodies mentioned in paragraph 3 of Article 15 for this purpose.

V. CONDITIONS AND ARRANGEMENTS FOR INTERNATIONAL ASSISTANCE
Article 19
Any State Party to this Convention may request international assistance for property forming part of the cultural or natural heritage of outstanding universal value situated within its territory. It shall submit with its request such information and documentation provided for in Article 21 as it has in its possession and as will enable the Committee to come to a decision.

Article 20
Subject to the provisions of paragraph 2 of Article 13, sub-paragraph (c) of Article 22 and Article 23, international assistance provided for by this Convention may be granted only to property forming part of the cultural and natural heritage which the World Heritage Committee has decided, or may decide, to enter in one of the lists mentioned in paragraphs 2 and 4 of Article 11.

Article 21
1. The World Heritage Committee shall define the procedure by which requests to it for international assistance shall be considered and shall specify the content of the request, which should define the operation contemplated, the work that is

necessary, the expected cost thereof, the degree of urgency and the reasons why the resources of the State requesting assistance do not allow it to meet all the expenses. Such requests must be supported by experts' reports whenever possible.
2. Requests based upon disasters or natural calamities should, by reasons of the urgent work which they may involve, be given immediate, priority consideration by the Committee, which should have a reserve fund at its disposal against such contingencies.
3. Before coming to a decision, the Committee shall carry out such studies and consultations as it deems necessary.

Article 22
Assistance granted by the World Heritage Committee may take the following forms:
1. studies concerning the artistic, scientific and technical problems raised by the protection, conservation, presentation and rehabilitation of the cultural and natural heritage, as defined in paragraphs 2 and 4 of Article 11 of this Convention;
2. provisions of experts, technicians and skilled labour to ensure that the approved work is correctly carried out;
3. training of staff and specialists at all levels in the field of identification, protection, conservation, presentation and rehabilitation of the cultural and natural heritage;
4. supply of equipment which the State concerned does not possess or is not in a position to acquire;
5. low-interest or interest-free loans which might be repayable on a long-term basis;
6. the granting, in exceptional cases and for special reasons, of non-repayable subsidies.

Article 23
The World Heritage Committee may also provide international assistance to national or regional centres for the training of staff and specialists at all levels in the field of identification, protection, conservation, presentation and rehabilitation of the cultural and natural heritage.

Article 24
International assistance on a large scale shall be preceded by detailed scientific, economic and technical studies. These studies shall draw upon the most advanced techniques for the protection, conservation, presentation and rehabilitation of the natural and cultural heritage and shall be consistent with the objectives of this Convention. The studies shall also seek means of making rational use of the resources available in the State concerned.

Article 25
As a general rule, only part of the cost of work necessary shall be borne by the international community. The contribution of the State benefiting from international assistance shall constitute a substantial share of the resources devoted to each programme or project, unless its resources do not permit this.

Article 26
The World Heritage Committee and the recipient State shall define in the agreement they conclude the conditions in which a programme or project for which international assistance under the terms of this Convention is provided, shall be carried out. It shall be the responsibility of the State receiving such international assistance to continue to protect, conserve and present the property so safeguarded, in observance of the conditions laid down by the agreement.

VI. EDUCATIONAL PROGRAMMES
Article 27
1. The States Parties to this Convention shall endeavor by all appropriate means, and in particular by educational and information programmes, to strengthen appreciation and respect by their peoples of the cultural and natural heritage defined in Articles 1 and 2 of the Convention.
2. They shall undertake to keep the public broadly informed of the dangers threatening this heritage and of the activities carried on in pursuance of this Convention.
Article 28
States Parties to this Convention which receive international assistance under the Convention shall take appropriate measures to make known the importance of the property for which assistance has been received and the role played by such assistance.

VII. REPORTS
Article 29
1. The States Parties to this Convention shall, in the reports which they submit to the General Conference of the United Nations Educational, Scientific and Cultural Organization on dates and in a manner to be determined by it, give information on the legislative and administrative provisions which they have adopted and other action which they have taken for the application of this Convention, together with details of the experience acquired in this field.
2. These reports shall be brought to the attention of the World Heritage Committee.
3. The Committee shall submit a report on its activities at each of the ordinary sessions of the General Conference of the United Nations Educational, Scientific and Cultural Organization.

VIII. FINAL CLAUSES
Article 30
This Convention is drawn up in Arabic, English, French,

Russian and Spanish, the five texts being equally authoritative.

Article 31
1. This Convention shall be subject to ratification or acceptance by States members of the United Nations Educational, Scientific and Cultural Organization in accordance with their respective constitutional procedures.
2. The instruments of ratification or acceptance shall be deposited with the Director-General of the United Nations Educational, Scientific and Cultural Organization.

Article 32
1. This Convention shall be open to accession by all States not members of the United Nations Educational, Scientific and Cultural Organization which are invited by the General Conference of the Organization to accede to it.
2. Accession shall be effected by the deposit of an instrument of accession with the Director-General of the United Nations Educational, Scientific and Cultural Organization.

Article 33
This Convention shall enter into force three months after the date of the deposit of the twentieth instrument of ratification, acceptance or accession, but only with respect to those States which have deposited their respective instruments of ratification, acceptance or accession on or before that date. It shall enter into force with respect to any other State three months after the deposit of its instrument of ratification, acceptance or accession.

Article 34
The following provisions shall apply to those States Parties to this Convention which have a federal or non-unitary constitutional system:
1. with regard to the provisions of this Convention, the implementation of which comes under the legal jurisdiction of the federal or central legislative power, the obligations of the federal or central government shall be the same as for those States parties which are not federal States;
2. with regard to the provisions of this Convention, the implementation of which comes under the legal jurisdiction of individual constituent States, countries, provinces or cantons that are not obliged by the constitutional system of the federation to take legislative measures, the federal government shall inform the competent authorities of such States, countries, provinces or cantons of the said provisions, with its recommendation for their adoption.

Article 35
1. Each State Party to this Convention may denounce the Convention.
2. The denunciation shall be notified by an instrument in writing, deposited with the Director-General of the United Nations Educational, Scientific and Cultural Organization.
3. The denunciation shall take effect twelve months after the receipt of the instrument of denunciation. It shall not affect the financial obligations of the denouncing State until the date on which the withdrawal takes effect.

Article 36
The Director-General of the United Nations Educational, Scientific and Cultural Organization shall inform the States members of the Organization, the States not members of the Organization which are referred to in Article 32, as well as the United Nations, of the deposit of all the instruments of ratification, acceptance, or accession provided for in Articles 31 and 32, and of the denunciations provided for in Article 35.

Article 37
1. This Convention may be revised by the General Conference of the United Nations Educational, Scientific and Cultural Organization. Any such revision shall, however, bind only the States which shall become Parties to the revising convention.
2. If the General Conference should adopt a new convention revising this Convention in whole or in part, then, unless the new convention otherwise provides, this Convention shall cease to be open to ratification, acceptance or accession, as from the date on which the new revising convention enters into force.

Article 38
In conformity with Article 102 of the Charter of the United Nations, this Convention shall be registered with the Secretariat of the United Nations at the request of the Director-General of the United Nations Educational, Scientific and Cultural Organization.

Done in Paris, this twenty-third day of November 1972, in two authentic copies bearing the signature of the President of the seventeenth session of the General Conference and of the Director-General of the United Nations Educational, Scientific and Cultural Organization, which shall be deposited in the archives of the United Nations Educational, Scientific and Cultural Organization, and certified true copies of which shall be delivered to all the States referred to in Articles 31 and 32 as well as to the United Nations.

Bibliography

UNESCO publications

On 18 April 1996, UNESCO began publication of the World Heritage Review, a quarterly, 80 page, color magazine that focuses on the *World Heritage sites*. The magazine is published simultaneously in English, French and Spanish.
The list of publications below includes those produced by UNESCO or in partnership with other publishing companies. All are available from the UNESCO offices in Paris. All enquiries should be sent to: The World Heritage Centre, UNESCO, 7 Place de Fontenoy, 75352 Paris, France.

Les villes du patrimoine mondial, CD-ROM, UNESCO Publishing/Cyberion, Paris.
The World Heritage Series for Children (recommended for children aged 8-15, available in English, French and Spanish), UNESCO Publishing/Childrens Press, Paris.
Patrimonio de la Humanidad (12 volume encyclopedia), Planeta/UNESCO Publishing, Madrid, 1995.
World Heritage Encyclopedia (in German), in 12 volumes, Verlagshaus Stuttgart/Plaza y Janes/UNESCO Publishing, Stuttgart, 1996/1997.
Schätze der Menschheit, Frederking & Thaler/UNESCO Publishing, Munich, 1996/1997.
The World Heritage Encyclopedia (in Japanese), in 12 volumes, Kodansha/UNESCO Publishing, Tokyo, 1996/1997.
Masterworks of Man and Nature, Harper-MacRae Publishing, Sydney, 1994.
Paradise on Earth, Harper-MacRae Publishing, Sydney, 1995.
World Heritage Twenty Years Later, by Jim Thorsell, IUCN, Switzerland and Great Britain, 1992.
World Cultural and Natural Property (available in Japanese), for children, Gakken, Tokyo, 1994.
Cultural Landscapes of Universal Value, by B. von Droste, H. Plachter, M. Rössler, Fischer Verlag, Jena, 1995.

Index

509

510

Photographic Credits

Gerard Clyde/Barnaby's Picture Library: page 228 bottom
P. Colombel/Corbis/Grazia Neri: page 376 center
Anne Conway: pages 158 top and bottom, 159 top, 158-159, 160, 161 bottom
Anne Conway/Archivio White Star: pages 50 top, center left and bottom right, 51 bottom, 210 top
Richard A. Cooke/Corbis/Contrasto: page 338 top
AND. Coppola/Panda Photo: page 381 top
Corbis/Grazia Neri: pages 58 center, 59 bottom, 98 center and bottom
B. Coster/Ardea: page 466
Guido Cozzi/Atlantide: page 85 top
G. Crabbe/AGE/Contrasto: page 450 bottom
A. Crandell/Corbis/Grazia Neri: page 381 center
D. Croucher/Bruce Coleman Collection: pages 365, 367 top left
M. Daffey/Lonely Planet Images: page 429 bottom
Alexis Daflos/Royal Collection: pages 20 bottom, 21 top and bottom
Giovanni Dagli Orti: pages 2, 68 top, 70-71, 70 bottom left, bottom right, 71 right, 72-73, 91 bottom, 218, 218-219, 219, 224-225, 236 left and right, 237right, 340 right, 350 top
S. Damm/Zefa: page 394 top
R. Dayton/AGE/Contrasto: page 451
Araldo De Luca: pages 220 right, 222
Araldo De Luca/Archivio White Star: pages 208, 212-213, 246 top, 246 center, 246 bottom, 246-247, 248 top, 248 bottom left, 248 bottom right, 248-249, 249 right, 250 top left, 250 top right, 250 center, 250 bottom, 250-251, 251, 252-253, 253 top, 253 center, 253 bottom, 254 top and center, 254-255, 255 bottom left, 255 bottom right, 256 top, 256 bottom left and bottom right, 257 bottom right, 260 top left, 260 top right, 260 bottom, 261, 262 top, 263 bottom left, 263 bottom right, 270 left, 270-271, 271 top, 271 center, 271 bottom, 272 top, 272 bottom, 272-273, 273 bottom, 302 top, 302-303, 303 top, 303 center, 303 bottom, 304, 305, 306 left and right, 307 left and right
M&C Denis Huot: page 387 bottom
M. Denis Huot/Hoaqui: page 380 bottom right
Gustavo Di Pace/Fotoscopio: page 360 bottom
Thomas Dix: pages 140-141
C. Doerr/AGE/Contrasto: page 484 top
A. Dragesco Joffè/Panda Photo: pages 377 top right, 378 top, 378 bottom, 378-379, 379 top
T. Dressel/Ardea: page 369 top
M. Dumas/Explorer: page 380 bottom left
D. Else/Lonely Planet Images: page 387 top
Martino Fagiuoli/CV Export: page 178 center and bottom
Ferrer & Sostoa/AGE/Contrasto: page 480 left bottom
AND. della Ferrera: page 423
Elisabetta Ferrero/Archivio White Star: pages 3-6
J.P. Ferrero/Auscape International: pages 486 left, 486 right, 486-487, 487 center, 488, 490 bottom, 490-491, 491 top, 492 left bottom, 492-493, 493 center, 493 bottom, 499 top
Kevin Fleming/Corbis/Contrasto: page 232
Florian Monheim/Bildarchiv Monheim: page 75 top and center
J. Foott/AGE/Contrasto: pages 482-483
J. Foott/Bruce Coleman Collection: pages 444-445
Gigliola Foschi/Focus Team: pages 47 top left, 48
Klaus Frahm/Artur: pages 41 left, right top and right bottom, 43 bottom
Ro Freck/Odyssey/F. Speranza: pages 108-109
B. Gardel/Hemispheres: page 426 top
Alfio Garozzo/Archivio White Star: pages 155 bottom, 157 bottom left and bottom right, 221 left, 226-227, 228 top, 228-229, 229, 230 top and bottom, 231 top, 231 bottom left and right, 235, 242-243, 243 top left and top right, 244 top, 244 bottom left and bottom right, 245, 266 top, 268 top, 269 bottom
Cesare Gerolimetto: page 42
Lowell Georgia/Corbis/Contrasto: pages 311 top left, 311 bottom
Getty Images/Laura Ronchi: page 320
Fausto Giaccone/Franca Speranza: pages 20-21
H. Goethel/Blickwinkel: page 472 center
Gohier/Ardea: pages 439 bottom, 444 bottom, 447 top, 455 top
Itamar Grinberg: pages 128-129
Itamar Grinberg/Archivio White Star: pages 286-287
Grafenhaim/Franca Speranza: pages 18-19
Grafenhaim/Simephoto: pages 24-25, 40, 44 center, 98 top
M. Gratton/Vision: page 124 top
M.W. Grosniek/Ardea: page 437 right
D. Gulin/Corbis/Contrasto: pages 449 bottom right, 478 bottom
D. Gulin/Corbis/Grazia Neri: page 447 bottom
H. Hamaya/Magnum Photo/Contrasto: page 497 top
M. Hamblin/Oxford Scientific Library: page 444 right center
M. Harvey/NHPA: page 382 left center
Jason Hawkes: page 193 bottom
Jason Hawkes/Corbis/Contrasto: page 186
Jochen Helle/Bildarchiv Monheim/©2002 Victor Horta-Sofam Belgique: page 38 left
C. Hellier/Corbis/Grazia Neri: page 399 center and bottom
Pal Hermansen/Franca Speranza: page 14
Angelo Hornak/Corbis/Contrasto: page 188
D.G. Houser/Corbis/Grazia Neri: page 441 center
H.P Huber/Simephoto: pages 69 top, 438-439, 496 right bottom, 499 center
Johanna Huber/Simephoto: pages 77 bottom, 487 bottom
Andrew Humphreys/LPI: page 126 left and right
R. I'Anson/Lonely Planet Images: pages 498-499
Index/Barbieri: page 110 top right
J. Johnson/Bruce Coleman Collection: page 392 center left
B. Jones & M.Shimlock/NHPA: pages 432 top, 433

Wolfgang Kaehler/Corbis/Contrasto: pages 310-311, 311 top right, 361, 410 bottom
C. Karnow/Corbis/Grazia Neri: pages 426-427
S. Kaufman: page 419
R. & J. Kemp/SAL/Oxford Scientific Films: page 371 left top
AND. Keskozommy/SAL/Oxford Scientific Films: page 412 top
B. Klein-Hubert/Panda Photo: page 439 center
C. Knights/Ardea: pages 460-461
F. Labot/Auscape International: pages 391 bottom right, 391 center
B. Lamm/Blickwinkel: page 447 right center
J. M. La Rogue/Auscape International: page 498 bottom
H.G. Laukel: pages 377 top left, 378 center, 379 center
Reiner Lautwein/Artur/©2002 Victor Horta-Sofam Belgique: pages 38 bottom right, 39
Kraig Lieb/Lonely Planet Images: pages 338-339
Charles Lenars: page 125 center left
Erich Lessing/Contrasto: pages 210-211, 224, 225 left and right, 238 top right, 240 bottom right
Marcello Libra: pages 369 center, 369 bottom, 370 top, 372 top 372 center, 372-373, 373 top, 373 bottom, 374 top, 374 center left, 374 center right, 374-375, 375, 385 center left, 412-413, 413 top, 413 center
V. Loi-S. Pisano/Panda Photo: page 367 center
A. Maniciati: page 413 bottom
Marka: page 241 top
N. Marven/Nature Picture Library: pages 410 center, 410-411, 410 top
J. Mason/Ardea: pages 467 left bottom, 467 right bottom
F. Mastracchi Manes/Panda Photo: pages 386-387
C. Mattison/Age/Contrasto: pages 390-391
C. Mauzy/Corbis/Contrasto: page 448 bottom
J. McDonald/Corbis/Grazia Neri: pages 381 bottom, 385 center right, 392 center right, 479 bottom
D. Meissner/Blickwinkel: page 444 top
S. Meyers/Ardea: page 444 left center
B. Miller/Timepix/PhotoMasi: page 461 center
C. Monteath/Auscape International: pages 484-485, 485 top left, 485 center left, 485 bottom left
C. Monteath/Hedgehog House: pages 420 center, 420-421, 421 top, 421 bottom, 483 center
B. Moranti/Age/Contrasto: page 407 bottom
J.C. Munoz/Panda Photo: pages 364 top, 364 right bottom
David Muench/Corbis/Contrasto: pages 338 bottom, 449 bottom left
D. Muench/Corbis/Grazia Neri: page 467 top
A. Nardi/Panda Photo: page 367 bottom
NASA: pages 408, 409 top and bottom, 410 top
Nature Picture Library: page 443 top left
N. Nightingale/Nature Picture Library: page 428 top
Nimatallah/AGK Images: page 206 top right
B. Norton/Evergreen Photo Alliance: pages 383 bottom, 391 bottom left
Oxford Cartographers/Archivio White Star: page 270 right
H. Palo JR/NHPA: pages 469 top, 474 center, 475 left bottom
Vincenzo Paolillo: pages 401 top, 402 center, 402 bottom, 402-403, 403 bottom, 404 top left, 404 top right, 404 bottom left, 405 top, 426 bottom right
Parlamentary Copyrights 1995: page 34 top
D. Parter & AND.Parter/Auscape International: pages 468 center, 468 bottom, 469 left, 469 right bottom, 470 bottom, 472-473, 491 center bottom, 492 top
C. Pavaral/Hoaqui: pages 400 top, 400-401
D. Paynet/Age/Contrasto: page 363
D. Peebles/Corbis/Contrasto: pages 464-465
D. Peebles/Corbis/Grazia Neri: pages 462-463
C. Penn/Corbis/Grazia Neri: page 372 bottom
Moose Peterson/Ardea: page 447 left center
Peterson/WRP/Ardea: page 436 bottom left
Daniel Philippe/Air Print: pages 40-41, 44-45, 56 bottom left, 68-69, 74, 100-101
Jean Charles Pinheira: pages 104-105, 105 bottom
Andrea Pistolesi: pages 43 top left, top right, 44 top left and top right, 436 top, 436 bottom right, 437 left, 450 right center, 453 left center
Alberto Pizzoli/Corbis/Contrasto: pages 206 bottom, 207 bottom
F. Poelking/AGE/Contrasto: pages 480-481
F. Poelking/Blickwinkel: pages 443 bottom left, 471 top
Josef Polleros/Anzenberger: page 13
G. Pots/Bruce Coleman Collection: page 443 bottom right
Pozzoli/Hoaqui: page 402 top
Hira Punjabi/Lonely Planet Images: pages 422 center right, 424-425
Nicolas Rachmano/Ag. ANA: pages 29 top, 30 top left, bottom left, 30-31, 31 top right and bottom right
Luciano Ramires/Archivio White Star: pages 62 top left, 75 bottom, 194-195
Carmen Redondo/Corbis/Contrasto: pages 284 top, 284-285
Carmen Redondo/Corbis/Grazia Neri: page 385 bottom
R. Ressmeyer/Corbis/Grazia Neri: page 462 top
Giovanni Rinaldi/Il Dagherrotipo: pages 176-177
Massimo Ripani/Simephoto: pages 117 top right, 364 left bottom, 453 top
P. Roig/AGE/Contrasto: page 485 top right
Basilio Rodella/BAMS photo: pages 216-217, 217 center
Laura Ronchi: page 296 bottom
Benjamin Rondel/The Stock Market/Contrasto: page 152 bottom left
SIE: page 127 bottom center
Hans Georg Roth/Corbis/Contrasto: page 240 top
Galen Rowell: pages 452-453
Galen Rowell/Corbis/Grazia Neri: page 422 center left
T. de Roy/Auscape International: page 473 top
Saffo/Simephoto: pages 116-117, 117 left
Kevin Schafer: pages 392 top, 393, 438 bottom, 440 top, 441 top, 448-449
Kevin Schafer/Corbis/Contrasto: page 360 center
Gregor M. Schmid/Anzenberger: pages 96 bottom, 97 bottom right, 99
V. Sciosia/Focus Team: page 371 right top
M.T. Sedam/Corbis/Contrasto: page 449 top
J. Sierra Antinolo/Oxford Scientific Films: page 368
Silvestris: pages 382 bottom, 396 top right, 397
Giovanni Simeone/Simephoto: pages 51 top, 55 top, 62-63, 90, 104 top, 120-121, 154-155, 155 center, 396-397, 446 bottom
G. Sini/Ag. Marka: page 69 bottom
P.A.Souders/Corbis/Grazia Neri: page 441 bottom
M. Spencer/Auscape International: page 492 right bottom
R. Spoonbill/Ardea: page 461 top
Henri et Anne Stierlin: pages 136-137, 137 top right, center and bottom, 143 bottom left, 151 top right and bottom right, 239 top right, 240-241, 241 bottom, 276 right, 277 top, 277 center, 278 top, 278 bottom left, 278 bottom right, 278-279, 279 top, 279 bottom, 280 bottom left, 280 bottom right, 280-281, 281 top left, 281 n alto right, 281 bottom, 299 top, 299 bottom, 300-301, 301 top, 301 center top, 301 center bottom
D. Stock/Magnum Photo/Contrasto: pages 496-497
L.M. Stone/Nature Picture Library: page 415 top
Keren Su/Corbis/Contrasto: page 310
K. Su/China Span/Lonely Planet Images: page 417 top
J.A. Sugar/Corbis/Grazia Neri: page 465 top
T. Svehsson/Corbis/Contrasto: page 395 bottom
J. Sweeney/Lonely Planet Images: pages 482 bottom, 483 top
S. Tauqueur/Franca Speranza page 18 top right
N.J. Tennis/Sime Photo: page 396 top left
Luca Tettoni: pages 430, 431 top left and right, 431 bottom
T. Till/Auscape International: page 496 left bottom
Timepix/PhotoMasi: page 452 top
Angelo Tondini/Focus Team: pages 198-199, 335 top, 335 bottom, 426 bottom
Prof. Gerhard Trumler: pages 58 top, 58-59
S. Turner/Oxford Scientific Films: page 383 center
R. Valterza/Ag. Franca Speranza: pages 370-371
Sandro Vannini/Franca Speranza: page 157 top right
S. Vannini/Panda Photo: page 367 top right
Giulio Veggi/Archivio White Star: pages 19 top, 25 top, center left, center right and bottom left, 26 bottom left and bottom right, 35 top and center, 52-53, 53 top, center left, center right and bottom, 54 top, center left and center right, 55 bottom left and bottom right, 57 bottom right, 60 bottom, 62 top right, 63 top, bottom left, bottom right, 64 top and bottom, 67 top right and bottom right, 96 top, 96-97, 97 top right and bottom left, 105 top, 106, 106-107, 107 top and bottom, 108 top and bottom, 110 top left, 110-111, 111 right and bottom, 112 top, center, bottom, 112-113, 113 top left and top right, 118 top, 119, 120, 121 top, center right and bottom, 122 top left, 200 bottom left, 202 top left, 203 top, 204 bottom, 205 left, 206 top left, 209 top left, 209 top right, 209 bottom left, 210 bottom, 211, 214 right, 215 bottom, 216, 221 top right and bottom right, 223 left and right, 228 center, 230-231, 234 top, 234 bottom left, 236-237, 262-263, 264 top, 267 right, 269 top, 290 top, 292 left and right, 292-293, 293 top and bottom, 294 bottom, 295 left and right
L. Vigliotti/Panda Photo: page 464 top
Brian A.Vikander/Corbis/Contrasto: pages 308-309, 309 left and right
R. Von Gotz/Bildarchiv Monheim: pages 34-35
U. Walz/Blickwinkel: pages 474-475
U. Walz/Bruce Coleman Collection: pages 446 center, 476-477
K. Ward/Corbis/Contrasto: page 418 top
A. Warren/Ardea: pages 434-435
M. Watson/Ardea: pages 439 top, 455 left bottom, 455 right bottom, 477 bottom
D. Watts/Nature Picture Library: page 448 top
K.M. Westrmenn/Corbis/Grazia Neri: page 163 bottom center
N. Wheeler/Corbis/Contrasto: pages 394-395, 395 center
A. White/Nature Picture Library: page 400 bottom
S. Widstrand/Corbis/Grazia Neri: page 425 bottom
S. Wilby/Auscape International: page 497 bottom
P. de Wilde/Hoaqui: page 401 bottom
Julian Wirker; Cordaiy Photo Library Ltd./Corbis/Contrasto: page 283
Christopher Wood/LPI: page 124 bottom
Roger Wood/Corbis/Contrasto: pages 240 bottom left, 282 right
D.Woodfall/NHPA: page 371 bottom
Adam Woolfitt/Corbis/Contrasto: pages 188-189, 238-239, 241 center
Shen Yu/Imaginechina/Contrasto: pages 414-415
Chen Yun/Imaginechina/Contrasto: page 416 bottom
Francesco Zanchi/Archivio White Star: pages 22 top right and bottom left, 23 top, 26 top, 27
Bo Zaunders/Corbis/Contrasto: page 195 left
B. Zhenjin/Imaginechina/Contrasto: pages 414 top, 416 top left, 416 top right, 416-417
G. Ziesler: pages 422 bottom right, 424 top, 424 bottom, 468-469, 470-471, 471 bottom left, 471 bottom right, 472 top left, 472 top right, 475 top, 475 right bottom, 476 center, 476 left, 476 right bottom, 478 center, 478-479, 480 right bottom, 487 top, 487 bottom, 487 left, 487 top right
J. Zipp/Ardea: page 460 left bottom

All maps are: Archivio White Star